Praise for Alejandro Jodorowsky and His Works

"... he creates a tapestry that is both linear and complex. The author manages to craft scenes of intense surrealism while never losing sight of the human experiences of love, loss, fear, and wonder. The final chapters [of *The Dance of Reality*] focus on how his ideas about creativity that he calls 'psychomagic' can be actualized; for him, art is a means of freedom from what he calls 'the prison of the rational.'"

PUBLISHERS WEEKLY

"Alejandro Jodorowsky seamlessly and effortlessly weaves together the worlds of art, the confined social structure, and things we can only touch with an open heart and mind."

ERYKAH BADU, SINGER-SONGWRITER,
ACTRESS, ACTIVIST, AND ALCHEMIST

"Jodorowsky is a brilliant, wise, gentle, and cunning wizard with tremendous depth of imagination and crystalline insight into the human condition. His work is a source of inspiration for me and for many of the most important and innovative artists of our time. *Psychomagic* is necessary reading for all who long to shock the world into awakening and remembrance of what has always been and what is still to come."

DANIEL PINCHBECK, AUTHOR OF
2012: THE RETURN OF QUETZALCOATL

"Jodorowsky is a psychotherapist for love rather than money, and he accepts no fees for his services. His unconventional and visionary way of being is in itself the truest recommendation of the path to freedom and creative evolution he foresees for us all."

Metagenealogy

Self-Discovery through Psychomagic and the Family Tree

Alejandro Jodorowsky
and Marianne Costa

Translated by Rachael LeValley

Park Street Press
Rochester, Vermont • Toronto, Canada

Park Street Press
One Park Street
Rochester, Vermont 05767
www.ParkStPress.com

Park Street Press is a division of Inner Traditions International

Originally published in French under the title *Métagénéalogie: La famille, un trésor et un piège* by Editions Albin Michel, 22 rue Huyghens, 75014 Paris
First U.S. edition published in 2014 by Park Street Press

The cards presented in this work are taken from the restored *Tarot de Marseille* of Alejandro Jodorowsky and Philippe Camoin, Camoin Editions (www.camoin.com).

Library of Congress Cataloging-in-Publication Data
Jodorowsky, Alejandro, author.
  [Métagénéalogie. English]
  Metagenealogy : self-discovery through psychomagic and the family tree / Alejandro Jodorowsky and Marianne Costa. — First US edition.
      pages cm
  Summary: "A practical guide to recognizing and overcoming the patterns and influences of the four generations before you" — Provided by publisher.
  Includes bibliographical references and index.
  ISBN 978-1-62055-103-5 (pbk.) — ISBN 978-1-62055-163-9 (e-book)
  1. Genealogy—Psychological aspects. 2. Families—Psychological aspects. 3. Self-knowledge, Theory of. I. Costa, Marianne, author. II. Title.
  RC489.F33J6313 2014
  616.89'17085—dc23
                                                                                2013046679

Printed and bound in the United States by McNaughton and Gunn

10   9   8   7   6   5   4   3   2   1

Text design by Priscilla Baker and layout by Virginia Scott Bowman
This book was typeset in Garamond Premier Pro with Helvetica Neue used as the display typefce

To send correspondence to the authors of this book, mail a first-class letter to the authors c/o Inner Traditions • Bear & Company, One Park Street, Rochester, VT 05767, and we will forward the communication.

Contents

Introduction

By Marianne Costa

The title of this work is a neologism. What is Metagenealogy? Why not use the word "psychogenealogy," since it is more fashionable?

Alejandro Jodorowsky coined the term "psychogenealogy" at the end of the 1970s. Since then, in Europe at least, its use has gradually degraded its meaning. The term has come to serve as a catchphrase for extraordinarily diverse practices—some that simply exempt psychology altogether, others that replace a less verifiable spiritualism. In this manner, the diversity of the word's usage has come to damage the subject's only suitable term.

What these approaches have in common is that said disciplines have emerged over the past several decades out of an awareness of the influence of lineage on the individual.

Interest in the genealogy tree on the part of therapists, as with the general public, has grown since the 1970s, when psychoanalysts tackled the question of transgenerational bonds for the first time. Although religious, magical, or shamanic forms of psychotherapy have always been present in the West, it is just now in the process of rediscovering what many other cultures assert: the inherited unconscious interacts with the individual unconscious, for better and for worse.

Presently, if someone makes an appointment for a psychogenealogy session, he could find himself in the presence of a licensed therapist, a medium, or an energist. And what would he gain from this session? A mere inventory of the important talents of five generations of ancestors? Perhaps there would be some strange intuitive messages from "energetic" memories, or the insinuation that he has descended from Charlemagne. In any case, he probably will be amazed by the relevance of the information he receives. And it is also likely to lead to the discovery of some recurring themes of which he was not conscious, family secrets or the origin of some obsession or phobia. In the worst case, he will find himself either tremendously frustrated by an excess of intellectuality and a frigid, useless diagnosis or end up quite skeptical after a session full of new age clichés, sentimental foolishness, and irrational ravings.

Metagenealogy, however, proposes to reconcile some apparent opposites by establishing its position precisely at the points of conjunction—where the rational collaborates with the irrational; where science dances with art; where "clairvoyance" means intuition rather than lucidity. In terms of of *neurology* (as far as we understand it nowadays) we could call it balancing the right cerebral hemisphere with the left.

But how does one account for a discipline that exists in the space between those extremes—that is as firmly rooted in psychology as in art, in science as in spiritual and esoteric traditions? This opus aims to summarize and present, in an accessible way, Alejandro Jodorowsky's thirty-five years of genealogy tree investigation and findings.

For more than ten years, we have both dedicated intense interest to this topic. It is an enormous challenge to share theories and practices that are in constant development. Firmly anchored in the psychological and scientific theories of the time, Metagenealogy reflects its creator's lifelong artistic trek and his inspired, insatiable search for meaning. This discipline suggests that all "illness" can be understood as a lack of beauty and Consciousness, and that the "cure" consists of authentically becoming one's self.

Rather than produce a manual, we wanted to create a book of a double initiation, the first of which is already complete—that of Jodorowsky's discovery of Metagenealogy through his own life path. The other, yet to happen, is that of anyone who wants to play along with us and take the journey to regaining his or her true identity. The two of us together have organized this narration as if it were an initiatory tale. And, given that it follows a pedagogical and exemplary chronology, it will serve as a guideline for any reader who wishes to study her tree and reflect on her own destiny.

Each part of the book starts with a chapter that is a first-person introduction reconstructing key moments of Alejandro Jodorowksy's crucial voyage. Each of the extracts of the author's life is followed by a theoretical chapter, supported by exercises and references to the Tarot— our founding model for work on oneself, which will, without a doubt, allow the reader to advance in understanding and in healing his or her genealogy tree. Likewise, there will be another series of exercises that can further the resources of attention, creativity, and imagination— qualities we believe essential to the work of recovering, and thus reinventing, the roots that we invite you to learn about here!

We hope with our whole heart that this double journey will serve you, like the heroes of old, in triumphing over all obstacles to attain the elixir that will forever transform your life, your existence, and your environment. Said elixir, in Jodorowskianism, bears the name "Consciousness."

PART ONE

Metagenealogy

Art, Therapy, and
the Search for One's Self

ONE

From Art to Therapy

By Alejandro Jodorowsky

One of the most intense adventures in my life began in the spring of 1979, and subsequently compelled me to create a therapeutic and artistic system based on the study of the genealogy tree. I was fifty years old at the time.

It is necessary to briefly return to the years leading up to that date. My upbringing was rich, complex, bookish, and autodidactic. Teachers and intuition followed one another, as did periods of study and periods of experimentation. The theories and practices presented in this book are based on the sum of these activities.

In 1947, after high school, I decided to register at the pedagogical institute of the University of Chile. I was attracted to philosophy and psychology, and after two years I obtained diplomas in the philosophy of mathematics and the history of culture. While attending a class taught by a North American professor who suggested we focus on adapting men to the conduct of machines, I left the university and dedicated myself to working with puppets.

My shows turned into psychodramas—I created dolls to represent my father, my mother, my sister, and most of my extended family. After creating several pieces I became interested in body language, theorizing that if emotions caused postures, postures could trigger emotions. I created a method of body language that began in a distressed, fetal position (wishing for death) and ended with the development of a mature human being, arms wide open, united with the cosmos—happy to be alive.

In the beginning, my purpose was to discover a sign language to help me tell stories. But as I concentrated on the mechanism of body language while practicing dance, meditation, and massage, I realized that countless memories—memories of childhood or the prenatal period, acceptance, defeat—and the psychic residue of different members of our families are nested in our bodies.

The following phrase from René Descartes's *Passions of the Soul,* published in 1649 in Paris, struck me.

> Some people, for example, can't bear the smell of roses, the presence of a cat, or the like; it's plausible to think that this comes from their having been greatly upset by some such object when they were infants—perhaps the smell of roses caused severe headache in a child when he was still in the cradle, or a cat terrified him without anyone noticing and without any memory of it remaining afterward; and yet the idea of the aversion he then felt for the roses or for the cat will remain imprinted on his brain till the end of his life. Or the person's present aversion may come from having shared a feeling his mother had when she was upset by a cat while pregnant. There certainly is a connection between a mother's movements and those of a child in her womb so that anything adverse to the one is harmful to the other.

In fact certain movements awoke in me my mother's depression, the shame of exile passed on from my grandparents, the anxiety of my having been threatened with death while still in the womb, and many other things. The pantomime rehearsals quickly became collective therapy. The contrast was intense between these performances, in which everyone's authenticity was revealed, and the outside world constructed of prejudices and appearances that submerge us into a kind of mental prison. I was twenty years old. I decided once and for all that art would, henceforth, be oriented toward my spiritual liberation. In spite of the success I had in pantomiming, I resolved to leave Chile, and I arrived in Paris determined to work with the mime Marcel Marceau, to work with the surrealists led by André Breton, and finally to audit classes conducted by the philosopher Gaston Bachelard at the Sorbonne.

Practicing pantomime with Marceau led me to investigate tantric yoga and the chakras, Chinese medicine and the meridians, the Kabbalah and the application of the Sephirot to the body. Are all of these practices imaginary? In any case, they help heal those who have faith in them, and they help develop Consciousness. With the surrealists, the practice of "exquisite corpses" (random text generation) allowed me to loosen the grip of the rational and get in touch with my Unconscious, which I no longer saw as a threat but as a powerful ally.

As for Bachelard's classes, his analyses of the primordial elements (water, fire, air, earth, and space) drove me to alchemy. I began to fervently read the work of Sigmund Freud, Sándor Ferenczi, Melanie Klein, Georg Groddeck, Wilhelm Stekel, and Wilhelm Reich. Carl Gustav Jung's *Symbols of Transformation* was a good guide. My still-young mind began to understand the close relationship between art and therapy. On the one hand I saw artists, separated from humanity like islands, engaged in the exaltation of their own individuality and seeking, above all, to be recognized and admired. And on the other hand, I saw devoted therapists who put themselves at the service of the mental and physical health of others.

When I had acquired sufficient knowledge and experience in Europe I flew to Mexico, where over a period of ten years I staged hundreds of shows, with a preference for theater of the absurd. I staged the works of Samuel Beckett, Ionesco, Tardieu, Arrabal, Strindberg, Leonora Carrington, Ghelderode, Lorca, Kafka, Gogol, and my own. Tired of creating shows with actors reciting in front of a passive audience, I decided to eliminate works written for theater and replaced them with books of philosophy and psychoanalysis. I began in 1970 by adapting Nietzsche's *Thus Spoke Zarathustra* to the stage, casting famous actors who performed in the nude under my direction.

Doing my best to go further still with this experimental search, I adapted *Games People Play: The Psychology of Human Relationships,* the founding book on transactional analysis by Eric Berne, who wanted to simplify psychiatric jargon into common language for patient and therapist. To this text I added Wilhelm Reich's *Listen, Little Man!* It was my first attempt at therapeutic theater. This work, which foresaw the ecological catastrophes to come, and which staged role-play between children, parents, and "adults" (healthy beings who choose to live completely in the present), had immediate success. Since its creation it has appeared without interruption in theaters in Mexico City, staged by different student groups year after year.

This desire to find methods of artistic healing caused me to leave the structure of theater, and I began to give impromptu performances in unsuspecting places: art schools, cemeteries, nursing homes, buses, and so forth. I no longer worked with actors whose goal was to dissolve into a character, but with human beings who felt diverted from their real selves by family, society, and culture— people who sought an end to being "characters," who wanted to find their true identity, their essential Being. This was accomplished by using shocking improvisations that showed stunned spectators the mental, emotional, and sexual obsessions of the participants, and their intrinsic fears.

I created a score of "ephemeral panics," most notably in Mexico in 1962 at the Academy of Art in San Carlos and in France at the Paris Festival of Free Expression in 1965, which gave birth to the therapeutic technique I called "Psychomagic,"* which consists of staging a healing act in daily life—similar to a dream—in order to liberate an unconscious block.

---

*[See A. Jodorowsky, *Psychomagic.* —*Trans.*]

With these acts I opposed the psychoanalytical attitude of transforming unconscious language (dreams, slips of the tongue, synchronicities) into an articulate language with rational explanations. I opted instead to teach the language of the Unconscious to the intellect, language that is to a large extent composed of images and actions that defy logic. Words reveal the problem but don't cure it. The only words capable of healing the Unconscious, because it understands them, are prayers and incantation. The way to transform the Unconscious into a protective ally is to seduce it by means of dramatic or poetic acts of nature. Just as the Unconscious accepts placebos, it also accepts metaphorical acts. Urges are resolved not by sublimation but by an act they perform symbolically.

In order to enrich my artistic activity I decided that rather than foraging among other artists, I would connect with purely spiritual sources. This is why in 1968, when I was eager to practice Zen meditation, I went to Ejo Takata, a Japanese monk who at the time had been living in Mexico City for four years. There were many doctors and psychiatrists who meditated in his *zendo* (meditation space) during that period, and they introduced me to Dr. Eric Fromm at a sanctuary in Cuernavaca. The eminent psychoanalyst and author of, among others, *Escape from Freedom* and *Zen Buddhism and Psychoanalysis*, lived in this village because the mild climate helped him to heal his heart condition.

After psychoanalysis turned into long conversations about the Bible and Buddhism, Fromm asked me to give body language classes to his students. I accepted. This allowed me to observe the profound separation that existed between the analysts' intense mental work and their lack of mastery over their physical capabilities. All of their exploratory work on the Unconscious took place only with words.

I poured this precious experience, along with knowledge gained from my time with Ejo Takata, into my film *El Topo* (1970), in which I address the conflict-love relationship between a son and a father. *El Topo* became a cult film, and John Lennon, through his American producer Allen Klein, entrusted me with the money needed to shoot my next film, *Holy Mountain* (1973). I began again to consider the possibility of an art that would be capable of enriching the Consciousness of the public. "Upon seeing my film, I want spectators to leave the theater transformed for the rest of their lives."

This exaggerated hope prompted me to conduct psychological, esoteric, symbolic, and religious research. For this I turned to many people, including Oscar Ichazo, founder of the human potential movement group known as the Arica School, who proposed a series of exercises involving the Enneagram, the metaphysical/psychological character type system of Islamic origin composed of nine distinct aspects of "I." Directing these films became spiritual development, an artistic experience, and psychological research.

At this time I plunged into the work of René Guénon and his analysis of traditional symbology, and I devoured the work of Fritz Perls, one of the creators of Gestalt therapy. The next stage of my search developed after 1974, when, strengthened by my North American and Latin American years, I again settled in Europe and began a new period of my life.

Michel Seydoux, a French film producer, contracted me to direct the film *Dune*, inspired by Frank Herbert's novel of the same title. A grandiose project, it was to be a super-production to compete with Hollywood's science fiction films. Backed by a colossal budget, I could contact the actors and artists I admired: the designers Moebius, H. R. Giger, Dan O'Bannon, Chris Foss; Salvador Dalí, Orson Welles, Gloria Swanson, David Carradine, and Udo Kier were to appear in the credits; the music would be by Pink Floyd, Tangerine Dream, and Magma. But after preparing the script for two years, the film could not be made due to problems with distribution in America.

This project, although unfinished, connected me with the esoteric community flourishing in Paris at the time. So, I studied the Kabbalah under the sage A. D. Grad, author of *Le livre des principes Kabbalisticques* (The Book of Kabbalistic Principles); gypsy magic under Pierre Derlon, specialist on the subject; and the work of mathematical physicist Jacques Ravatin, who theorized that waves emanate patterns, not only three-dimensional shapes. I also studied the work and ideas of the hundred-year-old alchemist and magician Pierre Cartier, famous among illusionists for his tricks with cigarettes, and the work in phytotherapy, chromotherapy, and aromatherapy of medical pioneer Dr. Jean Valnet. Guided by these insiders, for two years I went to the National Library every morning before going to work on my film; as soon as the library opened I would immerse myself in eighteenth-century books on the monumental metaphysical machine of the Tarot of Marseille.

Dr. Valnet introduced me to his main collaborator, the eminent phytotherapist Dr. Jean Claude Lapraz, who sent four of his patients to me every weekend to investigate the psychological roots of their illnesses by way of the Tarot. It was a period of intense learning in which the union of art and therapy was achieved in my soul.

When seeking to recover from an illness we cannot limit ourselves only to the scientific. The view of an artist balances that of a doctor who, able to understand biological problems, lacks the necessary techniques for detecting the sublime values buried in each individual. It is necessary for healing that the patient be what in truth she is, and free herself from the acquired identity that others have wanted her to have. All illness comes from orders received in childhood that force us to do what we don't want to, and a prohibition that forces us not to be that which we actually are. Ill health, depression, and fear result from a lack of awareness, from a forgotten beauty, from the tyranny of family, and from the weight of a world of outdated traditions and religions.

For a patient to heal or to receive help in becoming who he truly is, he must first become conscious of the fact that he is not an isolated individual but the fruit of at least four generations of ancestors. Without knowing the spiritual and material legacy of our genealogy tree, it is impossible for us to know ourselves, but the structure of the family clan should not be strictly analyzed or interpreted as if the individual were a biological machine. Although the extensive psychological theories of the twentieth century emanated from brilliant psychiatrists like Freud, Groddeck, and Reich, in their wake the false and pernicious belief developed that to get closer to the human soul every step should be based on the process of scientific investigation. Carl Gustav Jung was aware of this confusion:

> The intellect is effectively an enemy of the mind when it has the audacity to want to capture the legacy of the soul, which it is not in any respect capable of doing, because the mind is superior to the intellect since it understands not only the intellect but also the heart.*

The conscious human being cannot be analyzed as if she lacks the potential to change, a body-object without a spiritual reality. The Unconscious, in essence, opposes all logic. If reduced to scientific explanation or university education, it becomes a corpse. Jung adds:

> I know that is why the universities stopped working as a portal of light. We are tired of scientific specialization and rationalist intellectualism. We want a truth that does not restrict but expands, does not darken but clarifies, does not slide off like water but saturates and penetrates to the marrow.

It is for this reason that no diploma can guarantee the competency of a psychotherapist. In order to help another heal one must not only understand what she suffers from, but also put within reach the necessary elements that permit her to change. The doctor or the surgeon, attentive only to the body of the sick, establishes a diagnosis but then resorts to a prescription or an operation. Too often the alleged therapist is not capable of both arriving at a diagnosis and revealing the cause of the pain to the patient. If the patient responds, "Now that I know the cause of my problems, what should I do?" this therapist is not capable of helping her to find the answer.

---

*Jung, *Commentaire sur le mystère de la Fleur d'Or* (1929).

In primitive cultures, the shaman is usually an artist who is also an expert in medicinal and hallucinogenic plants that allow travel to other realities while exerting a therapeutic action. This medicine man or medicine woman is at the same time the healer and the remedy: the source of living information that allows the sufferer to rediscover her own resources.

From the moment that we are no longer slaves of university dictates, all styles and approaches have something to offer us. This is why I never denied myself the study of Eastern philosophies and religious or esoteric messages in my search for keys to universal understanding of the human being. My vision of the genealogy tree was guided by these words from the Buddha: "The world is burning! Your house is ablaze! So do not ask how the world is created or of its laws. Think only on how to save yourself!"

How to serve? How to be useful? How to accomplish this in a way that gives others the keys to healing, and does not limit us to merely explaining the problems?

Based on a hypothesis about the essence of therapeutic work—*truth is what is useful at a given moment, at a given place, and for a given being*—I said to myself, "More useful than thinking the universe exists by pure coincidence is to affirm that its purpose is to create Consciousness."

Although the existence of a mental zone imperceptible in conscious wakefulness and improperly called the "Unconscious," where primitive instincts, traumas, and memories of the past both personal and collective reside, has been accepted since Freud, this does not take into account designs of the future nested in matter since before the appearance of life due to a belief that the universe is unfolding without any conscious purpose.

Above all, the human spirit aspires to two things: wisdom and immortality. The Unconscious must then contain two zones: one that is the product of past experiences, including our animal instincts, that we can continue calling the "Unconscious"; and another that contains the potential power of mutations aimed at evolving beings with cosmic Consciousness. These mutations are not the result of past experiences but are future possibilities captured in poetic and prophetic states that we can call "Supraconscious."

We progress on a planet that participates in a cosmic dance where everything is emerging, disappearing, transforming. How then do we define this progress? In order to find the root of "one's self," this permanent self in the impermanence, we must look beyond the material universe and identify with the creative center, knowing that we were born to actively participate in the evolution of the cosmos. The individual "self" and the cosmic "us" can only unite in Consciousness, the ideal that alchemy raised in symbolic form: the effort to spiritualize matter and, at the same time, materialize spirit. Translated into psychological language, the Ego (the self) must be integrated into the Unconscious, while the Unconscious must be integrated into the Ego. Our individuality, established by family, society, and culture, is related to the base material—rot, *nigredo,* iron—that the alchemist transforms into gold, into the *essential Being,* into Consciousness.

I asked myself, how do I mutate? It seemed necessary to reduce my desires in favor of my health, to eliminate temporary things of little value, becoming aware of my immortality as a collective body and, in so doing, obtaining freedom by detaching from mental anchors so nothing subjective could separate me from the creative energy needed to reach union. Acting as if I were alive and, at the same time, freeing myself from worldly concerns as if I were dead, I ceased "pertaining to" my "identity," which "defined" me.

Developing a high level of Consciousness requires tenacious, continuous, intense, relentless effort. Through this process we must die to ourselves, being reborn transfigured, without defining ourselves as rational or irrational, young or old, women or men. No name or nationality should limit our impersonal events so we may enjoy the peace of anonymity under our individual masks, having no barriers between the human and the divine—we are as much that which we are as that which we are not.

Becoming completely devoted to these efforts, I began to understand that in order to heal myself, and others, the most useful hypothesis was one that considers each human capable of developing a Consciousness without limits.

If we examine a fertilized egg under a microscope, we can see a tiny red beating dot in the yoke: the beginning of a heart. The beat comes before the viscera. The heart exists thanks to the will to beat; it was created to serve as an instrument. Knowing this, how can we fail to understand that the brain does not give rise to Consciousness but is its instrument of reception? The genesis of what we are begins with this Consciousness, that inconceivable, all-powerful, unfathomable mystery we dare call "divine." Then comes its transformation into energy and, finally, into actual organs. For this reason, when we speak of the origins of the genealogy tree, we must also address its cosmic roots.

Our brain, probably the most complex object in the universe, contains more than one hundred billion neurons—cells equipped with a nucleus that functions as a miniature receiver-transmitter—which unite with others to form networks of connections that transmit information in the form of electric currents. We come into the world with the neuronal potential of a future human, but with shortages. A network is sewn, little by little, into contact with our relatives and the knowledge they transmit to us. We inherit experiences. However, being limited experiences, they translate into "national" or "maternal" languages that produce stagnant mental states comprised of very few connections, a cultural cell from which we can hardly escape.

The energy flowing through the neurons, which science defines as electric, may very well be thought of as a manifestation of universal Consciousness that creates in our brains a huge structure that is formed of all possible connections between its cells: the future human mind. Equally, we can think that this mysterious energy unites all Consciousness in the universe. The sociocultural family will fight to ensure that the individual obeys the will of his ancestors, but in the majority of cases, due to an accumulation of ideas, feelings, desires, and inherited needs, this adherence to the ways of the clan opposes the spiritual project and plunges it into lower levels of Consciousness.

The genealogy tree acts like a trap, imposing its material and psychological limitations on the perfection of the cosmic project of the descendants with fears, resentments, frustrations, and illusions. Already, in the mother's womb, the fetus receives orders to imitate the model inherited from its ancestors. The family simply does not accept that the creation comes from "nothing" without an exterior model.

Every individual is the product of two forces: the imitating force, directed by the family group acting from the past, and the creative force, driven by the universal Consciousness from the future. When parents limit their children, forcing them to submit to plans and orders ("you will be this or that," "you are just like such and so," "you will obey us and spread our ideas and beliefs"), they disobey future evolutionary designs, plunging the family into all kinds of physical and mental illness. Consciousness, from the first moment of individuation in the fetus, suffers from this conflict between "to create" and "to imitate." When at birth the child displays few of the psychological traits modeled by his parents, we can think of it as Consciousness overcoming the influence of the models shoved on him by previous generations of family. If, however, the child turns into a certified copy of his parents or grandparents, then Consciousness was defeated. Creative souls are scarce. Imitator souls are legion. The former must learn to communicate and cultivate their values, the latter must be released from the mold and learn to create: to become themselves, not what family, society, or culture wants them to be.

The clan acts as an organism. When one member experiences a change, the whole unit reacts, positively or negatively. Trees belong to the woods. A beautiful tree that gives poisonous fruits is a bad tree. A gnarled tree that gives healthy fruit is a good tree. The individual who expands her Consciousness becomes the good fruit and grants her tree a new significance. The sufferings of the ancestors—narcissistic wounds, humiliations, shame, and guilt—acquire a sense of purpose. When the family reacts, the society in which it develops also reacts. Each one has two primary purposes: to fulfill the biological need of procreation of children and take care of those in need, and to integrate into the social group, obeying its laws. If every family shrunk from contact with others, permitting separatist tendencies, society could not exist. This is why the genealogy tree becomes a prisoner of a web of orders and social and cultural obligations, among which the incest taboo drives the clan to mix with the rest of humanity instead of closing in on itself. However, in some cases these orders and obligations may not correspond to the being's essential nature. Based on its myths and religious beliefs or ideologies, each culture dictates different modes of conduct. From one society or culture to another, the family institutions can change. So not only monogamy exists: some cultures permit men to have multiple wives, others allow a woman to live with several men, some force the childless brother of the dead to marry the widow, others require the wife's younger sister to replace her upon her death. We were born into a given culture, at a given time, in a particular country. We would not be the same if we spoke another language, or were born into another civilization or historical context. These limitations, which depend on memory, encourage us to repeat patterns by stamping a cultural self on us. At the same time, the possibilities of the future, which work to drive man toward his mutation, transform the initial suffering into conscious energy, developing the essential Being.

The *cultural self,* molded by those who have raised him, must accept projections received from relatives who, driven by a desire to be imitated, expect him to embrace work in a given profession, belong to this or that religion or political group, and succumb to the clan's negative predictions: "If you do that you will destroy yourself," "If you do this you will end up a beggar," "If you have sex before marriage you will become a hooker." As the brain is inclined to satisfy these predictions, they are transformed by the Unconscious into orders and act like a curse demanding to be fulfilled in the individual's life.

On the other hand the *essential Being*, programmed by the Supraconscious, provides sublime aspirations for the mind that are usually reduced to simple illusions by clan memory: utopias, usually lived in anguish, or desires to change the world, usually lived in despair. The cultural self and the essential Being intermingle at all times, sometimes battling, sometimes joining forces. Great-grandparents, grandparents, and parents come together in us for better or for worse. In their dynamic endlessness, the forces of repetition and creation compel us toward both replicating the same *and* accessing that which we authentically are. Individuals can have received both a positive and a negative vision from their great-grandparents, grandparents, and parents, thereby turning each family member into a dual entity of light and dark comprised of two energy fields that, in spite of their opposition, are complementary. In the present, spirit that materializes adjoins with matter that spiritualizes, the Supraconsciousness with Unconsciousness, the intention to fulfill the future with the intention to repeat the past, the essential Being with the sociocultural self, the desire to create with the desire to imitate. The study of the genealogy tree under these simultaneous and complementary aspects, treasure and trap, is what I have called "Metagenealogy."

Because the study of genealogy is fundamentally an understanding of the essential meaning of the human couple, much like the Tarot—where the Pope completes the Popess, the Emperor the

Empress, the Sun the Moon—I realized the necessity of having a couple write this book. I found Marianne Costa, with whom I had already worked on *The Way of Tarot: The Spiritual Teacher in the Cards* (Inner Traditions, 2009), to be the ideal collaborator because she has a deep understanding of my concepts of the genealogy tree, and because she has practiced them with consultants for more than ten years. Without her collaboration, this work would have never been completed.

TWO

Orientation to the Work

Jodorowskianism: The Basics

Before beginning the initiation journey, which involves exploration of the genealogy tree, we believe it useful to establish some helpful theoretical concepts—not usually in the domain of classical psychology but, without a doubt, very familiar among spiritual seekers—and to also define what it is that we understand to be "work on the *I*, on *oneself*." We support our thinking with the essential contribution of the Tarot of Marseille as a "tool of reflection," and for this reason we will briefly look at some of its fundamental rules.

THE PRESENT AS THE ONE REALITY, AND THE UNIT AS THE ULTIMATE TRUTH OF BEING

Metagenealogy is not strictly a "therapy" but a work of awareness that involves understanding the elements of the past that have shaped us, and beginning a future pulse that we shape.

Truthfully, analyzing the genealogy tree requires changing our conception of time so that we may liberate ourselves from ideas such as past (before), present (now), and future (later). Reality is comparable to a trickle of water flowing from a fountain: there without being there, not turning into anything, and not transforming from a previous shape. It emerges incessantly. In the exact same way the universe does not have a past or a future, only an eternal present that never ceases to emerge.

Upon analyzing the genealogy tree the consultant is flowing, and her ancestors are in this flow: grandparents, aunts, uncles, and parents, and also her children, grandchildren, and great-grandchildren. The consultant is in a perpetual emergence, being at the same time fetus, baby, child, adolescent, young adult, mature adult, and elder. We live in the present, fundamentally as a unit, a cell. However, humanity is organized according to a consensus in which Time is divided into before, now, and later. We must be able to think of ourselves both in this dualistic vision of time and in the timelessness of the present.

In the chart below, we have represented the metagenealogical conception of the individual in the heart of his tree.

This allows us to quickly apprehend someone who is as much in his unit (or cell) as in the center of the apparent duality of the forces. In the extreme, we find ourselves with the alchemical principle of dual motion:

The Treasure {
Materialization of the Spirit
Universe / Pluriverse
Supraconscious
"Carry Out a Future Project"
Great-Grandparents
Grandparents
Parents
} To Create

——— Self / Present ———

The Trap {
Parents
Grandparents
Great-Grandparents
"Repeat the Training of the Past"
Unconscious
Earth
Spiritualization of Past Matter
} To Imitate

that of the spirit that materializes as matter is spiritualized. Alchemy should be understood here as a metaphorical reference to the work on the "I," oneself: the transformation of vile matter (neuroses, blocks, excesses) into precious matter (Consciousness, presence, freedom of the self). If we employ a more accessible terminology in order to designate the materialization of the spirit and the spiritualization of matter, we would do it with the concepts of *intention* and *attention*.

The practice of attention consists of concentrating our awareness on physical actions that spiritualize matter, as when we pay attention to movements or sensations in martial arts, Japanese tea ceremonies, body-oriented psychotherapies, and Gestalt. In this way the body quits being an inert vehicle, an exhausted server, and is converted into the perfect place for being present in the world.

Based on neuromotor response, intention is when an idea for a physical action is immediately interpreted as a nerve transmission, which induces a muscular contraction: an action. Consequently, the intentional process enables spirit to materialize. It is from here that all practices of intention like positive thought, mystical recitation, and repetition of mantra are derived, and we actively imagine a future reality in order to allow it to manifest in our lives.

Continuing on with the study of the above table, and observing the pairs of opposites, it can be understood that these are opposites only in appearance. In fact, in every moment:

- Universe and Earth are united.
- Unconscious and Supraconscious act in mutual agreement.
- We move with the tendency to repeat the known, what was lived for generations past, and with the aspiration to fulfill the new, unknown, future project.
- The essential Being (authentic and unique) coexists with the cultural self (acquired and collective).
- The capacity to create is built into the habit of imitating.
- We join in a family line that we recognize as a treasure, but we are conscious of being prey to its traps to varying degrees.

From the moment we focus on the present, we simultaneously experience the suffering of our ephemeral nature and the irresistible joy of being alive. One could say that the restoration of the tree justifiably consists in the acceptance of our own deaths, and of the permanent impermanence of things. This is the price we have to pay to be able to discover the great joy of life, and our existence as unit and union without faults. Accordingly, we are liberated from the anguish of losing anything known to be very valuable to us: loved ones, homeland, our own existence, our individuality, psychic or physical attributes that we associate with our identity, and so forth. In the same way the fountain accepts water, this is about our acceptance of the perpetual transformation that is our true nature and that of the universe—accepting the motto of surrealism, "Stop the certain with the uncertain."

Behold! This is why work on the genealogical tree is comparable to an artistic practice, and does not require the guidance of a licensed therapist. It is suitable, in fact, to choose a "tree-ologist" as we would choose a music teacher or martial arts instructor—according to affinities we feel for that person and according to her level of fulfillment in the art of being herself, which manifests before our eyes.

CONTRIBUTION OF THE TAROT

Although we won't go into many details of the formidable architecture of symbols that is the Tarot of Marseille, we think it important to remember some of its rules of use, for it will serve us as a valuable tool for thought during the study of the genealogy tree. The structures offered by the Tarot, foundations of Western symbolism, are presented as a mirror of realities: human and cosmic, physical and psychic, both infinitely small and infinitely grand. For our study, its structures give us a very valid conception of the human being.

Evolutionary Numerology

Without a desire for evolution, one cannot do work on the *I*, on *oneself*. A person who has completed her physical growth and has arrived at her adult dimension will have to decide whether or not she wants to continue growing on her psychic and spiritual plane. Because of this, at the time of requesting the help of a teacher, a guide, or a therapist, it is normal to fall into the trap of an "inactive patient" who wants to be treated, taken care of, caressed, and soothed as if a child. One could say that evolution consists in increasingly moving toward improvement: each day, less anxious than before. From this perspective, it is extremely useful to know the numerology dynamic of the Tarot, which summarizes in ten degrees the successive cycles of evolution.

Why ten? We all have ten fingers, but each one of these fingers has an individual existence. The number ten represents a totality that is subdivided into various stages, the thread with which one can build an entire process of growth that goes from the potentiality yet unrealized (the 1) to the totality fully deployed (the 10).

Every level emerges from the preceding level and is fulfilled in the next. In a state of good health we cyclically travel the series of levels in these dynamics, which could be compared to a spiral, and each step, by a certain numerology degree, allows us always to learn something new. Out of fear, because of an injury, because of laziness, or for a variety of reasons, we can eventually encounter blocks in a given state (stagnation) or, what is still worse, experience a withdrawal and oppose all evolution, convinced that the solution is to go back (regression). This dynamic model allows us to accept every stage as necessary, and to understand what is the next step. Let's look briefly at the levels of tarological numerology.

1: Potential, Strength

No experience, an immense energy. The point of departure from which the universe emerges (according to the Big Bang theory). It is the seed from which the future tree will emerge. Everything is possible.

Stagnation or regression: nothing is ever started.

2: Gestation, Detention

Stage of accumulation (of power, of data, etc.) in a protected space, just as the seed is in the earth or the fetus is in the mother's womb. A stable state, immobile even, prepares for hatching.

Stagnation or regression: death at the root, not born.

3: Creative or Destructive Explosion

First action without any experience. It is like the seed that surfaces or puberty that transforms the body, but also like a thorough cleaning or eradication of the useless. Acts without knowing where it goes.

Stagnation or regression: unceasingly explodes in every direction, unproductive, aggressive, invading.

4: Stability, Balance

The world grows stronger. A family, a government, a home, a stable economy, and so on. The conditions of life are there: soothing, protective, adult.

Stagnation or regression: dictatorial, coercive, cramped spirit, rigid mind.

5: Temptation, New Look

All exploration begins in this level, in which we can feel tempted to abandon the known and discover other horizons.

Stagnation or regression: lying, doomed to nullity, to death, or to deception (like Tartuffe in Molière's play).

6: Beauty and Joy as Reality Principle

On this level we have already surpassed the strict framework of survival and security to disembark on a reality that responds to other criteria. It is a new conception of life that opens before us, focused on beauty. In plant life, it would be the flowering: with its beauty, its color, its perfume, the flower prepares the opening of fruit.

Stagnation or regression: narcissistic and indulgent, it would dry up without coming to fruition.

7: Action in the World

The compilation of all of the previous grades leads to strong action not only individual and inexperienced, as with 3, but also collectively and firmly anchored in the world. The energy of 7 is young and dangerous, but it is mature through its experience. Acts as if it knows where it goes.

Stagnation or regression: action by action, destructive and excessive ego.

8: Perfection

Like a fetus, which at eight months is completely formed and only has yet to be born, 8 represents an unfolding perfection, horizon of all action, itself without need for action. Nothing to add, nothing to discharge.

Stagnation or regression: perfectionism, immobility.

9: Crisis of Transition

Like the baby that is at the point of birth in the ninth month of pregnancy, or like the ripe fruit at the point of falling from the tree, this grade evokes the abandonment of perfection to enter into a new, unknown world. It is the moment in which a crisis heralds the arrival of a new cycle.

Stagnation or regression: useless crisis, loneliness, agony.

10: End of a Cycle and the Beginning of the Next

The number 10, totally fulfilled, no longer has energy but has a vast experience. Symbolizing the moment in which the old and the new coexist: a chrysalis already torn with the butterfly already emerging, or the child who learns to breathe still united with the mother through the umbilical cord. It is the moment in which everything ends and everything begins. To be able to move into the next cycle, outside help must be accepted.

Stagnation or regression: blocked cycle, inability to move into a dynamic of evolution.

As shown in the chart below, after the 10 the 1 appears. In other words, this is another beginning in another world. For example, one can have completed the whole cycle in the intellectual aspect—to the 10, which represents the abandonment of fixed ideas and the openness to listen to others—and restart as a true beginner in the affective or emotional aspects, with a new link or a loving reorganization from this lesson in listening.

This evolving structure lets us contemplate the human being as a being in constant evolution. This is an essential attitude in working

Evolutionary Numerology of the Tarot

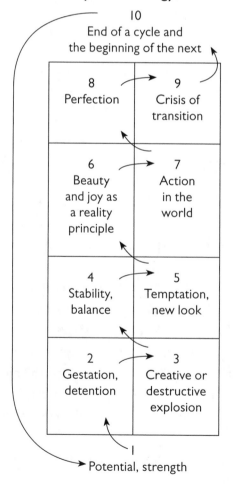

with the genealogy tree, where the repetition of the past corresponds to energies of stagnation and regression, and the fulfillment of the future to the dynamics of evolution.

Exercise: Where am I?

Mix the first ten cards of the Tarot's Major Arcana (from the Magician to the Wheel of Fortune) and draw a card randomly. Whatever the grade of the numerology that the extraction "randomly" sends you, ask yourself:

"In this moment, where am I in this stage of the numerological cycle? Am I in a fluid motion (evolutionary) or regressive (stagnation)?"

The Four Elements

The Tarot's Minor Arcana is divided into four suits (or symbols) that help us see, not as a monolithic entity where all are the same, but as a being provided with four energies, each one gifted with a distinct language.

Intellectual (Spades—Air): our ideas, beliefs, concepts, and ability to think about the world.
Its language: ideas
Its action: to conceive, believe, think, and orally define what it is.

Emotional (Cups—Water): our feelings and emotions, the full range of emotions that bind and separate us from others, our individual training in relationships.
Its language: feelings
Its action: that of love in all forms and that of the negative feelings that depart.

Sexual-Creative (Clubs—Fire): all possibilities of sexual or creative activity to beget a being or a project (a baby, a work of art, or any other creation).
Its language: desires

Its action: to create, but also to have the power (the creative and sexual processes go through refractory phases, which bring us through power and powerlessness).

Material (Coins—Earth): anything that keeps us alive (starting with our bodies), health and balance, the circulation of money, the territory in which we work and live.
Its language: needs
Its action: to live, to survive, to work with our fellows.

This division also allows us to address another aspect of the alchemical work: **dissolve and coagulate,** in order to isolate those specific elements we are made of and rebuild ourselves as a fluid unit, thus ceasing to believe we are a steady and monolithic entity driven by "mysterious" forces.

When our concepts conflict with our feelings—and in this very moment our material reality tells us to follow a path that goes exactly opposite to our desire—the four centers pull one another from side to side like four horses from the same draft but without a common objective. The first step in adjusting and guiding our energies toward a particular goal is to identify what has replaced each center. For example, for a long time Western morality, terrified by sexual energy, assimilated this energy into a feeling (specifically for women) or a necessity (specifically for men). In other words, it often happens that for cultural, social, and familial reasons, some energy is "colonized" by other. The intellect, invaded by emotions, fails to think clearly. Sexuality, overloaded by beliefs and prohibitions, turns into a fountain of anguish (like what happened in the nineteenth century when almost everyone practicing Western medicine produced pamphlets on the presumably fatal dangers of the healthy practice of masturbation). In some families, money or child support is the privileged or exclusive means by which the parents express affection for their children, who grow up prisoners of the terrible confusion of trying to separate the material and emotional centers, which can lead to destructive behavior with food or money.

Pursuant to the above, there are twelve variations or deviations of the personality, when one center is invaded (or colonized) by any of the other three centers. When work on the "I" is undertaken, it is very useful to ask which of these deviations are dominant in us. In this way we can study how our genealogy tree has produced them. The following list is intended to be not exhaustive, but rather a starting point from which to reflect.

When the intellectual center is invaded by the
- *Emotional:* affectivity makes thought too subjective, it becomes inaccurate and inconsistent, it excites without motive or, to the contrary, discourages or undervalues.
- *Sexual-creative:* competitive intellect, sexual obsessions, a boundless creativity that makes thoughts drift off into all directions.
- *Material:* ultra-materialistic thinking, incapacity for abstraction, incomprehension of all that is metaphysical.

When the emotional center is invaded by the
- *Intellectual:* emotional coldness, calculating, incapable of expressing emotions, detours due to rational explanations.
- *Sexual-creative:* passionate and possessive affection, jealousy, emotional dependence, sexual obsession.
- *Material:* blackmail, calculating, emotional manipulation to obtain something, love of a person for what he/she has and not for what he/she is.

When the sexual-creative is invaded by the
- *Intellectual:* cold, extreme ritualization of sexuality, sexual and creative impotence—knowing how to invent and analyze, but not being able to create.
- *Emotional:* tenderness takes the place of sexuality and refuses to enter the energy of desire, creativity becomes sentimental, libido and creativity are infantilized.
- *Material:* prostitution, overvaluing of the body or money in the field of sexual attraction, profit-oriented creativity or, conversely,

extreme material insecurity blocking access to creative and sexual energy.

When the material center is invaded by the

- *Intellectual:* obsessive disorders, living according to rigid rules without paying attention to the body's needs.
- *Emotional:* feeding, financial, and physical behaviors show a need for affection (overeating or malnourished, thoughtless spending, excessive attachment to a place, a house, or an object, economic distress or physical demands).
- *Sexual-creative:* systemically sexualizing the body, obsession with seduction, material disorder because of excessive creativity.

A person is prepared to evolve when he knows the language and the energy that corresponds to each of the centers: when he thinks with his intellect, loves with his heart, desires and creates with his sexual center, and lives in accordance to his needs. In Christian terminology we could say that the twelve deviations of the ego are the twelve "apostles" of the "Christ self," which would be a supreme ruler and a teacher, and in which the energy centers work correctly. This means that developing awareness of the deviations that exist in the four centers is a journey of discovery. For example, from the moment of acknowledging that "my emotional center is invaded by the intellectual, and I do not get to express my emotions, or I address the pursuant with endless explanations that do not serve me anymore, in order to get me away from what I love," the person can begin to mend the affected center (in this case, the emotional) and learn to express himself adequately. At this point the intellect (the clarity of expression) never again invades, but rather becomes an ally of the emotional. Below, I again show how this process is undergone:

As an ally, the intellectual center can accept the

- *Emotional:* learns to listen, opens the emotional intelligence, takes into account the more subtle aspects in one's reasoning.
- *Sexual-creative:* discovers mental creativity and the pleasure of

expressing ideas with abundance without necessarily finishing them.

- *Material:* the intellect anchors in the body and assumes its presence, which takes it to a silent regenerator.

As an ally, the emotional center can accept the

- *Intellectual:* chooses one's affections and understands that of others, clarifies one's emotions.
- *Sexual-creative:* discovers the pleasure of acting with feelings and of creating in oneself beautiful or sublime emotions.
- *Material:* learns to love not only similar people but everything that exists (since everything is alive, everything deserves to be loved).

As an ally, the sexual-creative center can accept the

- *Intellectual:* gets to know one's own processes of desire and enjoyment and also those of others.
- *Emotional:* is open to listening to others, creates and desires love.
- *Material:* learns to passionately desire everything already possessed, in other words, renewing one's view of what's already known. Learns also that money and health do not bring happiness but are helpful.

As an ally, the material center can accept the

- *Intellectual:* the intellectual, moral, or spiritual (dharma) permits the organization of one's time and one's existence; having our mortality in mind, we do not waste our lives.
- *Emotional:* acts for love and with love, knows the value of the caress, of the delicacy in relationships with others, of the affectionate care that gives a unique flavor to everyday existence.
- *Sexual-creative:* introduces beauty in daily life, allows oneself to be creative and understand that the best path to take from one point to another is not necessarily the shorter, but the more beautiful way.

Exercise: Hunting wild ideas

Now that we know all of us are more or less invaded by beliefs from scripted conversations, ideas, or obsessions that are not at all useful to our daily lives ("Life is really hard," "Men are boneheads," "Women are emotional," "Money is dirty," "It's better to die young," etc.), it is appropriate that we consider the following:

- What are, among my ideas, the wild beliefs that I inherited from my genealogy tree? (A wild idea is a main feature that constitutes an impediment, suffering, a reason to hold back, not knowing how to conceptualize the world in a way that is useful.)
- From a list I have made of ideas that routinely enter into my mind but with which I, truthfully, do not identify and do not agree, I should ask myself the following questions for each of these ideas: What person from my genealogy tree believed, or believes, in this statement, and why?

THE ROLE OF OBSTACLES

As we saw in the introduction, every individual is the result of two forces: the imitator (directed by a familial group) and the creator (which comes from the universal Consciousness).

In the diagram below we see this double influence on the Unconscious, as it fits within a concentric form:

- In the center is the individual and her personal Unconscious.
- Around this are members of the genealogy tree and the familial Unconscious, which is the focus of our study in this book.
- In turn, the tree is part of a society that also possesses a collective Unconscious, which is the fruit of a culture, which is, in turn, the fruit of mankind.
- Beyond the borders of Earth, the existence of a cosmic Consciousness is imaginable that reflects the Consciousness of

the universe and the "divine" or total Unconscious, which could be the origin of all Consciousness.

We can, therefore, visualize each individual as a center of a series of concentric circles that overlap in the different layers of Consciousness. On the planetary level (humanity as it exists today), we are all subjected to the forces of imitation: traditions, habits, rules, beliefs, and so forth. From the level of cosmic or universal Consciousness, we enter into pure Consciousness and nothing impedes the future project.

We could outline the dynamics between the forces of creation and repetition in the following manner:

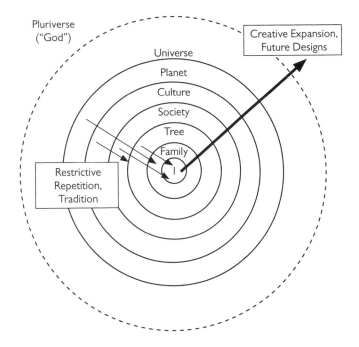

Every individual is constrained by a series of influences modeled from the outside, while the project of Consciousness (represented in the diagram above by the bold arrow) is performed creatively in an unknown way and in spite of the obstacles created by repetitive education.

Our genealogy tree, also complying with the pressures of society and culture, shapes us with forces of imitation, repetition, conformity, and tradition. The work of the individual Consciousness consists in undoing these limitations that do not correspond to our true personality in order to carry out a new, unknown, original project.

As can be seen, the path of the Consciousness goes through the tree, society, and culture in order to integrate with the universal plane. That is to say, if I quit repeating the prescriptions of my tree, of the society in which I live, of the culture in which I have been raised and established in a significant manner, my contribution will be of benefit to my tree, my society, and my culture. For example, in a family marked by ruin or exile, the individual success of one of its members, who now enjoys a good life, can contribute information on what all of them can do: prosper, do well in school, and so forth. Or in another case, when the capacity for bonding has been lost, if one of the members rediscovers the meaning of love and of human value, he could become the light that illuminates the rest of them.

The great artistic, scientific, or cultural revolutions are perceived in the beginning by society as being offensive to the established order. Similarly, at the global level, yesterday's utopian ideas about sustainable development and respect for natural resources are today considered beneficial. The circles of repetition always resist innovation because tradition (conservation of the familial, cultural, or social identity) demands reproduction of its own agenda by the members of the clan.

As we will see in chapter 8, the dynamics between the forces of repetition and creation can be interpreted in the following way: we are all children of our parents and, at the same time, the unique creation of the universe that exceeds the individual will of the parents, who simply serve as vectors or intermediaries. Therefore, the tree will be the result of the study of a series of *formations* and *distortions* imposed on this essential Being that we all are.

Second, we will study the **obstacles as both necessary and fruitful,** allowing our project to achieve its goal: the past wants to make the future make sense, but in reality, it is the future that gives meaning to the past, granting it a new significance. In short, this is the meaning of our work.

The role assigned to the inherited tree can be positive or negative, as, for example:

- The son or daughter who is appointed to carry on the family tradition in order to enhance the intellectual or social level of the family, to repair a series of deaths within the clan, or to repair the family reputation by having a good marriage or by maintaining a given social position.
- The "black sheep" of the family who is the carrier of all the stigmas the genealogy tree needs to expel from itself, which have fallen on this one member in particular, turning the tree into a negative inheritance. It is the one who has become an alcoholic or a drug addict; the one who has become a "prostitute," having chosen the path that does not conform to the ideology of the clan; the one who has become a compulsive gambler and ruins the family with failures that end in misery.

All of these cases, present in one way or another in all families, are the results of inheritance.

From the moment in which someone intends to incorporate new information into her tree, the resistance will manifest in the form of enormously varied obstacles, and at first, these obstacles are going to appear insurmountable. As occurs in myths and legends, we must confront them in order to transform them into stages of our liberation. There is an initiatory tale that pretty much sums up the essential function of the obstacle that interferes with our finding the way through Consciousness, God, or Nature, thus enabling us to strengthen and secure our beliefs.

A peasant receives a visit from his God. He kneels in front of him and thanks him for having granted him the gift of life. "I owe everything to you.

However, I need to file my complaints. I work for my land to make the wheat grow lush, but you send hurricanes, monsoons, hungry birds, mice, torrential rains, and pests. Can you, for once in my life, spare me these troubles?" God satisfies the peasant's pleading. When he plants the seed, no gale shakes the earth, the climate is mild throughout the year, it rains just enough, there is no sign of any bird or any harmful insect . . . and for lack of obstacles to overcome, the seed weakens, rots in the good soil, and fails to germinate.

The human being advances by triumphing over successive obstacles. The Zen monk, for example, manages to reach enlightenment as a reward for the titanic efforts put toward its achievement and the banishment of all parasitic ideas from his mind. The saint finds peace in his heart by refusing all forms of discrimination. The hero succeeds in triumphing over the fear of death. The triumph occurs when the champion submits to rigorous discipline. But these destinies are not an imitation of ancestors' destinies. Rather, they are stock of those men and women who knew to recognize in their spirits, their desires, and their bodies the universal Consciousness, the beginning of numerous universes.

These people have decided to live in eternity and infinity, and not to act through mechanisms and automatisms. They are not guided by fixed ideas, and they are capable of arresting the interior dialogue dominating the mind. They welcome each success with the admiration and candor of a child, and they open their hearts to sublime feelings. They exhale and scatter the ashes of all stereotyped traditions to then rekindle the fire that produces light and heat, here and now.

But on the path to the realization of one's true nature, habitual forces (of the genealogy tree, society, and culture) will put a multitude of obstacles in the way. The first of these will be the personal self, the acquired identity in all its forms, from the most seductive to the most terrorizing. Following will be the generally accepted ideas, phobias, worries, conflicts, accidents, failures, and so forth . . . the list of obstacles is too long.

But, independent of our training and our identity, life itself constantly presents obstacles and difficulties: unfavorable climate, a blow of bad luck, economic ruin, natural disaster, war, or an epidemic. Here, too, the list of calamities that can occur along the way is endless.

Before these obstacles, difficulties, or "wounds" we have, as did our ancestors before us, two possibilities of action. The first is to react by adopting the already existing attitude of applying a recipe, more or less effectively followed in the past, while remaining faithful to the forces of imitation and behaving in an inherited way. The second is dispatching ourselves to Consciousness, to creativity, to all there is within us, which is more innovative and a greater challenge, while simultaneously allowing obstacles to become our master, which prompts us to produce, in the face of them, unedited solutions whose origins are, in fact, the universal Consciousness. Then we will act as mutants, carrying new information to the genealogy tree. See the chart below.

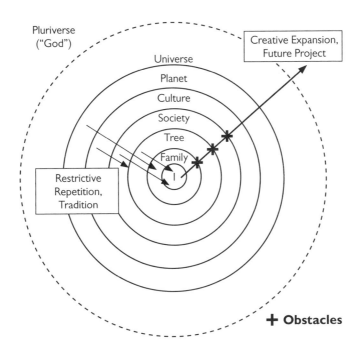

Exercise: Obstacles and the hero

What are the three main obstacles that you encounter in your daily life? Are they:

- Material? (problems with money, nation, health . . .)
- Creative or sexual? (frigidity or impotence, difficulty in creating . . .)
- Emotional? (feelings of inferiority, recurring conflicts . . .)
- Intellectual? (incomprehension, lack of education, verbal abuse . . .)

And between yourself and the society or culture in which you live?

For each obstacle, come up with at least six creative solutions that will allow you to overcome it, however improbable or bizarre these solutions in principle seem. For example, imagine the intervention of a supernatural character or imagine that we have superhuman powers. Put your imagination to work as if it belonged to a fictional character and not to you.

Then stipulate which among these solutions you feel are more feasible and which are absolutely out of reach.

Finally, going beyond your own history, return to take the "impossible" solutions and imagine a character superior to you (a lucky hero) who can put into practice said solutions. Visualize every detail of this triumph over obstacles as if it were a novel or a screenplay. This exercise will allow you to distance yourself from the limitations that your genealogy tree imposes on you.

Exercise: Setting my own limits: exercise for expansion of consciousness

In the same way in which one enters a foreign country—by first getting to the border—we have to first get to our own limitations before we can overcome them. Thus, we explore our own limitations in a symbolic way.

- Sit relaxed on a cushion and think of where the energetic center is: in the head? the chest? the solar plexus (at the tip of the sternum)? the hara (below the umbilical cord)? Any selection will be valid for this exercise.

- Now sanctify said center, and give it a solid existence by imagining a light, a flame, or a golden color there. (To stabilize your starting point a bit more, you can imagine yourself seated on a throne of light.)
- Then, from this center, begin to project six imaginary and subsequently luminous points (rays) as far as possible into space following the six cardinal directions:

1. One ray of light goes as far forward as possible.
2. One ray of light goes as far back as possible.
3. One ray of light goes as far to the right as possible.
4. One ray of light goes as far to the left as possible.
5. One ray of light goes as far up as possible.
6. One ray of light goes as far down as possible.

Also see yourself as far in each direction as your imagination will allow, and when you reach your limit (which is your actual obstacle to your expansion), be grateful that it has become apparent and then direct the beam toward yourself, already enriched by this wisdom, gratitude, Consciousness.

- Once you have explored each of the six directions, one after the other, return to the center and let the six imaginary rays rise together, creating a three-dimensional space around you that extends as far as possible. (This space will be that which defines your "bubble," which is to say, the space in which you are able to spread out into in the present moment.)
- Become aware of this bubble that surrounds you, and then return to the center and give yourself some time to be able to appreciate the time you have devoted to this experience before resuming daily life.
- It is perfectly possible to do this exercise repeatedly. As you go on practicing this, observe how the light rays increasingly go farther.

LESSON FROM CULTURES THEY CALL "PRIMITIVE" AND MAGIC POSSESSION

Genealogy Tree and Possession

This entire study will be peppered with references to various practices—from religion to magic to ritual—that, beyond possible cultural differences, shape part of humanity's heritage and, consequently, our own personal heritage. When addressing the question of ancestors, it is necessary to move away from the strictly Western or "civilized" method that assumes only a rational, scientific, medical, or obvious approach. In this way we will benefit from lessons provided by all of these practices, which use (in a special way or not) the human Unconscious as a reservoir of possible healing and of vital energy.

In summarizing the current discourse in neurology that concerns the function of the human brain, we can say briefly: we use the left lobe for rational thought (more frequently in our conscious activity), and we shift its directives to the "intuitive" right lobe when we sleep. Half of the brain predominates when we are awake, and the other when we are asleep.

But such a division is not absolute. It often occurs to us that we pass from a rational state to an emotional or intuitive state due to some commotion, accident, or other distraction. The quiet body of the brain makes a kind of "bridge" and is, symbolically, the location of the being of Consciousness, which learns to think and to live using both lobes of the brain at the same time. Artists and shamans function in a creative and intuitive way (one could say they open the door to the Unconscious with the practice of art or intuition) while retaining a rationality solidly anchored in the real, in relation to others and in the social context. To understand this, we could use the image of the staff of Hermes, the walking stick by which the two interwoven serpents climb toward still higher heights where the wings are deployed. The two serpents could be the two lobes of the brain and this winged summit the expansion of Consciousness. But such an expansion cannot be fulfilled by way of a hard and fast scientific "maneuver" based exclusively on repro-duced experiences. In everyday life, unique experiences exist that are never repeated but are no less certain. They belong to another order of events—if one must catalog them—that must be submitted to the credit of people in an artistic, not scientific, way. Contrarily, any focus based primarily on the right side of the brain (like the ecstasies of mys-tic leanings or surrealist experiments) can easily and at the same time fall into superstition and be perverted in relation to personal knowledge (as in human relationships), to a lack of awareness, and, one might also say, to common sense.

Our position, in this case, is that one cannot truly comprehend the human being and, consequently, the genealogy tree, if it is not studied from a point of view that unites the artistic with the scientific.

If we accept that *reality* and *dream,* two functions of the human brain, are in truth intimately merged, we have the possibility of using a strategy of comprehension and problem solving consisting of *rationally considering reality to be a dream.* That is to say, when facing a trau-matic situation or one we cannot resolve, we can ask ourselves: Why am I dreaming this situation?

This move from one perspective to the other can be boldly fruit-ful if the person has integrated the two aspects of his cognitive abili-ties. Likewise, with this same perspective, it becomes possible to *dream awake* in a particular situation, or to imagine an ideal outcome or a novel situation whose influence will be felt immediately in reality.

We can also point out that various religious practices (like the Bön tradition of Tibetan Buddhism) encourage work with the lucid dream, that is to say, the capacity in an awake Consciousness to penetrate the universe of the dreams and to control the developments. The objective of the lucid dream is not to artificially fabricate dreams worthy of a big-budget movie; rather it can serve to resolve very deep anxieties.

For example, with a recurring nightmare, we might propose to face the terrifying object (a monster, the thought of an accident, an aggres-sor) that haunts us—which is, in reality, nothing more than a request from our Unconscious—and drive into it with the question, "What do you want from me? Here I am at your disposal." Then this terrifying object reveals itself as a strength from the depths that has come to give us a very valuable message.

In the same way we can also propose, symbolically, to experiment in the state of weightless flight over a place, through a wall, or exceeding the limits of the atmosphere. When we practice exercises like these, whose objective is to detach us from our strictly rational spirit, we are united with the deep Unconscious, the great reservoir of the wisdom of humanity.

The contribution that "primitive" cultures have made in this regard is particularly important if we are interested in possession as a phenomenon. Classic possession consists of (in the case of the possessed) a person abandoning her own ego and personality and bowing to an archetype that has come to inhabit her, taking control of her thoughts, her words, and her acts. In the religions of possession (like in the cult of the Loa of the Afro-Haitian voodoo, or the orishas of the Cuban cult from which they derive) there exists a pantheon of different gods, each one brought about by a conduct, an attribute, or a much-defined power, and by a character, an aspect, or a singular rhythm.

Baron Samedi, Azaka-Tonnerre, Ogu, Èṣù, Ṣàngó, Ogun, Arere, Obatala, Yemaja, Oshun, and so on are spirits or deities with features that the person offered to be possessed (the officiant) does not have in his normal state. During the religious ritual, the officiant adopts the archetype's configuration, forgets himself and his personal features, and adopts the features of the deity or the archetype it possesses. The distance between the officiant who is voluntarily possessed and the personality that takes over during the ritual can be so great that it includes even a change of sex. And if the person is a medium he could *pass into deaths*—that is to say, the dead can speak through him and possess him in order to express themselves.

The shamanic cultures express their own possession phenomenon entity. A priest can, for example, be visited by the spirit of an animal, a plant, or a deity. In shamanism, a person equipped with very refined skills chooses the possession. In voodoo anyone can be possessed, in some cases even against one's will. The difference between the possessed and an actor is minimal. Essentially, the actor knows she is embodying a character, while the possessed *is* the character during the entire possession time. She has been invaded.

Families also behave by possession. It is often observed that a child not only adopts his parents' gestures, saunter, voice inflections, or postures but also their feelings and thoughts. Though these similarities could be due to an innate genetic component, they might be imitation or, more accurately, possession. Usually imitation is voluntary and conscious. This familial mimicry is instead inescapable, unconscious, and irreversible—unless a person can carry out hard work on the ego—and so it is related to possession.

If our parents have been "possessed" by their own parents who were, in turn, by theirs, it is easy to deduce that a child could be "possessed" by his grandfather or by his great-grandfather without ever having known him.

If a person mimics certain values that help him progress toward a goal or some objective, then he can speak of the transmission as a healthy one, since he is an adult in total control of his options. In this case, the imitated values in the genealogy tree may be considered allies.

But the characteristics of the possessor take precedence over those of the possessed, and this drives the possessed toward a suitable "character" rather than personal actualization, and what results is a deprivation of self in the interest of the persona or personas being imitated. And consultants frequently complain of a strong sense of self-devaluation and a negative self-image when this grandfather or that grandmother occupies the place of hero on the genealogy tree. That is to say, the model is always held higher than the person who has been possessed. It might be that this person, condemned to carry the identity of a tragically dead or terminally ill ancestor, will never be able to escape this sacrificial role.

The child's psyche tends to integrate and "duplicate" the feelings, ideas, desires, and acts of other people. This process of duplication is very much linked to fascination: when a more powerful ego (that of the adult) faces another less potent ego (that of the child), the more vulnerable of the two copies the other. This more powerful ego could very well be that of an ancestor, in which case said fascination will have lasted many generations. This same process then returns and replicates when, in adulthood, this person falls into the clutches of people who are dedicated to appropriating the ego of others: scammers, false "gurus," or power-hungry bosses. Accordingly, a person's degree of freedom from the possessions of the genealogy tree determines his degree of vulnerability to this kind of possession.

It is normal for an adult person who finds herself in a situation in which she does not recognize herself to feel totally blocked, and she may fail to carry out the desired changes. It is very probable in this case that one or more transgenerational possessions have been launched, and it would be advisable to clarify and deactivate them.

One example is a woman who had a weak, absent father and a dominating mother who attended to all the matters of the house. This woman ended up marrying a man whose father exerted power but whose mother turned out to be cold and distant. Each of them sought in the other's family the part they lacked: unconsciously, the wife projected onto her father-in-law her ideal father, while the husband wanted to be "adopted" by his mother-in-law, a closer and more attentive version of his own mother. At the time in which they met, both fell in love with the archetype that possessed the other. The wife fell in love with the "strong father" who possessed her husband (who was, in reality, actually crushed by his tyrannical father) and the husband with the "sweet mother" who possessed his wife (who actually resented her father and men in general). Some years later, in crisis, this couple came for a consultation unable to understand how the idyll they had enjoyed in the beginning had led to a marital hell. The study of their two trees helped them emerge from this double possession and find an authentic relationship.

Being clear about the tree can be indispensable for deactivating these "possessions." Sometimes, just one new insight is capable of driving away certain emotional, physical, creative, or sexual habits, including beliefs established over many years.

The genealogy tree can be compared to a "bath" in which we were submerged as kids, and whereby certain qualities and defects soaked into all the facets of our personality, in an apparently irreversible way. For example, we know that all predictions behave as curses do: they take hold of us, and we can't break free of their existence until we notice them. This holds true even for the many affirming predictions we receive from our birth until the moment we become autonomous people: "I will be a great orchestra director," "With these hands, I can build good houses," "Sad, what little faith it will cost to be happy."

Facing these traces of childhood possessions, we propose four therapeutic techniques directly inspired by popular, shamanic, or magical healing methods:

- *Initiatic massage,* in which the body is considered to be simultaneously a receiver of the past (therefore, its entire genealogy tree) and a vehicle of Consciousness (therefore, an essential or perfect body). The aim of this massage is to use touch to give the body the possibility of freedom from ill-fated or useless information of the past in order to integrate the missing information that will permit a materialization of body awareness.

- *The psychoritual,* which consists of "interpreting," as if in a theater with trusted people, a situation destined to heal the scars of the past, which as we will see further on is mainly concerned with our gestation and birth. This staging, which should be prepared and carried out with great care, is intended not to repeat negative information but more to integrate, insofar as it is possible, something we lack.

- *Psychomagic,* an act that fosters an individual situation in which a major shift in reality is achieved. This "waking dream" consists of inoffensively fulfilling an unfeasible fixation of the Unconscious (death wishes, incest, etc.), repairing a traumatic situation (reliving a situation in which abuses were inflicted in order to overcome it), or integrating information and positive qualities thought to be impossible (embodying a heroic character, living through a certain experience, etc.).

- *Psychoshamanism,* where a competent guide mimics the shaman's own interventions (purification, operations, etc.) but then sheds them from his superstitious and dangerous character in order to directly act on the physical Unconscious or "phantom body."

WHO AM I?

From the Personal to the Transpersonal, from the Four Egos to the Essential Being

When speaking of the individual as an object of study, it helps to refine the aspects to which we refer, so we distinguish three levels: the personal self (ego), the transpersonal self (which takes the past into account), and the essential Being.

All of the paths of personal development set out from the ego, pass through the transpersonal self, and flow into the essential Being (which we could also call one's Self or inner god), where things happen harmoniously within ourselves.

The four energies are the physical (material), sexual-creative, emotional, and intellectual, and they manifest in the ego and in the transpersonal self. We all have needs, desires, feelings, and personal thoughts, but we can also cultivate necessities, wishes, feelings, and transpersonal thoughts that—overcoming the limited sphere of egoism—embrace not only the individual but also the group and all of humanity.

All of this occurs in the majority of people in a disorderly and undifferentiated way. Putting everything in order requires personal effort that always involves a certain kind of pain, dissolving the chaos of this undifferentiated imbalance in order to rebuild, or "coagulate," as they say in alchemy, the unity of one's Self.

One of the elements essential to undertaking this is the will to "meet" one's self, to become truly *oneself.* This will is fostered in us by the examples of others we see who are further along the path of the authentic I, who manifest generosity, openness, or devotion in turn, who emanate an irresistible happiness in being alive, and who are peaceful and know how to sit in silence and listen. Moreover, they have a very unusual energy and a wisdom that confuses us.

Suffering exists only on a personal level, and we can also say that everything that is personal is suffering. All of that which is "I" returns, in one way or another, as attachment, as the deprivation of liberty, as limited perceptions, as the impossibility of a truly independent investigation, as surrender to existential schemas imposed by family. This entirely or in part negates *that which is*. Thus, one lives as a totally isolated being. This essential suffering can only be overcome in the transpersonal, in that which is valid to all of mankind. The human being is really humanity. The notion of the solitary individual is an egotistical vision. The lone individual cannot exist. Insofar as she remains captive to the illusion (positive or negative) of living as an isolated individual, she lives in an artificial and imaginary world.

Very frequently, work on oneself begins with an awareness of suffering. Then resistance arrives. We resist change, and often personal needs enter into conflict with transpersonal needs. It also happens with desires, emotions, and thoughts. At the point of departure, everything presents itself as an intricate and confusing whole and helps to clarify desires, needs, feelings, and ideas that cheer us up. Some of us are unique, but the majority of us are the inheritance of the genealogy tree.

At the end of intense and persevering work it is possible to open each and every one of these centers, allowing them to enjoy the magnitude of humanity and not only that of individuality. But it is necessary to have the will to create an objective perspective that is cut off from the four elements, an outlook that is not only that of one's needs, that of a being (which is, for the moment, self) agitated by desires and emotions, or that of one's intellect. This new outlook is divided into two stances, one directed toward the ego and the other toward the transpersonal self, in order to dissolve and know each one's aspect separately.

In the first moment, the outlook on the ego is certainly painful, because here we recognize the triviality of our false identity. "I am not this" is what happens to those who start Zen meditation. Sitting for twenty minutes in absolute silence, they discover a huge multitude of disordered ideas that churn in their mind, or the ocean of chaotic emotions that follow one after the other in their heart, and suffer still the impatience and inconveniences of a body unaccustomed to immobility.

It is at this moment when it is truly useful to look toward the transpersonal self, for this backcombing of sublime emotions does not only say "self" (or I) but includes "us" (or we). As a general rule the personal self learns, in this process, to collaborate with the Unconscious and the Supraconscious. Meanwhile, the transpersonal self starts to discover the collective Unconscious, moving beyond the childish feeling of "everything for me" possession into the adult altruism of "nothing for me that is not for everyone." The transpersonal self begins to consider that everything humanity enjoys comes from the universe and passes through "me" in order to be transmitted. From a first "solid" and personal state (reinforced by borders and protected with bolts), it switches channels.

This free outlook that the will has produced is going to integrate the transpersonal self into daily life little by little. From now on the actions and individual decisions will be stained by impersonal intent, like caring for and protecting our ecosystem and the planet, giving to those in need, resolving conflicts by recognizing our part in them, and promoting harmony. This regard, which simultaneously separates and unites everything, is going to turn into the foundation of the Consciousness of the essential Being, and, finally, it would be wonderful if the transpersonal self-lived "I am not this either" is finally concluded.

If we rely on the subdivision of four energies, we can see that four egos exist: one physical, another sexual and creative, another emotional, another intellectual. Each one of these four egos has two aspects, a personal and a transpersonal.

The Physical Ego

Personal: Aspires to immortality, infallible health, eternal youth, invulnerability, abundance, and wealth.

Transpersonal: Accepts illness, old age, and death, although realizing that humanity, in oneself, is immortal. Age is a contribution of culture and wisdom for the youth of humanity. Each inflicted illness turns into a lesson that makes us conscious of the existence of internal conflicts, including problems that are still unresolved, like cholera and other epidemics that are directly linked to the extreme poverty in which part of the planet lives. The transpersonal self eliminates absurd needs inculcated by media, society, or culture.

The Sexual and Creative Ego

Personal: The wish to possess everything, to create everything. Aspires to be the best lover, the greatest artist, the most formidable healer, and also to blast all competitors. Seeks the satisfaction and the victory.

Transpersonal: Tames its urges and cravings, learns to collaborate in acts of collective creation, perceiving clearly that nothing one creates will belong to oneself and that one is simply a channel. This is sacred art, useful action, healthy sexuality, and a medium for union with the divine.

The Emotional Ego

Personal: Wants to be loved exclusively and to be loved with exclusivity. Confuses love with possession.

Transpersonal: Understands that love is universal and learns to transmit that which is received, and whatever is received is distributed. Has had the experience of a love without possessions or borders, where everyone is the same (the Christic love). "If you take sand and you put sand in a closed hand, you don't keep more than a handful of sand. But if you open the hand, all of the sand of the desert will be able to pass through your fingers" (Arab proverb).

The Intellectual Ego

Personal: Wants to explain everything, control everything, and shred everything. Clings to beliefs, opinions, fears, and above all else the craziness.

Transpersonal: Learns to be quiet and listen. Renounces understanding everything to be able to understand the notion of Everything, like this African proverb suggests: "The truth is not only in the head. It then passes from *to create* into *to know.*" As the nineteenth-century Indian saint Ramakrishna responded to a question about his faith, "I do not believe in God, I know God."

In the end, the transpersonal self arrives at a point in which it realizes its limits: "I am nothing, I can do nothing, I know nothing." It is then that one recognizes one's origin, the Self, which says, "I am Everything, I can do Everything, I know Everything."

In this completely whole center age does not exist, there is only an eternal youth; nothing of ignorance, only total wisdom; nothing of beliefs, only total abundance; nothing of individualism, only the unified totality. Some people, nearing this state, form a new individual illusion about the universal center. They fall into an ego trap that glorifies, and they imagine themselves being "elected" or exclusive depositaries of the unified Consciousness, which, in reality, is a universal treasure. This way, they create certain deviations of saints, gurus, master egotists, and so forth.

The essential Being is not the privilege of anyone but a benefit for everyone, in exactly the same way that the fragrance of a rose does not pertain to any of the petals in particular but is owed to the generic essence of the totality of the rose.

When a person is able to dissolve into the essential Being, it produces that which the Evangelicals call transfiguration. The body loses the weight of suffering, emotions become sublime, and ideas are fluid and awarded the happiness to live. This transfiguration can be permanent or timely, and if it doesn't last, it at least leaves behind a taste, which permits the frequent return. When this state is made permanent, the essential Being folds in turn into the personality, the personal ego and transpersonal ego, like the hug of a mother supported by a great tenderness. "This person with my name exists, this person with my name is going to die, but in the end this person who has my name and is mortal is an illusion." This is the message of all the great spiritual traditions.

PART TWO

Your Tree

Individual Faces Lineage

THREE

The Magic Carpet
By Alejandro Jodorowsky

In the summer of 1979, I still did not know that I was going to create an entire therapeutic system based on the study of the genealogy tree. My films *El Topo* (1970) and *Holy Mountain* (1973) had just begun to have a bit of success in France, and the producer Eric Rochat asked me to travel to India to make a film about the story of an elephant who, born into slavery, frees himself little by little by expanding his Consciousness and becomes the divine elephant Ganesh, worshipped by all. I spent three months in Bangalore, India, surrounded by elephants to make the children's movie *Tusk* (1980).

Upon returning to Paris in early fall, I received the crushing news that my producer would not pay me what my contract stipulated because he had declared bankruptcy. With the little bit of money I had left, I rented a little house outside of Paris in Joinville le Pont, and I had to read Tarot cards so I could feed my wife and kids. Many might have considered this a disgrace, but it was a benefit to me. If my producer had not been the swindler he was, I never would have created Tarology, Psychogenealogy, Psychomagic, and Psychoshamanism.

For my consultations I painted a room white, ceiling and walls, and polished and varnished the floorboards. I bought a purple tapestry about five feet long by thirty-one inches wide and spread it out in the middle of the floor of this clean space, free of furniture and paintings on the walls.

Opposite the purple rectangle, the consultant—seated like me on a *zafu,* a Zen meditation cushion—would listen as I read his Tarot cards. Why the purple rectangle? At this time, I had a close friendship with an extraordinary man, Pierre Derlon, author of the book *Secrets of the Gypsies,* published by Robert Laffont in 1975. French by birth, Pierre was a specialist of gypsy magic. His concepts were very useful for me, although, at times, he said things that were hard for me to believe. For example, although he appeared to be thirty years old and his gypsy wife sixty, he claimed that they were the same age. . . . *Thanks to the magic spell from a tribal Elder, I age only once every two years!*

Among other things, Derlon showed me a purple (the color for inherently mindful gypsies) anti-insomnia pillow, a calendar made of matches, a special way of cutting apples for use in love rituals, and a way to predict the future with chicken bones. This did not interest me very much because, from the beginning of my Tarology work, I rejected the dubious activity of reading the future and dedicated myself instead to reading the consultant's present: his current problems, fruits of a conflicted past.

However, what did pique my interest was the magic carpet. Derlon told me that when gypsies want to concentrate, they nail four stakes into the ground, join them with twine to create a rectangle about thirty-one inches wide by a little over five feet long, and use it to "stash" empty cans, stones, pieces of wood, and so forth, arranged in geometric shapes. Seated opposite this rectangle, with a fixed stare, they eventually depart from space and time, traveling to another reality. Pierre was convinced that this practice was the origin of the flying carpet story that appears in some Arabic fairy tales. The day we moved to Joinville le Pont, Pierre came to our house unannounced, stuck four forks in the yard, and tied them together with a cord to make a rectangle in which he arranged some stones, dried branches, three bottles of cola, and half a dozen potatoes that he took from his pockets, and he invited me to kneel down in front of this magic carpet to meditate and leave my body. The experience interested me. I had just read in *Wittgenstein,* by William Warren Bartley III (1973), about a dream the philosopher Ludwig Josef Johann Wittgenstein had in 1919. The dream had left him with a riddle that he was unable to solve.

> It was night. I found myself outside of a house over which light beamed. I got close to a window to look inside. There on the floor, I noticed an exquisitely beautiful magic carpet, which I imme-diately wanted to examine. I tried to open the front door, but a snake blocked my path. I tried to go through another door but another snake launched out at me, again blocking my path. Snakes also appeared in the windows to block my efforts at reaching the magic carpet.

According to Bartley, Wittgenstein interpreted the carpet as a phallus and the snakes as moral barriers to his homosexuality. A carpet a phallus? Why not a womb in which we are allowed to die in order to be reborn in another dimension? The carpet in the dream presented the philosopher with the possibility of exceeding his rational mind, and of entering into the magic of life. Avoiding his feelings and desires, and identifying with his intellect by way of condemning the snakes, he rejects entrance into a world that goes beyond words. The guardian reptiles are his rational limits. Stagnant concepts impede the flight of his imagination into the depths of his Unconscious; Zen monks call this *stepping into the void.* Determined not to be overcome by the terror of freeing myself from the rational prison, I sat facing the rectangle that Pierre Derlon created with the firm intention of decapitating my mental serpents and surrendering to a magic trip. We remained immobile with fixed stares until night-fall. I did not leave my body or time or space; I did not *fly* as he wanted. Pierre left without hiding his disappointment. I never saw him again. He died in 1989.

Nevertheless, that experience was essential for the future development of my therapeutic techniques. Upon kneeling and facing the rectangle to meditate, I felt my psychic shadow project onto it. A vertical axis divided the left and right sides. Three horizontal axes divided four parts. My head was reflected in the top part, my chest in the next, then hips, pelvis, and penis, and finally, in the part closest to me, the fourth part, my legs and knees. The vertical axis turned these four parts into eight. Those on the right corresponded to my active energies, and those on the left to my receptive energies. The section closest to me, the first section, reflected my material life (my necessities, my upbringing); the next section corresponded to my sexual and creative desires; the third to my emotional life; the fourth to my intellectual life.

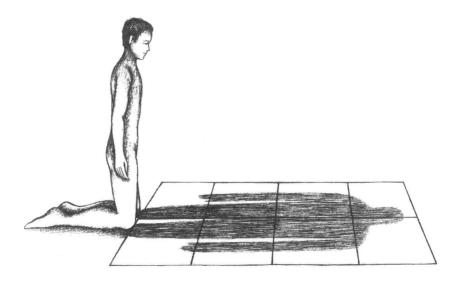

Drawing by Pascale Montandon

This way of projecting myself onto a rectangle—which originated with my use of the purple tapestry—broadened my horizons and changed my way of reading the Tarot. At this time I invented

Tarology to distinguish my work from that of fortune-tellers; my goal was to interpret the graphic language of the Tarot without attributing any psychic gifts to myself. This practice would later give birth to another discipline that I would call Psychogenealogy.

From then on, I organized my readings in the following manner.

The consultant put five of the Tarot deck's twenty-two Major Arcana in each of the four sections. This made twenty cards. The remaining two, placed off the tapestry, symbolized what the consultant had been in the past (the bottom one) and what the consultant wanted to be in the future (the top one). The consultant revealed her doubts to me, her problems in choosing between several options, and so on. I began by analyzing her material needs, then going up, step by step, her creative or sexual conflicts, her emotional life, and, at the top of the tapestry, the ideas that govern her life.

I can attest to the fact that as soon as we started examining her material area of health, work, and territory, the consultant would want to address her childhood, birthplace, and sibling relationships, until finally ending up talking about the circumstances into which she was born.

In the second section, the parents appeared as a formative influence on both the consultant's capacity to create and her sexual attitude. Meanwhile, the parents' creativity and sexuality often depended on the relationships the parents had had with their own siblings. The maternal and paternal aunts and uncles proved to be of vital importance for the consultant even if she had never met them.

In the third section, after scrutinizing the consultant's feelings, I realized the importance of the four grandparents and the great-aunts and great-uncles. They passed their emotional successes and failures on to the next generation, who passed them on to their children.

The last section, which clarifies the intellectual space, I found to be made up to a large degree by absurd ideas and out-of-date morals transmitted by the great-grandparents. Always prevailing was some religious book poorly translated by misogynist priests with political objectives—be it the Torah, the New Testament, the Qur'an, Buddhist texts, or sacred books of other religions.

In this way, while going section by section, I came to visualize the consultant's genealogy tree on my carpet. Enthusiastic about my discovery, I put aside the purple tapestry and the Tarot cards and devoted myself to the exclusive study of my consultants' genealogy tree. I investigated their family details and wrote down the data on a sheet of rectangular paper. In general, the solicited information included first and last names, dates of birth and death, causes of deaths, marriages, adulteries, abortions, divorces, illnesses, abuses, accidents, land loss (domicile changes, exile, war), economic ruin, injustices, professions, awards, and failures of each member of the consultant's family up to his great-grandparents.

With few exceptions, I did not try to search for the fifth generation or later because family memory fades beyond the great-grandparents. It is nearly impossible to find accurate data on these tumults of personality because data gets wiped out, only fragments of a personality are transmitted, and hardly any images and few words still exist. As we have eight great-grandparents, each previous generation doubles to a total of sixteen great-great-grandparents. Generation after generation, our ancestors are increasing: 32, 64, 128, 256, 512. In thirty generations, our ancestors equal 1,073,741,824—more than a million. Going too far back in time with this multiplication of ancestors abandons the dominion of the family as such to the multitude of society, encompassing all of humanity. After a number of consultations, I realized that with little exception the Unconscious organizes itself over a familial terrain that covers only four generations. Thereafter, the tree descends into anonymous ghosts.

I could also verify that the whole family, from great-grandparents to the consultant, formed the unit that was the basis of all of each individual's problems and virtues. One could not treat anyone without also treating the family, which nests in the darkness of the Unconscious. Astonishing repetitions emerged, as if on photographic paper where the image contained is revealed under acid. From the first to the fourth generation names, illnesses, losses, and conflicts are reproduced. Obscure zones appear: relatives are expelled from the clan and, from those, nothing is transmitted; secrets are jealously guarded; there are sibling rivalries, resentments, neuroses of failures, shame, economic ruin, and so on. But the tree was not only a war zone and a place of sorrow, it was also a place of fulfillment for moral and spiritual values and the capacity to confront difficulties and resolve conflicts. I realized that the genealogy tree was, at the same time, a trap and a treasure.

Such was the impact of this work that my consultants organized workshops, which I called Psychogenealogy. In 1980 a small group of volunteers, among them therapists, psychologists, and psychiatrists interested in my theories, began to meet so as to undergo experimental exercises using their genealogy trees. This allowed us to see deeper aspects of the family trap, for example, programming. Programmed childbirth: "My mother had her first child at thirty-six, I am twenty-six. I have ten years left to enjoy life." Programmed indifference: "My father never loved me. I have such bad luck. It is certain I will end up living with a selfish and indifferent man." Programmed death (an example from Freud's correspondence): "Do not be surprised if I don't, at eighty-plus years old, ruminate on whether I will reach the age of my father and of my brother or exceed them to live to be as old as my mother when she died."*

The family is a clan to which we want to belong, perhaps due to our proclivity as warm-blooded mammals to die if we are separated from the herd. Fearful of being excluded for being different, we repeat the mistakes that flow out of our ancestry. If a grandmother suffers from liver disease, her grandchildren say they have a weak liver, thus affirming their membership in the group. If a great-grandfather returned from WWI trenches with his lungs eaten away by gases, many of his descendants will suffer with lung illnesses.

---

*[Translated from Spanish by Rachael LeValley. —Trans.]

A social ascent that does not enter into the family's conscious or unconscious plans can drive a person, at the height of success, to self-destruction. I recall a case of laborer parents who criticized their daughter for graduating from veterinary school and earning plenty of money; the girl ended up working as a supermarket cashier. Or the miner grandfather who died from an accident that shattered his skull; his son and grandson became hairdressers.

For more than a year, I gave these seminars twice a month. At the same time, I began to give free lectures every Wednesday, which very quickly became known as "Mystic Cabaret." At first these took place at a small dance studio on Malebranche Street; in the 1980s at the School of Mimes; in 1992 on the Jussieu campus of the Pierre and Marie Curie University; and finally, in Paris at the karate *dojo* of my friend Jean-Pierre Vigneau.

During a visit to the Rodin Museum, another image solidified the next part of my experimentation with and study of the genealogy tree. I intuited that the family, dead or alive, organizes itself in each individual Unconscious and becomes like a statuary group sculpture—this came to me upon viewing Rodin's monumental sculpture *Les Bourgeois de Calais* (*The Burghers of Calais*).

We each have a subjective perception of time and space that depends on our genealogy tree. For example, many women, feeling that the moment has arrived, marry at the age at which their mothers did; many men succeed or fail at the same age at which their grandfathers did. There are those who feel old at forty, while others believe they are young at seventy. Some people are satisfied to live in 200 square feet of space, while others feel they are suffocating in 3,300 square feet. Certain characters confine themselves to a small mental island, while others exist on a broader scale, and some rare individuals live in the middle of eternity and infinity. The limits we impose on our temporal and spatial imagination come from our ancestors' morality, religion, social status, and levels of Consciousness. The interior space where we organize our memories has a bright center that expands outward while becoming darker and darker, and this is where we arrange our family. The important ones we put in or near the center; the less important ones we place nearer the dark edges—as in medieval art. Whomever exercised more power is granted more love and is given greater stature. What is important is to discover where we place ourselves. Are we at the center of our tree, the essential fruit, or have we been disposed to secondary darkness?

The family group nests in all of us, in our interior spaces, arranged according to our prejudices, frustrations, and desires and the moral values that have been transmitted to us. In the same way that the family could be symbolized on the purple tapestry and in the Tarot cards, I imagined the family could be portrayed three-dimensionally.

My weekly conferences, which had become populated with something like two or three hundred people, offered the ideal context for this experiment. In 1980 I created the *dramatization of the tree* by randomly choosing a spectator and asking her to pick people to represent her family members from among the rest of the group present. I had her identify people as siblings, parents, grandparents, and great-grandparents and organize them into a whole—with absent or unknown relatives positioned far away from the group; important or dominating relatives seated in a chair; humiliated relatives crouching; the rejected, for whom only a name is known, with their backs to us; for the stillborn, spectators lay on the floor in the fetal position; the loved ones, very close; the hated ones, separated or with their backs to us; and so on.

Once this group was formed, I asked the chosen one to take her position among them, thus revealing the problem of adjustment within the family: the feeling of exclusion, the acknowledgment of a preferred or rivaled sibling, the forced worship of a grandfather (who was built up as the only true man of the family). I asked the consultant to talk with each *actor*. The actors almost always responded fittingly because of the inexplicable mystery that the chosen actors always had something in common (in experience, in character) with the person they were chosen to interpret. For example, if a grandmother had died of cancer, the person chosen to embody her would have a grandmother who had developed a tumor. I came to the conclusion that the Unconscious telepathically captures each person's family drama.

My experience as a theater director allowed me to moderate these sessions and to take into account each of the collaborators present on *stage*. Once the tree had been formed, as well as the understanding that every performance should culminate with a conclusion—the most positive one possible—I strained to direct them in a way that would permit the consultant and his benevolent helpers to not have performed in vain. This is how I began to explore a vast field: the healing of the tree.

During these dramatizations, after gaining an understanding of the family's level of Consciousness and having seen the problems, I asked the consultant to grant each relative that which he or she lacked. To those who died young, give them a long life; to those who failed, allow them to triumph; to the sick, provide them with good health; to the poor and unloved, bestow upon them prosperity and love; to the excluded and the absent, give them back their place in the family.* Always attuned to the harmony of the characters in this exterior space that reflected the consultant's inner space, I asked him to balance the position of the actors—lowering those who were perched in chairs and raising up those lying on the floor or squatting—to grant the same dignity to everyone. Straight away, I advised the consultant to take a position in the group that would make him feel happiest. The consultant always, after searching for different solutions, stood between his father and mother. The consultant then added his siblings, aunts and uncles, grandparents and great-grandparents. Generally the work concluded with the consultant, surrounded by the actors embodying relatives, forming a compact group, united in a general embrace.

---

*The essence of this work I later presented in my novel published in 2002 by Siruela, *Donde mejor canta un pájaro* (Where a Bird Sings Better).

Over the years I realized that some of the frequent attendees to my conferences had ordained themselves "genealogy tree therapists" or "psychogenealogists." Having no desire whatsoever to guarantee a so-called profession of something that was for me only a vast search, I quit giving seminars and public conferences and carried on with my work in private. I decided to receive one consultant every day. Together we would establish her genealogy tree and I would do my best to guide her healing.

I believe it necessary to clarify why I opted to use the word "consultant" when talking about my Tarot readings or my genealogy tree analyses: I reject the use of the word "patient" because it seems to me to be reserved for the medical domain and because, according to what I feel, in the context of psychotherapy it devalues the person's eagerness toward self-fulfillment. To heal, in psychological terms, is to find yourself. A "patient," being essentially passive, cannot cure himself because he waits for his health to be returned to him by a doctor or by a charlatan. A "consultant" is capable of converting himself into his own healer. He knows that his accomplishment (finding peace) depends on his own efforts. A therapist should behave not like a prideful master, but instead like a humble guide.

I began my sessions reading the consultant's Tarot, which allowed me to quickly identify the central problem. Then, on a big piece of paper, I wrote down as much data on the family as possible, and I analyzed it. Once this history was in order we theatricalized the tree on a circular table using a variety of small dolls, sometimes twenty or more for large families. Having positioned everyone, the consultant identified her ancestors one by one, giving them voice and holding conversations with each of them to bring the problems out into the light. I added small objects: a little black ball symbolized breast cancer passed down from grandmother to mother to granddaughter; a small, broken sword symbolized intellectual failure suffered by three or more generations of relatives who could not achieve the coveted diploma; a little tube of red dye represented rejection or disregard of menstruation in misogynist trees. The consultant identified with these objects and passed them from one doll to the next, also giving them voice.

Finally, I asked the consultant to draw a depiction of the whole family, including herself, on another piece of paper, but without speaking or the use of anthropomorphic shapes. It often occurs that an outright prohibition made in childhood impedes the consultant's ability to verbally express her desires or aspirations. When she is allowed to substitute drawings for spoken descriptions with drawings, the consultant can draw that which was forbidden. For example, she can draw a half-page circle (the mother) and a small square in the far corner (the weak or absent father), placing them in the center of a big circle shaped very much like a fetus to express, in a way, a feeling of not yet having been born. This intuitive drawing session completes the *theatricalization of the tree* and ends with asking the consultant to readjust the drawing so that the picture is satisfactory.

These experiences confirmed for me the idea that these genealogy tree structures should be observed with an artistic eye capable of capturing this miracle.

FOUR

Clarify the
Genealogy Tree
Collecting and Organizing Information

In this chapter, we propose various forms of collecting and organizing information to create different outlines of the genealogy tree that will allow the consultant to carry out the analysis she wants to perform.

Collecting information is very important. The quality of the concrete data we collected will depend on many factors: age (a "young" tree has more living witnesses); the country or the countries in which the family is rooted (available data differs according to region, society, and culture); and particularities of the family data (a propensity to transmit information soiled by dysfunction or violence, loaded with secrets, etc.). Whatever the situation, it comes down to collecting as much information as possible in order to have a very clear idea of what escapes—and will always escape—from our desire for objective knowledge.

Once we have carried out this research, we can let the unconscious information (some would say imaginary or fictitious) emerge, which in due course also finds its way into the tree. The information, memories, or subjective inventions should not intervene until we have accomplished and established the actual frame and purpose of the tree as has been indicated so far. In the end, our work is about enabling a harmonious dialogue to occur between the two halves of our brain: the rational and the intuitive.

The next stage will be organizing the various forms of the tree so as not to be partial to any particular representation. We will do this first in a rectangular and rational scheme to clarify the position of everyone in the lineage, before tackling the more organic and intuitive representations that account for our conception of the family at the time we begin the work of increasing awareness. Thus, we will face various images of the tree, which are intended to continue to evolve even more in the course of our "journey."

COLLECTING INFORMATION

Three principal difficulties arise that we must accept and overcome:

- **A lack of objective information.** Whatever our efforts, we can never know "the whole truth" because many objective, tangible traces have been erased by the vagaries of life. This applies to all families and all cultures.
- **Family resistance.** The living witnesses cannot or do not want to provide accurate information because of embarrassment, shame, exhaustion, loss of memory, denial, and so forth. Contrarily, certain members of the family are so eager to express themselves that their subjective narration, inevitably biased, becomes the tree's official truth—although not necessarily the truth that will give us a balanced view of the lineage. Family memory is based on a certain number of myths and legends, which are, in reality, more or less deliberately concocted to strengthen the cohesion of the clan. For example, we might say of a child that her birth "went really well," but she was born prematurely, by way of forceps, or after two days of labor. Another common myth might be the woman who, when asked about her childhood, responds, "I was loved," and then provides a list of idyllic relationships, when in reality the relationships were marked by many shortcomings and

abuse. And we frequently come across the myth of noble origins: a woman whose father lost all his money gambling might invent a myth in which the man was a saint who gave all his money to the needy; a person who made a pact with the oppressive forces during the war could be presented, once peace is restored, as a resistance fighter.

- **Our own resistance.** In one way or another the tree inside each of us refuses to give up certain information. If we discover a truth, an unknown fact, that we do not acknowledge because it clashes with our resistance, the truth can fade away as if only a dream. We "forget" or "lose" very useful details, certain steps seem insurmountable, we constantly reject asking certain questions, we imagine that too much investigation could endanger the physical and mental health of the people we want to question, and so on.

These three obstacles will always be present in some measure. But with calm perseverance we can learn a lot from our genealogy tree, whose purpose is to gather information and to identify all that is humanly possible to know about our genealogy. Essential are prudence, lucidity, and method, above all else. Subsequently, the imagination or unconscious memories can play a role, but not before we have clarified all the objective information available.

Consider the extreme case of an orphan who thinks it impossible to establish her genealogy tree. In reality, this person has more of a chance than one could imagine on the surface.

To begin, she has an **educator tree,** and she can establish the genealogy of the people who took care of her. The genealogy of the adoptive parents makes sense for the adopted child since she became a member of the family, while a person who was brought up by several people or successive institutions must ask, "Who mostly played the role of mother, father, brother(s), and sister(s) in my life? Who represented my maternal and paternal grandparents?"

Frequently in the genealogy of an adopted child, family secrets or unspoken pain led to the couple's sterility. The adoption then was designed as an act of salvation, and the child, like the parents, may not want to dig into this genealogy if there is a risk of revealing the suffering.

When a child is raised in an institution, she is marked by the beliefs and cultural habits of members of this institution and can therefore be considered, for better or for worse, an unwitting heir.

Every person also possesses a **genetic tree,** even if there is little or no information on the tree in question. Eye color, ethnicity, hair type, size, and possibly certain peculiarities or genetic diseases can be precious signs. If someone was adopted during a certain era or in a specific place it helps to look into history, geography, and sociology, clues that allow us to build possible scenarios. For example, a child abandoned at the social services office during WWII may have been the result of adultery, and the mother feeling guilty, wanted to hide this from the husband who was away, fighting for his country. If someone is adopted in a foreign country, it helps to know what was, at the time, the relationship between the country of birth and the country of adoption.

For example: A man with Eurasian traits was adopted in French Indochina during the colonial years. He knew his mother was Vietnamese and that she had confessed to the orphanage that she gave him up "because I cannot take care of him," but he never thought to ask who his father was. However, an abundant hairiness on the back of his hands indicated Western genes mixed with his Asian genes. Recognizing that his father was probably, in all likelihood, a French soldier forced him to envision several painful hypotheses: that the father had abandoned the mother while she was pregnant, or even that perhaps he was the child of a rape. This perspective led him to eventually reconsider his own role as a man and father of a family. His values, his sense of responsibility, and the entire question of his own virility were hit by culpability, even on the unconscious level. "My mother was a victim of my father. I must not become like this man." All of that was hidden beneath the initial declarations: I don't know anything. I was an orphan.

Finally, an orphan who has little information about his family of origin often has an **imaginary tree,** which he dreamed of during childhood: genealogy as fairy tale. He imagines himself the descendant of a wealthy family, or a child of a forbidden love between someone from the upper class and someone from the lower class. In reality, it is often the child's idealized version of a scandal: rape, prostitution, or incest. In the conventional imagination, the father abandons the mother, and the mother abandons the child. These daydreams often also include forgotten memories or suppressed information.

When approaching the gaps in our trees, in some ways it is useful to behave as if we were orphans. We can use our educator tree, not to be confused with the dominating ideology that the family wants to present itself as; our genetic tree, which begets us, sexually, with its trail of secrets, among which the most frequent are hidden abortions or illegitimate fatherhood; and an imaginary tree, which lives in our individual imaginations: my dad is the strongest in the world, my mom is the most beautiful in the world, my parents are famous.

In practice, these are the elements to be collected when studying the family tree. If possible this information must cover all ascendants of the direct line (great-grandparents, grandparents, and parents) as well as oneself and one's brothers and sisters.

Notice the Given Names and Surnames of All Members of the Tree

Our given name is the sum total by which we are identified. Consequently, our given name is a key element of our acquired identity, to which it can have attached various illnesses (we may carry the first name of a crazy person, a dead person, a sick person, or a betraying friend) and projections (we are named for such-and-such person because we represent a flame, as if we are accomplices to something we did not do). Certain cultures give several first names to a child at birth. In many societies, a child carries the given names of his grandparents, of his godfather or godmother, or even of his parents. During Francoist Spain, adding Maria to girls' given names was obligatory in accordance with a political and social system that confined women to the role of wife and mother in the strictest Catholic tradition. All of these elements must be taken into consideration and not minimized: in every case, the given names reveal something of the transmission of unconscious work in the family, as we shall see in detail later.

Specify Important Dates (Births, Marriages, Deaths)

Also of interest is when each couple met (date, era), the circumstances of this encounter, and whether a marriage took place before or after the conception of the first child. This is, in reality, intended to build a simplistic and, at the same time, concrete vision: How old were my ancestors when they died? How old were they when they married? Did births take place outside of marriage? Who was the eldest and who was the youngest of the siblings? At what age did they lose their parent(s)? Frequently, if a firstborn sibling was conceived before the marriage of his parents, that fact is, even if it is not, strictly speaking, a family secret, never mentioned. Comparing the parents' date of marriage and the child's date of birth permits the reality of these facts to be restored.

Often, we have the tendency to think of members of our families as frozen at the age or in the role in which we knew them when we were children. But it is possible that the woman whom we know as a kind, sixty-year-old, peaceful grandmother was, for our father or mother, a difficult, overwhelmed, controlling, or hysterical mother whose personality has nothing to do with the "granny" we know. Similarly, sibling rivalries or even hatred between brothers and sisters is sometimes reversed in adulthood, so the father or grandfather's hated little brother can become someone who now is always welcomed at the family table. But even if as adults the hatred is resolved, the trace of this childhood conflict can mark the genealogy tree in a way that will directly affect us; for example, a father or mother may project onto his or her own offspring the rival sibling.

Clarify the Causes or Circumstances of Deaths

Beyond a specific medical diagnosis, and in the event of an accident, one must have the most accurate image possible of "what happened." Death remains a major taboo in our society, more so if it is a premature or accidental death. If someone from the genealogy tree lost his life in a car accident, one must know who was driving and what the circumstances of the accident were. If the deceased was driving and no collision took place, it is likely that the death was partly seen as a suicide by his relatives. If, on the other hand, another person was responsible for the accident, the death verges more toward a murder—with or without the guilty being named.

With ancestors whom we know little about, it is common for the circumstances of their deaths to inform us of their character, their secret wounds, their levels of Consciousness. In the same way as in ancient China, where a good man made sure to utter in his last breath a final poem by which his relatives would remember him, one can say that the way we die is our last poem, our last message to subsequent generations.

For Each Couple, Note the Number of Children

How many pregnancies did each woman have? Among her children, how many are alive? How many are dead? Miscarriages? Abortions? This information is sometimes difficult to obtain, but more women than one might think are willing to speak of their terminated (intentional or not) pregnancies.

Every child conceived exists in the familial Unconscious as a sibling, even if he did not pass the fetal stage. A miscarried or aborted fetus is often transformed in the mother's mind, or in the mind of other members of the family, into an "angel" or potential savior, unsurpassable. This is why abortions, miscarriages, and premature deaths in a family of several children can psychically influence the rest of the siblings, especially if the mother did not have the time or the emotional means to mourn.

Take Note of Everyone's Profession

Clues can be found in the information surrounding issues of social recognition and achievement, the reproduction of parental models, and standards of living. For women in the tree it is important to know the circumstances of their lives as the mothers of the family: with or without domestic help, working outside the home or not, and so forth. The shift between a declared vocation, or studies undertaken, and the profession by which a person has earned a living may also be interesting.

Investigate Ancestors' Major Life Events

Grand voyages, exiles, accidents, religious vocation, imprisonment, war, illnesses, handicaps, important successes or failures, love affairs (sexually consummated or not), political affiliation—the genealogy tree is also a socio-professional portrait of the family. What worldviews, conceptions of money, social relations, and work have we inherited? What concepts of good luck and bad luck, of health and illness, of strength and weakness does our tree guard? A short biography of each of its members, to summarize the major events of their existences, is useful to characterize the lines of force that maneuver our destiny. Are we heir to a professional tradition? Are we asked, instead, to repair a social injustice? Are we haunted by the prospect of failure, an epidemic that took place in the past? What are our ideas about exile—was our genealogy tree "nomadic" or "sedentary"? All of these questions find very clear responses if we commit to retracing the paths of all members, not just the paths of certain positive or negative "heroes," like the uncle who made a fortune in America, the great-aunt who was a prostitute and died in destitution, or the respected, notable ancestor who was her town's mayor. Often, some prominent characters attract all the family's attention, but one must ensure the completion of the chart.

Get an Idea of the Relationships between Members of the Same Household

Even if attachments are taboo they exist in certain families, especially rivalries or privileged relationships between brothers and sisters or between parents and children: solidarity, complicity, or conflict. It is inevitable that these elective affinities occur within a family.

The web of preferences and conflicts is the basic dynamic of a family unit. We are, in general, conscious of the connections and oppositions at work in our own childhoods. It is crucial that we understand who was, in the childhoods of our parents and grandparents, the "preferred" and "unloved," the "kind" and "mean," and how each was forced to play his role in the family economy.

Take into Account Historical Circumstances (War, Revolution . . .)

If the tree is seriously affected, it is necessary to examine in a basic way how society interacts with the tree. If your tree suffered World War I in France, it is necessary to have an idea of the conditions of life in the trenches, of the practice of gassing, of the way in which life was organized for the families without a father or elder brother, to see the inequalities between the different regions. For example, in Corsica, unlike the rest of France, a father of more than five children was not exempt from the draft, and a Corsican could not return for a year, while the rest of the French had permission to return every three months. This trauma from inequality heavily marked Corsican society and, in certain measure, resulted in their reclamation of identity in the 1970s and the accompanying violence.

Other Elements to Include

If one or more persons, although they are not related by blood lineage, had a decisive influence, it is well to note their existence: priest, friend of the family, boss, lover, late marriage, godfather, godmother, and so on.

If we possessed the totality of this information (which is never the case), we could approach our tree as a documentarian or as an omniscient novelist who then somewhat observes all the characters in the saga according to the actual conditions of childhood, adolescence, maturity, old age, happiness, strife. At the end of the day it is this broadmindedness that we aim for in order to understand all the elements of our upbringing.

Resources We Can Use for This Investigation

- Documents: identification cards, correspondences, military records, diplomas, report cards, diaries
- Collections, pictures, and films, which provide us with the missing persons' physical attributes and sometimes clues about their personality
- Family albums and civil status records
- Cemeteries, where tombs generally carry names and dates
- Archives of local newspapers
- Internet resources, including genealogists in other countries and community associations and their archives
- Conversations with members of the family or relatives

Interviewing our parents, cousins, uncles, aunts, and family friends is often the best resource. While those who hold this information may be reluctant to deliver, we can nevertheless ask them objective questions detached of emotional issues, which do not require a personal response.

- When did each event take place?
- How old was so-and-so when she gave birth?
- How was his or her financial status?
- Did the father's occupation take up a lot of time, or did it allow free time?
- How was the house arranged? Was there one room for each child?

We can also pose very personal questions in a way that does not sound inappropriate. Instead of "Who was your mother's favorite?" we can ask, "Did one of you have a particular affinity with your mother?" Instead of "How did your parents get along?" we could ask, "What kind of couple were your parents? What was their union based on? What were their common values?"

If family members do not wish to talk about past events, it is fair to observe their modesty. But we can however insist upon obtaining objective information, like dates, places, and the circumstances of important events like trips, accidents, or hospitalizations.

Often, the tree's trauma is designated in a vague way because at the time of the accident, failure, exile, death throes, or mourning, being silent was a way to suffer less. But ten, twenty, thirty years later, it is necessary to know more: in the case of death by car accident, for example, we want to know who was driving the vehicle, who appeared to be at fault, if the person died instantly, who discovered the body, and so on. Continuing to comply with vagueness maintains a pain that no longer belongs to us, a pain that if expressed once and for all will affect us in a different way and no longer as a phobia, shame, or mistaken belief. For the Unconscious, and specifically the childlike part of the being, a premature death (violent or accidental) is remembered as suicide ("He or she could have been saved if . . ."), abandonment ("How did he or she not have the strength to live for me? Didn't he or she love me enough?"), or murder (for example, with someone responsible for a woman dying in childbirth, be it the baby, the husband who impregnated her, or even an incompetent doctor).

Thus, even the gaps in the tree inform us because they always reveal a lack of transmission (lack of information, lack of love, lack of Consciousness) between one of our parents or grandparents and their ancestors.

In order to punish a tyrant or unjust pharaoh in Egypt, one did not kill him but removed his name from the shrine, thus erasing him from history. Similarly, in an emotional conflict, one punishes those who are considered guilty by not transmitting their names or other information to their descendants.

THE RECTANGULAR DIAGRAM

Once all of the information is gathered, one finds oneself generally face to face with an abundance that may itself seem unmanageable: heaps of more or less readable papers, yellowed photographs, letters, documents. It helps then to organize a coherent diagram to summarize and gather this data in a way that one can take in at a glance. To do this, each character in the family must have his or her own box in which we can legibly write essential information about him or her.

- First name and family name
- Birthdate
- Profession or principal occupation and sources of revenue

For example, someone known as "an engineer" probably makes his living by his trade. On the other hand, if for example a brother is a "guitarist" but lives essentially by subsidies from his parents, that fact should be noted and differentiated from an artistic activity that would be profitable. For housewives, their at-home work corresponds to that of an employee. Another example is the person who is supported by the state through a disability pension. This is to simplify, in a clear way, how a person spent his days and how that person survived in the material world, the two not necessarily being tied together.

- Marital status: ∞ for married couples; ~ for couples in a committed relationship but not legally married; ⊕ for a divorce; ♨ or ⚖ for widowhood; ⊹ for a separation between a couple in an open relationship.
- Important relationships: specific relationships merit notice, like a breakup leading to a long celibacy, or the relationship between a married man and a mistress, or a marriage after widowhood.
- For siblings, uncles, and aunts, note the first and last names of their offspring. Each one has a designated box. Use ▼ for abortions and ⚴ for miscarriages. Use ■ for persons without descendants.
- Illnesses or significant accidents.

- Cause and date of death. Death is noted with a normal-sized cross if later in life and of natural cause, and with a larger-sized cross if premature or violent.

The symbols below will be used to interpret the family trees illustrated in this book. Of course you are free to invent your own symbols, particularly if you belong to a culture or religion in which the cross, for example, is not a relevant symbol.

∞ Marriage   ▪ Childless

~ Committed relationship   ▼ Abortion

φ Divorce   ⚊ Miscarriage

⟊ Separation

⚭ or ⚮ Widowhood

To grant each member of the family a space that corresponds to him or her, and to create a diagram in which all the members of the family relate to one another, we use the rectangular diagram inspired by the gypsies' magic carpet and by the shape of the Tarot cards.

Base Diagram

maternal great-grandparents		paternal great-grandparents	
maternal great-uncles and great-aunts		paternal great-uncles and great-aunts	
maternal grandmother	maternal grandfather	paternal grandmother	paternal grandfather
maternal uncles and aunts	mother	father	paternal uncles and aunts
my siblings and I			

As you can see, the maternal branch is always to the left of the paternal. This mirror position respects the orientation suggested by the Tarot (and by many other religious or symbolic representations of the West), which places the maternal female to our left and the paternal male to our right. The most striking example is Judgment (XX), which represents a birth or rebirth: the new being arises midway between a woman placed to the left of the reader and a man to the right. Each of the members of the genealogy tree is thus in the position of the central character, between his or her mother to the left and his or her father to the right.

Ideally, the siblings of each cental character of the family should be placed next to that character, as is the case with the uncles and the aunts. For practical reasons, we have put the great-uncles and the great-aunts above the grandparents, but on your paper, you can make a small lateral component for each of the grandparents and register the siblings there. In this case the great-grandparents are just above the grandparents.

Each generation finds its place on one level of the rectangle.

First Level: My Siblings and I

At this level, we place the siblings in order of rank (oldest to youngest), each in the same-sized box from left to right. By "siblings," we mean the ensemble of brothers and sisters from the mother and/or the father, living or dead, and we include pregnancies (abortions and miscarriages), as well as adopted brothers and sisters. Abortions, miscarriages, and stillbirths are inserted into their corresponding places in a narrower box. A dead infant who played an important role in the familial imagination must have a whole box for himself with a cross, his age, and date of death, and the cause of death if possible.

If there are half-brothers and half-sisters, two cases present themselves: they were raised together with the other siblings, in which case they are written into a box the same size as is used for the other siblings, or they were raised separately (for psychological reasons, due to geography, or because of age difference) and they should be mentioned in a narrower box.

Thus, an only child "has a lot of room," whereas smaller boxes are required for a family with many siblings. When they are represented in such a clear way, the differences between these types of siblings become obvious. In large part siblings determine our conception of space, territory, and division in daily life. This first environment is that in which we learn to live, even to survive or struggle to find our place. The genealogy trees below, illustrating typical cases, are genealogy trees from four different cultures (Spain, Italy, France, and Mexico) that illustrate different situations.

Tree: Maria-Jesus

Maria-Jesus came to consult with me forty years ago. She had always lived with her parents. She said, "I have the feeling I haven't lived my life." She had never had sexual relations. The study of her tree made clear the very deep permeation of the Catholic religion in the choice of first names, which constitute all the variants of names in Christ's genealogy.

Apart from the great-grandmother, Ana (named after the mother of the Virgin Mary), all the women in this tree bear a name representative of the name Mary. The male first names refer to God the Father (Domingo), to Christ (Salvador), or to Joseph, particularly the father of the consultant, who is the second of his siblings (the first is justly named Salvador). Furthermore, this tree carries a strong endogamous component since the two pairs of grandparents are first cousins. The study of this data confirmed Maria-Jesus's feeling of confinement. All of the tree's ambitions led to creating the perfect child—that is to say, Christ—out of the only child.

Ana	José	Maria	Luis	Pura	Domingo	Carmen	José
Maria Pilar 1901		José-Luis 1900		Maria Concepción 1899		Salvador 1890	
	Maria Concepción 1927				José 1927		Salvador 1925
Maria-Jesus 1960							

Tree: Carmen

The siblings are many, even excessive. The mother remarried after becoming widowed, and the age difference between the first and the last child is twenty years. One can say that the eldest and the "little last one" did not have the same parents, not even the same mother, so much had the situation changed between the siblings' childhoods. Moreover, Carmen's case illustrates the "replacement" child who comes after a death, and to whom the surname of the deceased is given.

Carmen is a woman with remarkable energy. A true Amazon who left Mexico for the United States, first as an illegal immigrant, she became very successful directing a transport company. However, she complained of a deep lack of self-confidence and dreamed of blossoming. The study of her tree revealed the limited space she had in which

?	?	?	?	?	?	?	?
?		?		?		?	
Maria-Paz ⚭ Antonio			Rosa + Salvador +			Fernando	
Juana (1) Antonio † (2) Ana (4) Antionio (5) Concepcion (6) José (7) Maria-Paz (8) Luis (9) Luisa † (10) Francisco (11) Soledad (12)		Rocio (3) + Antonio + Rex		⤨ Hector (12)		Salvador (1) Gabriel (2) José (3) Carmen (4) Jesus (5) Maria-Ana (6) Rosa † (7) Emmanuel † (8) Dolores (9) Rosa (10) Victor (11) ▼ ▼ ▼ ▼	

Carmen †	Maria-Paz	Juan	Antonio	Ana	Rocio	Hector	Gabriela	Victor	Lola	Maria-José	Carmen	Paquita	Sally	Daisy	Charlie	Sonny

to flourish during childhood; in the middle of a number of siblings, she came to replace a dead one. A sister, an elder by twelve years, raised her and ruled over her with an iron rod. Thus, she unknowingly envied all kinds of men who "had the right and the freedom to do anything they wanted." In effect the tree is marked by the absence of fathers, who are simple progenitors without conscience, who disappeared, leaving the mothers to take care of the children they had made. Three men followed one another in the life of Rocio, Carmen's mother. All three eventually deserted the matrimonial home. Carmen's work will consist of getting out of the sacrificed "surrogate/hen" fate, which characterizes the women of her tree, and revaluing her femininity in order to avoid excessive "virilization," which tends to fuel its undervaluation.

Tree: Roberto

Before each birth the mother had a miscarriage, abortion, or ectopic pregnancy. All of the children were thus preceded by ghosts, which could partly be explained by the fact that Roberto's mother comes from an extramarital union and is not "her father's daughter"—something that she ignored until the birth of her third child.

Roberto is an established therapist. He came to study his tree in order to complete a long journey that had allowed him to recover from death wishes, and in turn to guide him in his practice as a therapist. The work on his tree allowed him to make a link between the tragedies that affect each generation. To begin, his mother Renata never knew her father; she was born of a premarital union or rape and the secret remains intact, the father's identity unknown. The husband of her mother adopted her

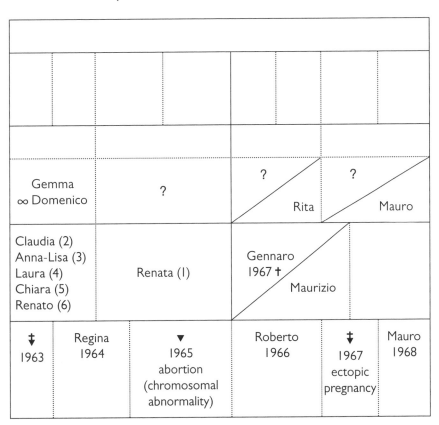

while she was still an infant. Roberto's maternal grandparents then had five more children. Like her mother Renata was pregnant six times, but each live birth was preceded by a death: a miscarriage before Regina, the eldest; a therapeutic abortion before Roberto; and an ectopic pregnancy before Mauro, the youngest. Roberto discovers soon enough that his mother's husband, Maurizio, was actually impotent and all of the children are the product of an extramarital affair between Renata and Gennaro, a priest who died just before the birth of the third child.

Tree: Jean-Paul

Two siblings, very close in age. The brothers share a "place for two." This false twinning resonates with the fact that Jean-Paul's maternal grandmother successively married brothers. The first husband died of tuberculosis after three years of marriage, which left her without any children; she then married his brother, with whom she had one child.

Jean-Paul came to consult with me to, in his own words, "move away from the anger inside me," which drives him toward different self-

Simone	Victor	Adele	Honoré	?	Jean	?	Paul
Pierre 1897		Pierre 1895–1928 †		?		?	
Éva 1899 ♂ Pierre (1925–1928)	∞	Paul 1897 (1929)		Paulette		Marcel	
♱ 1930		Pierrette 1931	∞	Marcel (1) 1925		Yvette (2) Jean (3) Robert (4) Annie (5)	
Jean-Paul 1954				Jean-Pierre 1955			

destructive habits: alcoholism, drug addiction, and smoking. The study of his tree reveals that his younger brother (born barely one year after him) took the very important place in the heart of his mother, Pierrette, and in some way robbed him of his birthright. The two brothers, in permanent conflict, created a rivalry. Jean-Pierre was the "good boy" and Jean-Paul the "rebel." One excelled in school, the other in manual labor. The study of the tree reveals that Pierrette's mother, Éva, successively married two brothers: Pierre, the elder, who died at thirty-three of tuberculosis, then Paul, his younger brother, who inherited the widow. Her first pregnancy (which she always fantasized had been a boy) ended as a miscarriage at four months, after which Pierrette was born and named after the deceased first husband. After the birth of Pierrette, the couple ceased communicating and lived in separate rooms. The emotional issues of two brothers gathered around one woman and the failure of a couple after the birth of a child weighed heavily on her sons two generations later, when Pierrette always favored Jean-Pierre as the idealized image of her deceased great-uncle.

Second Level:
My Parents with Their Brothers and Sisters

Starting at this level the tree will be subdivided into two halves: to the left the maternal, and to the right the paternal.

In each case it helps to note significant life events that correspond to the two parents. For example, if my father and mother separated when I was two, and my mother remarried, my stepfather will be noted as an additional marriage in my mother's box, even if my stepfather was more important than my biological father in my childhood. Any marriage, divorce, and/or separation dates are placed between the two parents' boxes.

On the other hand, if someone grows up with an adoptive or assumed father and discovers the truth later—that the adoptive or assumed father is not the biological father, even though according to his mother the man was his real father—it helps to separate the parent boxes with a slash mark to reflect this dual relationship.

One could then eventually do the same for the grandparents. The nonbiological father will be in the lower triangle (in contact with the children), and the biological father in the upper triangle (in contact with the mother who guarded the secret). It is obviously the same in the more rare case where the mother who raised the child is not the biological mother. (See Roberto's tree.)

In cases where a parent is completely unknown, one writes down the little bit of information, real or assumed, that one has: hearsay, memories, or hypotheses. One can then adopt a color code to separate the objective information from the hypothetical information.

A rectangular box is used on the side of each parent to record the uncles and aunts in birth order: the eldest at the top, the youngest at the bottom. One does not re-record the parent among his siblings. Next to his first name, in parentheses, record his order among his siblings. If not raised together, step- or adopted siblings are separated from the other siblings by a dotted line.

In cases where the child discovers that his parents are really his grandparents (less rare than one might think) and that his big sister is really his biological mother, a preliminary and simplified diagram of the "official" tree is established whereby the grandparents take the place of the parents. One will work on the "real" tree, in general, from where the biological father disappeared. The work will consist in large part of recovering information about the paternal family.

The sexual relationship of our parents is the founding act that creates us. As Freud and all of psychoanalysis established, the Oedipus complex is the basis of all attraction. It is at this stage where the tree's **sexual and creative keys** can be found.

Third Level:
My Grandparents and Their Siblings

The grandparents find their place at this level with whatever data we can collect about them. All the scenarios (adoption, remarriage, illegitimate parenthood, etc.) described for the consultant apply to his or her parents' boxes, too. We also mention the great-uncles and great-aunts.

At this level the boxes become much smaller, and the information is simplified, since in general as one goes back in time there are fewer details available about the lives of these ancestors. Don't forget to record the date and cause of death for deceased grandparents.

It is important to have an idea of who the siblings of our grandparents were because it permits us to imagine them in the context of their childhoods, and thus to better understand the bonding that they wove with our parents. One reaches the genealogy tree's **emotional key** with one's grandparents.

Examples: Jean-Paul's tree illustrates a case where the grandmother, becoming a widow, remarries her brother-in-law. Maria-Jesus's tree shows the case of grandparents (as it turns out, both sets of grandparents) who are first cousins.

Fourth Level:
My Great-Grandparents

Oftentimes one possesses little information about the great-grandparents; however, it is advisable to include at least some information in the boxes. If one cannot find the first names or other significant biographical facts, then at least include cultural, social, and ideological data such as ethnic background, religion, and significant historical events during their lifetimes.

Contrarily, in some cases we have a lot of information, which allows us to reconstruct a life history and measure how social, cultural, and historical circumstances of the time—together with the morality and beliefs in effect in this branch of the family—could shape the destiny of our ancestors and that of their descendants.

If one has no idea who this or that ancestor was, one can leave his or her box empty or write in a question mark.

Even if we are very detached from our ancestors' beliefs or values and the remoteness of time makes them almost unknown, their ideas, their morality, and their ideologies affect us more than we think. Most of the ideas that burden and serve us originate in the world of our ancestors.

This rectangular diagram of the genealogy tree is an excellent way of illuminating every relationship between the protagonists and our own role in the lineage. Don't hesitate to redo it several times. Progressively, it clarifies as we go along. You can also prepare several trees with more or less detail—one with only first names and birth dates, marriages, and deaths—gradually adding other "layers" of information about major events, professions, illnesses, accidents, successes. You will then see different data highlighted depending on the chosen angle.

YOUR OWN TREE

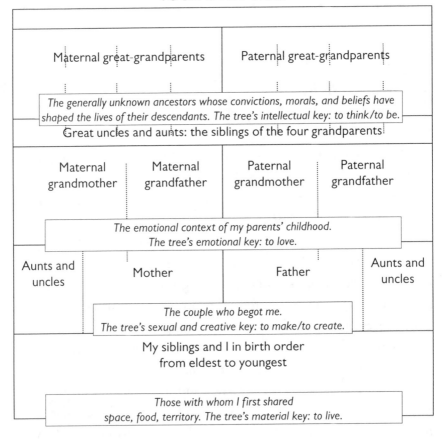

Exercise: The Metagenealogy conversation

Begin by calmly creating your tree as a rectangular diagram on your own. Once you have finished the most complete and clear notation possible, ask someone to serve as your benevolent witness. This person should listen to you attentively without commentary, and from a neutral position, for twenty to thirty minutes while you "present" your tree to him, "filling in" the rectangular diagram before his eyes on a previously blank page. Once this presentation is complete and before your witness makes any comments, compare the newly obtained tree with that which you completed alone. Are some elements clearer? What have you learned from this sharing experience? Oftentimes, in describing one's tree to someone else, information previously overlooked comes to light.

You can then reverse roles. Using whatever information your witness possesses on his family, help him to create a first version of his genealogy tree. Then, taking care to make only neutral or positive comments (all judgment is excluded), each person takes ten minutes to say to the other what he retained from the presentation. These commentaries must be formulated with prudence and compassion, ensuring a neutral attitude. As soon as we are interested in the genealogy tree a series of aggressive, unconscious behaviors tend to lash out at our unleashed knowledge, so it is important to remember this and to not give these behaviors free reign.

Once you have drawn your own genealogy tree, it is very useful to construct the genealogy trees of your mother and father on two individual blank pages of the same size in order to clarify your family vision.

Exercise: My father's tree/my mother's tree

The recommendations will be the same as for when we draw our own tree, but this time our father and the mother will be placed in their own framework, on the first (not the second) level. This simple exercise will allow us to envision our parents as children, among their family group, and thus broaden our view of them. If we possess information on the great-grandparents of our parents (our own great-great-grandparents), we can fill in the fourth level of the genealogy tree. If parents are living, it helps to ask them what their life's goal is (see chapter 6).

INTUITIVE AND CREATIVE METHODS

Presenting the Tree in an Intuitive Way

In addition to the rectangular diagram, it is also helpful to create several imagined depictions of one's genealogy tree. The metagenealogic process is facilitated by a dual effort—one to clarify and rationalize, the other to allow the intuition to express itself. It is in this collaboration, between the human capacities of rational understanding and creative imagination, that all achievement and all healing can take place.

Therefore, we are going to embark on the work with several intuitive depictions of the tree. It is possible that these depictions will evolve during the course of this search, and it is precisely this evolution that interests us. Our experience with hundreds of respondents has shown us that the images evoked by the family, ancestors, and lineage of genealogy trees are always original and different.

We now enter into a domain where it is impossible to do "good" or "bad" work because this is about externalizing the images we carry within us, permitting them to speak to us like dreams do.

Basic Visualization

What is the first image that arises in your mind when you think of your genealogy tree? Write, describe, or draw this image; it will evolve gradually based upon the extent of your work.

Basic Representation

Take out several colored pencils and, like a child, without thinking, draw the first thing that comes to your mind to represent your genealogy tree as you might for a person of goodwill from a very distant culture who does not understand your language.

After you complete this first step, if you feel like going deeper the suggestions below for representation and visualization can help.

Pictorial Representations

Reimagine your genealogy tree as a drawing or painting. It is good to make at least one sketch even if you do not know how to draw. Draw your tree as:

- A landscape: How? With what colors? What elements? What light? What season?
- An abstract: What shapes? Colors? What relationship between the different elements? What shape could represent each character? Who will be present and who will be absent in the painting?
- A still life: What elements should be present? What should the atmosphere of the painting be? The moral?
- A family portrait or an everyday life painting: Who would be represented? What clothing would they wear? Where would they be? The decor? What would the relationship be between the characters?

The Race or Tree Rivalries

Imagine all the characters from the tree, including yourself, running a race on a long path, everyone trying to pass the other. Visualize each person's position, attitude, and everything you feel as a witness to this race. Are you always losing, or are you in the middle of the pack? Can you imagine yourself in the lead?

The Ball or the Connections and Collaborations in the Tree

Visualize the scene as a grand ball, to which you have invited all the members of the genealogy tree. What is the decor like? What kind of music? Who dances, how, and with whom? What makes the atmosphere festive? What is your place?

Other Artistic Suggestions

Following your artistic sensibility, don't hesitate to probe your creative imagination for all the incarnations of collective art that you know of in order to represent your genealogy tree. Some examples:

- If my tree were an orchestra, who would play what instrument? What music would emerge?
- If my tree were a dance company, who would dance what? Who would be the choreographer? What would the movements of the ensemble resemble?
- If my tree were a museum full of sculptures, who would be what? Would there be groups? What era? What style?

Creative Exercises to Fill the Gaps

As we have already said, sometimes we have less information on the tree, or on one of the branches, or even on one of the people in particular. People who have the most gaps in their genealogy tree tend to believe they are at a disadvantage compared with those who obtain lots of data. Actually, everything is not so cut-and-dried. That which we call the tree, according to the Metagenealogy approach, is not the sum of objective information collected about our ancestors but rather the **traces** left for us by previous generations. In other words, I am my family tree as the product of my ancestors and as the sovereign individual who was shaped by these influences, and in spite of them.

One of the most useful hypotheses in our work is to consider that the Unconscious knows everything. That is to say, our individual Unconscious is connected with the familial Unconscious and can have access to information that we don't have in conscious reality. This is obviously not a demonstrated scientific truth, and we do not claim it as such, but it is a base effort of what is typically called "imagination," which fills the gaps remaining after the initial rational inquiry. In other words, the moment to turn toward the interior arrives once all available exterior information has been collected. One is allowed to imagine if one does not know. The work can then take several more intuitive shapes intended to reveal not *the* truth, but *our* truth.

We mention here a few possible techniques for filling family tree gaps, which you can experiment with at your choosing:

Visualization

Lying on your back, calmly concentrate on a specific issue and allow twenty minutes for an imaginary scene to emerge (you can set your clock to sound a soft alarm). For example, you can ask, "Who was this person for whom I have no information?" "What happened to him during those years?" "What took place in this scene?"

If a scene emerges, like a dream, write it down in detail at the end of the meditation. If nothing comes, you at least opened the question in the Unconscious. You can therefore write it down as an unresolved issue along with a brief account of the experience. An opened question sometimes "works" inside us with as much strength as a response.

Consult the Body

Figuratively speaking, memory is not only nestled in the brain, it is embodied in various parts of the body to which we can attribute a symbolic function. The head traditionally represents the father; the throat, whereby we ingest our first food, evokes our initial relationship with our mother; the hands are our means of action in the world; and so on.

If pure imagination does not bring you anything, try to concentrate on different parts of the body and let different family characters enter there (invite this, or let it emerge). As in voodoo rituals of possession, where the gods of the pantheon express themselves through the body of a medium, perhaps you'll notice that some characters of the family are more comfortable in some parts, in some energy, or some rhythm.

Here again, give yourself a time limit (fifteen to thirty minutes), sufficiently long for the relaxation and concentration to permit you to leave the state of habitual vigilance, but sufficiently short so that you can return to your daily Consciousness, take notes, and continue your day normally. It is not necessary to overwhelm yourself!

The *active method* consists of voluntarily calling a person into a place in the body.

Example: I invite my grandmother's hands into my own hands. What memory lives in these hands? How do they feel? What do they know how to do?

The *receptive method* needs to focus on a body part and allow a character to come. Who lives in my legs, my sex, my back? Am I, to a certain extent, possessed by certain events of my tree?

Example: A man complains of erection problems. Focusing on his sex, he realizes that it is inhabited by the sex of his father, in an overwhelming way. Each time he has an erection, his sex becomes that of his father (a violent man and a runner who left his wife when his child was eight years old). His mother remained single and instilled in her only son her own hatred toward the sexual man, whom she saw as the executioner. Our consultant realizes that he has voluntarily castrated himself in order to not lose his mother's love. He asks for a psychomagic act to free him of this possession. He is instructed to wrap a photocopy of a photograph of his father around his penis, which he glues to the skin with honey, and to sleep that way through the night, thereby metaphorically fulfilling the possession of which he has become aware. The following morning the consultant puts the photo in an envelope, closes it, and places it on his mother's tombstone (if she had been alive, he could have sent it to her by mail). He gives the negative thoughts about the male erection back to his mother.

Automatic Writing

Why use spiritualism when the surrealists left us a marvelous method for letting the Unconscious speak? After all, *everything* is still a matter of a contract with yourself. If you wish for one of the tree's characters to say something through your own pen, sit in front of a blank piece of paper and resolve aloud, "I write the name of this person." Then let the ideas string together on the paper. If you are more comfortable being verbal, you can do the same thing by making a recording of yourself talking to let this person "speak."

Example: A schizophrenic is possessed by several of the family characters, in particular the grandmother. The psychologist who follows his progress at the psychiatric hospital knows the Tarot de Marseille well and comes to ask advice from Alejandro Jodorowsky. It is recommended that he teach the Tarot to his patient in the company of four students, one of whom represents the grandmother—the internal characters of the family learn the Tarot along with him. Each character will be able to make commentaries on the cards, ask him to give a reading, and so forth. Putting the internal characters to work will be beneficial to the patient, who thus attains more coherence with the organization of the internal voices.

Intuitive Drawing

Painting a portrait of an unknown person, or re-creating a scene from your memory, uses the same process as automatic writing: let the pencil, pastels, or paintbrush roam freely on the paper, and watch what results emerge.

These exercises have the common purpose of bringing awareness to the fact that all of our family characters live within us and can speak to us at will through our own voice in the same way that, as in religions like voodoo, the spiritualist speaks on behalf of the pantheon's different deities.

It is possible that you will obtain astonishing results, or, to the contrary, seemingly disappointing results. Either way, keeping the results of your research—both the objective information and the intuited material—is essential.

It is also possible that the resistance of the genealogy tree will make your productions look flat, banal, contrary, or otherwise confusing. But as you progress in the study of the tree, you may discover a revealing detail. Similarly, specific concrete information that may have escaped you the first time can suddenly assume important significance.

PART THREE

The Role of the Future

*Personal Goal and the Goal of
the Consciousness*

FIVE

The Call of the Future

By Alejandro Jodorowsky

The first time I understood the importance of the future on our mental and physical health was in 1972, during the shooting of *Holy Mountain*. Due to unfounded rumors, the filming of this movie became a real nightmare. Looking to shoot the colonial architecture in Mexico City, I found the venerable Basilica of Our Lady of Guadalupe, in front of which I shot a truckload of naked corpses—gunned-down students in the film. Word spread that I had conducted a black mass inside the temple, defaming the Virgin. A campaign of insults and threats in the tabloids began. I was summoned and threatened by a minister of government who demanded the removal of said black mass, and I was not given the chance to prove the scene's nonexistence. At dawn, following this disagreeable discussion, a group of police in civilian clothing, the "Falcons," stood in front of my house screaming, "Jodorowsky, we are going to kill you!"

The next day, I put all of my negatives in the trunk of my car and, with my wife, my kids, and my cats, drove to New York via Tijuana. There, I began editing my movie. These unjust persecutions, along with the sadness of having lost my territory and my friends, and legitimate doubts about the quality of what I had shot (I wanted nothing less than to revolutionize cinema), caused a state of anxiety that made me sweat gallons of water each night. I soaked at least seven T-shirts each night. None of the pills prescribed by doctors were effective against these night sweats.

One day, while I was buying Taoist treatises in an esoteric bookstore, the clerk recognized me and struck up a conversation. In light of the subject of my night sweats, the clerk mentioned a Chinese sage living in New York who, apart from being a famous t'ai chi chuan master and teaching the art of calligraphy, gave free consultations each week to Chinatown's sick. His name was Cheng Man Ch'ing, but his students nicknamed him "Whiskers Man."* I went to see him in a gym lobby. He was seated at a table covered with a thin cushion. He listened to the sick talk about their symptoms while also listening, with his fingertips, to the different heart rhythms in their wrists.

After standing in line for a couple of hours—there were at least fifty consultants—I sat down in front of a beautiful elder. He emanated an extraordinarily gentle energy. He looked at me as if he had known me for a long time. He felt my wrists and asked me about my problem. I told him, "I perspire all night long."

He stared into my eyes and asked this unexpected question: "What is your goal in life?" That bothered me, and with a lack of respect I regretted immediately, I answered, "I came to you for a remedy against sweating, not for a philosophical conversation."

Calmly, he responded, "If you do not have a goal in life, I cannot cure you."

This came as a shock to me, psychologically. The first thing that came to mind was: I want to finish my film. But I quickly felt that this was a very circumstantial desire. It changed to: I want to be an international success. This goal collapsed at the very moment when I realized it was the cause of my social neurosis. I then thought: I want to find a woman who loves me and make a happy family . . .

In those few seconds in front of this sage I realized that all the

---

*Cheng Man Ch'ing wrote *Lao-Tzu: "My Words Are Very Easy to Understand": Lectures on the Tao Te Ching.*

goals that pushed me into action consumed my physical and spiritual energy, and were goals in search of all of that which my family had deprived me. The children of Russian-Jewish emigrants, my parents and their parents never achieved their dreams in Chile, their adopted land. My mother wanted to be a famous opera singer, and my father thought of himself as having the potential to be a great philosopher.

Emigration engulfed both maternal and paternal sides in poverty, which destroyed any possibility for using their talents. At a very early age they were limited to obligatory work and they became shopkeepers, locked in a small, ready-to-wear clothing store from 8 a.m. to 10 p.m., every day. Any success of an artist or intellectual would awaken terrible jealousy in them. Furthermore, dark doubts about my mother's virginity on her wedding night sparked a deadly hatred between the two families. As far back as I can remember, my father and my mother fought, heaping abuse onto one another. The product of two antagonistic clans, I was treated badly by both sides. That is why my goal was to accomplish everything they were unable to accomplish. At the same time, I prevented myself from success because in my Unconscious success was prohibited due to the risk of causing my parents immense pain, and even worse, jealousy.

Since my genealogy tree prevented me from fulfilling my goals, achieving success, loving and being loved, and having a united family, I asked myself, "If all of this were achieved, what would be my true purpose then?" I think I caught a raw glimpse of the complete universe in Cheng Man Ch'ing's profound gaze, full of tenderness and compassion for the lives of others, and an absolute selfless availability to all of mankind. I realized that my purpose in life was not that of an isolated individual, but that of the entire human race: past, present, and future.

Timidly, a bit ashamed, I ventured to say, "I want to know and understand the whole universe; I want to live as long as the universe lives; I want to become the Consciousness of the universe in order to eternally create." I thought the wise man would laugh at me, accuse me of delusions of grandeur, but it was the complete opposite. With a loving smile he said, "You have a purpose in life.

Now I can cure you." Then he wrote down a list of herbs, seeds, and bark that I should buy at the pharmacy in Chinatown and boil into a decoction to drink.

I stopped perspiring. I don't know if it was due to the effects of the remedy or to the spiritual peace the medicine man transmitted to me. Still, his silent message, communicated by his example, made it clear to me that individual fulfillment is impossible if the individual has only a personal, selfish goal. His call for me to state my purpose under the pretext of healing a mere ailment seemed to be an invitation to free myself of my purely selfish interests, replacing them with a goal that encompassed not only the human race but all sentient beings wherever they are. For him, no purely physical disease existed: the root of disease was located in any Consciousness shackled by the intellect.

Years later, I decided to give free Tarot consultations at a public café every Wednesday and, imitating Whiskers Man (who, with just one look and one seminal question, became my teacher for life), I began by asking my consultants to tell me their life's purpose. Physical and mental problems are responses to the trauma the Unconscious keeps secret. In order to heal, it is necessary to know what we truly want. This question stands for two arcs that represent our life's path: Where am I from? Upbringing, family, acquired personality. And where am I going? My true goal, unknown to me at times. Likewise, for my genealogy tree sessions, I took note of the consultant's goals in the beginning of the meeting in order to guide our search.

Traditional medicine, like traditional psychology, focuses on the patient and his symptoms. It seeks to "repair" or "organize" that which does not "go away": the products of the past. Psychological work is still oriented toward the memory buried in the Unconscious, the origin of problems, the psychological knots and the formation of trauma. Gestalt therapy* and all theories of "Here and Now" fall in behind Eastern meditation techniques, taking a leap forward in

---

*Developed and introduced in Big Sur, California, in 1966 by Dr. Fritz Perls.

working primarily with the present: How does the patient feel? What does he want? But, it seems to me that even these techniques are incomplete: they omit the importance of the future.

How then to heal the tree and bring it into fulfillment? Foremost, we must ask ourselves what concepts we have of mental health. Freud told of several cases of neurotic patients but did not include the sick society in which he lived. He wanted to relieve the suffering of his patients by giving them the key to adapt themselves to the destiny generated by family, society, and culture. But he never proposed the revolutionary act of mutating.

At a conference on the teachings of the Islamic mystics, I heard this short Sufi story, which corroborated that which I had understood with Cheng Man Ch'ing.

A tourist visits a construction site where two masons are hard at work. The tourist asks the first worker, "What are you doing?" The first mason responds angrily, "Don't you see? I was ordered to cut the damned stone into a cube! It's ridiculous!" Then the tourist asked the same question of the second worker, who calmly replies, "I was hired to carve the first stone of a magnificent mosque."

The first worker is furious because he does not see the purpose of his work. The second knows what his work will serve.

Because of this story, I saw a carved stone as the symbol of a life. We fall ill due to our lack of conception of our purpose. Basically, all of our troubles come out of our ignoring the mutation we call the future essential Being. In other words, **all illness is a lack of Consciousness**. It would be a mistake to limit ourselves to believing that in freeing ourselves from physical and material ailments, we can achieve happiness. Only through the evolution of Consciousness does suffering end. The physical and psychic pain of experiences lived in Consciousness simply remains pain without becoming suffering. From the moment we no longer cling to pain as if it were an object, we enter into Consciousness: a state of unity and non-duality where we exist in situations not "to see," but rather to live. As soon as I look at myself and define myself, I am no longer in Consciousness. The ego is suffering because it is a limitation of the essential Being.

As already mentioned, what we commonly call "Consciousness" is actually awakened individuality: a rational prison of the mind that makes us believe we are only what we are aware of. We believe we see what we see without realizing that our eyes communicate data that is registered only by the Unconscious. The same happens with all the other senses. We live overwhelmed by what we call "Consciousness": a multitude of thoughts, feelings, desires, and emotions that cling to us like shadows.

Consciousness is not Consciousness of or desire for a purpose, but rather **Consciousness of oneself.** One achieves this when one frees oneself from all desires, not for the purpose of Consciousness itself.

SIX

Work toward the Goal

Repetition, Creation, and Levels of Consciousness

In tackling this next level, you will formulate your goal or purpose in life into words. In other words, if you could write the "program" for your future existence, what phrase best summarizes that to which you most deeply aspire? Of course, this wording is not definitive and may evolve gradually, commensurate with your work, over your lifetime. But to use Lao-tzu's famous maxim, "The journey of a thousand miles begins with a single step." In the case of the genealogy tree, the first step is responding as clearly as possible to the questions "What is my purpose in life? Where am I headed? And what would I say if I could describe in words what I hope for my future?"

Don't worry about knowing, for the moment, whether this goal is sufficiently elevated or sublime. What counts is that you deeply agree with the sentence in which it is summarized. Some people have difficulty summarizing their aspirations. They say, "This is useless," "I have no goal," or "I am unable to plan for the future." In general, this is an indicator that one was not welcomed at birth, that the parents did not know or could not think of this newborn as anything but a goal in itself. It is possible to remain a prisoner of this deficiency, depriving ourselves of our futures because we unconsciously, as our main purpose, want to be the center of parental attention. We remain dependent on this impossible desire instead of stating a purpose. In other words, if we fail to state a purpose, the tree traps us in the past.

If this is the case for you, part 5 is devoted to methods for overcoming this deficiency. For now, though, you can express the goal of "finding my purpose in life."

THE PURPOSE

Traction in the Work on the Tree

The simple sentence that you wrote stating your purpose represents a decisive step for the study of your genealogy tree.*

In the rectangular diagram titled "Base Diagram" (see page 80) you may have noticed that the top box remained empty. This box is used to register the goal that will serve as a compass to guide you in working with the genealogy tree. On the one hand the goal will consist of working with what your genealogy tree as a whole needs most on the material, creative, emotional, intellectual, or spiritual plane; and on the other hand, it entails working with that which this same genealogy tree forbids or prevents you from doing. If the genealogy tree forbids the goal—does not allow it or makes you believe the goal is impossible—the study of the tree turns into **a gathering of hints and ideas about the hindrances and impediments to the fulfillment of your true project.**

Now read the phrase you wrote again in light of this proposal: My goal in life is everything the genealogy tree opposes and/or is unable to accomplish and/or forbids me from fulfilling.

In fact, our goal is either something not yet achieved, like finding interesting work, or the continuation of a process in which we already find ourselves but which we fear, consciously or not, to see disrupted—this could be raising children in the best way possible and continuing

---

*Unless you work on your purpose, studying the genealogy tree will just be working with your past.

as a couple. This future project then is, to some extent, linked to a ban or threat. Occasionally, this ban or threat is so well integrated in our upbringing that we don't even see it. For example: "Of course I'm afraid of losing what I have—life is made of losses and accidents!" or "I would like to have an interesting profession, but we must go with the evidence that the majority of people do work that bores them."

However, the very fact that we can make a wish for our future is evidence of a deeply creative aspiration to introduce actions and new information into our lives and, therefore, into our lineages. It is through our own fulfillment that the tree evolves. And the obstacles presented by the tree, once we manage to go beyond them, form our initiation path: **a victory over inertia.**

The goal then is to begin to see the traps laid by the tree, but also the potential treasures if we succeed in accomplishing what we deeply aspire to. That is why we define our goal in a simple phrase that can serve as a guide in this metagenealogical study. For this work cannot be an in-depth psychotherapy for each member of the lineage; an entire lifetime would not suffice to analyze the intricacies of multiple lives, and we run the risk of losing ourselves to the point of not being able to understand anything. Contrarily, the metagenealogical work must lead to a concrete realization, oriented toward solutions, and the possibility of real change for the person who questions his tree. It is more precisely the result of an outline summarizing the present psychic forces rather than a precise painting on which the details are superimposed to the point of an unreadable mush. The following initiatory story (maybe Chinese) offers a perfect metaphor for this process.

An emperor loved paintings. One day, the overwhelming desire came upon him to adorn the throne room with a painting of a rooster fight. He called for the best painter in the kingdom and the master of masters appeared.

"How much time would this painting take?"

"Your majesty, if you want the best representation of this noble animal, you must give me six months!"

The emperor accepted, and the painter enclosed himself in his studio.

Once six months had passed, the ruler demanded his oeuvre. The master announced that the painting was not yet finished and asked for another six months. Though angry, the emperor agreed nonetheless. He then waited twenty-four weeks in a state that bordered obsession. On the specified day, followed by an impressive procession, the emperor went to the studio. The artist apologized profusely and asked for three more months. The emperor, red with anger, muttered, "That being so, if my painting isn't finished after this last delay, I will cut off your head!"

Ninety days later, the emperor, followed by his executioners, rushed to see the painter who was in his studio with a big blank canvas.

"How is it," vociferated the ruler, "you have done nothing yet? This time, you are finished! Cut off his head!"

The painter, without a word, seized his brush and, in one stroke and at breakneck speed, painted the most beautiful rooster ever seen in the kingdom. The beauty of this bird was so intense that the delighted emperor fell to his knees before the masterpiece. Once he recovered from his emotion, anger again seized him.

"You are the best, I'll give you that! But you still deserve to be decapitated! Why have you made me wait so long if you could have given me satisfaction in just a few minutes? Are you playing with me?"

The master then invited the ruler to visit his home, where he discovered thousands and thousands of sketches of roosters, anatomical studies, mounted roosters, bones of this fighting bird, countless representations, pages and pages of notes, specialized books on their breeding, and a paddock full of living roosters!

Experience, observation, and hard work will lead to the expression of essentialization. They will also orient us toward a goal, which will point all the work of the genealogy tree in one vital direction for the consultant.

Goal: "To Cure Excess of Materialism"

Below are brief examples taken from a variety of real situations that illustrate the way in which the goal expressed by the consultant can orient itself toward interpreting the tree as a trap and as a treasure. Of course these interpretations do not hold universal value and must be modified according to each person. But for each example the treasure provides an awareness that can be valuable for anyone, and this universal dimension goes beyond a tree's specific limitations.

Example: The grandparents of a consultant, who were animal breeders, worked very hard to feed eight children. Their eagerness to work and the spareness of the energy they spent on family and on tenderness (in other words, their emotional unavailability) were at the time, nothing more than an expression of their primary concerns of survival and raising their children. Following their own logic and the circumstances of their existence, there was no "fault" on their part—it can be argued that they lived honestly and did the best they could.

Their third son became a butcher and accentuated this work ethic to excess. He did not pay any attention to marital and family relationships and he amassed gold bullions in his cellar, obeying what mattered most to his parents: hoarding wealth in case of potential shortage, to shelter the family.

In the third generation, the young daughter of the butcher became a vegetarian, kinesiologist, and masseuse, and she strove to "cure" this excess of materialism in her own and others' lives by restoring emotional balance, especially through touch, which she really missed (she was never taken into her father's arms, who himself was never cuddled by his parents).

From her point of view (the only one that interests us in the study of her tree), there was a "failure" or rather an "absence" of information, of contact, of affection. It is this loss that she strives to fill in her life and the lives of others. According to her, she counterbalances her genealogy tree by abstaining from meat in favor of a more sustainable diet, and by providing her customers with a benevolent connection.

Her goal: "To form a peaceful and magnetic relationship, and to create a family."

Trap: This genealogy tree offers no example of a magnetic relationship. Through two generations, all the unions were dictated by necessity (to continue the exploitation of a herd or to run the butcher's shop). Slaughter and butchering meat is associated with a violent climate. The marital and family relationships were anything but peaceful. The women in the genealogy tree, overwhelmed by multiple pregnancies and work, passed on the unconscious message that one would be happier to avoid motherhood. This tree's trap is that it reduces the consultant to isolation by presenting the marital union as a place of conflict and breakup, and her only escape is as an assistant or caretaker for her patients (mothering her clients in a sublimated way).

Treasure: In addition to the Consciousness work already done by the consultant, her desire and her emotional quest reveal a vital need, as much for her as for her tree, to reinvent the family unit as a place of exchange, love, and Consciousness. Though her ancestors lived by physical survival logic, our consultant becomes aware of equally compelling but subtler needs. She replaces the omnipotent fear prevailing in her tree, like a key value, with omnipotent love.

Goal: "To Be Happy"

Trap: The tree carries a deep sadness—indeed, several well-hidden breakdowns. It is without a doubt the base of many sadomasochistic links and its preferred maxim could be "Life is made of suffering."

Treasure: To seek one's own way to happiness, which is to say, to celebrate at every instant the miracle of being alive. Then the consultant carries this crucial information to the tree: Life is joy, not suffering.

Goal: "To Be Rich"

Trap: The tree passes on no spiritual value whatsoever and sees material success as supreme. At the same time, becoming rich (which no member of the tree has thus far succeeded in doing) would be a source of anxiety and guilt because it is a betrayal of the poverty that has afflicted the family for generations.

Treasure: Money is only a concrete symbol of an exchange of energy. In refurbishing the "love of money" in the genealogy tree, the consultant restores a deep respect for vital energy and abundance.

Goal: "To Live in Holy Poverty"

(As Have Those from Wealthy Families like Saint Francis of Assisi and Buddha)

Trap: The family has not passed down the joy of humility, of simplicity. The descendant who has a model of a perfect poverty that opposes excessive materialism establishes poverty as a value itself, and the only way to summon the divine in human existence.

Treasure: By arriving at a state of simple abundance at the heart of poverty, the consultant discovers deep prosperity (vital energy itself), which transcends all notions of "rich" and "poor" and accepts abundance in all forms.

Goal: "Be Able to Earn Money While Doing What I Love"

Trap: The tree leads to a fierce economic anxiety. Work is approached as an obligation, maybe as a sacrifice. The concept of work and of money instilled in the consultant terrifies him and reduces him to an infantile state instead of supporting him.

Treasure: In discovering a satisfying way of being in the world, the consultant surpasses the limiting opposition between work and leisure and gives himself completely to the joy of working and relaxing alternately.

Goal: "To Be Useful"

Trap: The genealogy tree is egotistical. It denigrates the consultant who had to earn every expression of love or attention in order to demonstrate that she deserved it. Whatever efforts she made, she always felt empty because no one ever gave her a sense of place or value.

Treasure: In discovering the joy of service, the consultant will be driven toward understanding another view of the Christian maxim "Love thy neighbor as thyself." She will understand that her sacred obligation is also to love herself and to be useful for her own development. She will thus leave behind her role as sacrificial victim and relieve her relatives by becoming a spiritually mature, joyous, and radiant being.

Goal: "To Be Able to Travel and to Discover New Places"

Trap: The tree produces confinement. The family does not have a horizon and lives enclosed in its territory. Those ancestors who left never returned, so any distance is seen as a threatening split.

Treasure: Having overcome the tree's taboos, our traveler becomes a conscious traveler and not a postcard tourist consumer. The consultant's path in the world is marked by significant chance encounters. He may become an environmentalist because he has come to understand that the totality of the planet is his home, and that he has to try to protect it.

Goal: "To Be Able to Leave My Husband Whom I No Longer Understand and Become Financially Independent"

Trap: The tree gives the woman very limited options—spouse and mother—at the price of personal development. Maybe all the women in the tree have played the same role. Maybe there are many missing mothers, whether deceased, ill, or otherwise absent.

Treasure: In overcoming cultural taboos that reduce the woman to a spouse's assistant and eternal victim, this woman frees her husband, who is also imprisoned in this schema; her children, who finally have a liberated adult for a mother; and herself, who participates in the necessary evolution of humanity, which is the equilibrium of masculine and feminine.

Goal: "To Recover Health"

Trap: One must ask: What are the benefits in the tree to getting sick? Are there people for whom sickness was their way to get attention or love? Is illness the only known way to create links between members of the family?

Treasure: Healing (definitely physical in certain cases, psychological and spiritual in others) becomes a lesson that one can share. Illness becomes a teacher, a reason to evolve, and not the calamity it seemed at first to be. No matter what, the consultant and his kinfolk will die someday. But the ordeal of the disease, and the sense of having learned something, helps them get closer to their future death with a new wisdom and live more authentic lives.

Goal: "To Be Famous"

Trap: The tree suffers from mediocrity and failures. This suffering is transferred to the children, who are not seen by their parents and must become their "public." In some trees, being famous is experienced as an obligation because a parent or an ancestor was famous and so fame was incorrectly presented as the only way to surpass a predecessor. Fame then is approached as impossible, and the consultant could even wish, consciously or not, for the death of the famous person who preceded her because it is the only solution to finally becoming an adult.

Treasure: If the consultant becomes famous or remains anonymous, she is no longer duped by this recognition frenzy. She focuses on the most essential values: talent or creativity (if she is an artist), her deep values, the quality of human relations. And as such, whether in the spotlight or not, she ceases to be toxic in her relationships and instead becomes a good person, one way or another.

You may not arrive at such a clear interpretation at first glance. But more important is to begin to see how the goal (the call of the future) interacts with the repetitive conditioning at work in the tree (repetition of the past).

A SYSTEM OF REPETITIONS

The genealogy tree is, above all, a system of repetitions. Tradition, culture, transfer of name and heritage, conservation of inheritance—all these values are an integral part of the very notion of family. The clan is above all a hierarchical system of solidarity and affiliation whose members must be identifiable as elements of the group. The injunction to "Be like us!" is present in all social and familial systems.

From a very primitive point of view, conditions for survival in the first societies necessitated extreme dependence, so the clan affiliation was a condition sine qua non for survival. Being rejected from the village, from the tribe, or from the maternal breast meant dying of hunger, of cold, or attack of savage beasts. In a number of real cultural contexts, being rejected by the family also equals social and economic danger.

This first condition is recorded in our Unconscious and establishes a universal terror of the prospect of being excluded. The fear of exclusion goes hand in hand with the fear of the future: there is no future except within the clan. But this future is possibly nothing more than a repetition of the past, since above all else the clan passes down its values, even though this threatens individual values. The clan attaches to us and does not allow us to evolve in but one set direction.

One finds the echoes of this schema of forced affiliation in a number of actual families:

- Conditioning: You will be a doctor like your father and your grandfather before you.
- Prohibition: There are no homosexuals in this family.
- Forecasting: If you are not married by thirty you will become an old maid.
- Affliction: In our family no one has ever earned a living as an artist, and if you follow that dream you will fall into misery.

All of these warnings to maintain the integrity of the clan are traps that keep us in the past. Basically, a clan is driven by fear of the other, who is seen as an enemy or a potential aggressor. Whoever dares to wreck the culture of the clan and invent a new destiny is perceived as a traitor or an outsider, and the clan's reaction is to disown—this fear of the unknown dictates that we must always stay the same.

In certain cases this prohibition and these afflictions are not even stated aloud by parents and grandparents. These things are so ingrained in the family logic that each member feels, reproduces, and recalls a distant past; it is not uncommon for people to act according to the orders and prohibitions of deceased parents.

From here, your work will be to drive out the repetitions at work in your genealogy tree. Several types of repetitions exist:

- **Repetition, pure and simple.** One is a member of one's clan and, as such, one directly reflects its values. Example: I take the first name of my father, grandfather, and great-grandfather; I study the same thing they studied; I work in the same field as they do; I am my aunt's "spitting image" and my destiny is modeled on hers.
- **Repetition by interpretation.** In childhood one interpreted the family codes in one's own way. As an adult, one transposes these codes into one's own reality. Example: My grandfather is an illegitimate child who never met his father. My father, unloved by his father, always felt that he was not really his father's son and doubted his paternity. In my turn, as an adult, I married a woman who claimed to be pregnant with my child, but I realized after some years that she was actually pregnant with another man's child, and so my first child is actually the biological child of another.
- **Repetition by opposition.** One is an unloved or mistaken member of the clan, a black sheep, and, as such, one expresses one's differences with blatant opposition, which paradoxically allows for identification as a member of the clan. Example: In my family everyone is wealthy and lives in a twelve-mile radius of their parents' home. I, the next-to-last daughter, always considered myself the "rebel." I live by my wits in a foreign country. Paradoxically, I do respect the role handed to me. So everything is in order, and I have a secret wish, which will probably be a letdown, to inherit part of my parents' estate after their deaths.
- **Repetition by compensation:** One is a member of this clan and,

as such, must accomplish that which one's ancestors could not accomplish. Example: Three generations tried, without success, to climb the social ladder and leave their hometown. My grandfather left for the city and returned to raise sheep. My father worked for some time in the city before returning to open a town grocery. They both say nothing beats our region's air. I live in a different country where I have a thriving business, but they refuse to visit me under the pretext that the trip is too tiring.

We will return to these four forms of repetition. For the moment, we see how they fade into each of the four centers.

Physical and Material Repetition

From the time of an infant's birth, everyone seeks **similarities** between the baby and the other members of the family. The mother may wish for the child to look like her or the father, to confirm the child is really his. The father may also wish to be reproduced in the newborn, or to find the mother's traits in the newborn, or perhaps the traits of his own mother and father. In general, we obtain a kind of fragmented family portrait where we pretend that the child has the eyes of one, the nose of another, the laugh of a third person. There are skinny lineages and fat lineages, families in which everyone is more or less a blonde or a brunette, more or less hairy. When the child grows up, real or imagined similarities can be detected in his or her attitudes and gestures.

When an offspring falls ill, the **illness** is immediately accepted as part of the clan: "We all have delicate throats." Or to the contrary, as a deviation from the clan: "This child is always sick." Thus, even in the most tender of childhoods, we receive unconscious orders that force us to think of our most basic elements of being in the world as signs of belonging.

Later it is the **relationships with money** or **profession,** the **domicile,** and **territory** in the greater sense that become the subject of repetition. Certain people live as if it is their inevitable duty to take over the family business, or to study the same subject the mother or father studied, with the intention of succeeding where the other failed. The town, region, or country of origin can represent a stake in clan membership or, to the contrary, a child who was emotionally excluded may be likely to emigrate.

Sexual and Creative Repetition

Some psychologists who work in the area of **sexual abuse** point out that rape, incest, and pedophilia tend to repeat. Sexual abuse experienced by a child (often in guarded silence) has the possibility of becoming a sexual fixation for that child as an adult, which pushes the previous victim to perpetrate acts of the same kind. A father who was molested in a Catholic school (symbolically raped by his "father") can in turn be irresistibly impelled to commit pedophilic acts in his own family.

There is also a tendency to repeat **the manner of giving birth**: repeating the mother's age at her first pregnancy, the type of delivery, the timing of the birth, and postpartum depression. However, this is not something that necessarily moves from uterus to uterus—a daughter giving birth like her mother—but one does see, for example, the lineage's first male child (first patronymic heir) born by forceps "like his paternal grandfather." The manner of birth reinforces the membership in the clan and, particularly, the name's lineage.

An unwanted, first-born girl can very well be caused to abort her first pregnancy or to abandon her first child, symbolically fulfilling her mother and father's desire to get rid of her. Similarly, abortions and stillbirths are repeated. For example, a woman has five abortions and later discovers that her grandmother had five children who died in infancy.

Sexual problems like frigidity, impotence, or sterility can also be repeated because taboos and frustrations are transmitted from one generation to the next. It is often difficult to trace the sexual history of one's genealogy tree because it is the most taboo subject in the family, but with certain clues we can imagine the degree of a couple's sexual satisfaction. Were there mistresses or lovers? Illegitimate children? Did the couple have separate bedrooms? What was said about women in general? And men?

In the **creative domain**, we often see an artistic practice repeat from one generation to the next, or skip a generation. Who played piano, or would have liked to play? Who painted? Who had a beautiful voice? The question of talent in the genealogy tree is also part of our inquiry. Was talent recognized? Encouraged?

In artistic families, the most active creative energy of a member of the family (the "official" artist) can often eclipse the creative aspirations of his descendants. Occasionally an artistic child will find it extremely difficult to detach from his mother or father's style, producing pale copies of the work of his predecessor all of his life. There are notable and inspiring exceptions. For example, Pierre-Auguste and Jean Renoir—in passing from painting to cinema this genealogy tree begot two great creators, father and son, both innovators and completely fulfilled in their artistic practice.

On the creative plane and in the broadest sense, there is often a repetition of failure. If an ascendant does not succeed in overcoming such demise, future descendants may find themselves blocked by a drive toward failure.

Emotional Repetition

By definition, our **way of expressing affection** is passed down to us and forms our emotional learning. Similarly, emotional trauma tends to create repetitions that unfold over many generations. Among the most blatant repetitions are those that affect the way we express love, sometimes in a roundabout way through, for example, money or food, or even taboos tied to the expression of love, such as talking or embracing. These negative emotions are repeated, and it is not uncommon to carry another's shame, anger, or depression.

The **notion of partnership** is also very dependent on the tree, including the repeating of conflictive relationships, divorce, or abandonment. Sometimes the abandonment suffered by a child (orphaned or given away) will translate into the abandonment of the spouse or the family one or two generations later, and so forth.

Emotional repetitions are equally governed by our **projections**. Instead of establishing a relationship with a child based purely on the love she bears, one projects another member of the family onto her, and the innocent child becomes the battleground for unresolved emotional conflicts. This situation is extremely frequent in genealogy trees.

Some childish feelings, like preference, contention, and rivalry between brothers and sisters, can then affect adulthood. It is not uncommon for a parent to project one of his brothers or sisters onto his son or daughter, and this uncle (or aunt) is sometimes even the child's godfather (or godmother). The parent will, more or less knowingly, treat this child as a "double" of the parent's brother (or sister), and the parent-child relationship will suffer the weight of that with which it has nothing to do, even if the dynamics of the relationship are not hidden. One common case is that of the parent who projects onto his child a secretly hated little brother or sister. The child is subjected to wildly imbalanced destructive rivalry due to the parent's complete authority over the child.

It also happens that a parent projects a childhood romance onto his offspring, to the point of naming the child after a lost love. Here also the child will receive emotional messages not directed toward him specifically, and his whole range of emotions will be disrupted.

Intellectual and Ideological Repetition

The premier, traditional repetition in many cultures is that of the **first name.** The first name is a word used to designate us, like the word "table" designates a table. If we think well on this, in our way of viewing things the first name contains all of our identity. Tradition or not, it is thus evident that if someone names us after one or more members of the tree, he clandestinely passes on to us something of these characters' identity. Experience shows that the first name induces a series of repetitions in such cases, as much material as sexual-creative or emotional.

The most powerful repetition in the genealogy tree is that of **beliefs.** Insofar as they are supported in language, ideas are expressed through words, and these vital elements integrate our identity. If I spent my entire childhood listening to my mother say "all men are bastards," something of this belief will continue into my adulthood. Similarly, it is understandable that fear, shame, religious prohibitions, moral systems, and politics continue to impact people's lives even if they have abandoned the practices and organizations that trained them in these beliefs.

In a genealogy tree, these beliefs want to unify—we are not of such political affiliation, not that color, not from that town. But each time the family is defined as such, it shuts off the opportunity to open the world to its descendants. Sometimes fanatical beliefs mutate from one generation to the next by a mechanism of opposition. If the grandparents were religious fanatics who oppressed their children in the name of this ideology, it is possible that the tree will produce militant politicians, anarchists, or anti-clericalists who are equally fanatical one or two generations later.

Another recurring element is in the **usage of language**. Dialects, slang, and regional expressions are, as such, elements of identification with the clan. In a bilingual residence, the choice of language can become a gamble and the object of conflict. This also goes for subtle verbal aggression: a child who is raised in an atmosphere of regular verbal abuse may become an adult who is totally unconscious of his own verbal aggression. In developed countries, all of the stakes bound to scholastic and university education become elements of repetition. Being "intelligent" in France is the key element for membership in an educated tree. Similarly, the decision to go to school or not, and even the rank awarded in this competition, determines membership in a clan. Woe to the heir of a lineage of engineers who although more gifted for skilled handiwork, gardening, or the cello is forced nevertheless to pass the same exams as his ascendants and fails miserably; his difference will be experienced as a sign of nullity and failure.

Tradition, folklore, and religion are ties to the past, as are regionalism and nationalism, with their share of culinary habits, customs, and sometimes chauvinism.

In short, **refusal of the new** is what is primarily repeated in the four centers. The tree pushes us to redo what already exists and forbids our working to transform the clan to make it a conscious society, unified with the totality of humanity. It commits us to focusing our thoughts, actions, and emotions on the known.

Work on the tree depends upon an understanding of the finer repetitions. To begin to identify them, we note the most obvious:

- First names
- Key dates, ages, and gaps in time (length of a marriage, age at the time of a car accident, age gaps between brothers and sisters)
- Professions
- Circumstances of deaths, accidents, life crises
- Number of siblings
- Territory of the tree, established or temporary

But the repetitions can also be subtler, with one or more elements changing from one generation to the next. A first name can:

- Be a full or partial anagram of another first name: the father named Hermann, the daughter Maren. All the letters in the daughter's first name come from the father's first name.
- Begin with the same first letter and contain the same number of letters: Veronica, Valerie, Vanessa; Rita, Rosa, Rafa.
- Repeat a syllable: Joanne, Josephine, Jonah.

Dates can also be examples of repetition.

- The date of a baby's conception can be the birth date of another. For example, a son born in April was conceived in July on the exact date of the maternal grandfather's birth date: the mother unconsciously includes her own father in this sexual act that will beget a son.
- Date of death: for example, the father who dies the day the daughter marries or gives birth.

Choice of professions, location choices, and attractions can also have influence.

- Some professions are opposites of one another. This opposition can be interesting symbolically. For example, a hairdresser suddenly emerges from a lineage of cobblers, as if head and feet seek to join or oppose one another.
- An obvious opposition can betray a connection. For example, my father is tall, blond, blue-eyed, and European, and I don't like anyone but short, olive-skinned men who are from other continents. I do not therefore dethrone my father by falling in love with someone so dissimilar to him.
- The tree is also about rearrangement. For example, if my ancestors migrated to Spain at a time when the country seemed very distant, it is possible that subsequent generations will choose Latin America as the new horizon to conquer (but the language is the same).

These figurative cases are as numerous as the pictures of human diversity. We can scarcely begin to explore the system of similarities and differences, heritage and compensation, that is the genealogy tree. But before we become absorbed in a search for the repetitions at work in our own tree (see the exercise at the end of the chapter), we will identify the ingredients that permit us to dissolve these very powerful repetitions, overcome them, and fulfill our own destiny.

KEY TO THE SERVICE OF A FUTURE PROJECT
Levels of Consciousness

One can summarize the process at work in the genealogy tree in the following way: Parents, in a given generation, find themselves facing a material, emotional, sexual-creative, or intellectual (moral) problem. Facing this problem, they react by adopting **the best solution that**

their level of Consciousness at that moment allows them to find.
Often, this solution is a *repetition*. That is to say, they apply a known
formula, already proven and validated by their familial, social, and cultural milieu. For example:

- Facing shame (imprisonment, psychiatric internment, illegitimate
  child) or emotional distress (relationship trouble, betrayal), they
  will choose to guard a secret.
- Faced with mourning, they will choose to never again speak of
  the missing person or, on the contrary, to make him the center of
  domestic attention, retrospectively transforming the missing person into a saint or hero.
- Facing extreme material difficulties, they will choose to
  immerse themselves in their work and make their children
  work, or the father will live alone in exile, in a foreign place
  that is considered a paradise, from where he will send subsidies
  to his family.
- Facing adolescent rebellion or conflicts among siblings, they will
  choose violence and coercion.
- A woman, abandoned by her husband and attempting to fill
  the emotional void she feels, will turn to her son or daughter. A
  divorced couple can force the child to bear the weight of the conflict as each one says abominable things about the other.

In every genealogy tree, we find examples of these false solutions
that have worked very well for the parents, but by the second generation, the ravages are felt: violence, secrecy, frenzied materialism,
breakups, or impossible emotional demands will become, for children
who later become parents, new wounds for which they must find their
own solutions. If these solutions conform as those of the previous
generation did, the grandson or granddaughter will, in turn, pay the
consequences.

When studying our family history, it is not difficult to identify elements that could be the source of suffering. But, in general, our initial

reaction is to justify them by saying, "In those days, they did things like that." "My mother (my father, my grandfather) didn't have a choice." "But there are a hundred families in which those things also happened." Or to the contrary, facing similar facts, a more perceptive or a more rebellious person risks locking himself in permanent anger toward his ancestors and dwelling on infantile troubles by always asking, "How could they have done that?"

Often, these two positions—the rationalized forgiveness or the hopeless resentment—coexist in one person. In one part, mental judgment justifies the tree's events. In the other part, the heart (the child's psyche) still suffers without the ability to overcome the trauma. Many people find themselves in this paradoxical situation when they begin therapy or spiritual work.

When we have a metagenealogical attitude we will be in a place beyond hopeless resentment and rationalized forgiveness. Our goal is to understand why and how these false solutions have emerged; what familial, social, and cultural repetitions are at work; and from an ideal perspective, what could have been the attitude of an adult confronting the obstacles manifested in his or her genealogy tree.

In other words, we are going to ask what level of Consciousness our ancestors had at the moment of these events, and what might have happened had they acted with a greater level of Consciousness independent of the socio-economic-historic circumstances that, in a way, define the limits of individual freedom. We recall that one can always express a resistance to the family's prevailing cultural ideology even if one's actions are restricted, for example, by an authoritarian regime.

An Evolutionary Concept of the Human

More and more Consciousness will mean more and more freedom for an individual. The more one becomes mindful, the more one refuses to accept being narrowly defined, and, in fact, by ceasing to identify strictly with the clan one becomes unified with the totality of the universe. All self-definition is, in reality, the cause of suffering because it makes us sick. If I am strictly French (or American, or Spanish . . .), I am nothing else; if I live exclusively as "man" (male) or "woman" (female), this will be a cause for suffering because I turn my back on anything beyond my gender. All definitions cause conflict with possibility. In reality, it is possible to recognize one's origin without relating to the definition.

The notion of **level of Consciousness** returns us to an evolutionary concept of the human being. We have the potential to be in permanent evolution until the moment of our physical death. It is therefore logical to conclude that the spirit can evolve to a supreme point at which, having given up physical life in full awareness and joy, our individual Consciousness fuses with that of the universe. The various spiritual and religious traditions each have their own vocabulary to describe this ideal process, which is illustrated by accounts of the deaths of the great saints from every culture.

A low Consciousness level manifests as permanent dissatisfaction, from the person who has lost all joy in life, to the person who offsets this deep dissatisfaction with illusory purchases (accumulations of material or immaterial assets, successes, or objects). Without the development of the Consciousness, there can be no authentic satisfaction.

To progress, it is necessary to propose a goal that allows us to unify our interior world (our true identity) and our exterior world (fulfilling our true destiny, acting authentically in the world). But the genealogy tree can inoculate us with fictitious goals on which we deploy enormous amounts of energy—to become a millionaire, to find our soul mate, to top everyone on the creative or sexual plane—and awaiting the results of a false goal once again produces a deep dissatisfaction. This is why people who are rich with money, honors, or glory are often also depressed and can self-destruct or commit suicide. Unconsciously, the person who repeats the goals of the tree, even if he accomplishes the goals, remains dissatisfied.

Example: The great-grandfather ruined himself, creating misery and shame in the family. A descendant can strive toward amassing a fortune, giving up his purpose (to practice art, study medicine, find emotional fulfillment). Even if he amasses this fortune, he will feel like a failure because the true goal is not to obtain something in particular but **to grow and to develop**.

This purpose does not have to be abstractly formulated ("I want to develop my Consciousness" doesn't mean anything to the majority of us), but one activity in particular can be a vehicle for this growth. In Zen stories, it is common for the dying master to designate the cook as his successor as the head of the monastery. Through this humble, concrete, daily activity, the monk has developed his Consciousness to match his master's. He will be chosen, not because he is a cook, but because he demonstrates the interior qualities of goodwill, discipline, and detachment and does not live under illusory values like power, nationality, age, sexual orientation, or national or racial identification; this release of definitions is a sign of awakened Consciousness.

As the saying goes, all roads lead to Rome. Similarly, all paths in life (intellectual, artistic, material, financial, service to others, etc.) can be a way to develop the Consciousness, provided that one develops one's degree of concentrated attention, perseverance, detachment (letting go), and above all, discipline. This discipline, called *dharma* in Eastern traditions, is the set of actions and rules to which one bows in order to put oneself at the service of the essential Being, to be face to face with oneself, without seeking the approval of others or a master.

Naturally, we cannot exactly quantify a person's level of Consciousness, and the way in which we make diagrams should only be used for our own work. In this way we can look at our genealogy tree not as a lineage from superiors (ancestors) to cadets (us), but as human beings who together equally confront their destinies while being unequally capable of coping in a mature way.

This part of the work is essential because it disrupts the traditional hierarchy in effect in the family that requires the younger to respect the older. However, we imagine for a moment that the less conscious (more immature) must respect the more conscious (less immature).

This respect is a legitimate ambition, and a possibility open to everyone to become the light and the Consciousness of the genealogy tree. But for each one of us, this work also represents a litmus test because it forces us to leave the complaint and the established order and poses fundamental questions: "Am I capable of recognizing the level of Consciousness in which I ordinarily live? Am I ready to bow down before the superior level of Consciousness of a person more evolved than me? Am I capable of evolving?"

At this stage, and as you will see in the proposed exercise at the end of this chapter, work on your goal can have already begun. Without having to depart from your personal or material goals, you can offer to add another goal: the most elevated goal you are capable of conceiving, at the highest level of Consciousness possible from you today. The majority of people have an individual purpose. Some have a social, humanist, and generous purpose. Very few people are capable of spontaneously conceiving of a goal that encompasses all of mankind.

From Animal Level to Divine Consciousness

A six-month-old child naturally will have a different Consciousness level than adult. Each age, each stage in life, corresponds to a radiant, healthy level of Consciousness. A level of Consciousness does not become toxic unless one continues to live according to it instead of moving to the next level, and growing up. It is a tragedy to have to act, think, work, or manage information as an adult while still an infant, so say the psychologists. But what they say less often is that it is equally tragic to act and to think like a child or an adolescent while still an adult.

Each level of Consciousness implies a **central unit,** or reference point, that helps a person define what his own world revolves around.

Animal–Survival

This is the primitive level of Consciousness of animals or babies. At this level priorities consist of eating, defending, and sheltering oneself. For warm-blooded animals (humans), this first level inscribed the need for the clan, the family, in our history.

If a human who has passed the infant stage finds that he remains in this level of Consciousness, it means that he lives exclusively along the axis of predator/prey. This is the case for major offenders, criminals, and people whose education or the environment in which they live has returned them to a state of struggle for survival and ongoing violence. A very depressed person who is totally dependent on others and is incapable of communicating can have also regressed to the level of animal Consciousness.

Central unit: the governing body (the mouth for the infant, the stomach for the animal); if this level of Consciousness is regressive, the governing body may become, for example, the genitals for a sex offender or the brain for a fanatic who becomes a criminal in the name of his ideas.

Infantile–Consumer

This level is that of the ultimate child: dependent and playful, she consumes without ever producing anything; she does not work but plays like she is grown up. Dream and imagination are adjacent to reality. The infant receives regardless of whether or not she gives, and her favorite phrase might be "Give me!" At this age we have the right to be useless to society, and it is vital that those who take care of us like parents and teachers accept us.

All of these ingredients in adulthood define the consumer type, which an industrial society needs to survive. Dependent and materialistic, she is convinced this or that product is indispensable. Willingly irresponsible, engrossed in video games or television shows, she feeds off illusions and products of no real value. She is also the subordinate (imaginary) in the company hierarchy. On the emotional level, she is incapable of putting others' interests before her own.

Central unit: the head of the household (the love between parents) or its symbolic representative, like a hierarchical superior or other person of authority.

Adolescent–Romantic

Adolescence is an age marked by three main concerns: love (idealized in general and considered eternal); death (an opponent that one tries to defy in a more or less definite way); and the aggregation into a new group (a circle of friends, a fan club) that will serve as an airlock between the family, the infant's enclosed world, and human society at large, toward which the adult being moves. This level of Consciousness is thus characterized by extreme romanticism, the temptation for danger or a willingly morbid aesthetic like skulls or gothic fashion, and the strong desire to identify with a "posse" through clothing, lifestyle, or other means. A claim to freedom or originality, based on opposition to the established education system, is also symptomatic of this age.

Once past adolescence, this level of Consciousness sends us back to the tyranny of fashion and youth culture, to the film industry of action and romance movies, and to all kinds of idealism and fanaticism, including self-destructive and revolutionary paths.

Central unit: the leader of the new clan (rock singer, group leader) who approves of the person's departure from the family.

Selfish Adult

This first step into adulthood is not negative in itself; above all there is a moment to reflect on one's own safety, to build a nest and a heritage that we try to maintain for safety reasons. The first act in an adult's life is to make a place for oneself, even at the detriment of a competitor.

The exclusive concern of anyone content to remain at this level of Consciousness will be hoarding to ensure his own security (or that of his own family), without sharing anything. Freely offered generosity is not part of this level of Consciousness. He lives mostly to profit as much as possible without giving anything back: he buys cheap to sell high. This is the level of Consciousness of business and economics. Its maxim could be "Everything for me, nothing for anyone else." The community is hierarchical and inevitably becomes the ground for fierce competition. The key values are stability, protection, and the defense of interests.

Central unit: the top of the hierarchy, the CEO or president of the company to which one belongs.

These four first levels are the most widespread. As products of the inertia of the past, these alone suffice to organize a hierarchical human society in which the strongest laws prevail.

From the moment at which the Consciousness comes into play, we begin to explore the following levels.

Social-Altruistic Adult

This level of Consciousness represents any adult with a social conscience and concern for collective well-being, which becomes a central focus in his or her life. The purpose of life for an altruistic and social adult is to unify human society. Initially, this union can be nationalistic or corporate, but then it can lead to a vaster union. The main principles of equality among people—pacifism, freedom of expression, the abolition of slavery—are fulfilled at this level of Consciousness. Examples of altruistic and social adults include a resistance hero who dies for her ideas without betraying her comrades; an honest person who, at the risk of her own life, provides shelter for the persecuted; a tireless social worker. At this level, generosity is a necessity, not a luxury. These adults understand that everything they give to others is, in reality, given back to them—and they deprive themselves whenever they hoard or reject anything.

Central unit: the exemplary beings, heroes, geniuses, and saints who are the most dear to us, and who demonstrate the principle of action in the world (Gandhi, Nelson Mandela, Mother Teresa).

Planetary Adult

At the next level we find an adult endowed with a planetary Consciousness: a part of the whole planet and everything experienced on the planet, he takes care of it as he takes care of himself, living closely with the natural environment. The great sages of early religion, the shamans, medicine men and medicine women—all convey this level of Consciousness. It is also the authentic level of ecological awareness. Naturally, this level of Consciousness aims to live in close union with everything on the planet (even minerals), in an effort to experience all of daily life far beyond a simply theoretical position. To share, to not waste, to find durable solutions, and to respect life in all forms are the requirements of this level of Consciousness. In some Zen monasteries, for example, monks live so that nothing is thrown away, and they strive to create the least amount of waste in the most useful way. On a collective level, this refers to fair trade (not only in service to those who produce but also to the consumers) and to sustainable living. The master word of this level of Consciousness could be *service.*

Central unit: the center of the planet, anchor of everything living on Earth.

Solar Consciousness

This level of Consciousness extends to the limits of the solar system. This person considers the solar system and not Earth to be her natural environment, transcending time and terrestrial space. She wants to affect not only his own generation, but within and beyond the previous and subsequent generations. This level of Consciousness is at peace with all the events that have affected the history of humanity, and with all the past, present, and future energies that contribute to the arrival and appearance of life. She is driven to live in the company of the major archetypes and the incarnation of symbols, which are thus considered (à la C. G. Jung) elements of a whole and of a single unit designed as a life principle in the same way as the sun diffuses heat and light. Irrespective of religion or spirituality, the person who has reached this level of Consciousness lives in close relations with the principle creator, whom she calls "God" or "life force."

Central unit: the sun as a symbol of Consciousness around which Earth turns.

Cosmic Consciousness

This level consists of leading a life in full awareness that life is not our exclusive prerogative or right. It consists of being in full awareness of the certainty of the existence of other life forms and other habitable planets, which enables us to embrace the immeasurable multiplicity of the universe and to envision life beyond planets, in interstellar space. All prejudices are shattered as we sense life nestled even in black holes. At this level of Consciousness, we understand the dissolution of individuality into the Whole of which the great mystics spoke.

Central unit: the Center of the universe (everywhere and nowhere).

Divine Consciousness

While the divine Consciousness is experienced in everyday life, the principle of all action is the god within. It is difficult to speak of this level of Consciousness because one enters into the unspeakable and unimagined. It is the diamond: it brings all the facets together, the absolute unity of everything. Borders are abolished. One becomes transpersonal and moves beyond one's own ideas, feelings, desires, and needs, in order to create God. The unthinkable, indescribable unity that one feels in the depths of Consciousness is in everything. The center is built not of the mind but through an entirely intuitive knowledge, a feeling of unity, love, and compassion for limited beings.

Nevertheless, one can identify what level of Consciousness is at work when fear disappears and the being is seized with a permanent and absolute zest for life. Until that moment one has been terrorized by the world. In discovering that the world and the self are one and the same thing, this terror is abolished by joy, a state of happiness.

Central unit: the heart, both literally and metaphorically speaking. One is born out of the heart: the heartbeat emerges from the rhythm of the universe. In the divine Consciousness, one is tuned into the whole, which beats like a heart: the whole universe is a loving heart.

These levels do not specifically describe a spiritual or religious reality; a person who has reached a high level of Consciousness can be an artist, farmer, or manual laborer. On the other hand, the understanding and implementation of religious dogmas change dramatically according to the level of Consciousness. We will see how they express themselves in religion, dogma, and mysticism.

- The **animal level** produces superstition and violence in the name of religious beliefs. Whoever is not of my faith threatens me; religious affiliation becomes the logic of survival and a person will attack someone simply for being of another religion.
- At the **infantile level** we find "blind faith," naïveté, the type of religious devotion in which one uses little dolls, figurines, idols. Prayer or rituals are used to ask for help from a deity conceived of as a benevolent parent who protects us.
- At the **adolescent level** the expression of faith is exhilarated and partisan. Proselytizing and claiming one's own faith feels unique, or the most authentic, in nonaggressive but intense ways. It is also the level of collective celebration and self-mortification practices—flagellation, imprisonment in darkness, rigorous fasting, painful yoga, meditation marathons—which augment the intensity of the faith.
- The **selfish adult** invents the religious hierarchy, politicizes religion, and, in effect, is the basis of social order. In its name he will deliver the Inquisition, religious colonization, the crusades, and the formation of secret societies like Opus Dei. He will not hesi-

tate to make financial profits in the name of religion and adopt partisan attitudes by the construction of temples, mosques, and churches and the beatification of saints, which conform not to political and economic logic as much as to acts of pure faith.

- The **social-altruistic adult** establishes missions, public works, hospitals, and orphanages. Mother Teresa and the worker-priests represent this level, as do the social works of Indian gurus like Amma. It is social action in the name of religion, and it is accompanied by ecumenism and tolerance. The monastic life, when it is opened to the outside by its works, also corresponds to this level.

The social-altruistic adult considers a miracle to be an extraordinary manifestation appearing outside of that which he believes to be the laws of the universe. But at the planetary level of Consciousness, one begins to notice the miracle everywhere, to witness it, and to be able to act in a miraculous direction. For example, collective unions can produce inexplicable results, like when masses of people pray together for rain during a severe drought and it rains the next day.

- For the **planetary adult**, there is no "one" religion better than the others; she is far too conscious of the unity of questioning and of the diverse forms of faith. Thus, she supports the fusion of religion with nonreligious approaches, including science. It is the level at which the scientific and religious can talk in peace because the level of Consciousness of the planetary adult becomes attached not to words or to ideologies, but only to the mystery of living. On the individual plane, the planetary adult adopts the attitude of the Bodhisattva or the enlightened shaman; he forever blesses the totality of living.
- From the level of **solar Consciousness**, one enters mysticism and ecstasy: the temple is a body and the body is a temple. One finds God within and one knows impersonal love and universal compassion. Every human being is a priest, every place is an altar,

every act is sacred, and every obstacle or deed is a lesson along the way.

- From the **cosmic Consciousness** one witnesses miracles, inexplicable coincidences, bodies that do not rot after death.
- The **divine Consciousness** is, in essence, the core of every religion.

We summarize thus:

- **Animal**: Survive. "Eat or be eaten."
- **Infantile**: Consume. "Obtain everything, to be able to live dreaming and playing."
- **Adolescent**: Be loved and admired; defy distant death; integrate into a group. "Love always/live fast, die young."
- **Selfish Adult**: Preserve security and private property; defend one's own interests. "Everything for me."
- **Social-Altruistic Adult**: Share. "Nothing for me which is not for others."
- **Planetary Adult**: Ecology, service, and sustainable Consciousness. "Everything is living, everything is part of me and I am part of everything."
- **Solar Consciousness**: Have an effect on the past and future generations, and understand the principles of life. "Time and space do not exist."
- **Cosmic Consciousness**: Understand that we are not the only form of life. "My pain never becomes suffering: I dissolve into the Everything."
- **Divine Consciousness**: "I am love."

Exercise: My five genealogy trees

On five sheets of paper, trace the base diagram of the tree (see page 80). Label each tree:

1. One level of Consciousness tree
2. One intellectual tree (ideas, morals, religions, studies)
3. One emotional tree (bonds between people, injuries and major joys, dominant emotions)
4. One sexual-creative tree (the role of creativity, sexuality, the enjoyment/disappointment dynamics in your tree)
5. One material tree (money, place, illnesses, sports, eating habits)

For each of these trees, insert the phrase formulating your goal in the top box. Reflect upon this, and then add a sentence that states the purpose of the material (the fifth tree), sexual-creative (the fourth tree), emotional (the third tree), and intellectual or ideological, moral, etc. (the second tree). Notice how the goal declines with each energy level. For the first tree, ask yourself, "If I, as a social adult, put myself at the highest level of Consciousness that I am capable of attaining, what collective goal can I offer that complements my personal goal?"

For example, a person's personal goal might be, "Self-fulfillment." And the specifics might be:

5. Material tree: To live in the country in a big house with a garden. To earn three times my current salary.
4. Sexual-creative tree: To exert my creativity, my sense of beauty, in my work. Paint again.
3. Emotional tree: To better my relationships with my partner and with my children. To be more patient and available.
2. Intellectual tree: To have more confidence in my ideas. To find my curiosity again.
1. Consciousness tree: To promote peace in the world by every possible means in my power.

Once, center by center, the objective is specified, insert all the main characters into the tree—all direct ascendants and any very influential person among the siblings. Then, for each tree, determine what key elements occur in each center. As a guideline, here are some useful questions to ask for each member of your tree (the list is not exhaustive):

1. Level of Consciousness tree
   - What was this person's level of Consciousness that determined the majority of his or her actions?
   - What level of Consciousness influenced this person's life and that of his or her descendants?
   - In my opinion, what was this person's goal in life?
   - In what level of Consciousness do I live most of the time?
   - What is the highest level of Consciousness that I have attained in my life and under what circumstances?

2. Intellectual tree
   - What were this person's religious and political opinions?
   - What might have been this person's favorite maxim?
   - What ideas or ideologies did this person bequeath to me, or to one of my parents?
   - What was this person's education level?
   - What was this person's native language? How many languages did this person speak?
   - How did this person communicate (with or without violence; verbosly or tersedly; clearly or confusingly)?
   - What was "intelligent" or "informed"; what was "stupid" or "no education"?

3. Emotional tree
   - What were this person's dominant emotions?
   - With whom was this person most closely tied?
   - What were this person's main injuries in life?
   - What were this person's greatest pleasures?
   - What was this person's emotional maturity? Did he or she act like an adult, an infant, an adolescent?
   - What conception of love, what emotional bonds, did this person have?
   - Was this person "kind" or "nasty"?
   - How did this person express emotions and feelings?
   - With whom did this person communicate effectively?

4. Sexual-creative tree

- Did this person express his or her creativity? If yes, how? If no, what could have been?
- What were this person's sexual relations?
- Where were the taboos, shame, or bans this person faced?
- What were this person's major frustrations?
- In what ways did this person experience pleasure?
- What were this person's successes and failures? How were they experienced?
- What was this person's conception of art and beauty?
- Was this person talented? In what?
- Was this person beautiful or ugly?
- In what conditions, at what age, did this person conceive children?
- Under what conditions did this person give birth or abort, if any?
- In what social, moral, and cultural setting did this person experience puberty or the beginning of sexuality?

5. Material tree

- Did this person have a physical resemblance to anyone else on the tree? How did this person experience that resemblance, or the lack of it? An infant may be preferred by a parent because of his resemblance to another member of the family, while a lack of resemblance can call into question—real or imagined—a child's paternity.
- Did this person have illnesses, accidents, or physical deformities?
- What was this person's relationship with money?
- Was this person "strong" or "weak," thin or fat, rich or poor?
- What place did sports, the body, and physical activity take in this person's life?
- Where were the significant places in this person's life? The climates? The trips? The exiles?
- How did this person eat? What this person's relationship with food?
- At what age did this person die and why?

If these trees remain incomplete, don't worry. They will continue to serve you as a reference throughout the work.

These are only suggestions designed to differentiate the mass of information you have about your family, and this subdivision into five distinct areas allows you to make a first go, to ask questions differently. Thanks to this, you can clarify your tree's legacy and then start driving out the repetitions at work.

LEVEL OF CONSCIOUSNESS AND FAMILY SECRETS

Many consultants take on the genealogy tree with the intention of exposing a family secret. But we must understand what we are talking about when we are talking about this kind of secret.

Some critical new information may appear that even modifies parentage. For example, "My father had illegitimate children," "My mother abandoned a baby before her marriage," "I am not the biological child of my parents," "My grandmother was a Jew during the Occupation and has hidden her origins until this day," "Our family name comes from a great-grandfather who was an orphan," and so on. Often, these facts concern a social or familial shame, or a major taboo like a death or incest. "This person went to prison," "My aunt was crazy, they locked her up," "An uncle was a priest and had four biological children," "My grandmother was an alcoholic and prostituted herself," "My father killed a man," "My grandmother witnessed a murder," "My great-grandfather raped his daughter and she gave birth to his child," and so forth.

But a family secret can also be existing information that is not supposed to be mentioned. "My mother was a widow when my father met her. I do not know anything about her first husband," "My parents adopted a fourth child in Latin America. We have never been to the country of his origin and he does not speak the language of that country. I do not know why they wanted to adopt him," "My grandfather dreamed of being a priest. He was not allowed and he spent his whole life regretting his vocation," "My father was in love with a man and he never stopped loving him. He married my mother to escape his homosexuality. She always criticizes him and treats him like a 'dirty queer' in big arguments," and so on.

In all of these cases, it is the **treatment of this information** and **the concrete emotional and psychic consequences of the secrets in the following generations** that should interest us. As such, everything left unsaid in the genealogy tree is a kind of "family secret." It is not necessary to bring up the great-grandmother who was a single mother and raped by a member of the local nobility in order to resolve her suffering.

In other words, one must not wish for the study of the tree to remove all of the family secrets. Instead, one must remember that one's own personal purpose carries this work, and the fundamental questions are "Why can't I live the life I truly want to live, have the experience I want, feel at peace in my heart, think freely, and live a fulfilling life?" If there is a secret, it will be connected to the consultant's deep, authentic, intimate questioning. The rest is anecdote.

Several secrets can emerge by dint of inquiry, questioning, and awareness. But certain family secrets are not revealed in a person's life until the moment arrives by way of dreams, encounters, and/or spontaneous clear-sightedness.

When a suspected family secret resists one's inquiry, the best attitude to adopt is to study the tree as it is with all the emotional, intellectual, sexual, and material nuances. It is also essential to open one's eyes to the social circumstances surrounding the tree, because they are often determinants in the constitution of the secret, according to what society approves of or punishes, with the traps being the deciding factor in which secrets are more likely to be kept. For example, if someone was raised in a religious institution, one must ask him about his living conditions there; if a family was very poor and the children were sent to work when they were very young, it is likely they were subjected to a variety of abuses.

Many secrets consist only of the pain of being unable to express an inner truth—for example, love that is condemned by the society of the time, an activity or sexual orientation that clashes with family morality, or abuse suffered in a context in which said abuse is so common that it is believed to be normal. A person then guards the secret out of obligation and, ultimately, seeks an understanding ear to open up to. Through peaceful dialogue with members of the family, we are sometimes surprised to hear these secrets revealed for the first time.

From the metagenealogical perspective, all work with these family secrets is oriented toward the perspective that **the whole tree, like the individual, tends toward Consciousness**. When succeeding generations are bestowed with a very low level of Consciousness, the later generations seem to be eliminated:

- The tree no longer reproduces. The parents had pathological and toxic behaviors and their adult children refuse to procreate, or become psychologically or physically incapable of doing so.
- All members of the tree enter religion, either to find a substitute family or to reconnect with their spirituality.
- They self-destruct through alcoholism, drug addiction, or other problems. One can even say that when society has too many sick families, it starts to become self-destructive because the trees destroy one another. Very serious studies have shown the influence of nineteenth-century German education, founded in corporal punishment and similar approaches, on the emergence of Nazism. This pattern also applies to civil wars, which can be considered "fratricides."
- They exile due to unfavorable economic conditions, which drive members of the tree to emigration to take their chances in a wealthier country; the family then continues on new terrain, but breaks with their traditions.

To counteract the tendency of self-destruction, the genealogy tree begets one or more conscious descendants who save themselves. Paradoxically, these genealogical mutants are often considered by the family to be "black sheep." If inheriting the tree requires perpetuation of the low level of Consciousness, the family will initially reject the descendant in search of meaning.

Consciousness progresses by meeting obstacles. Aspects of the past slow the progress of Consciousness, and, inversely, Consciousness battles the inertia of the past, which produces an equilibrium. Descendants who seem to come "out of nowhere" correct the massive tendency of the genealogy tree toward its different forms of inertia. This is how a scientist can be the lifesaver in a tree of artists, and how a financier can generate a tree of irresponsible bohemians.

Study of a large number of genealogy trees shows that they function following a system of equilibrium that permits contradictory personalities to emerge, sometimes a few generations apart, as if one person's destiny comes to compensate for the destiny of someone else. One can thus find a saint on one branch and an assassin on another, or else a tree crippled by sexual dissatisfaction can produce someone with a very energetic sexuality in the next generation.

For the person who lives as the black sheep of the tree, it can be very reassuring to realize that he embodies the potential that the tree needs in order to experience the equilibrium that has been missing throughout the genealogy.

Returning to the family secrets, we realize that everything that was hidden for four generations ends up manifesting at a given moment, whether by repetition, a revelation, or some other process. We can call this the **genealogical confession**. Just as the individual Unconscious tends to manifest itself through dreams in the absence of action, or in repetitions, encounters, or coincidences, the familial Unconscious will express itself through the most sensitive subjects—through art, a personal search that uses therapy, spiritual research (motivated or not by suffering), or even compulsive acts. Orgies, parties, drug use, and other secondary states, like an awake-dream or a psychodrama, can produce the repetition of the tree's secret.

Following are the **major secrets** found in family histories.

- Incest
- Homosexuality concealed under a traditional marriage
- Crimes, robbery
- Sexual abuse (pedophilia, rape)
- Sexual deviation (betrayal, prostitution)
- Disease thought to be "shameful"
- Abortions, infanticides
- False paternity
- Bankruptcy
- Imprisonment
- Insanity and psychiatric confinement

The tree's **minor secrets** are essentially emotional secrets, but they can also have a considerable influence on the lineage. Namely:

- Clandestine romances, including those not consummated
- The nationality or true denomination of an ancestor
- A physical defect
- Surgery (aesthetic or otherwise)
- Professional, academic, or artistic failure
- Secret or imaginary guilt (to have wronged someone, to have treated someone badly before their death)
- All minor sexual secrets (impotence, frigidity, premature ejaculation, marital rape, aversion, but also unacknowledged unbridled sexuality)

In general, something repeats in the next generation, or if a repression has been very well maintained in one generation, it repeats also in the third generation, with the children therefore reviving the secrets of their grandparents. The tree proceeds as an individual who, incapable of really hiding his secret, owns up to it in different ways. This revelation passes through people who have knowledge of the secret and filter it or compensate for it with something in their lives—their gestures, their beliefs, their way of loving and interacting.

A family secret can also serve to screen an even bigger secret. For example, a mother who was a widow and apparent exemplar raised a daughter pretending that she did not have a man in her life. The mother closely monitored the child's relationships. The daughter, until age fourteen, grew up with the idea that her mother was a saint. One day, returning earlier than planned from school, the girl found her mother—a tall, distinguished woman—in the kitchen having sex on all fours with a short, fat, ugly "friend of the family." The psychological shock was so strong that the young girl experienced a psychotic breakdown (delusions of persecution). For the next ten years, she fought against a tenacious frigidity that finally ended after several therapeutic approaches combined. But the true secret, discovered thanks to the "indiscretion" of a healthy family member, was that she was not the biological daughter of her father, who had disappeared when she was seven years old—the unbridled sexuality of her apparently very wise mother began, in reality, much earlier than had been revealed.

Shame, imaginary crimes, unconsummated romances, and the like can all have significant effects on the next generations just as if they were real acts. For example, on a whim, a little girl refused to hug her father before the trip during which his plane crashed and he died. The feeling of omnipotence specific to children drove her to firmly believe that she was responsible for his death. Until she reached adulthood, she believed with mute certainty that she had killed her father. Her own children felt threatened by this mother who thought herself a criminal—one became a police chief, the other a criminal attorney, and every day they face the murdered and the murderers.

A family secret is motivated by one person's inability to surpass the level of Consciousness of the society and of the family in which he lives. His individual destiny conflicts with the values in which he evolves, so he finds himself at odds with his family tree, its society, and its culture. In such a situation, the only truly healthy solution is for him to access a more elevated level of Consciousness. If he is able to accept the actions or circumstances of the secret, finds a way to communicate with the family, and circulates the truth among the adults at all costs, the price his descendants have to pay will always be lower.

If incest, agreed to or not, took place in the family it is better to be honest and open with the family community. Each member will be free to think, to react, according to his or her own beliefs and personal maturity. It is possible that a victim of abuse, of a maddening situation, of an injustice, et cetera, will not receive the family's support once the secret is shared. For example, a woman married for twenty years to an impotent man conceived an infant with the sperm of an anonymous donor. The husband obviously recognized the child. Tired of living in complete sexual dissatisfaction, the woman decided to tell the whole family the truth about the situation. The family absolutely refused to take advantage of the "perfect" husband: in the familial culture, the woman's sexual satisfaction was negligible. But this action allowed the consultant to divorce quite peacefully and to choose her own path in life.

Our conviction is that whatever the situation, whatever the apparent severity of secrecy, **the truth is always preferable to silence**. Not because of any moral virtue, but because the familial Unconscious is always informed of the secret and, consequently, each member of the family carries it as his or her own destiny even without knowing it.

From the point of view of Consciousness, shame is just a social artifact. If one asks an artist to design (write, perform) that which shames him, he will produce a series of erotic designs of extraordinary quality or a book of shocking truths or a hilarious show—creators know that shame is an airtight door that leads to the deep Unconscious.

All that we store inside ourselves as shame is a hidden treasure repressed by the desire to "be seen," which is similar to the infantile desire to be loved. A person who has shame over her sexual actions or desires in reality has the need to undertake the power of the libido, which is experienced, and to shape it into something that is right for her. A person who has shame over his social exclusion has, in reality, the need to find his place in the world. A person who has shame over having been a victim of abuse, of an injustice, or any other experience in reality has a deep need to have her suffering and humiliation understood, and to be reassured of her capacity to be loved for who she is.

The family secret, motivated by shame, corresponds to the difference between the being's deep truth and the social pressures he must face.

PART FOUR

The Couple

Origin of Lineage

SEVEN

The Magic of the Encounter

By Alejandro Jodorowsky

The whole study of the genealogy tree is based on the emotional encounter, in the romantic sense, and on passion, in the sexual sense, of men and women—almost always unexpected, and sometimes miraculous. One generation after the next couples who are driven by an unconscious desire to experience a love that they could perfect battle the traps of their genealogy tree in an attempt to fulfill their union. The circumstances of these encounters are innumerable and almost always extraordinary, to the point that we doubt the strength of our reasoning.

"Because, to fight off a cold, she removed her shoes in the five-star restaurant and spread mustard on the soles of her feet." (The meeting between Andre Breton and Leonora Carrington.) "Because she came to my pantomime lesson in square spectacles." (Marcel Marceau fascinated by his future wife, Huguette.) "Because at her painting exhibition, I discovered a word written in lowercase letters on a little canvas attached to the ceiling. To read it, one had to climb a ladder; the word was *yes*." (John Lennon on the moment he discovered that Yoko Ono was the woman of his life.) "Because, during a performance of my piece *The Games People Play,* a woman laughed so loud I felt obliged to meet her." (Myself, the day I discovered Valerie, the mother of three of my sons.)

In spite of our resistance, friends convince us to come to a party . . . a beautiful stranger runs into our car . . . the voice speaking in the office next to ours seduces us . . . seemingly impossible encounters, accidents, coincidences . . . these are details that fascinate us.

When François feels in love with Françoise, Louis with Louise, Claudio with Claudia, it is arguably the names that are in charge of a magnetic force, so that it is not a man and a woman who fall in love, but first names that mutually seek their reflection.

The ideal woman can also fall from the sky. The famous singer, Libertad Lamarque, in a moment of depressive loneliness jumped out of a fourth-floor window and fell on a man who, for the first time in his life, had walked down that street. The singer, unscathed, broke several of the man's ribs. Full of remorse, she accompanied him to the hospital and visited him until his rehabilitation. They fell in love and were married.

Dr. Arthur Janov, creator of primal scream therapy, says in his book *Sexuality and the Subconscious,* "The universe is indifferent. Our existence, our mode of living, our suffering, our personality, doesn't interest it. . . . The universe is only interested in one thing: the perpetuation of life. On the cosmic plane, only sex is important. We are here to make love, to be fruitful and multiply. Each one of us is a genetic machine whose fundamental purpose is to reproduce. . . . Sexuality is vital and all the rest is secondary."

If we think **the truth is useful,** we prefer to say that the universe is indifferent compared to the egotistical and isolated individual, but truth is nevertheless a project for the human species. The goal of humanity is not only to procreate, but also to mutate and to create Consciousness. Janov says, "We embellish our sexuality with broad terms like morality and love but it is ultimately for procreation. Everything probably passes on better if the partners are in love but what counts is that the couple mates and has children." And, we should add here, that they become **aware.**

In the future couple's first encounter, even the incident that appears to be the most insignificant has causes, similar to roots, that span several generations. Human beings do not unite like other animals, motivated by rutting. In their union, there is an unconscious desire to give birth to offspring capable of one day achieving impersonal love and universal compassion. Sometimes with awkwardness, sometimes in suffering, from one generation to the next we advance toward the development of Consciousness. The genealogical trap often triumphs and the process of evolution seems to stagnate. However, through successive generations evolution slowly carries out the intention of the future.

Anne-Marie, totally normal in appearance, tells us the story of how she met her husband: "During a party he tripped and spilled his orange juice all over my white gown with an incredible clumsiness." But how can a glass of orange juice unite two beings? This link created by the incident, is it as absurd as it seems?

The young woman with the white gown stained with orange juice, Anne Marie, is the daughter of Christian, a professor of literature and director of a school in Marseille, who died during WWI. In childhood, he lived with his mother, Marie-Anne. With Marie-Anne (metaphor for the Virgin Mary), an absent father (metaphor for God) generated the perfect child—Christian (metaphor for Jesus Christ). Thus the professor of literature, who was guided by a powerful religious morality, married Marie-Madeleine (comments are unnecessary), who was also zealously religious and a professor of literature. These parents, fleeing sexual sin, took refuge in their heads and floated above their bodies, consequently restraining all the natural urges of their daughter. So, alone in the middle of a party and ensconced in her starched white dress, she felt imprisoned in her cold, dry body. The orange juice—fruit of heat, of the big sun—reversed that, revealing the passionate moisture nestled in her vagina. She realized that, since puberty, she had longed for a relationship with a foreigner bathed in the sunlight of his country.

Meanwhile, Octave was not born in an exotic country but in France. He was a failed musician, a bad student, a slacker, immature, himself the grandson of an Octave who, because of his audacious, strong, and adventurous character, left for Morocco to amass a fortune selling oranges. After a sumptuous life, he was assassinated and no one ever learned why or by whom. Octave Jr. cowardly fled to France, where he squandered the fortune and became a police officer (perhaps with the unconscious desire to continue looking for his father's assassin). Octave III, our lover, grew up feeling he was as small a man as his father, raising the level of the mythology of his grandfather's virility. One must add that our young man's mother died of pulmonary cancer before he was five years old. To conquer the virgin dressed in white (metaphor for the mother transformed into an angel), he used orange juice: the strength of his legendary grandfather. As for Anne, she satisfied her desire for a foreigner's heat through a compatriot, and he was very useful because it was indeed under these conditions that the in-laws, full of prejudices, accepted the fiancé to whom they could teach literature. He accepted this teaching, which before his own eyes elevated him above his "son of a cop" condition.

Alfred Richard Orage (1873–1934), an English disciple of the occultist George Gurdjieff, in his work *Of Love and Other Essays,* developed Gurdjieff's theory that we are three people: "The three principal systems—cerebral, emotional, instinctual—coexist and sometimes cooperate but most often fail to cooperate and have opposite intentions in general." The result of this inner fracture is that three totally different people compete inside of us for the governance of our actions and, refusing to cooperate, make obstacles to impede one another. "It is rare that the three antagonists fall in love at the same time with the same object: one is in love and the two others are not or they resist or, while the lover is not on guard, they push the organism to infidelity. Under these circumstances, what is a lover?"

In responding to Orage's question, one must distinguish between seven kinds of love: physical, sexual, emotional, intellectual, conscious, cosmic, magic. Everyone can experience the first four; the fifth and the sixth are rare and take effort and perseverance. Regarding magic love, it is independent of will and is only known once the six previous loves are achieved.

Physical love is, basically, the meeting of two bodies motivated by the necessity of finding a companion, a physical link that does not include the other dimensions of the human being. The couple sleeps, eats, works, and fornicates without passion; the couple is incapable of exchanging ideas. Each one lives enclosed in the prison of his or her egotistical individuality and can only give his or her physical presence to the other. It is a form of love similar to that of domestic animals. Any attempt of one to develop his or her capacities provokes in the other reactions of anxiety, anger, or illness in an attempt to prevent the partner from moving forward on a new path.

Sexual love is based on the attractions and impulses of the reproductive instinct. Men seek power (the satisfaction of power) and women seek satisfaction (the power of being satisfied). Behind the lure of pleasure and attraction, procreation is the primary function of sexual love: the universe desires the proliferation of the species. Once they cohabitate, satisfied, the lovers reject one another until the sexual drive resurfaces. All spiritual development extinguishes this passion.

Emotional love is often the reproduction of a situation in childhood. A woman who had an absent father weds a man who lives in a remote city. A man who had a cold mother is attached to a woman who is incapable of love. Those who were once humiliated, beaten, abused, or deceived later seek relationships that reproduce similar suffering. These unchecked affinities are sooner or later shipwrecked in jealousy and passiveness. The lover becomes an object of indifference or of hatred.

Intellectual love negates the body, emotions, and sexuality for the benefit of mental communion. The man loves an ideal, impossible, distant woman. The woman needs a man to hand over his life to be able to love her. An ancient Arabian tale tells such a story:

A poet fell in love with a princess upon seeing her portrait. To her, he dedicated sublime verses. Learning of these poems, she was offended: a miserable poet cannot entertain such feelings for a woman of her rank. Meanwhile, he decided to cross the ocean in a small boat to see his beloved. During the passage, storms fell upon him and he lost all hope of accomplishing his goal. He was lovesick. The winds deposited him, in agony, upon the shore. He was incapable of going any further. The princess, alerted to his arrival, considered him with disdain and, just the same, went to meet him and to punish his arrogance. Upon discovering him at the point of death, she fell in love with him . . .

One might say such facts belong only in the realm of fairy tales. Yet they occur in real life, as in the case of Teresa Wilms Montt (1893–1921), a poetess of aristocratic origin and one of the most beautiful women in Chile. Horacio, a poet of nineteen years, fell insanely in love with her. Teresa rejected him. He would not listen. For a year, he called to her, pursued her, dedicated poems to her. She, with haughty coldness (she told a friend, "Love of the living interests me not"), told him again that she did not love him. Horacio killed himself by slashing his veins. After his death Teresa's coldness ignited. She observed a strict mourning and wrote passionate poems for Horacio: "Why have you gone? Why? I ask myself one, two million times each day. And I cannot find the response to relieve my soul's fierce pain."

These four kinds of love can join forces more or less completely. For example, intellectual love, associated exclusively with emotional love, consists of a union where the passionate or physical interests are lacking. If the union is completed only by sexual love, the couple will miss out on kindness and material security. If associated only with material love, the couple will miss out on human warmth and will descend into cruelty. As for emotional love, united with sexual love, the couple will miss mental and material organization that may lead to excess passion, like jealousy. An emotional and material love leads to possessiveness. And if sexual love and material love finally unite, the relationship will not have a soul.

Even when three kinds of love unite, if the fourth is missing the couple will live with the feeling of incompleteness: the absence of material love evokes abandonment; the absence of sexual love evokes dissatisfaction; the absence of emotional love evokes indifference; and the absence of intellectual love condemns the couple to misunderstanding.

It is possible to arrive at material balance and spiritual peace if the once-separated four loves unite. For this to occur, self-sacrifice totally devoid of selfishness must be developed.

Material love will forfeit the desire for ownership. The two partners will share a common space with pleasure, and in that, each will maintain a territory of his or her own. Each will commit to not invading the private space of the other and to respecting his or her need for solitude.

Sexual love will be complicity based on trust and the dissolution of jealousy. The pleasure of both partners will be mutual and without borders, and it will allow them to express their desires. Each will work to satisfy the fantasies of the other but will be equally free to refuse, in which case "no" will be a compromise and will allow the other to seek satisfaction elsewhere. Sublimation and abstinence, where appropriate, will be sincere, not to be confused with disguised frustration.

In emotional love, the desire to disappear by dissolving into the other must be abandoned. Any symbiosis leads to a struggle to eat each other. The partners love one another without aspiring to a chemical fusion, without pretending to be everything for the other. They do not lock themselves in an exclusive relationship. To their mutual affection, they add what they are to their family, friends, colleagues, and humanity. They recognize that love is a search not for equality but for a complementary difference. Neither is the owner of the other. Their attachment is made of knots that are untied at will. They protect each other without ever depriving themselves of freedom, and they move forward together, blessing every step. If their paths do part, each accepts this and wishes the other all possible happiness in his or her new life.

Intellectual love can only be achieved by renouncing the narcissistic search for the twin soul. In mutual understanding, without a doubt, and far from verbiage, the couple will reach a shared rapture of essential silence. Each respects the other. Each always gives the other the right to express his or her own vision of the world and, even if the one doesn't agree, allows the other to develop his or her thoughts in whatever direction is suitable to him or her.

It is possible to achieve all this by conscious work that leads first to living in harmony with oneself, then with the other: leaving behind immature attitudes; learning to forgive; loving ourselves as we are; obeying intuition rather than reason; living in the present moment; accepting what is presented to us without holding back; giving without ever expecting anything in return; being sincere; not lying to ourselves or to others.

Thus, we can reach conscious love. In setting the goal of improvement, we allow the loved one the possibility of accessing his or her personal improvement no matter what the consequences are to the relationship. With humility and tolerance, we look at the other with understanding (of what the other is and of what the other can become when following his or her own inclinations), and we provide today the loved one's future needs, never thinking about what these needs cost or take away from us.

If the couple achieves conscious love, which includes the previous four loves, the couple can then experience cosmic love. The lovers go beyond the borders of their personalities, feeling the unity of everything: the immeasurable force that leads the universal dance. In time, which elapses incessantly, they are capable of detecting another time in which neither space nor movement can exist; they feel the unimaginable Consciousness that fills the totality with life.

Each person loves, not only the other's body, but also the mysterious energy that drives the other; not only the other's feelings, but also that infinite love that created matter and Consciousness. Each obeys sexual attraction, knowing that their goal is not only to create offspring but also to capture, through orgasm, the creative joy of the universe. Each lover loves the other's mind but also the other's wholeness, which is passed on by moving beyond anxiety about death. These lovers can then say, "In the center of the silence of the soul, the invisible garden where nothing is, I welcome your silence, I respect it and I understand. Our words acquire a dignity and, in purifying them, we share the pleasure of growing together, of offering the fruits of emptiness. We are accomplices in the quest for a treasure—universal wholeness—and we pave the way to the light without seeking to possess it. We are free to expand beyond the ultimate limit and to humbly accept constant change, to open our doors and our windows, drawers and closets, and to offer everything in a feast for others, without withholding anything for ourselves of that which is impossible to give: the eye of Consciousness, able to see the self."

Together, united by magic love, in a state of detachment, without possessing anything or being possessed by anything, they represent spiritual androgyny. The deepest desire of the human race is to reach a perfectly complementary union between a man and a woman capable, in their internal and external interactions, of bringing physical and spiritual fulfillment to humanity. The mystics, the alchemists, the magicians, and the poets desired this supreme love that words cannot describe. Each civilization illustrates this by figures or symbols: the mythical Chinese emperor Fou Hi and his sister, Niu Kua; the Hebrew patriarch Abraham and his wife, Sarah; Jesus Christ and his mother, Marie; the god Shiva and his companion, Parvati; Manco Capac and his sister-wife, Mama Ocllo; the yin and the yang of the Tao; the double triangle of the Kabbalah, which forms a six-pointed star; the union of the square and the compass in Masonic symbolism; the Rebis or the alchemical hermaphrodite; the marriage of the Egyptian Nut (mother-sky) and Geb (father-earth).

Without thinking that this feeling is mythical or impossible to achieve, the lovers recognize magic love while establishing perfect trust in the meantime. They stop trying to rationalize and instead invest in, and happily accept, who they are without trying to change the other into a mirror image or an audience. Each moment together passes in peaceful happiness. They work together without competition and they quite naturally agree without the need for debate. They travel toward the same purpose and make helping others a fundamental duty. They take responsibility flawlessly, and contact between their bodies and their souls is a heavenly pleasure.

It goes without saying: if the couple reproduces, each kind of love offers the children a different destiny.

EIGHT

The Couple in My Tree

Encounter and Fertilization, Conflicts and Cooperation

A genealogy tree is essentially the product of seven couples: four couples of great-grandparents, two couples of grandparents, and one couple of parents. Naturally, the further back one goes, the number of couples multiplies and a fantastical number can be reached, even exceeding the population of the planet for each family. This extrapolation sends us back to human origins and indicates that we are all children of the same source, as is evidenced in the many creation myths where the central figure is an original or archetypal couple, divine or human: Adam and Eve; Marduk and Sarpanit in Mesopotamia; Isis and Osiris in Egypt; Shiva and Kali in India. As we saw earlier, beyond four or five generations, the genealogy tree dissolves in collective memory.

So the seven couples we want to talk about here are personal couples, unique to our tree, who represent the lineage through which we came to this world. Whatever the relationship between these men and women—from the ideal situation where "they were happy and had lots of kids" to the tragic situations of rape, abandonment, widowhood—each one of us is the product of seven sexual encounters between women and men. At the root of the tree is the couple.

160

How do we look at these couples who created us? Here again we distinguish and unite two opposite and complementary visions:

- If one refers to the forces of repetition of the past, **we are the product of our parents**. Two scenarios are then possible: "I am a wanted child" or "I am an accident." The wanted child's mission is to accomplish the goals set for him by his parents. The accident's mission is to have his birth pardoned by developing compelling qualities. For example, very frequently "adult children" take responsibility for the adolescent or childish parents overwhelmed by the birth they had not expected.
- If one refers to the creative forces of the universe, **we were not created by our parents but through them**. Instead of saying that a mother "made" a child, we would say that an infant "is made" inside the mother. Our arrival in the world goes beyond the parents' individual will: they are no more than the vehicle or the means of expression. In such cases, whatever happens we can say, "I had to be born," indeed, "I wanted to be born." Thus the parents' encounter, whatever the nature, is an event that made this essential birth possible.

Throughout the study of the tree, these two myths about our origin will intertwine. One assists our repetitive formation and determines the fate of the tree's **heirs**: "My parents gave birth to me, and I must give them back their invested energy by accomplishing the goals they have set for me or by repairing the mistakes I have made." The other indicates a creative power that will make us **mutants** of our genealogy tree: "I was born and my parents allowed this. My mission is to express, in the unique way that I have been granted, the project of Consciousness as it manifests through me. My creative acts are a vital contribution to my family tree, for society, and for humanity."

To be able to undertake the work, we must understand both aspects of the couple in our tree: the aspect inherited from the past, soaked in romantic dreams, traditions, resentment, conflicts, and repetitions of every kind, and the aspect corresponding to the call of the future, wherein every couple carries the seed of a sacred union, either made in the history of the previous generations or not.*

THE ORIGIN MYTH

Fertilization

The genealogy tree's destiny, above all, resides in the idea that the family is the sperm and the egg. To move beyond the war of the sexes, in order to perceive the miracle that we beget, it is helpful, above all, to revise our idea about fertilization. Indeed, the way in which scientists describe the manner in which each of us came into the world is taken from the Darwinian notion of survival of the fittest, which in varying degrees leads to the following description: With each ejaculation, an army of sperm warriors rush to the conquest of the fortress (the female genital structure), where the ovum (the coveted booty) lounges softly among the folds. At the entrance of this stronghold the troops face many obstacles (vaginal secretion, cervical mucus) that help select the most robust sperm. Then there is the endless procession toward the uterus as the attackers are depleted by crossbow flagella. When the most deserving finally arrive at the huge egg, they engage without mercy in a final combat to penetrate the egg. A single and unique victor will finally perforate all lingering opposition.

This masculinist and warrior-centric metaphor presents fertilization to us as a conquest, almost a rape, where the sperm engage in merciless competition while the ovule (stupid and passive) waits to be conquered: raped or violated like women vanquished during war. However, recent research states that the female orgasm may in fact facilitate progress of the sperm in the uterus and the tubes. Again, this is the latest of the most progressive theories.

---

*We focus here on the heterosexual couple to the extent that the genealogy tree is the product of man-woman couples. But this chapter can absolutely apply to the homosexual couple today, which is frequently also a parental couple.

We are all marked, consciously or not, by the creation myth stemming from twentieth-century science, itself marked by Western social and cultural concepts. What happens if we look at our design according to other, more useful and universal criteria? Recently some scientists, among them Professor Lars Hamberger, a Swedish gynecologist and obstetrician, became more interested in the details of this conception adventure and began developing in vitro techniques to allow for closer observation. This is how we propose to rewrite history in light of their scientific observations.*

We imagine for a moment that far from being a tug-of-war between sperm and egg, fertilization is the product of an incredible cooperation between masculine and feminine at the service of Consciousness, a theory based on the Tarot, in which the Major Arcana unfolds between the two essential principles of the Fool (masculine) and the World (feminine).

Aided by the impulse of his dog and carrying his little bundle, the Fool launches out in search of the World. The World looks at

---

*See in particular Nilsson and Hamberger, *Naître*.

the Fool and seems to tempt him. The encounter between these two archetypes gives birth to the totality of the Tarot. Each is at the same time active and receptive: the Fool, pure energy, obeys the call of the World, which is peacefully spread between the four cosmic energies (the four symbols in the card's four corners) and actively receives the Fool's energy.

And was it the same with the gametes that made us?

One might think that the egg selects and draws in the sperm, one way or another, choosing the sperm most adaptable and capable of giving birth to a being that must come into the world. Obeying this powerful call, the sperm collaborate with one another like a sports team to facilitate the chosen individuals who advance toward the egg: the success of one is the triumph of all.

Each ejaculation produces a discharge of seminal fluid filled with five hundred million sperm. A large number of these sperm, even in a young subject, contain what scientists call "flaws that prevent the fertilization of the egg."

But are these flaws, really? If we put aside the original sexist, Darwinist prejudices it becomes clear that not all sperm are destined to achieve fertilization: millions mobilize to neutralize the vaginal acidity as they travel through the neck of the uterus. Those that continue climb back up against the current of vibrating cilia lining the wall of the uterus. Actually, these apparent obstacles produce a secretion that induces maturation of the sperm, which changes their energy as they advance. Indeed, the sperm initially carry a certain number of mitochondria (the "energy centers" of the cell), allowing them sufficient energy for twenty-four hours. When necessary, however, they can also "recharge" in the tube.

When they are finally at their goal there are not more than a hundred remaining, the others having sacrificed themselves to help a small group advance. Meanwhile, the egg descends into the fallopian tube, where it is surrounded by a viscous layer of nutritive cells, most of which have been used up. Those that remain will help the sperm clear a path to the thicker, more elastic layer of the egg. To accomplish this, the sperm must get rid of the acrosome, the protective coating that covers its head and whose enzymes dissolve the wall of the egg. This task involves another sacrifice of the many. The last dozen sperm are able to cross the wall of the egg and stay planted there, stirring up the flagella, which results in the egg turning in the opposite direction. This rotation, which is the same as that of the planets, the sun, and the universe, unites the egg with the cosmic dance and the charge—an enormous energy, one might imagine. It is at that moment that the egg chooses (by reasons which may have to do with the mother's Unconscious or Superconscious) which will become her ally in the creation of the new being. The chosen one, with whom all the others collaborated, is pulled inside the plasma cell, and at breakneck speed the composition of the shell of the egg changes, closing the passage to the others. As it approaches the egg's genetic core, the chosen sperm loses its flagellum, which has now completed its mission. Attracted to one another by what could be described as infinite love, they merge. What makes them stay together is the vigorous movement of the remaining sperm, which continue to rotate the egg for several days. Before dying, they allow the fertilized egg to slide along the tube and find its way into the uterus. Thus, five hundred million beings collaborate so that one of them has the privilege of giving rise to the human being.

According to this interpretation, which uses only scientific facts and has merit for being more comforting than the currently accepted myth, one can say that in the sperm-egg relationship there is no rape or conquest but rather an incredible mutual relationship fueled by a tireless collaboration among the sperm and the female reproductive tract. One can even imagine another kind of orgasm produced at the moment when the egg opens and the sperm is absorbed: together, they create a new unit.

Whatever the circumstances of our arrival into the world, the modern origin myth (which is a product of science) serves to affirm the miraculous need for our existence. So, rather than devaluing ourselves and imagining humans as the product of blind chance, perhaps we should change our perceptions.

MASCULINE AND FEMININE

Two Acquired Identities?

The notion that our genealogy tree is made of masculine and feminine sides will determine how we see ourselves as sexual beings and, therefore, how we see the couple.

Two concepts essentially oppose one another. The first is a universal (or sacred) concept of the feminine and masculine in which one finds, for example, roots in religious archetypes and the divine couple. The second is a more restrictive cultural, social, and familial concept of the respective roles of man and woman, which varies according to family and culture.

The family always has a position—stated or implied—about the signs and manifestations of sexual identity. In other words, the concept of male and female in our genealogy tree begins with the concept of the sperm and the egg together with all the secretions and secondary sexual characters. In general, previous generations did not have access to contraception. In every genealogy tree the tension between such diverse elements as love, sexuality, the social organization of marriage, and the risks of pregnancy created a certain number of problems, even tragedies, whose consequences in particular we carry in our ideas of male and female.

Stigmatization of the Male

Frequently, sperm can be considered "dirty," absorbed in unhappiness, a curse. When women have more pregnancies than they can bear it is not uncommon for them to curse the male sperm. Similarly, if for example a grandmother dies in childbirth while delivering her first child, the tree can form a concept of sperm as assassin. Sperm is also the enemy of love, since unwanted or socially unacceptable pregnancies can actually cause disasters: shame, abortions that put the mother's life in danger, expulsion from the family, poverty, suicide to restore family honor, abandonment, and so on. For this reason, it is not uncommon for men in pain to live with a devalued conception of their genitals, like the feeling of having feces on their testicles or of rejecting their own sperm.

Example: A man, having fought testicular cancer, came to me for a consultation. Studying his genealogy tree, we find that his mother made a child (the consultant) behind his father's back in order to attach herself to this man. The man felt betrayed and imprisoned by the kidnapping of his sperm. But, faithful to the established social morality, he never left this woman, with whom he had one other child, a daughter. This man lived with the feeling that his testicles carried something susceptible to imprisonment. His son (our consultant) decided very early that he would not have children, and he asked at the age of thirty (the father's age when his son was conceived) for a vasectomy to prohibit any woman from imprisoning him like his mother imprisoned his father.

A woman who gets pregnant against her companion's will does not make the man a father, but rather deprives him of paternity. In the case of our consultant, the mother put off her son's demand for affection and nourished his fear of abandonment, which reinforced the anguish of imprisonment that the father had bequeathed him.

Conversely, use of sperm can also be a means of aggression. Group rapes are used during civil wars. For example, during the war in the former Yugoslavia the Serbian nationalist soldiers, driven by an ideology of ethnic cleansing, were ordered to rape the Bosnian Muslim women to thus purify their bellies. Ejaculation then becomes an affirmation of power, a revenge that is definitively exerted on women of a foreign tribe, but whose origin is actually a stubborn hatred of the mother.

Denigration of the Female

In this same tradition, many women live with a vague and negative conception of "what is in her belly." If you ask a woman in pain to concentrate on the feelings and images that arise from her genital tract, she frequently has a truncated vision at first, and the Consciousness of the totality of her organs—vulva and lips, clitoris, vagina, uterus, tubes and ovaries—is often fragmentary and imprecise. Many women feel that their sex is dirty, dark, vulnerable, full of knives, a coffin, brambles and thorns. Menstruation, which is a concrete manifestation of organic fertility in a woman's life, is painful, described as foul smelling, a source of embarrassment, shameful and disabling. The taboos and repugnancies associated with menstrual blood in many patriarchal cultures are evidently no stranger to these insults. The statistics concerning clandestine abortions in the twentieth century are not precise, but in France figures vary between 90,000 and 250,000 per year. Practical experience shows us that in our grandparents' generation these facts were totally absent in our genealogy trees. If we refer to family memory, there were no abortions. There may, however, be mention of an ancestor (a grandmother or great-grandmother) who died prematurely from "uterus cancer" or "stomach pains"—in other words, a botched abortion.

These secrets tied to reproduction weigh heavily on the transmission of the female and male in the genealogy tree. Yet when placed in the temporal perspective, sexual organs and sexual indifference confer on us the power to launch ourselves into eternity. When faced with an unplanned pregnancy the sperm-egg encounter can frustrate the man and woman, who may feel themselves deprived of their liberty, their personal destinies. If, contrarily, the pregnancy is wanted, the creative power of one or the other can be fulfilled. From the moment of insemination, the potential of the egg and sperm is fulfilled. One could even argue that the famous "penis envy" on which psychoanalysis is based is in reality the irresistible desire of the egg to host the sperm—unifying the breeding power of the masculine sperm and the feminine egg. As such, it can also be argued that man has an irresistible desire to unite with the power of gestation in the female organs.

All of this can result in very distorted concepts of both the feminine and masculine. The weight of social ideology is also very important. What are the traditional roles imparted on the girl and the boy, the woman and the man, in the culture and family from which we come? Finally, the manner in which the couples in the genealogy tree lived together and managed their inevitable tensions or conflicts also gives rise to our heritage.

These are the basic elements to consider when summarizing the notion of the two sexual polarities transmitted to us by the genealogy tree. Some questions may help clarify the acquired concepts:

- What are the social roles occupied by the men and women in our tree? Were the relationships with money, career, and housework equal?
- In what way was girls' education different from boys'?
- What are the supposed skills of each sex?
- For women, is their femininity defined only by childbearing and other "specifically feminine" criteria according to the culture in effect, like beauty, seduction, and sweetness, or by a universal criteria such as elegance, vivacity, and intelligence?
- For men, what are the signs of virility favored by the tree: physical strength, wealth, skill, Don Juanism, intellectual competence, or some other attributes?
- Is there someone in our genealogy tree who held animosity toward a particular gender throughout his or her life? Did the tree carry dictums to reduce what is feminine and/or masculine?
- What was the tree's reaction toward the passage into adolescence and the appearance of secondary sexual characteristics? What happened during a girl's first menstruation? Was it even noticed? Did parents condemn masturbation, or did they respect the adolescent's need for privacy?

The tendency of every novice reading the genealogy tree is to say "Yes, of course I see in my lineage things that I find aberrant or unacceptable today, but in those times and in that context they were normal. Everyone thought and acted like that." In reality conscious, free, generous beings, visionaries, have lived in every age, every era. It could be then more useful to ask oneself, "What prevented my ancestors from uniting with the pioneers instead of enclosing themselves in hardened practices and beliefs?"

Today's gender studies present extreme theories of masculine and feminine as purely political or social constructs. In feeding girls less protein and pushing them to take care of their appearance at the expense of other qualities, or in giving boys war toys or cars and telling them they have no right to cry, parents become accomplices in a social and political order that arbitrarily produces the "male gender" or the "female gender." An increased vigilance as to our own upbringing can be drawn from these ultra-critical theories: How did they make me a "boy" or a "girl"? In the formation of my own identity, what part did mimicry play in my search for acceptance? What aspects of myself have I neglected, or even rejected, in order to be accepted into the family, society, or culture? Conversely, current theory argues that this conformation of identity ("nice" and receptive for girls, "aggressive" and active for boys) is good and, in reality, prepares children for their social roles. But this directed upbringing forces individuals to adapt to a prearranged society and forces them, once again, to live their future in conversion and application of the past.

COMPLEMENTARITY AND CONFLICT

The complementarity of the female and male is affirmed in all the great religious myths, not only in terms of reproduction, but also leading to a combined action in the world. Conceiving a child is not the only way to bring Consciousness into existence—every couple wants to create shared Consciousness, to embody a project, a discourse, a body of work.

The Wedding at Cana from the Gospels is an excellent example of this. The Jesus and Mary couple is not a couple in the sexual or parental sense of the word. Nevertheless, it is Mary who in this circumstance became the engine: when the wine ran out she pushed Jesus to perform his first miracle, not as a mother but as a feminine energy complementing the active male. He had the ability to change water into wine. She had the intuition that the moment had arrived for him to manifest this capability. Jesus then replied, "Woman, my time has not yet come." He implicitly recognized the significance of the feminine and began to put her on equal footing. Mary insisted and managed to convince him, taking the position not only as mother, but also as wife. The miracle took place, and a new Consciousness appeared in the world.

Similarly, Scheherazade in *One Thousand and One Nights* delayed her execution by telling a story each night to the sultan who cut off the heads of women. She became his wife, and the feminine twin to this powerful man, by defeating his cruelty and hatred through art and the imagination. Once again, two complementary polarities meet not to produce a child but to engender Consciousness.

In the Tarot of Marseilles, in addition to the Emperor-Empress power couple and the Sun-Moon mythical couple, the Hierophant is preceded in numerical order and bordered by the High Priestess. The couple functioned inadequately in the Christianity of that time, and thus the Tarot essentially fills a gap in the Church: bringing the Holy Father his female counterpart, and recognizing the capacity of woman to take her place as a spiritual guide.

Eve led Adam and awakened his intelligence by making him eat the fruit from the tree of knowledge. Unlike medieval interpretations of the myth (where Eve becomes the source of the fundamental fault of all women, guilty as a result of original sin), we can say that she awakened Adam's intelligence. She plunged the human couple, the divine essence, into the reality of soul and reproduction and gave her companion the purpose of making a garden of planet Earth.

Finally, in the mythologies of religion's hall of fame (Indian or Greek, for example), the adventures of the divine couples are dramatized, in all their detail, showing the couples struggling with a daily life full of conflicts and reconciliations (Shiva making fun of Parvati because of the color of his skin, Zeus's infidelity to Hera)—the argument itself is an initiation.

The dream of a couple without conflicts reveals infant and adolescent levels of Consciousness. The child must imagine his all-powerful father and mother, unbreakable, securely fastened one to the other, as one entity devoted to the child's happiness and safety. It is the reason for which fairy tales end with a reassuring formula: "they lived happily ever after and had many children." But this version only relates to the infantile level of Consciousness. To the adolescent the dream becomes romantic with the discovery of first love, accompanied by the expectation of a passion that will last forever at the same level of intensity as the energy level of an adolescent in a growth spurt, in full hormonal buzz, free from all responsibility in the world. This vision of the couple is the formula used in romantic comedies of cinema from the West and from the Orient.

One can look at the couple in the light or through the shadows, but the adult attitude is that of accepting that there is always a moment in which conflict can also be fruitful.

This complementary union of dissimilar elements, whose collaboration produces a harmonious whole, is also found reflected in the age of Tao, where the yin and the yang interpenetrate endlessly.

In the genealogy tree the maternal lineage spreads out to our left, the paternal branch to our right. The left, side of the heart, is more receptive and in our predominantly right-handed humanity has the more maternal role of stabilization, while the right reveals itself to contain more of the paternal roles of dexterity and strength.

As we have already seen modern neurology teaches us that the right side of the brain, which governs the left side of the body, is also the seat of present awareness, of the language of images, and of music. Its cognition is that of union: we see ourselves united with everything, in states that return us to love, to ecstasy, to enlightenment. It allows us to experience totality, beauty, and perfection; it learns by the five senses and kinesthetics.* The right hemisphere of the brain does not differentiate between "me" and everything. Contrarily, the left hemisphere, which governs the right side of the body, lives in memories of the past and in plans for the future, learns and thinks in language, dominates linear and methodical thinking, and categorizes and organizes details; it is the site of intelligence that calculates and records.

---

*Kinesthetic intelligence includes a deep sense of the body and its movements, together with a feeling of balance.

The left hemisphere allows us to think in the capacity of *I* as a unique individual, separate from everything; it clearly makes the distinction between "me" and the rest of the world, and it establishes the differences.

In our civilization sensorial and kinesthetic learning experiences in the right brain are in the domain of the mother, first in utero and then at the moment of lactation. Initial aesthetic experimentation with individual values, learning, and methodical thought are in the father's domain of action in the world, assertiveness, acquisition of language, and mastery of reality. That is why we retain the traditional rules of orientation when representing the family tree, while accepting the fact that they are dependent on a common cultural past and not universal or eternal.

The corpus callosum, situated between the brain's two hemispheres, is the place where the hemispheres unite—like the two parts of the genealogy tree in the rectangular diagram studied in part 2—and is a central line leading to our own existence. This collaboration between the two brains, like the collaboration between the individual's two parents, is essential to the individual's living as a whole being. In the same way that the union between the left and right brain capabilities allows the human being to live a complete experience, the combined intake of the paternal and maternal world determines every child's mental balance.

Symbolically, the meeting between the left and right hands represents a complementary union: they are able to explore and caress each other, but they are also capable of working together in a common action, and in the case of attentive and evolved individuals, each one can attend to its own occupation without disturbing the other. It is an excellent metaphor for love and for relationships. When both hands unite, the person bringing them together feels immense pleasure. One can imagine that any couple represents the "left hand" and the "right hand" of universal Consciousness, and their encounter is a joy.

THE ENCOUNTER AND AFTERWARD . . .

Couples are rarely united like two hands. And it is rare for a couple to achieve the level of Consciousness of a sacred couple. Work on the couple in the genealogy tree consists of clarifying several key moments in the relationship: the circumstances of each encounter, the way in which each relationship was established, and the balance the relationship found to sustain it. We also work on conflicts and oppositions in order to understand if the couples in our tree were able to learn from their differences, or if they failed to deal with conflict.

The Grandparents:
The Origin of Our Concept of Love

Of the tree's seven relationships, generally that of our parents is best known to us. To better understand the relationships of our grandparents and great-grandparents, a little genealogical trick can help us: as a general rule, one chooses one's spouse according to a more or less conscious dynamic of **repetition**, **opposition**, and **compensation**, relative to the parental couple. For a man, this means the girlfriend's mother will be, to some extent, his own father's ideal woman, and his girlfriend's father will be, to some extent, his own mother's ideal man.

Thus, in our genealogy tree there is a potential union between the maternal grandmother and the paternal grandfather, and between the paternal great-grandfather and the maternal great-grandmother. This union can be deep or superficial, and can uncoil in any of the four centers.

Example: "My maternal grandmother never wanted to have kids. She wanted to travel, to read, to write, to discover the world—kind of a frustrated Alexandra David-Neel—yet she found herself the mother of a large family. My paternal grandfather never had a fatherly bone in his body, and he was very bothered by the incessant demands of his wife, who wanted to have many children. He dreamed of hiking the mountains and escaping into his reading." In the case of this consultant, we see symmetrical a link emerging between the maternal grand-father (a noted, honorable man, a good father and husband, who was very engaged in his family life, ambitious, and happy to be) and the paternal grandmother (a perfect hostess, exhausted by her husband's immaturity and infidelities, who dreamed of dinner parties and hav-ing a stable place in society).

But the complementarity can be more anecdotal: a maternal grand-father hairdresser and a very tidy paternal grandmother, or a pater-nal grandfather gourmet and a maternal grandmother graduate of Le Cordon Bleu. Once these complementarities between the grandparents are discovered, we can also trace the great-grandparents, who play the same game of union but about whom we usually know little; this can help humanize our picture of our great-grandparents, which is often fixed on some key detail.

Honeymoon and Conflict in the Relationship

We have already seen again and again that the genealogy tree's trap drives us to reproduce the suffering experienced during childhood gen-eration after generation, which can manifest in three different kinds of repetition:

- **Outright duplication.** A daughter marked by the absence of her father spends her life falling in love with absent men; the son of a cold and indifferent mother gets into relationships with women who are incapable of loving him . . .
- **Opposition.** The son of an invasive and enmeshing mother falls in love with elusive women who are not likely to invade his space; a girl inflicted by a strong Oedipal relationship with her brilliant, industrious blond-haired, blue-eyed father mar-ries the opposite of her father: an illiterate gardener of another ethnicity . . .
- **Compensation.** The daughter of a physically disabled father, with whom she could never have contact or share real life adventures,

marries a great athlete who became a physiotherapist; the son of a loving mother who was often absent because she worked outside the home marries a woman whose ambition is to become a house-wife and mother . . .

When others do not match the projections that inspire us, we pass them without notice. But if the pattern matches, we immediately feel attracted by a mysterious force. When we study a couple's genealogy trees, it is not uncommon to find striking similarities.

Example: She suffers from psoriasis; he has acne on his back. In her family, the maternal grandmother died of skin cancer; in his family, the maternal grandmother met an African at a school dance and, from this fleeting relationship, a mixed-race child was born (proof, in their family, of "sin"). The "mixed-race question" affects the man, himself born with white skin. He does not reveal the blemishes that bother him. His wife is ashamed of her psoriasis, like her grandmother was ashamed of her illness, cancer. The woman with psoriasis and the man with pimples on his back seek to resolve their childish neuroses in order to form a relationship where both traps fit perfectly together. In a lightning bolt, the problems of thirty ancestors unite.

During the process of nesting, at the moment of encounter the relationship often appears to be the miracle solution to all problems. This is the "honeymoon" phase, when one idealizes the other, and unconsciously makes the other a savior or soul mate. Biological processes, hormonal changes, and alterations in brain chemistry work to put the lovebirds in a state of maximum availability for one another. But once the psychophysical euphoria dissipates, the family tree does not hesitate to call them to order: if the couple reproduces the past without evolving their level of Consciousness, the relationship soon becomes the preferred breeding ground for unresolved conflicts and continuous challenges between the intellectual, emotional, sexual, and material egos. During courtship, everyone has agreed to play the role that the other needs in order to yield mutual desirability. But the moment arrives when the differences erupt. Incapable of withstanding, they clash. What happened? Each one wanted to find in the other their complement, a source of what they lacked.

Example: He has a kind of intellectual dexterity and a vigorous sexuality, but he is incapable of expressing his emotions and he does not know how to cope with daily life. She, on the other hand, can easily organize daily life and express her feelings. But she is blocked sexually and intellectually devalued. They complement one other by uniting their egos (intellectual and sexual for him, physical and emotional for her). But their complexes also collide: he feels inferior physically and emotionally, she sexually and intellectually. It is here that conflicts emerge, with each one bound to complete some part for the other while waiting for the other to complete another part. Thus, it is impossible to attain satisfaction; the relationship is caught in a trap similar to that of childhood's "a place for two," and the rivalry becomes as ferocious as it sometimes is among siblings.

Here, we distinguish between four main types of conflict, summarized briefly.

The Fight to Exist

The childish assumption could be summarized thus: "My parents did not pay enough attention to me so that I could form my own individuality. I do not truly know who I am or how I am. I feel empty. I don't know what the meaning of life is. I give myself to the other without even possessing myself, and I do not feel worthy nor do I value myself. My happiness is in your hands."

The person who gets into a relationship with this attitude is an ambulant trap, an empty adult who feeds the demands of the abandoned baby, waiting for his partner to say, "You exist!"

But an empty and devalued person will meet another in an emptiness/devaluation symmetry. If one is passive ("I leave it to you! You will be my Me!"), the other is active ("I accept that you come to fill my nonexistence since, for you, I am someone. I will become your guide and model.")

In the beginning, one adores the other and the other lets him. Gradually, the "weak" partner starts to manipulate the "strong" partner, until eventually leading him. One day, having gained the necessary confidence, he demolishes his idol's pedestal. The partner falls. Or else he eventually blames his partner for not giving him room to grow.

The War of the Sexes

This type of conflict is inherited from the social and cultural concepts we talked about earlier: everyone is dissatisfied with their sexual identity, and if at first each relies on the other to feel better, it does not take long for war to erupt.

As a general rule, a conscious man experiences the desire to express his feminine side and a conscious woman her masculine side. But it is necessary for the basis of sexual identity to be balanced.

For example, a devalued woman—her father did not accept her or she had a "manly" mother who was envious of male social prerogatives—simulates a femininity that she does not feel. At her opposite, a man, castrated by an almighty father or otherwise suffering from his father's physical or psychic absence and essentially raised by his mother or grandmother, simulates a virility he does not know. The moment arrives, the masks fall. She takes back the masculine role that she saw her mother take, and he, passive, childish, or depressed, sinks into a neurotically "feminine" attitude. It is possible that the conflict will affect their sex life (frigidity for her, impotence for him), and they may lose their desire, or continuously criticize one another. He might find that she drains his energy, and she may reproach him for his inability to perform. The relationship can become very violent if they lose respect for one another.

The Impossible Satisfaction

Both, at the moment of the encounter, confused enmeshment with love. We want to be only one. In reality, they projected onto one another a primitive dissatisfaction that could date from their early childhoods (they were not breastfed, or not enough; they were not fed; or they did not receive the attention they needed at a crucial moment).

So they are both hungry, and their hunger knows no satiety. By all appearances, they are adults. But in reality they are children who demand to be supported, materially and emotionally. They both want to make a relationship not with a man or a woman but with a father or a mother. Often, the frustrated baby takes on the features of an adult who sacrifices himself: "I do not need to suckle, and to prove it I will sacrifice myself for you and become your ideal father or mother. So that you will love me I will give you everything you ask for, provided that you do not grow up: I will protect you, but if you become independent, I will fall into a depression because I will have lost my job. I do not exist unless I take care of you."

Conflict can erupt when the one who holds the role of the child decides to take a turn as a father or mother. The dethroned partner weakens, gets sick, is the victim of a horrible accident or bankruptcy: as one grows, the other shrinks. Those who are in search of this quixotic satisfaction become a bottomless pit and their demands have no end. In constantly asking for more, one demonstrates an inability to be satisfied to the other. The other one suffers because he needs to be thanked as proof of love, but someone who makes constant demands and is unable to be satisfied is equally unable to appreciate anything.

The Struggle for Power

This relationship is based on the question, "Who dominates whom?" Both, in childhood, were not able to be themselves but were forced to satisfy the requirements of their dominating parents. They grew up with an immense desire to triumph over another. Sometimes sibling conflicts aggravated this competitive spirit. But if a partner gives in and "loses the game," the other will quickly lose all interest. A dominator/dominated dynamic can alternate in the same individual.

Occasionally, the one who abandons the struggle—who lets go and submits—is not fooled. "I know if I give in, like I eventually always gave in to my parents, you will abandon me. So, I am going to insist on contradicting you even if this should provoke a fit of rage. I will go as far as threatening to commit suicide so you do not restrict my movement. In spite of all your insults, I cannot separate myself from you. I am struggling in a cruel game to which I am chained."

The one who occupies the dominant position is justified by the belief that in a couple, one must dominate. "I assume the role. As a child, I always lowered my head and I was forced to abandon my most authentic impulses in order to satisfy the tastes of others. I do not want to go that way. I treat you as you treated me for fear that it is you who imposes your will on me."

One who continuously plays the dominated role will have the hope of being defeated one day, while one who plays the dominant role is plagued by unacknowledged insecurity. Due to the fear of separation, each one backs down and it is not uncommon to see the roles reverse.

This state of conflict and incompleteness is that of the majority of couples in the genealogy tree. We may believe that based on an instinctive need the simple family (mother-father-child) obeys the biblical advice, "That is why a man leaves his father and mother and is united to his wife, and they become one" (Genesis 2:24). However, that would mean the collapse of the two family trees. And so that is not how things happen: the man and the woman, affected by the family, carry it within. They are, for better or for worse, in happiness and sadness, heirs to entangled generations. They may come from loving and conscious clans, or from clans of interest, duty, or the reproduction of social and familial models, in which case they only live as their cultural being and are separated from the essential; union with another may then only be a failed attempt to escape the trap.

Conflicts should be considered **necessary obstacles** that couples encounter in order to grow up. Union with another is a privileged situation that offers an opportunity to deepen work on ourselves. Rather than asking to be recognized, desired, loved, and supported by another, we can—with hard, personal effort—decide to acknowledge ourselves. By becoming free from the judgments made against us by our trees and desiring ourselves, we can accept once and for all that our coming into this world is essential, regardless of what our parents think, and revere the energy that keeps us alive. To love ourself means acceptance without reservation, seeing in full awareness what part of our own being is fueling the conflict. And finally, by taking charge, we accept our responsibility and become aware that we must stop making someone else responsible for our happiness or sadness.

Conflict then becomes something that drives us to grow in Consciousness, through love for ourself and for another. Finally, it comes down to recognizing each other and forbidding all judgment, our own and those of others, appearing before the other in the total nakedness of an authentic self, and truly desiring that person. By recognizing in the romantic encounter the energy of life at work, and together giving birth to embodied Consciousness—whether in a child or in a body of work—truly loving one another is possible. By thanking each other for his or her existence, in completely accepting each other's strengths and weaknesses without ever entering into any calculating or emotional blackmail, the couple can emerge victorious from all conflicts, taking charge like healthy, independent, adult entities destined to go on to a new Consciousness.

These conflicts can become initiatory and lead the couple to collaborate:

- For each person, the struggle to exist becomes a peaceful Consciousness of his or her own existence and the path to fulfillment.
- The war of the sexes leads each person to accept his or her sexual identity, and to realize the androgynous core of his or her essential Being.
- Perpetual dissatisfaction leads to a happy acceptance of hunger and satiety, both physical and psychic; each one learns to give and to receive.

- Struggle for power leads to the ecstatic experience of letting go, and a resulting increase in power—that which is accomplished through me is the work of a superior will.

Clarifying the Dynamics of the Couples in My Tree

The language of the tree is made not only of repetitions, but also of mythical images and archetypes. As such, it is very useful to be able to account for as accurately as possible the circumstances of the encounters of the seven couples in the genealogy tree because they constitute a kind of origin myth of our existence. For each couple then we are going to ask:

- Under what circumstances did these two people meet?
- How old were they? What was their social background?
- What did they see in each other that would be the solution to their problems? What united them: interest, desire, love, or a common ideological problem? At what level of Consciousness? Were they united by the desire to kill their solitude, to reproduce, or for economic security, or by a great spiritual love?
- Was their union founded on a bolt-of-lightning attraction, feelings of love, a kind of familial or social contract, or an arrangement for lack of anything better?
- What work did they make together (Consciousness, a child, and/ or other work)?
- What happened to the couple after the birth of their first child? What became of their relationship after the birth? How did it change over time?
- Which of these couples from our tree have we known? What kind of testimony have these relationships been?

If the question here is of the progenitor couple (father and mother of the family), it is also necessary to be conscious of all following unions that took place that strengthen the family relationship, this includes secondary unions of stepfathers and stepmothers, but also the nonsexual, functional couples created between mother and daughter, mother and son, brother and sister, and all other possible combinations between two people of the same family living under one roof and sharing daily life.

- What have we heard about the couples we did not know (generally the great-grandparents)? What concepts of the relationship filter through these stories?
- Are there any exemplary couples? Any cursed couples?
- How has this legacy influenced our own vision of the couple?
- What rituals and habits, passed down from generation to generation, define the couple (one serves the other breakfast in bed; we must respect a father's silence while he eats; do not invade the kitchen, which is the mom's territory, and she is the head of the household)?

The couple begins the work of genealogical relationships. The human relationship is complex, but we can make a diagram to later clarify the relational chains that affect the tree's balance, a little like the chains of muscular tension that condition an individual's posture.

To do this, we suggest reducing the relationships to four fundamental dynamics symbolized like this:

- Union ●——●
- Conflict —→ ◄—
- Separation —┤ ├—
- Domination or protection ●——◖●

For each couple it is worth asking: What dominates in each center? For some couples, the tone is the same in almost all centers; for example, they may exhibit mental, emotional, and sexual separation but material union. It also happens that the four types of relationships are divided between the four centers. A couple can be very united on the intellectual front, but emotionally conflicted, and have a sexually separated point of view, while in their material life, only one partner earns all of the household's money and protects the other partner. So then we have the following diagram:

- I (intellect) ●——●
- E (emotions) →► ◄—
- S (sexuality) →| |—
- M (material life) ●——●

Exercise: The couples in my tree

Even if you are missing details, you can clarify the status of the couples in the tree, integrating the following elements for each into the diagram:

- The circumstances and the date of the encounter.
- The length of the relationship. If there was a separation, whose choice was it? In the case of death, who died when?
- A simplified diagram of their relationship in the four centers.

A couple's relationship can change dramatically over time. For each couple, we propose that you establish a portrait of the couple when their children were still totally dependent (up to age six to eight) and, if necessary, to correct this portrait according to the future of the couple. For example, for parents who separated when their kids were twelve years old, you must determine if the relationship was contentious or not when the kids were younger, and if the separation had actually taken place well before it was formalized.

The diagram is not easy to create. It represents an unvarnished vision of the couples in the tree. But it helps to identify which relationships are clearer for us and which relationships remain unclear. The well-known relationships are often official models (positive or negative) and the unclear relationships deeply influence the Unconscious.

An example is maternal grandparents who are "the gems" that give the tree its idealized model, the unsurpassed "perfect" couple, and yet their children grow up to become parents with a contentious relationship.

We must then ask about this tight-knit couple: In what center (intellectual, emotional, sexual, or material) was the union genuine? And in what center was the relationship more problematic? After this we must turn to the paternal grandparents to understand what the diagram of this relationship means to this work. Finally, if possible, revisit the history of the great-grandparents to better understand the grandparents' upbringing.

The alchemists' dream was to become a perfect couple—in other words, a harmonious alignment of intellect, heart, creative sexuality, and material life that allows union of one Consciousness with another.

In fact, no union of two can sustain itself on the lone project of "being a couple": they will both eventually end up devouring each other. A couple's goal is to stretch out into a common Consciousness, whether it is in raising a family (becoming parents with the joint mission of raising their children) or, if the couple cannot or will not procreate, by projecting themselves into a body of work or an artistic, economic, political, practical, or even spiritual project, with this work becoming the anchor for the family. Naturally, the couple can have neurotic behavior toward this collective project exactly like couples in the genealogy tree can have toward their children. Then we see the rise of competition, self-destruction, or the tendency to make the other responsible for one's own unreality.

The **alchemic couple** is a successful union of the four centers in service to the unborn Consciousness. We have seen, in general, that this union does not exist in the tree. Marked as we are by the repetition of models, we have limits that do not allow us to spontaneously imagine the ideal couple relationship.

Exercise: The alchemic couple

Write down on a plain sheet of paper, with a minimum of fifteen lines per center, how it would be between two partners in each of the following types of union:

- An ideal intellectual union (ideology, freedom of thought, curiosity, language, communication, mutual learning, intuition, a mental union beyond words)

- An ideal emotional union (marks of affection and proof of love, exclusive love or not, family relationships, friendships, loving and being loved, giving and receiving, compassion toward the world)
- An ideal sexual and creative union (a sexual contract between two people, freedom or creative exclusiveness, cooperation, creating together, a sense of beauty)
- An ideal material union (tastes and eating habits, sharing space, money management, body care, dependence and independence)

This project, which can take shape as a contract or by traditional wedding vows, must seem valid to any couple, including the couples in your genealogy tree. Without a doubt you will encounter difficulties when imagining a union in a particular center. In all likelihood, these difficulties will refer to what happened in your family: the standard that you cannot get over, or the traumatic.

For each person, the vision of the ideal couple will vary according to personality, needs, ideas, yearnings, and feelings. For example, some people need more exclusivity in one center than another: some couples function very well living in two separate homes; others with complete independence of political, religious, or philosophical opinions; some with tolerance of sexual infidelity. Still others have multiple love objects under one roof (biological, animal, community) and do not necessarily seek emotional exclusivity.

Essentially, for this exercise to be useful, ask yourself honestly what the circumstances are for a relationship to be lived in Consciousness, and at what point your individual concept differs from the genealogy tree's models.

The couples' failure in the genealogy tree marks us individually and also marks society as a whole. In many trees, the couple is synonymous with suffering, conflict, and separation, rather than fulfillment. From the moment in which we ourselves form a relationship with a partner we are attacked by these negative examples. Our entourage is no exception. The creation of a new relationship can more or less consciously wake up hostile reactions in the familial or friendly entourage. If our family histories have not known authentically happy and fulfilled couple relationships, it is difficult to imagine that anything beyond a childish and romantic concept is possible. Thus, if we aspire to create an adult and Conscious relationship, it is necessary to reasonably protect ourselves from external influences and "well-intentioned" opinions, and to get clarity on the influences running through us. This is why the preceding exercise includes a personal conception of the most actualized, perfect relationship: one in the four centers that would be suitable for us individually and for society as well.

People who have not experienced a fulfilling relationship (and this includes therapists) tend to doubt the couple to the point that they seek the relationship's destruction, motivated by jealousy or simply ignorance (that which I do not know cannot exist). Against this aggression, the couple must then build a system of psychic defense that is based on complicity and solidarity.

PART FIVE

To Be Born

When the Child Appears

NINE

Birth:
Toward Air and Light

By Alejandro Jodorowsky

The problems of previous generations affect the baby's gestation from the moment the sperm penetrates the egg. At this key moment not only is the mother's psyche present, but so is that of the father, grandparents, great-grandparents, and any social upheaval.

In my case, the most significant influence was perhaps the anti-Semitism of emperor Alexander III on Russia from 1881 to 1884, when he made the Jewish people scapegoats to appease the discontent of his subjects, accusing the Jews of slaughtering children to make bread for their black masses with their blood. A wave of pogroms broke out, during one of which my maternal grandmother, Jashe (a Sephardic brunette), was raped by a Cossack. Pregnant, she fled Russia and landed in Argentina, where she brought a daughter with marble skin and big blue eyes into the world: Sara, my mother, the child of an infamous rape. Jashe, in order to justify her daughter's abnormal beauty, invented a ballet dancer who gave up a promising artistic career to flee with her to South America and who died, unfortunately, while climbing on a barrel of alcohol in order to light a lamp: the lid gave way under his weight. Jashe married the brave man Moises, with whom she had two ugly daughters (brunettes) who despised my mother. They settled in Iquique, Chile, a port whose wealth was due to the precious potassium nitrate cargo. Moises and Jashe got rich in the gold trade. Once Sara became a woman, she made a love faux pas with a non-Jew (a duplication of contact between the Cossack phallus and the Jewish vagina). To avoid scandal, she married Jaime, a poor young man who—in exchange for the family's established trade—accepted her torn hymen (as Moises did with Jashe).

Regrettably, the day after the wedding night my father's mother Teresa entered into the nuptial chamber to examine the sheets. Upon not finding any trace of blood, she leaned out of the window to publicly insult Sara the whore. Jaime, to avoid public humiliation, threatened to declare that he had been duped. A new sum of money silenced him. Together, Sara and Jaime, bound by "what people might say," moved to Tocopilla, far from the gossip of the Jewish community. They lived in this strict town feeling oppressed, hating one another. My humiliated mother refused any attempts my father made to possess her. Each intercourse was turned into a rape. Jashe was raped. Sara was raped. Like my mother, a violent sperm and a victim egg created me.

The terror of male brutality is engraved in the cellular memory of my grandmother, my mother, and then me. Nevertheless, the feeling was theirs, not mine. I was born afraid of my father. Whenever he approached the cradle, I pushed out terrorizing howls. I never ceased fearing him. But I never stopped imitating him either. In my film *El Topo* I shot a scene in which my character, a brutal bandit, rapes a woman. Later, the bandit shaves his beard and his locks, breaks his revolver, and turns into a saint. Unconsciously, I wanted to prove to my mother that not all men were scoundrels, and so I gave myself the right to leave my childhood and become an adult.

A violent sperm and a victim egg cannot provide for the individual the same vital energy born of a generously opened egg and a sperm filled with love. Everything is written in the cells—suffering—as well as ecstasy. Throughout all of existence the repeating past and the creating future will fight, constantly reproducing the moment at which life nestled itself into the first cell.

Our work consists of becoming conscious, freeing ourselves from emotions, ideas, cravings, and feelings that do not pertain to us. "Family, I give you back your fears, anxieties, failures, violence, intolerance, and dissatisfaction, your mental blinders that prevented you from seeing the suffering, and your belief that happiness resides in this suffering."

The project of Consciousness—which is to create a perfect, harmonious being, destined to live a long life full of vital joyfulness—can be interrupted in countless ways during the development of the embryo.

Sara managed to convince herself that a legendary dancer had created her to overcome the anguish over being the daughter of a Cossack rapist. Pregnant with me, it wasn't me she awaited but rather her imaginary father: I was born with skin as white as milk, with an abundance of blond hair that she refused to cut until I was four years of age. One day my father, furious that I looked like a little girl because it reminded him of his younger homosexual brother, secretly brought me to the barber. When I returned home with my peeled skull, Sara screamed and locked herself in the kitchen to cry. Seeing that my hair grew back darker, she lost interest in me. She never hugged or kissed me again. When I was around eight, my mother cut her finger on a bread knife and told me, without giving it much thought, that on the fifth day of her pregnancy she bled a little. Neither she nor I realized (as I now know) that this small hemorrhage was the eviction of another egg: that of my twin brother. This should shine light on this story I loved so much as a child: the half chicken.

There once was a half chicken who had one wing, one leg, one eye, and half a tail. He had half a beak, half a body, and half a head. He retained nothing of what he ate so he was always hungry. His half--a-stomach let everything escape. He spread sadness everywhere he went. The half chicken devoured whole plantations of wheat, corn, and rice, as well as salad and vegetables, absolutely everything. Moreover, even if he swallowed a lake, a river, an ocean with all its fish, his thirst never was quenched. After having desperately traveled the whole world, he returned to his village, where he met another half chicken just as hungry and thirsty as he was. They instantly loved one another like brothers. Every day, satisfied, they shared a drop of water and a grain of rice.

I took pleasure in calling myself "half chicken." Reacting to this nickname, I felt incomplete and looked for a brother. My father's shop was next to a fire station. The humble security guard of the building had a son my age, Orlando, with whom I established a deep friendship that allowed me to feel whole for the first time in my life. Thanks to him, I explored the abandoned Cerro Don Pancho mine, I climbed up sixty-five feet where the fire hoses hung, I entered through a hole in the wall in the back of the cinema to watch horror films, and finally, I masturbated in a circle of boys whose idol was Orlando. This symbiosis lasted five years. At ten years of age, as my parents suddenly tore me away from Tocopilla to bring me to the capital, Santiago, I felt that which my generator egg had to have experienced in losing his twin—a wave of cold that seemed to freeze me to the marrow of my bones. I ceased feeling incomplete when I met Enrique Lihn when we were both ten years old. I recount my adventures with this friend, brilliant poet, and teacher in my book *La Danse de la Réalité*. For five years we were inseparable brothers, and then I felt mutilated again and cut my ties with Chile. Today I think what caused my departure, besides my need to explore the world, was Enrique's sharp drop into alcoholism because he, like so many drinkers, locked himself away on an emotional island with no bridge.

In Paris, I found my twin again: the Canadian sculptor Jean Benoît. An authentic surrealist, he presented to the whole world an homage to the Marquis de Sade. Under André Breton's horrified but fascinated gaze, he burned a big "SADE" into his chest with a hot iron. For five years, we enjoyed ourselves like brothers. We made liberating scandals at bourgeois parties (Benoît, to the guests' general indignation, went so far as to sodomize a roasted chicken). Suddenly, driven by an irrational urge, I went to Mexico, once again feeling that well-known coldness in my bones.

As if by miracle, in that great Mexican capital I found a true Zen master, Ejo Takata,* who was also my age. I never could project my father onto him (like all his other disciples did); he was once again the mysterious twin. With the help of this Japanese saint I learned to go beyond my mental limits and to make, as he said, "footsteps in the nothingness."

In my usual abruptness, I went to New York. It was only then, in studying cellular memory, that I encountered evidence that my mother had expelled my twin egg. It was this very painful absence that forced me to cut ties with my friends: it wasn't they who disappeared, but me, the perpetual immigrant. The fear of not being able to handle the loss or death of a friend pushed me to erase myself. My mother, who could not rid her mind of the Cossack rapist, imagined herself as having been inseminated by two men—the bandit and the sublime dancer—at the same time.

In general, little girls want to have a baby with their fathers. My mother had two fathers, so she became pregnant with twins. Her organism chose between the two options: she would give birth to either the reincarnation of the Cossack rapist or the mythical dancer. She chose the second, and eliminated the first. I grew up feeling incomplete, glorifying my artistic activities but suspicious of myself, and distrusting my obscure tendencies toward violence.

Before the birth of Adan, my fourth son, I was an egocentric artist and therefore a "psychological barbarian," and I had not really

---

*I relate my adventures with Ejo Takata in *Mu: Le maître et les magiciennes,* later published as *The Spiritual Journey of Alejandro Jodorowsky* (Rochester, Vt.: Inner Traditions. 2008).

been interested in the birth of his older brothers. The first was Brontis. At six in the morning I received a call from the clinic inform- ing me that Bernadette, his mother, was delivering. I went there by car as fast as I could. On my arrival, I was guided toward a window where a nurse, with a mask covering her mouth, lifted my son to the window to show him to me. That was all. The mother was asleep. When later I saw her, due to the anesthesia she had no memory of the experience.

What effect did this monstrosity have on Brontis and me? For forty years, I had to make an effort to reach true intimacy with my son. He built his character to lean toward emotional solitude. A genius actor, humble and pure, he accepts the roles offered to him like the monk of a powerful religion, never pretending to be the main actor.

I cannot speak about my second son Cristobal's birth because it was in Mexico while I was in Paris for a big Panic Movement per- formance. My inability to speak of my son's birth means I was an absent father, which represents a psychological catastrophe. He had to supplement this void by re-creating me in himself, at a distance, in a manner more sublime than what I am.

As for the birth of Teo, it was very different from that of Brontis. Having become a little bit more aware, I was asked to attend the event. At this time I had become a celebrated artist due to my con- troversial theater direction and the scandal that followed my first film, *Fando y Lis*. The obstetrician, who was by chance a fan of my work or who wished to do some publicity, consented to my being present on the condition that the clinic film the delivery for its archives. And so it was done this way. They made me wash with antiseptic soap; I donned a tunic, shoes, cap, and surgical mask. I was relegated to the corner so that my presence would not interfere with the doctor, the nurses, and the cameraman. I was unpleasantly impressed by the fact that Valerie's bountiful pubic hair had been shaved. The nurse, while encouraging Valerie to push, tried to stick a needle into a vein in Valerie's left hand. The vein in question was so tiny that the nervous nurse began to stick the hand painfully. I also saw, in one stroke of the lancet, the doctor slash from the bottom of the sex to the anus. This gesture suddenly transformed this sacred gift of bringing a child into the world into an act of defecation wherein my baby could be compared to excrement. The mother suffered more from this medical intervention than from the natural contractions. They treated her like she was gravely ill.

Naturally, Teo was born protesting. They drove a tube through his nose and into his mouth to absorb the amniotic fluid he had swallowed. The clinic reeked of disinfectant. The neon lights hurt his eyes. The obstetrician, taking him by the ankles and pushing his head down, dealt a few blows to Teo's bottom. The child began to cry in rage: a rage that lasted twenty-four years, until the accident (perhaps unconsciously caused) that forced him out of the life that made him so angry.

After Teo's birth, his mother and I swore that if ever again she were expecting a child, we would offer this child a conscious birth.

The years passed. I was fifty years old and Valerie was thirty-three. We lived in France and time wore down our relationship. To restore the emotional bonds, we decided to conceive another child. After a very painful examination, the gynecologist told Valerie that her fallopian tubes were blocked. We decided to trust the power of the Tarot of Marseille. On our bedroom walls, we posted thirty-five-inch by seventeen-inch reproductions of the Ace of Wands (an active, sexual symbol) and the Ace of Cups (a receptive, emotional symbol). We chose a precise date guided by the Aztec calendar. This date indicated to us in what position we should fulfill the sacred act of intercourse. We lit incense and three candles (black, white, and red, the three colors of alchemical work), and after we had caressed for an hour, we began the ritual. At midnight, concentrating body and soul into this act of love, we heard little sounds from the window overlooking the balcony. Quickly sneaking a look, we saw the silhouettes of Brontis, Cristobal, and Teo, who were spying on us. What to do? We said, "They see us. We are trying to fulfill a sacred and therefore beautiful act. There is nothing to be ashamed of and no reason to feel guilty. We do as if we had not noticed their presence. We continue." And at that moment, with our three children as witnesses (and one could say, miraculously), we begot Adan.

During the nine months of pregnancy I made sure to always be present, to talk to the fetus, to caress my wife's belly, and to share with her the experience of the process from the baby's point of view, allowing him to be the leader of his own birth. We read with great interest the following passage from the book *Birth without Violence* by Dr. Frederick Leboyer: "From the instant at which the sperm enters the egg, where mitosis occurs, everything is alive and moves and is transforming. Birth is a change. That is why we must stop looking at birth as a medical, biological, physiological problem. We must not look at it with eyes of a doctor, or even as a human being. It is of another language, another dimension; like death."

Leboyer, an obstetrician, was the first to investigate birth trauma and the insensitivity with which childbirth is practiced in hospitals around the world. At a clinic in Neuilly, we found Dr. Paul Bertrand, a fervent admirer and practitioner of Leboyer's theories. We adhered to the birthing conditions: delivery will not be forced (no preterm arrangements, no nurse will break the amniotic sac); the baby will decide the moment of arrival in the world; the room will be lit with soft, indirect lights; there will be no use of synthetic anesthesia; the baby will not be hit and made to cry but will be given a soft, loving massage; once out of the mother's body, the baby will be placed on the mother's chest and then in a tub with water at the baby's body temperature; finally, once the baby's heart rate is normal again, we will cut the umbilical cord.

Even though all of these propositions seemed just, I discussed them and others of his teacher's statements with Dr. Bertrand. At the time I thought all this was based not on scientific certainty, but rather on beliefs. In effect, Leboyer said, "Most of the anxiety experienced by the woman during pregnancy is that of the man, which the woman absorbs unconsciously. This anxiety is much greater in men because pregnancy for him is intolerable, inaccessible, and an absolute mystery. Then suddenly an intruder appears in the couple. He feels betrayed and abandoned. The man, because he doesn't have any other option, should be wise enough to let the woman go with this perfect, absolute lover in her womb. The man tries to relive what comes naturally for a woman. Men can only do this by returning to their own birth, as they are incapable of giving birth. All initiatory paths are a return to the womb to relive this state of total fusion."

I objected. "Leboyer does not value the father. He recognizes the quality of the inseminator only as a helpless and often jealous witness. In spite of his good intentions, just like all the other doctors, he usurps the father's position and assigns him a role comparable to the high priest. But no one can deny that the tree's power is in the seed. So why deny that the child is fully incarnate from the moment the sperm and the egg unite? Those who separate the soul from the body can argue that during his first weeks of life the fetus is only matter, and then the being descends from a spiritual dimension into this mass of quivering flesh. The sperm, exploding in the egg, does not disappear but gives birth to the male cells that unite with the female cells created by the egg. Fetal growth is the product of continuous intercourse between masculine and feminine cells."

Psychologically, the father is "pregnant" with the baby along with the mother. His spiritual food is as necessary as that provided by the mother. If the father is absent during the pregnancy, denying his wife or himself, the new Being will develop through anxiety. In that case, Dr. Leboyer was right to declare, "Birth is like crossing a storm. For the child, the fact of birth is insomuch intolerable that he refuses in every way to see the light. He refuses with his body, closing his eyes, clenching his fists. He is not there. Symbolically, he continues to be a fetus. How to overcome this fear of the world?"

This question finds its response as soon as we value the father's contribution during pregnancy. If the father participates with all of his soul during the nine months of pregnancy, and during the delivery, the child will not cross any storm during birth and will not feel any fear. If the child comes into the world in a state similar to orgasm, he will deeply wish to be born into a world that seems like Eden. Upon emerging from the vagina, the baby ceases to be a fetus and no longer wants to return to the womb, like a butterfly not wanting to remain in the chrysalis where it developed. However, if the father was absent during the pregnancy and the delivery, then the mother, accompanied by the doctor, becomes invasive and is made owner over the child. This baby will remain a child for all of his life and will indeed crave a return to his mother's womb, not because he considers it a place of happiness, but to find what he needs: the paternal contribution that will allow him to be more than a perpetual fetus.

My beliefs, although they were not supported by scientific study, had enough merit to persuade Dr. Bertrand to allow me to attend my wife's delivery in the company of my three sons. Brontis was fifteen, Cristobal was twelve, and Teo was eight.

No one made us dress us like surgeons; instead we dressed in everyday clothing. Instead of using antiseptics, we simply took showers. Then we were able to be near Valerie, the boys at her side and me facing her legs. Although the clinic imposed a metal table on Valerie, the doctor and midwife remained discreetly behind us, ready to intervene in case of complications.

Valerie, surrounded by her family, anxiety-free, experiencing a pain that mingled with sexual pleasure, pushed intensely four times. I saw my son's head appear, looking toward the earth. He began immediately to harmoniously turn around. He let his right arm out, then the left. Thus, arms outstretched, face turned upward, he seemed to be waiting for me to take him in my hands to finish pulling him out, and that's what I did.

We decided to accept the child that the universe gave us. So as to serve any child regardless of the sex, the clothes we had prepared were pale purple, not pink or sky blue. Seeing his testicles, which seemed enormous to all of us, I exclaimed, "Adan!" without having thought about it before. Later, I realized Adam (Adan in Spanish) was the first man to be born with such ease in Valerie's genealogy tree and in mine.

I put this smiling little Adan on his smiling mother's chest, with Brontis, Cristobal, Teo, and I each with the same smile. After having bathed him in the little tub of warm water, where he pretended to swim, it was time to cut the umbilical cord. I was handed a pair of scissors. I started to cut the tube, solidly. But I stopped myself, feeling it the mother's place, not mine, to complete this important act. In the animal kingdom, the females chew through the umbilical cord with their teeth. Adan's mother, assuming this cut, recognized that the child was no longer one of her organs or viscera but a complete individual who, thanks to her care, mine, and that of his brothers, would achieve independence and become an adult, responsible for his own destiny, not enclosed in a family's fate but opened to the world.

Today, Adan still remembers his birth with pleasant emotions. He tells me, "Birth is not the painful loss of an intrauterine paradise. It is the same pleasure a flower experiences upon opening."

TEN

From Birth to Nativity
Gestation, Delivery, Birth, Rebirth

From the beginning of pregnancy, life happens like an explosion of joy. If nothing objects to its development, the fertilized egg transforms into an embryo, then into a fetus that grows for nine months until the total joy of birth, cooperating completely with the mother. This is our ideal course of arrival into the world.

The essence of our organism is not the matter it is composed of or the energy it produces, it is that which we might call **the will of Consciousness**, which precedes both matter and energy and will exist before the gestation of the fetus. Without it, our birth would not be possible. If the father and mother have not reached a higher level of Consciousness, they procreate motivated by the instinct to propagate the species and by the unconscious desire to be imitated. In this case, before the flesh-and-bones child exists there is an imaginary child without a real individuality who is expected to meet the family's needs, not becoming his true self but completing his parents. But parents who have high levels of Consciousness will respect the individuality of this Being who has come into the world, and they will do so without hassling him with plans, projects, and a mapped-out destiny, complete with their projections and repetitions, in deeds and in words, at any cost.

In reality, gestation and birth are often affected by a series of more or less painful accidents and traumas whose consequences affect our future lives to varying degrees. One of the essential steps in understanding the genealogy tree consists of revising some of the circumstances of our own conception, pregnancy, and birth, then taking an interest in the way in which members of our genealogy tree were also conceived, expected, and born into the world.

The impact of prenatal trauma is the crux of the matter and endures in the lineage. As with the other themes addressed in this book, we first look to see how the weight of the past has distorted this process, then go on to repair our birth with this awareness and by the symbolic means of integrating information: the memory of traumatic birth might be completed by new elements that allow us to metaphorically "rebirth," free of these mortifying footprints.

FROM FERTILIZATION TO BIRTH

The Weight of the Lineage

In eight weeks the fertilized egg turns into an embryo and then into a fetus. During this short period the initial cell divides and multiplies eight hundred million times at a constant speed. Gradually it develops emotional and sensory receptors whereby the fetus interacts with the mother and the liquid environment. This stimuli will shape the nervous and endocrine systems: sensory and motor areas, the thalamus, the pituitary, and the still mysterious places nestling the Unconscious and Subconscious.

The energy that induces the growth of the nervous system during the first eight weeks of pregnancy is so powerful that if the momentum were to continue for the nine months of gestation, the brain would grow to the size of the planet Earth. It is the same force that gives birth to the suns, the galaxies, and the universe.

If the parents are prisoners of the past, of genealogy tree demands, or of a limited level of Consciousness, their physical and spiritual breaks will oppose this joyful vitality, a suffering the embryo absorbs in one way or another. These breaks can be very concrete in the form of beatings, assaults, toxic food, drugs, alcohol . . . one can suppose that the thoughts, feelings, and desires metabolized by the mother's body as muscle tremors and chemical information can very much influence the embryo's development.

Science tells us the mother's behavior has a decisive influence on the unborn child. Thirty years ago no one would have thought smoking during pregnancy was harmful to the unborn child, whereas today we know it can have a very negative impact on the developing baby. One day it may well be proved that thoughts, feelings, and cravings may also be part of the child's harmonious development, or otherwise obstruct it.

The life force of an unborn child is already that of a full-fledged human being. Just as the seed contains the power of the future plant in total perfection, the sperm and egg, similarly united, contain the person in absolute potential. The person begins to take shape together with its share of cosmic Consciousness. And the whole universe comes to life.

However, one pregnancy out of six (or out of four, according to some statistics) does not make it to term. Most miscarriages take place during the first eight weeks, and doctors agree that this is for the best because the Being who disappears was not sustainable—the carrier of a chromosome abnormality, for example. Nature, it seems, proceeds "by accidents." Should we then deduce that these fertilized eggs were not destined to live?

In all cases, we can postulate that the mother's belly and uterus, and the developing egg inside the mother, are not only private territories but also familial and social nests. The mother and the father's genealogy trees are present in the parents' DNA, and regardless of the mother and father's desire to conceive a child, a past conflict that prevents or deforms conception may exist in their cellular memory. In this case the struggle between the developing Consciousness of the two adults who want to become parents and the contradictory injunctions of the past (various conflicts related to the conception of a child can exist in the genealogy tree of both parents) can produce an accident at the precise moment of fertilization, which condemns the egg to being unsustainable in the long term. But no matter how painful a termination of a wanted pregnancy is, this little short life is also a potential source of Consciousness: the body of the mother re(learns) to create an implantation. On the spiritual level, the parents need to understand that the coming of a child is independent of their plans, their personal will, and that they are only the spokespersons through which Consciousness is embodied.

This letting go is essential for all pregnancies, viable or not—we do not create a child; we allow the child to create itself through us. Parents must accept this to become, in these circumstances, a channel of cosmic Consciousness while remaining, in large part, receptacles of the lineage's traditions and injunctions.

The dynamic between these two forces, past and future, is the work of the four centers. Physically, it can produce fetal deformities, miscarriages, and many interferences during pregnancy and birth: a hole in the neck, phlebitis, abnormal placental position, premature or late birth, or the umbilical cord wrapped around the baby's neck. In the other centers it can cause various types of internal conflicts or conflicts with the couple, whether emotional, ideological, or sexual. Most common is intense anxiety, to which most parents are subject.

In fact, when preparing to give birth to a child, one is dedicated to the human condition. Which is to say, the child is also gifted the fate of death or, if the human is separately mortal, the human species (which is a perennial). Anyone who thinks of herself as an individual will live in anxiety over her own death. But, inscribing herself to humanity, her own death becomes a joyous sacrifice granted to future humanity. This transpersonal position not only is the mind's view but is an essential conviction that once reached allows a person to consider her own demise with a lot more serenity.

Thus, to the parents who have not yet reached this transpersonal Consciousness, the arrival of a child is a powerful reminder of their own mortality. Birth closely mingles with death and awakens fears. Some fathers who have not had the spiritual preparation necessary to understand that life is united with death experience an incomprehensible guilt for having impregnated someone. They can express this anxiety, for example, by fearing that the birth will be fatal for mother and child. The father's anguish, and that of the mother, multiplies and divides.

The only way to avoid this anxiety is to understand that the unborn child resides within the power of life that exceeds the child's own generation and moves toward successive generations. In this sense, death is also a contribution. It allows the continuation of other lives. We accomplish this by developing a feeling of love for all of humanity, moving from the genealogy tree to the **genealogy forest**.

The whole pregnancy will be a battlefield (or, in the best cases, a playground) for the forces of the past, which want to make the child a continuation of his lineage, and the forces of the future, which call him toward self-actualization like a promised being.

As soon as conception occurs, the genealogy tree memory pushes the mother and father to project their expected hopes and fears onto the infant. They prefer a girl or a boy; she wants to give her jealous and suspicious husband a child who looks like him to convince him that he is the only one; he wants to see a little girl born with blue eyes like his own mother, who died when he was only a child; they dream of giving birth to beings who will have everything they never had, or kids who will become what they could never become. Parents, caught in the genealogy tree's trap, are lost in fantasies instead of offering the most free Being possible to the world. The more conscious the parents are, the more they will be able to help their child develop into his essential Being, accepting that he will become an adult, knowing that he belongs not to them but to the world. Very often, in spite of the parents' initial best intentions, the genealogy tree's trap wins, and the adults end up using the child like an instrument of compensation in their own unresolved problems.

When we refer to **the genealogy tree's trap** we are speaking of parents who, because they lack awareness, have fallen back into habit, mediocrity, defeatism, and suffering, instead of leading the project of Consciousness. If, at the time of their union, their vision of the future consists only of "making a family"—repeating a manner of living established by previous generations—the family in question will be distorted and fully characterized by the repetitions of the past well before the moment of insemination. If a child is conceived with the intention of continuing the lineage, saving the couple from separation, giving a woman who doesn't know what she wants to do with her life something to do, providing the family with an heir, continuing the family business, filling the emptiness made by the loss of another child, serving as the receptacle of the soul for a deceased ancestor, then that conception takes place in a pathological atmosphere, and from the moment of fertilization the new Being enters into the genealogy tree's trap. Many neuroses begin at the moment in which the egg is fertilized by the sperm.

If we look at our genealogy tree with lucidity, we can begin to imagine the atmosphere in which each member of the tree was generated, expected, and delivered.

Even if it is impossible to make a list of all the possible circumstances of the first two months of pregnancy that distort the momentum of life of the unborn child, we can enumerate some of them.

- Children of duty are not children of pleasure: a child begotten of a violent or tedious sexual act can be deprived of his natural joy of life; an unwanted child can spend his life feeling like an intruder in the world, looking for love without ever finding it or building relationships with those who do not want him.
- All attempts to eliminate the fetus remain etched in the cellular memory as a programming for death. How many adults who received the order to disappear from the womb now live an exquisite, successful life in all appearances, but also live with the nagging impression that they do not have the right to life?
- When the mother is a drug addict, a compulsive smoker, or an alcoholic, the embryo develops with the nourishment of toxic substances that will be absorbed as if they contain legitimate energy. This can cause the child to be born worried and anxious, eventually seeking relationships with self-destructive people.

- When parents do not grieve the death of a previous child or miscarriage, and they create a new child with the desire to replace the absent one, the child spends her life dragging around in the shadow of the other's ghost like a kind of living dead. The person in this situation often describes a kind of paralysis before certain things she wants to accomplish, a general malaise and confusion accompanied by the feeling of living a half life, or of being a vampire, driven by an unknown force.

- When the mother "forgets" she is pregnant for the first crucial weeks, either because someone in her entourage demands all of her attention (because of a serious accident or illness, for example) or because her work or actions in the world take all of her attention, the child risks being born feeling unloved and incapable of holding his parents' attention. The child may then develop chronic maladies like an eczema that is impossible to heal, or any other malady that requires that the mother fixate on him.

- Emotional conflicts also have an influence on the embryo. If the parents hate her, the child will be born incapable of loving, with immense difficulty staying in a long-term, intimate relationship, or even in the same job. If the mother is secretly in love with another man—the one who created the child—or if someone other than the official father created the child, the secret will affect her in various ways; for example, she may constantly use justification, or constantly feel unreasonable guilt or contempt.

But, we can also envision the ideal situation: that of two parents who are profoundly in love, free of the dictates of their genealogy tree, conscious of their future projects, and eager to give birth to a Being who can fully realize his potential. This child is created in the great, erotic pleasure of lovers who possess a high level of Consciousness. Knowing how to navigate the political, economic, and social difficulties of their time with ease, this child's parents can protect him. It must be admitted that these circumstances are not met in most genealogy trees.

In any case, the quality of the relationship must be taken into account, as well as the presiding intention at the time of the child's conception and the adults' living conditions during pregnancy and at the time of birth.

During the nine months of gestation, all of the psychic forces will continue to act on the fetus. In many cases the womb is not the mythical paradise sometimes described, but rather an aggressive prison where the child receives contradictory information. The amniotic fluid, the placenta, and the uterus transmit the state of the mother. If the mother considers, even unconsciously, that the fetus is not welcome, the body will respond as if it is a disease or an intruder and will attack it to try to eliminate it. Protected somewhat by the placenta, the fetus protests in its own way but remains misunderstood. It is also possible that this prenatal alliance with the placenta, which assumes the role of the fetus's true defender, can remain etched in the infant's psyche as a full-fledged relationship. The child will then experience an inexplicable feeling of having lost a twin or a double, and separation from the placenta, protector against the genealogy tree's aggression, will be experienced as a loss at birth.

While childbirth is difficult, it is common to use language that attributes responsibility for this event to the baby:

- You were too big. You took twenty-four hours of labor. Your mother suffered.
- You came out wrong. We had to have a cesarean.
- You had wrapped the umbilical cord three times around your neck.
- You were in a hurry to be born. You came at seven months.
- You didn't want to be born. The doctor had to pull you out with forceps.

All of these stories are false and blame the child unnecessarily, not to mention the injustice of ignoring the suffering she endured upon leaving the only world she had known—the womb—to enter a strange and unfamiliar place.

In reality, we should tell these stories of birth in the first-person plural to cover the parental couple and all of the genealogy tree's negative influences on the mother and the baby:

- We had to make you fat beyond reason. You had to have suffered a lot during that twenty-four-hour delivery when you were forced to be born.
- We had to turn you and impede you from being born the way you wanted.
- We had to wrap the cord around your neck. Forgive us for having strangled you.
- We had to oust you at seven months while you were still entitled to two more months to develop fully.
- We forced you out and we hurt your skull with these forceps.

For all of the distortions made during pregnancy and childbirth against the baby's impulse for life, the being only asks to be allowed to grow harmoniously and to be born into pure bliss.

Some analytical theories, and some common Buddhist theories, support this first tragedy—the suffering of birth. To the contrary, we believe this first tragedy, due to neurotic repetitions of the genealogy tree, should not have happened. We support **feeling the immense happiness of birth**.

All of these distorted births produce the additional anxiety of not knowing how to leave one world for another. The person born prematurely or late, by cesarean or with forceps, or strangled by the umbilical cord, will find key moments in his life that resemble his birth—and this "born-wrong anxiety" will prevent him from moving from one reality to the next without suffering. In order to avoid reproducing the circumstances of his birth, a person can organize his life so well as to never experience any mutation, therefore eliminating all risk of reliving the intolerable anxiety associated with his notion of birth. This fixation can localize into one or more of our centers: a person may never evolve emotionally and will remain in a persistent childhood; a person will irrationally freeze his ideas; a person will live out a sexuality that never develops into its adult form; a person will fossilize in the body and remain fixed, for example, on an eating behavior from which he cannot separate.

However, the genealogy tree is not the only potential influence on birth—society and culture can intervene in an extremely harmful way. A feeling of impotence and sometimes jealousy by men in the West, in respect to the essentially feminine process of pregnancy and childbirth, has produced an over-medicalization of birth. This has had a negative effect on the twentieth century, and still exists to this day despite valuable efforts toward developing self-awareness under way since the 1970s. How many women still complain of having undergone abnormal treatment like a cesarean, or induced labor, to accommodate the doctor's schedule?

All of the initial care given to infants (cutting the cord, bathing, feeding) are crucially important actions and are registered in cellular memory forever. Throughout the twentieth century the medical institution committed a series of extraordinary errors of which many people today bear traces: cords cut too soon, unnecessary suffering inflicted on newborns, and delusional ideologies related to breastfeeding—including disinfecting the breasts; forbidding breastfeeding in the first twenty-four hours and giving the newborn sugar water instead, and claiming that infant formula is better for the child than the mother's milk.

One might also mention the cultural aberrations that drive parents to, for example, kill or abandon female infants in countries where they are considered negligible. Even in the West, however, how many girls are born and in their first few minutes of life feel the disappointment of parents who wanted a boy? This disappointment is so tangible that it is still a clear and vivid memory for many adult females.

These pregnancy and childbirth traumas leave lifetime marks. Without pretending to provide an exhaustive picture, we can give some examples:

- **The threat to the fetus,** if the mother actively or unconsciously tries to terminate the pregnancy, engenders depression, worthlessness, and self-destructiveness.

- **Strangulation by the cord,** deemed in some cultures to produce artists, is also the vector of creative anxiety and a neurosis about failure or failing: at the moment of success, one is restrained by a link to the past (the symbolic cord), which produces a fear of imminent death. The person may live with a fear of reality, which is in fact fear of the mother. Suicide by hanging is also an echo of this initial constriction.
- **Every birth with respiratory distress produces immense anger.** An infant who choked on the amniotic fluid will experience it as a betrayal by the mother, who, involuntarily or not, did not collaborate actively enough in the birth. Scientific studies show that more than one hour of respiratory distress during birth produces an increased risk of suicide in adolescents.
- **Breech birth** sends the baby back to the past and records a fear of the future, or a sense of powerlessness in regard the future, in the child's memory. It can cause the child or the adult to stagnate thereafter. And again, scientific studies have proven breech birth to be directly related to learning delays and repetitions. As a rule, correlation exists between traumatic birth* and a number of diseases and/or criminal acts.
- **Premature birth** can cause existential weakness, the feeling of never being prepared, and the feeling of an ever-present risk of being ousted. Having arrived early, these people have great difficulty in completing their work. It can also lead to chronic dissatisfaction linked with overdependence: memory of when the baby, too weak to survive, had to receive intensive care, which was, however, inadequate to his or her essential needs.
- **A late delivery** where the baby is too big and the amniotic fluid disappears little by little so the baby is born dehydrated, or "burned," can produce persistent anger, inflicting upon the adult the tendency to always arrive late but also the phobia of confined places: the mother's uterus, in the end, became a

---

*See Janov, *Le corps se souvient.*

painful prison. This initial confinement can generate a fear of commitment and a series of physical ailments linked to a terror of the womb, including erectile dysfunction or problems ejaculating for men.

- **Birth by forceps**, where the doctor intervenes like a painful *deus ex machina,* can render adults incapable of "moving on to other things" without outside help, restricting them to unsatisfactory situations rather than risking a mutation that is, in their eyes, doomed to fail. These people may suffer a chronic lack of will. They constantly feel in conflict, or feel as if they are clashing with a more powerful obstacle and are therefore unable to help themselves.

- **Cesarean birth** is not a birth, it is an extraction: the baby is removed from the mother's belly like a tumor, which can subsequently produce intense self-deprecation. As a product of a cesarean, the adult will live with the feeling of having never been born, of not belonging to this world, of never having known the final caress of the maternal vagina, all of which fosters a deep dissatisfaction. Not having been able to experience this initial collaboration with the mother, the adult will have difficulties collaborating in future endeavors. We also know, according to Arthur Janov, that children and adults who experience a cesarean birth are inclined to respiratory trouble.

- **Trauma related to breastfeeding,** where it was interrupted or problematic, or where there was exclusive use of the bottle, can produce eating disorders, alcoholism, or drug addiction, symbolizing the search for withheld food or the nectar of a toxic substance. The trap of the genealogy tree can force the mother's body to produce acidic milk unfit for consumption, at which point the child suffers from diarrhea, regurgitation, and other symptoms. Infants who were badly breastfed can become chronically dissatisfied, unclear adults without obvious cause but with a deep reason: the loss of the first feed. There are also people who were not breastfed and, as adults, most often have problems with their teeth and gums.

Those who have suffered such difficulties, who were badly brought into the world by an unwelcoming team of soulless technicians, will feel a deficiency that will continue all their lives. The future will feel threatening because the birth stage increased their agony, and they place any hope of their own fulfillment in the hands of others, secretly trying to play the role of victim, feeling that things happen to them for reasons beyond their control. Having struggled to emerge from the womb, they unconsciously arrange their lives so that everything becomes a struggle, even inventing difficulties if necessary. Many of them cling to a small space, a few square feet, feeling protected from life's turmoil in a cramped room. Very little can satisfy these adults. They will feel ugly, frustrated, useless, incompetent, unloved; they believe themselves to be indifferent to the world and that no one cares if they are dead or alive. On impulse, or sometimes in desperate attempts—as before when trying to get out of the womb—they will sink into ceaseless activity, killing themselves with work without ever ridding themselves of the catastrophic loneliness. Unloved, they seek the help of others but require senseless rescuing, never thinking they might start by helping themselves. Both demanding and ungrateful, they lose the ability to trust others, and they don't believe in anything, especially not in themselves.

At the end of this chapter, we see that it is never too late to **heal our birth.** Understanding the events is the first step, but then we must stage a therapeutic act and psychoritual rebirth, a delivery that integrates the positive missing information into the body and into cellular memory.

Initially, it is helpful to gather as much information about our own birth as we can, and if possible, information on the births of other members of the tree. Information on traumatic births occurring in previous generations is quite valuable for this process.

BECOMING A FATHER
AND A MOTHER

We must pause for a moment to study the situation of a pregnant woman from the metagenealogical perspective. Pregnancy, particularly the first, is a tremendous physical, mental, emotional, and hormonal upheaval. Moreover, for the growing child the pregnant woman becomes the place of suffering, frustrations, beliefs, and wounds not only of her own genealogy tree but also of the father's.

We have seen that when the weight of the past is too strong, the baby's development will be affected. We must be particularly aware of blaming the mother and the mother alone: during pregnancy and birth she is at the junction of two lineages, and it is sometimes impossible for her to stem the neurotic wave engulfing her without some assistance. The role of a woman expecting a child, and that of her entourage, begins with the man who accompanies her. Ideally, he would do everything to help the child develop and be born without the genealogy trap interfering.

In energy medicine, as with homeopathy, practitioners note that during pregnancy the mother "integrates the father's energy information," at which point she becomes inhabited by the dominant energy of the baby's "generator" and can suddenly change behavior or character. Hormones are not the only culprit; the woman hosts the child's entire paternal genealogy tree for nine months, in her body and in her psyche.

Until the 1970s (and in many cases even today), Western genealogy trees were particularly susceptible to accidental and unwanted pregnancies. It is still very rare for the family history to openly mention these facts. One must learn to read the genealogy trees according to what is mostly left unsaid . . . that there were illegal abortions—often true butchery—many of which ended tragically.

As was already briefly mentioned, a woman who died as a result of an abortion is generally not designated as such. It is said that she died of exhaustion, cancer of the "uterus," a gastrointestinal disease, being kicked by a horse, hemorrhage or other "unexplained" bleeding, or any other accident involving the belly.

It is also sometimes found that a woman died six to eight months after childbirth. One might suspect then that the death is actually the tragic consequence of a spontaneous abortion due to getting pregnant again too quickly after the previous childbirth. The last living child can be permanently and unnecessarily blamed for the mother's death.

In the same vein, over several generations one can follow the effects of a death during childbirth of the grandmother or great-grandmother: descendants marry doctors, sterile men, or men who feel guilty about their sexuality (the husband's sperm symbolically killed the woman through the child).

Rather recently the secret has been uncovered that infanticide occurs with unimagined frequency. Just as it was once thought that children do not suffer (do not feel anything, do not have feelings), that is slowly losing popularity. Equally so, the idea that the full-fledged person already exists at the moment of conception, as a fetus, and as a newborn child, is a rather recent introduction into human Consciousness.

Our task will thus be to explore the emotional and physical suffering of women over several generations, as well as the gap between their individual experiences of motherhood and the cultural belief of women's alleged "natural and innate" motherly role and "instinct." Throughout the twentieth century, this ambivalence has been widely explored in the field of psychology.

The role of the idyllic Mother established by society and religion as the homemaker and nurturer who will always listen, tirelessly and courageously, with patience and endless kindness, elegant and dignified, is so similar among cultures that several dedicate a particular day to it—Mother's Day! Similarly, the agreed-upon role of the idyllic Father is one of a model and refuge, a valiant and sure guide, a financial provider and guarantor of security, infallible and generous, loyal and inflexible, full of compassion but a guardian of laws, severe but just.

In the shadow of these two archetypes, we would like to cite a long list of elements at work in maternity and paternity that can be identified as constructs of both past experiences (one is a parent like, against, or in spite of one's parents) and the arrival of one or more children. When studying the family tree of several siblings, one quickly notices how parents are not the same for each child. They develop and react just as their growing brood of children do. For each child the challenges of the parenthood they experienced are based on where the parents were in life, the evolution of the parents' levels of Consciousness, and each child's unique personality, which provokes changes in its own way.

There are different kinds of mothers and fathers and, moreover, **different levels of maternity and paternity**. Each is healthier and more informative if it leads to the next level. But many parents in the genealogy tree stop, or are blocked, somewhere on their paths as fathers or mothers. So they stay in a stagnant position (the first, second, third, or fourth level) and become toxic to their children.

First Level:
Progenitor Mother/Progenitor Father

Insemination is a tangible reality. The woman acknowledges she is pregnant and joyously accepts this change in her personal identity: now she carries within her a life that is not hers, which was created by her union with a man. She acknowledges that the sole purpose of her sexuality was not the momentary pleasure of orgasm, but to provide the sperm with the opportunity to meet the egg with whom it would make love and generate a living being. Things change for the man, too, but not in the body: he begins to imagine the future child, usually with a temptation to make a better picture of himself. If he becomes conscious, he accepts the difference, above everything, as a contribution and not as a shortage, and he has no intention of appropriating the future child.

*If the parents shrink before the changes brought about by the situation and stagnate at this level, the **assassin mother/vicious father** appear.* She has no desire to be a mother; she wants only to make sure she is a fertile woman. Maybe her genealogy tree has overly favored men, giving women a secondary role. Neglected by her father, she competed with her mother or with the men in her family and is plagued with a sense of impotence and sterility. Once reassured of her capacity to conceive a child, she could abort her heavy heart. This episode was necessary to prove that she could, that is to say, to reassure her of the vitality of her sexual-creative center. If she keeps the child, she risks becoming an assassin mother with no desire to be pregnant, to bring a child into the world, or to take care of a child.

Father assassins could also qualify as *futureless hedonists:* men who hate their mothers or women in general, who take refuge either in an immature escape or in sadistic claims. In the first case, frightened of the responsibility of establishing a family and having the impulse to flee, if he is forced to stay he will cover this unwanted woman and child with sarcasm and contempt, or he will refuse to communicate with them, enclosing himself in an aggressive silence. The second category covers unrepentant seducers, those with sadistic behavior, rapists, and all men who use their sperm like a weapon. For example, in the early 1950s, a Chilean sculptor of German heritage and fanatical Nazi ideas seduced young Jewish girls, got them pregnant, then presented them to their parents dressed in SS uniforms, proposing to marry these unfortunates or—for a substantial amount of money—to leave their lives forever.

Second Level:
The Incubator/The Provider

Pregnancy is seen as a happy time. The pregnant woman puts all of her energy into the incubation as the child gradually grows in the womb. She honors and protects this life that depends on her, taking particular care of her lifestyle and her eating habits, but also in her thoughts, feelings, and cravings. As such, she legitimately asks to be protected. The man builds the nest around her and provides for her needs. Perhaps for the first time in his life, he gives to this woman and child as he gives to himself. His generosity is a captivating part of the adventure he is taking part in. In providing for the physical and psychic needs of the pregnancy, he begins to start his family, even if it is not yet a tangible reality for him.

*If the parents shrink before the changes brought about by the situation and stagnate at this level, the **consuming mother/absent father** appear.* She loves her pregnant-woman belly, but not the baby inside of it. The baby is nothing but an object of power for her. Refusing to accept that a life independent of hers is developing in her womb, she lavishes care on herself and denies the individual existence of the baby, who is just a way for the woman to be the center of attention. If the expected child is a boy it is possible that he will represent the phallus that she never had, and that she finally carries in her body. She risks disavowing the child completely at birth or making it a tentacle, creating a symbiosis in which the child will be an extension of her own body, her own desires, and her own power. This kind of mother can come from a genealogy tree in which several generations of women sacrificed their lives to generate many children; some of these women may have died at childbirth. It is thus possible that she and her companion, driven by a complementary neurosis and believing that he is the carrier of killer sperm, face enormous anxiety during the pregnancy. These anxieties can obstruct progress, can produce premature opening of the womb, and may cause the mother to be bedridden or create immense difficulties during birth. The mother may also experience post-partum depression because the arrival of the child deprives her of the care that was given to her during pregnancy. In this category of mothers we also find some who are ashamed of their pregnancy and fear the child's birth, conceived of it as the product of sin or treason. This could be the case of many "child mothers" of the past, and also of women who carried mixed-race infants in a racist genealogy tree.

The man who stagnates at this level can be described as an absent inseminator. It is possible that as an infant he did not receive all the necessary care from his mother, that he will project himself onto the fetus of his pregnant wife, and once the baby is born, that he will be jealous of it like a little brother or sister. He attempts to steal the attention of the mother away from the child, but when disappointed in his desire to be adopted by his wife he becomes absent and invests his affection elsewhere. This is a man who accepts feeling needed but is unable to connect with his family: he continues to meet the needs of his wife and child without being really involved, depositing money into the account and reporting back will be the only kind of payment he will be capable of. Sometimes he succumbs to rage and risks taking revenge, becoming violent or otherwise completely absent. He may choose friends over family, or a mistress who will appear to be the true love of his life. This category includes men who marry in order to comply with their parents' and society's wishes—because they got a girl pregnant, or were forced to marry a woman of the same social class in the framework of an arranged marriage.

Third Level:
Biological Mother/Legal Father

The parents, like society, recognize those contained in the family register. The mother brings the child into the world, and ideally this birth is an enchanted collaboration between the child who wants to be born and the woman who wants to give birth. In the same way a chick emerges from an egg—pecking from the inside as the hen pecks from the outside—the setting of the child into the world is experienced as a wonderful realization, with the newborn perceived as the most beautiful being ever. For the father, this is the first concrete meeting with this other being who will carry his name; the child has entered into his lineage in a tangible way. It is the same with adoptions, where oftentimes the real or metaphoric trip that unites the parents with the adopted child is experienced symbolically as an initiatory proof of a happy ending comparable to childbirth. The moment of recognition between parent and child, which seals their belonging to one family, is often narrated with a lot of emotion: "From the moment I saw her, I knew it was her," "I got lost in this little boy's gaze and I knew I was his mother."

*If the parents shrink and stagnate in this level the **dry mother/castrating father** appear.* Once the child is born, the story is finished; the parents are by no means ready to go beyond the narcissistic satisfaction of "having made this." This little one who cries, screams, defecates, and wants to suckle is an extreme bother. They will once and for all have placed the child on the throne to sit still in their lives like an art object or a pet. The mother refuses to breastfeed or suffers from diseases that prevent this; she rushes back to work or suffers from an illness that prevents her from taking care of her child, so she entrusts him to a sitter or another member of the family. This does not prevent her from having conversations about it: "This child is what I do best in my life." In some cases she will say the delivery was "marvelously easy," using formulas like, "You came so easy," "You came through like a letter in the mail slot." Indeed, "it didn't take longer than going to the bathroom"—in a way comparing the child to a turd. The child is her sculpted, soon discarded "artwork." A woman who refuses to breastfeed might say, "Having a child hanging from me like that makes me feel like an animal," or she invokes the fear of damaging her breasts, her assets of seduction. The objective for this dry mother is to recover her individuality as quickly as possible, to the detriment of the child, who is thought of as a pain—she may even criticize the child for having deformed her body. All that remains for the child to be accepted is for him to become a resource, to be "wise" or "nice." Parents can go so far as to use the child as an audience, servant, or advisor, forcing him to live his childhood as a little adult as if to force him to pay for his care.

The father is an accomplice to this denial. One might think of him as a *proud anti-father,* authoritarian and strict, who sees only the continuation of his own name in the child. The situation is not that of a loving relationship, but of a hierarchical transmission where the child is the father's subordinate or, later, his employee or clone. He submits the child to being trained in order to mold the appropriate image, in contrast to the child's true identity, because he considers this heir to his name a mere extension of himself. In many dynasties, the children are responsible for their role as heirs and, at the same time, denied their own individuality. If the child does not meet the father's expectations, if he is "fundamentally bad" (like a daughter in a lineage of men, or a sensitive child in a willful and conquering lineage), he will find himself victimized, abused, locked up, humiliated, or treated like a criminal by a narcissistic father who himself has a deep thirst for attention.

Fourth Level: Mom/Dad

Once the child is born, the parents feed him, raise him, and busy themselves with helping him grow up. They understand and support him at each age throughout childhood, playing with him, offering him a stable, tender, reassuring, kind environment.

If the parents shrink and stagnate in this level the **possessive mother/ infantile father** *appear.* Stagnation at this level, when the parents seem to be perfect, includes not letting their child become an adult, whether after puberty when the offspring is to become financially independent, or when as an adult the descendant finds a partner and becomes a parent. The infantilizing parents cannot bear to lose their "little one," so they punish their offspring in various ways: with guilt, illness, seemingly inexplicable aggressive behavior, or even disinheritance. We can put a parent who suddenly dies at the time of the marriage of a son or daughter, or at the time of the birth of a new baby, in this category. It is also here where we find mothers who breastfeed their children until four or five years of age. In short, infantilizing parents refuse to see their children grow up, like the father who calls his nineteen-year-old child "my baby" and will tuck him into bed at night.

Occasionally one of the parents considers the child to be his or her exclusive personal property and undertakes to invade the child's psyche by presenting him- or herself as the omnipotent father or perfect mother or by exaggerating distress and requiring the child's commitment under all circumstances. These parents are truly leeches, incapable of letting go of the "treasure" they created, and they convey a terror or distrust of the outside world to their child, causing him to be antisocial, turning him into a misanthrope or a misfit. They refuse to see that they have not brought this child into existence for themselves, but for this child to become a full-fledged member of human society.

Fifth Level: Mother/Father

These loving and responsible adults traveled the entire parenthood track and integrated authentic issues related to becoming parents. They accepted themselves as the channel for a life not their own:

during pregnancy they wisely took care of the growing life; calmly and joyfully allowed the child a healthy birth; accompanied the child's growth with benevolent care, striving at every moment to help the child develop her truly unique qualities; and prepared her to fly with his own wings.

Once she is independent they continue to love their child selflessly and tenderly, without any requirements, and gradually establish an adult-to-adult relationship. They will be understanding, not overbearing grandparents who will know their roles and limits, and they will never allow anyone to criticize the manner in which their child raises her own children.

Pediatrician and psychologist Donald Winnicott alludes to "the good-enough mothers" or those who are "ordinary, normally devoted." Healthy in mind and body, and satisfied with their own sexuality, these women give birth and raise children with consistency and in full collaboration with the father. These parents do not seek to teach their children an obsolete model of the past, do not make themselves owners, and allow their children to form their own worldview. For them, to be parents means sowing the future of humanity.

When speaking of our genealogy trees' mothers and fathers, it helps to know what level of maternity and paternity these parents reached. It is rare, in our genealogy trees, for the parental couples to reach the fifth level that we have just described.

FROM BIRTH TO NATIVITY

Each of our birth experiences, suffered through or enjoyed, is closely linked to our parents' state of Consciousness, our genealogy trees, and the society into which we emerged. Our conception of all forms of birth depends upon our experience of coming into the world. That is to say, our concepts of all change, real or symbolic, of status, identity, place, situation, and even of the last change we know, death, will depend on our own personal experience of birth.

So work on our birth is a crucial element in our ability to evolve, since a big part of our resistance to becoming ourselves dwells in the trap of our birth as it is etched into us.

On the other hand, if Arthur Janov's work was fundamental to evidencing the influence of birth trauma on an adult's life, primal therapy and all forms of conventional therapy lean, more or less directly, toward operating from the presupposition inherited from psychoanalysis that by reliving trauma (in the reptilian brain) and releasing regressions (forgotten memories, endured suffering), the adult could free himself. But this proposition once again only takes into account the relationship with the past.

A large part of traditional psychology is based on the idea of birth as a disconnection, an injury, and a separation. But if one uses common sense, being born is a joy, a gift, and a privilege: from the time of birth one enters into the world of Consciousness, into a state of love and happiness. According to all Eastern philosophical traditions, represented in the Hindu pantheon by the divine Trimurti of Brahma, Vishnu, and Shiva, a threefold law to create, preserve, and destroy governs the universe. This Hindu triad of happiness teaches us that the moment of decline is not a drama of nature, because winter will give birth to spring, with plenty of new possibilities for life and creation.

The mistake made by psychoanalysis was in rearranging this trilogy, putting preservation first, and postulating human Unconsciousness as a place, where things must not change: let the child maintain his nostalgia about the original fusion, and let him believe being "born" is an awful thing, a separation, trouble. But if one replaces that with a transpersonal perspective, human life follows both a linear logic (I was born, I live, I will die) and a cyclical logic (my individual death allows the continuation of the species). While every individual perspective is tragic (because it returns us to the indifference of the universe by way of our demise), the transpersonal perspective says every birth is joy and every death is joy: an investment into Consciousness, a moment in the cycle.

That which has happened, what we were not given, is the way it is. It is useless to explore the past. The real reason to return to the necessarily imperfect maternal womb will be the irresistible desire to overcome the barriers imposed on us by gestation and a pathological birth, to heal our genealogy trees' neuroses, and to finally obtain the birth we deserve.

We see certain adults faithfully taking care of parents who abused them during childhood, persistently begging for the affection and attention they did not receive. These adults crave a return to the more or less welcoming belly to curl up within. This desire actually reveals a deeper need: **to be born into what one truly is**. Only identification and staging a future project can connect us with this so desired birth.

All of the "paradise in utero" theories* reveal a limited understanding of a fundamental necessity: the essential Being, nestled within each one of us, is eager to emerge into full light and full freedom and drives us to replay our birth, but with a higher Consciousness this time. Many so-called primitive cultures have established rituals evoking pregnancy and birth that are aimed at purifying members of the society, making them more human, stronger, and more capable.

The Christian rite of baptism was initially a ritual of rebirth, as evidenced in the conversation between Jesus and the Pharisee Nicodemus: "Jesus answered and said unto him, 'Verily, verily, I say unto thee, except a man be born again, he cannot see the kingdom of God.' Nicodemus saith unto him, 'How can a man be born when he is old? Can he enter the second time into his mother's womb, and be born?'" Jesus answered, 'Verily, verily, I say unto thee, except a man be born of water and of the Spirit, he cannot enter into the kingdom of God. That which is born of the flesh is flesh; and that which is born of the Spirit is spirit'" (John 3:3–6). This "birth of water and of the Spirit," which originally used full immersion, symbolizes a return to the motherly water with the blessing of a priest: symbol of the paternal Spirit par excellence, which is to say, divine Consciousness.

In the same sense, one might also see this connection in the Native

---

*See the "weaning complex" of Jacques Lacan: "Metaphysical mirage of universal harmony, mystical abyss of emotional fusion, social utopia of guardianship totalitarianism—all outputs of the obsession with a pre-birth loss of a paradise and an even more obscure dream of death."

American and Mesoamerican sweat lodge ceremonies, the *temazcal*. In a sacred place, a fire burns for several days in the middle of a circle of stones. Mineral, the most ancient element of embodied existence, absorbs the fire's energy, which brings the stones to life, united by the fire. They metaphorically become magma and can transmit their basic message of love. The burning rocks are then transferred to the interior of the circular hut, symbol of the matrix, where the whole community unites in a spiral movement. The intense heat gradually encourages participants to curl into a fetal position on the ground where the air stays fresh in order to breathe. Chairing the ceremony is a couple, medicine man and medicine woman, representing parents of an elevated Consciousness. They purify the air and register nonverbal olfactory information by burning sacred plants (especially sage), chanting and recounting initiatory stories both for the individual and for the cohesion of the social group. By sweating, participants free themselves of contaminated liquid representing amniotic fluid, which contains the whole tree's neuroses. Leaving the hut, participants ladle on blessed water to wash away past influences. This water flows untamed, never deviating from its natural flow to the ocean, toward wholeness.

Several "rounds" of sweating may follow to complete the purification, and to more deeply record positive information in the form of songs and stories. This ritual, experienced collectively, provides each adult with a healthy regeneration, but there is also a transpersonal dimension: the concern is not only for an imperfectly born baby, but is rather about the whole society, collectively, caring about birth.*

We have seen that as soon as the sperm enters the egg the future child begins to be modeled, mentally and physically, by the genealogy trap. Ritually replaying our birth consists of finding that which we truly were

---

*The ritual described here is a transcription of an annual practice led by Charlie "Red Hawk" Thom on Mount Shasta in northern California. This visionary and generous medicine man used to host people of all communities, Native American or not, in this ceremony. In addition to the elements described above, it is Red Hawk's intention to heal the wounds of the Native American genocide by uniting the colonized and the colonizers in the same act of rebirth.

in the maternal womb. This luminous information is registered within us in the same way that our distorted and inherited personality is. This search for the true Self, which goes beyond our physical form and our spiritual boundaries, is the visible or hidden motor of all the work, on all paths, in any quest. In extremely neurotic cases this quest can reach "delirium filiation" where a person believes he was brought forth by exceptional beings and expresses through this certainty a deep and contrasting desire to manifest the essential Being.

From the metagenealogical perspective, one could say that everyone is of divine nature, of "royal blood." One might recognize this in order to live as an agent of future humanity and no longer like a product forged into the image of known models. Once work is completed on the birth (that is to say, on the past), it is possible to be reborn in the future, to recognize oneself as an essential fragment of cosmic Consciousness, as a being involved with the divine. "Nativity" refers to the birth of a god; if one cannot change one's birth, one can invent one's nativity.

In order to accomplish this we must go back to the attributes that characterize the divine nativity: annunciation preceding conception, ecstatic or exceptional delivery, perfect body, and sacred name. As we have already mentioned, in the Tarot's arcana Judgment (XX) illustrates the birth perfectly—or rebirth, if one considers it to be like a painting of the Last Judgment.

Either a man or a woman, a being of undetermined sexuality, with light blue skin (like that of some Hindu deity), emerges: life from the irresistible appeal of an angel who represents cosmic will. This birth occurs under the influence of a spiritual entity between two parents presented in their purest authenticity (they are naked and on the same level) who are under the influence of a spiritual entity, and the child being born, before being male or female, is primarily a body that is the color of the clouds in the sky that surround the angel. The three human protagonists pray while the angel waves a flag with the cross on it: the symbol of the union between horizontal human reality and vertical spiritual reality.

Annunciation

An ideal birth requires an agreement with the will of universal Consciousness and the acceptance of those who welcome it on the earthly plane. That is why in religious traditions the mythical nativity of gods is often preceded by an annunciation where a heavenly being proposes and agrees to accept an earthly being. The best example in Western culture is the Annunciation to Mary. The angel Gabriel announces the birth of Jesus to Mary, who responds: "I am the servant of the Lord. Be it unto me according to thy word" (Luke 1:38). But we might as well mention the birth of Hatshepsut, queen of Egypt, whose birth is attributed to intercourse between the mother-goddess Mut and Amon, god of Thebes, who announced to the queen once the sexual act was completed that she was carrying his heiress in her womb. "She will exert this illustrious and benevolent royal function throughout the entire country; for she will be my value, my power, my strength (...) and I will ensure her magical protection every day."*

Every birth involves two facts: a revelation of universal Consciousness (annunciation) and the consent of human will (reception). If Mary had responded to the angel, "I want to be free, I refuse to accept your proposal," the Savior could not have been born. But when

---

*Taken from Lalouette, "La naissance divine de Hatchepsout" (The miraculous birth of Queen Hatshepsut).

Mary pronounced him "Magnificent," she embodied a universal truth: **it is not the mother who makes the infant—it is the infant who is made in the mother's body.** The child does not come into the world but is already the product of the universe, in the same way fruit does not come from the tree but is produced by it.

When Mary accepts the annunciation, when the molds of past and future designs are complete, she shows herself willing to produce a unique and changing being—she makes herself available so that this incarnation takes place.

Every newborn has the mission of changing the world, beginning with the mother. The emerging body, impregnated with spirit, frees itself from the orders of the past. After a happy and generous life, this being will give back to the universe all of its borrowed energies; the impersonal essence will survive the individual death.

We will see when we discuss the healing of the genealogy tree that it can be lifesaving to replay the scenario of one's own birth, to somehow perform an autonomous and nonreligious adult birth into Consciousness. This psychoritual (which we describe in detail in part 9) is supposed to re-create an annunciation by choosing surrogate parents who agree to symbolically put their lives into the service of this nativity.

Orgasmic Childbirth and Ecstatic Birth

We have seen centuries of masculinist ideologies result in the turning of women's uteruses into passive, inert (in the best case), often suffering, and even toxic nests. Most women from patriarchal cultures, even today, do not know anything about their uterus except for pain during menstruation, a direct consequence of the societal devaluation of the female. In 1982 the psychologist Françoise Dolto made a stir by describing the function of uterine contractions in a complete orgasm (which she refers to as little pleasurable "utero-adnexal orgasms"). Every woman who has regained the integrity of her body has experienced, sometimes in the greatest secrecy, this voluptuous dimension of the uterine contraction. And more recently, in the case of orgasmic births, they have begun to be described and studied in broad daylight and have thus collided with skepticism and sometimes outrage: the unthinkable mother's orgasm caused by the birth of the child touches the core of the incest taboo.

Common sense tells us that since these harmonious uterine contractions indicate the female reproductive tract's good health, the height of health then is childbirth in ecstatic pleasure. Let's imagine for a moment what this experience could mean for the unborn child. The contractions begin at the back of the uterus and move to the front, like the waves of muscle movement steeped in happiness. The child sinks his feet and pelvis into this magnetic current and, without resistance, lets it carry him. Little by little the contractions increase and the child is integrated as part of one effort and is propelled forward, prompting the orientation of the skull toward the widest part of the maternal pelvis, to gradually slip into the birth canal. In total darkness and bathed in ecstatic effort, the cellular memory reminds the child of the existence of light. And by gyrating and undulating his whole body, assisted by the maternal contractions, he pushes his head toward the light awaiting him. A flood of oxytocin (the mammalian neurohypophysial hormone also known as "maternal love") causes a relaxation of the ligaments between the two halves of the pubic arc and facilitates the descent. The baby's mouth touches, like in a kiss, the walls through which it spirals and the baby leaves behind the amniotic fluid: what was nourishment becomes the lubricant to help him slide out more easily. The baby can then turn his head to avoid bumping into the sacrum. This last turn allows him to rub against the walls of the vagina, stimulating friction in the urinary, gastrointestinal, and respiratory systems, among others. The last and strongest contractions (around his chest) help the baby to empty his stomach of liquid and help him to breathe. With all of the joy of a job well done, the baby enters the world. The first contact with oxygen is neither painful nor forced but is made gradually through the still-beating umbilical cord that no doctor or nurse cuts before the time has come.

If the motherly waters and the darkness of pregnancy bind us to the mother, the light that the child discovers and the first breaths of air taken upon leaving the mother's body represent a bond to the father: wind and sun. "And the Lord God formed man of the dust of the ground, and breathed into his nostrils the breath of life; and man became a living being" (Genesis 2:7). This first contact with air, where one ideally learns to breathe deeply and freely, will later determine one's sense of freedom—freedom to breathe, to come and go, to be. It is the assertion of individuality, the exchange between air common to all and to the unique organism. In Greek myths, even if painful wanderings often precede childbirth, the god or the hero just out of the maternal womb sprang toward the light in an explosion of joy. Here, birth is synonymous with freedom and perfection, such as when Athena sprang from Zeus's skull, fully armed and screaming a victorious war cry. No one meddled in this: no one hit her or stopped her from breathing.

Then comes the moment of breastfeeding, corresponding to another basic need: eating. Ideally, milk flows from the maternal breasts in explosions of joy, as it does in one of the versions of the birth of Ganesh, whose mother Parvati (wife of the god Shiva) gave birth to (or, in some versions, recognized) their first child Karttikeya, an event that provoked such excitement that sacred milk began to flow from her breasts, and mixing it with sandalwood paste, she sculpted Ganesh. This sacred milk, a verifiable elixir of life, can give balance to a woman, releasing her from the traps of the genealogy tree. Her nipple adapts perfectly to the child's mouth. The suction creates voluptuous sensations that, directly aligned with uterine movements, allows the womb to recover its place and original size. The mother spontaneously knows how to hold the child in her arms, and the child receives exactly what the child's taste buds and body depend on.

The Perfect Body

All myths give us deities with perfect bodies: Jesus's perfect body is the vessel of his perfect soul. The Buddhist sculptures assigned thirty-two body marks that reveal physical perfection. Hindu deities have super-natural attributes that correspond to miraculous abilities (multiple arms, bluish color, a third eye, a place in the body to which a second-ary divinity can be created). In Judeo-Christian monotheism Adam and Eve, made in the image of God, represent the original perfection of all human bodies.

Our previous hypothesis states that, at the moment of our concep-tion, a diagram of the human being with a perfect mind and body is immediately formed. However, the memories of the genealogy tree, through the mother's psyche and body, appear to deform this original diagram in a subtle and organic way by marking it with traces of the repetitions, orders, prohibitions, punishments, sufferings, neuroses, traumas, and so on. We can thus accept as the basis of the work the belief that, in each and every one of us, this embryo that we were was diverted at some point from its original perfection. Most people feel spiritually limited and physically imperfect. It is easy to imagine that said feeling is the basis of an intuition, of a kind of body-mind original lodged in the Superconscious, of that which we should have become and that in which the ideal trace remains.

The genealogy tree largely shapes our artificial personality, which conforms to what society, culture, and the family want from us. But we also live in an inherited subjective body, which is moreover our concrete objective body (deformed or not), **our self-image**—that is to say, the way in which the spirit feels the body in accordance with the limited Consciousness. The five senses suffer familial and social injunctions on their fundamental acts of seeing, hearing, smelling, tasting, and touch. Our posture, our movements, our muscular orga-nization conform to what the genealogy tree wants us to become. For example, a woman from a society dominated by a centuries-old patriarchal ideology cannot live in her real body without cleaning away these impositions. This work applies of course to her genitals (including the perceptions of uterine contractions already discussed) but also to her whole posture, to her sense of self in daily life. One can use a number of postural techniques and internal or external martial arts to render the human body "independent of heritage,"* as Moshé Feldenkrais very rightly said about judo.†

The body is connected to both our artificial personality (our self-image, our imaginary body that most people live in every day) and our essential Being (the sublime body, the fully human body just as it is, which nobody can feel or live in in its entirety). We can get close to the essential Being (see the exercise at the end of the chapter), but to purely embody it, we must eliminate all familial and social prejudices. Certain spiritual practices, like tantra, offer meditative postures and exercises to help understand this body as a "unified space" that resonates with the universe.

The essential body cannot be modified. We live in the notions we have about our bodies, which depend in turn on our level of Consciousness. As the level of Consciousness rises, we perceive the perfect body more and more, which is an inner feeling that superimposes on our concrete, deformed body. This feeling of the perfect body can even be experienced in a mutilated, amputated, aging, or ill body because in the sense of self one is neither ugly nor beautiful.

The aesthetic judgment of the body depends upon the social context in which it is seen. Western culture today is based on the cult of appearance and thrives disproportionally on cosmetic surgery: a sign of our dependence on the gaze of others, of society's gaze. If society looks at our bodies as defective, we are forced to adapt to this limited view. Thus, certain eras produce waves of body modifications such as the current fashion of breast implants and rhinoplasty, which is nothing more than an example of a total transformation. Body transformations (from the necklaces of Thailand's "giraffe-women" to the common "touch-ups" in today's cosmetic surgery, from Western culture's corsets to the bound feet of women in earlier Chinese culture) present perhaps nothing more than social and normative traces often

---

*Feldenkrais, *Higher Judo.*

†Western culture, imposing the chair as a place of preferred seating, has, for example, massively uprooted its members' real center of gravity (the hara) by depriving them of mobility in their hip joints.

perpetrated against women whose autonomy poses a real or imagined threat. Within this nostalgia for the perfect body we seek to find reality by gaining or losing weight, dying hair or skin, removing hair, and enlarging or grinding this or that, depending on the fashion of the time.

The perfect body is potentially capable of actions unthinkable by people today, yet humanity collectively dreams of flying or levitating, phenomena sometimes attributed to saints or magicians. Recent scientific discoveries confirm that the human brain, when it calculates a movement to make, never takes weight or gravity into account. Neurophysiology and action potential currently confirm that the human brain is organized so that we may live outside of this heaviness, that we are virtually independent of gravity. Cosmonauts, after spending several weightless weeks in outer space, undertake muscle rehabilitation upon their return to Earth but do not suffer any brain damage or disorientation. This example illustrates the fact that the perfect body is also potentially a total human body, and it is advisable that we get as close to it as possible!

The First Name

In all cultures, the first thing the family does when a child is born is give it one or more first names. In some cultures, the birth name can grow as the person grows. But in our so-called advanced societies, we generally have a name to reference for life that we repeat and hear repeated for a long time, from our first to our last breaths. To a certain extent this name acts like a mantra of Eastern traditions, a repetitive sound that can be beneficial if it is a call to the forces of life and of Consciousness. However, the opposite is also true, and it can be terribly toxic in its hypnotic power.

In most cases, the first name consolidates a limited identity. Gods themselves have several names. Jesus Christ represents both the incarnation (Jesus) and the divine nature (Christ). Indian gods can have thousands of names, or sometimes precisely one hundred and eight, to designate various aspects and strengths of their various qualities.

A number of gods are also represented by a periphrasis, which refers to their magnificence and the extraordinarily sacred character of their name. Ra, the Egyptian god of the sun, is He-who-is-in-his-disk; to avoid pronouncing the sacred tetragrammaton, Yod-Hey-Vav-Hey, Jewish people use Adonai (eternal), Elohim (the powerful), and so forth for God. Conversely, an object has only one name to describe its usefulness. If a "scarf" turns into a "turban," its essence changes because its function changes. But for humans, any changes or additions made to a name moves closer to the person's essence. It is in this spirit that in some Native American tribes a member receives a new name at each milestone in life: He-who-is-born-with-the-rain as an adult becomes He-who-climbed-the-high-mountain, named for his actions and skills, not according to the clan's all-or-nothing gaze held on him.

We should therefore consider whether the name we received does justice to who we truly are. In chapter 12 we will develop the mechanism by which the genealogy tree models the child's identity by assigning it one name or the other.

In order to undertake this work on birth we must determine to what extent we can completely identify, as a fulfilled and autonomous being, with the first name we received. For anyone who feels the need to do work on the first name, there are three possibilities:

- **Purify and exalt the first name.** For example, a first name making reference to a dominant religion (Marie or Joseph in Christian culture) may well be a limiting and frustrating factor if the genealogy tree has absorbed a narrow and mutilated understanding of these archetypes: Mary as a frustrated and suffering virgin, Joseph as an old, ineffective, castrated man. A sense of well-being can be achieved by deeply reworking one's own in-depth understanding of the archetypes whose name one carries. Mary then becomes the divine Mother in all aspects, and Joseph, the incarnation of faith par excellence, becomes guide and protector, the symbol of stability and construction as expressed through his profession as carpenter.

- **Once the first name is exalted add another name**, public or secret, to complete it. Western disciples of Indian gurus often carry a Sanskrit or other Indian-language name opposite their original birth name. But one must ask, is being newly baptized by a spiritual master truly freeing? Would it not be better to find by and for oneself a sacred name, rather than to accept a newly assigned name? In naming a disciple, the guru risks infantilizing the disciple, once and for all taking the parental figure's place.

- **Change the first name**, whether by adopting it informally or by following legal procedures to enforce it. Later we will see with psychomagic healing of the genealogy tree what symbolic procedure a person can undertake for a name change. Thorough work on the first name is required, and should proceed without hastiness. Nothing is worse than falling between two names, recognizing one's self in neither the old nor the new. The first name is the preeminent mark of the individual's membership in the clan. It is even sometimes necessary to mourn the death of our birth name when it is so toxic and deadly that it prevents us from living fully. This work is action that requires courage and determination.

THE BODY'S MEMORY
AT THE SERVICE OF HEALING

To heal the birth we must be truly aware that work on the self consists not only of identifying and reliving past traumas, but also of letting the immense pleasure of living emerge, which is nestled in our bone marrow. Just as a plant pushes its roots down into the soil and its foliage rises toward the sun in order to grow, **work on the self is like diving into the depths and, at the same time, elevating.**

With respect to birth, negative information that we have registered goes far beyond the rational: there are cellular memories engraved in the body and mind. We must also begin by communicating as much as possible with our perfect bodies, registering new psychic and physical information into our experience using verbal and nonverbal means to add the memory of a well-lived birth to the whole of the individual.

This staging of the ideal birth that we call **psychoritual** is a therapeutic, theatrical, and religious act, which in the etymological sense of the term allows us to connect to a higher dimension. It also provides for the anchoring of a new reality in the life of an adult by providing missing information about the moment of one's birth in a tactile, experiential, and verbal way.

The exercises of the recovery of the perfect body and of the psychoritual birth (detailed below) are intended to allow everyone to metaphorically recover information damaged during pregnancy and birth. This work might at first seem superficial or fictitious, but in reality, the Unconscious accepts the metaphor and feeds on it. By performing these two acts of voluntary healing we regain a part of our potential and our integrity, which helps to free us a bit more from the genealogy tree's trap and, in gaining distance from the clan, to observe it from a relatively independent position. This position is indispensable for continuing the study of the family dynamics, and for facing the emotional issues that developed over four generations.

Exercise: Feel your perfect body

You can record the instructions for this exercise (which is akin to a visualization), then listen to them played aloud with your eyes closed to carry out this exercise with all the resources of your active imagination.

Sit or lie down in a balanced and comfortable position, preferably with your eyes closed and the soles of your feet planted firmly on the ground. Take three deep breaths: the first to calm the intellect, the second to calm the emotional center, the third to calm the sexual-creative center. Next, immerse yourself in the feeling of your body with the intention of allowing yourself to express in the four centers the memory of the perfect body: the original form, destined to be yours, which is always there, powerful, unchanged, available.

Let yourself feel, visualize, imagine. What is your size? Your shape? How do your legs feel? Your feet? Your toenails? Do you have two arms? Two hands? What size? Color? Shape? What is the texture of your hair? What color is your hair? Your eyes? What are your ears like? Can you feel your organs? The beating of your heart? The tireless work of your lungs—inhaling, exhaling? What is your gender? Your sexual power? Are you man? Woman? Both? Can you change your gender voluntarily? Do you have superhuman qualities? How is your life energy? What can you do? What do you wish to eat?

Now that you are firmly installed in your perfect body, let the character come to you who corresponds to your perfect intellect. What is the character's age? What does the character look like? How does the character move? Let this character melt into your interior from the head. Knowing that this character is at your service, what intellectual energy emanates from you now? Visualize its speed, color, shape; in which direction does it unfold?

Now, let the character come who represents your perfect emotional energy. Welcome and observe it: what is the age, appearance, dynamic?

Let this character melt into your interior at the heart level. Knowing it is at your service, what emotional energy emanates from you now? Visualize its speed, color, shape; in which direction does it unfold?

Finally, let the character come who represents your perfect sexual energy. Age? Appearance? Movement? Let the character melt into your interior at the level of the pubis. Knowing this is at your service, what sexual energy emanates from you now? Visualize its speed, color, shape; in which direction does it unfold?

Slowly, with your eyes still closed, begin to move your arms: How does the perfect body move? Little by little, stand up and feel how your perfect body unfolds. What is its weight? How does it stand?

Then, let the life partner who suits you come freely, for the body lives not alone. Imagine, visualize, feel the perfect body that can make a couple with you and accompany you.

Similarly, the body does not live in nothingness, so let an animal come to accompany you. Then let a vegetable that suits you grow near you. Finally, let a mineral element rise from the earth, which is, like you, a perfect creation of the universe.

Standing in the center of your world, take a few steps and make a few gestures, then slowly open your eyes while tasting the movements of your perfect body. When your eyes are opened, take a few minutes to notice how you see what surrounds you. What is your view of the world now that you have taken back possession of your perfect body?

For the healing of the genealogy tree, which will be the culmination of all our work, these are the elements on which to work in order to prepare for the birth psychoritual. With the help of this chapter, and the summary below, you can design your own nativity psychoritual and imagine in detail the pregnancy and birth that will allow you to come into the world as a perfect body.

- In the first trimester the parents still do not perceive the baby. This period is primarily about the physical transformation of the woman's body, but the parents' expectation and joy are key elements. In the first month, when the egg becomes an embryo, the heart begins to beat. During the second month the embryo develops into the fetus and the major organs are formed. Then, in the third month, the sex is defined. The parents who monitor the pregnancy accompany all of these events.
- In the second trimester, as the mother feels full of energy and the baby begins to manifest in his first movements, a presence becomes tangible. At the fourth month, the size of the baby's head decreases relative to the body, his limbs lengthen, bones harden. In the fifth month, the baby begins to move and his senses develop; he begins to perceive sound, including his parents' voices, and his hands open and close. In the sixth month, the sex organs are completely developed and the brain continues to form, preparing for, among other things, the ability to smell.

- In the third trimester, one prepares for the arrival of the baby. Is the room ready? How are the parents? Are they communicating with the baby? The mother needs more rest. During the seventh month, the fetus's skin thickens and his fingerprints form. In the eighth month, the infant is already formed and ready to be born, but he grows and prepares; all of the audio and tactile information reaches the baby as if he were already born. At nine months, space is reduced and the baby has almost no more room to move; he cannot stretch his legs or arms. The baby's digestive system is formed, as are his lungs and eyes. He smiles.

When the baby is ready, at the moment of birth he turns and places his head down. The mother is listening; the being decides the right time to be born. The mother continues to work with the baby. The baby, at birth, emerges into the collaborating father's hands to enable him to learn to breathe without stress; the cord is not immediately cut. The baby can be breastfed without first being washed; the protective layer covering him gives off a delicious aroma.

Exercise:
Preparing for the birth psychoritual

Questions to ask regarding the circumstances of your conception and birth:

- What information do you have on the meeting between your parents? If you have none, how do you imagine it? What is the ideal scenario of their meeting as you would film it or describe it in a novel?
- How was your gestation? Have you collected the information described in this chapter? Are you missing anything? What would be the ideal gestation if you were to relive those nine months? Write out a scenario for each month to correspond to an ideal gestation that equally benefits the fetus (on the biological plane) and the parents (on the spiritual plane).

- How were you born? What kind of birth would you like to have experienced? How was your breastfeeding experience? What care would you have liked to receive in those first weeks or first months of life? Given these elements and your own personal research, compose a brief scenario that represents your pregnancy and your ideal birth.

PART SIX

From Triad
to Brotherhood

Family Dynamics

ELEVEN

Conflicts between Siblings

By Alejandro Jodorowsky

Every human being's deepest desire is to fulfill, by internal and external interactions, a complementary union between an ideal and capable man and woman in order to bring material and spiritual growth to society. This wish is for a union where absolute trust reigns; where each person accepts the other with joy, without seeking to change the other; where each partner advances toward a common goal; where agreement is born spontaneously without the need even for discussion, without any competition except a healthy rivalry; and which emerges directly from the child's need to have perfect parents. In other words, a couple that is exclusive property. Even the last of many siblings will consider parents to be exclusively "his," feeling himself in the center of the "father-mother-child" triad.

Not having the parents' total agreement causes the child deep anguish, and in the majority of families, this agreement is impossible to attain. From the moment of a child's birth, extreme attention is required. Any distraction by the mother causes tears. The child lives in the absolute present and requires the same of his parents, but parents tied to their past by multiple knots due to unresolved obsession on their own parents may see the child as an "intruder" and turn him into deceased grandparents, or project the identity of a "dead child" or sibling rival onto him, well before his birth.

My own father, whose younger brother Benjamin "stole" his mother from him, all his life called me Benjamin instead of Alejandro. Motivated by this jealous projection, he saw me as a rival and wished to crush me psychologically.

Every child sees himself as the center of the world. And loudly (if necessary) cries or falls ill and is treated as such. This intense demand for attention covers the need to be seen as he is, and not to be mistaken for a projection. If one does not see the child he is but rather projects onto him an imaginary personality, he feels devalued and invisible. He thinks he is not worth anything and suffers under the weight of this fictitious character that he must carry around in order to be loved.

When I started analyzing genealogy trees I realized that most of my consultants, although adults, still lived as prisoners of their "mommy-daddy" troubles. Most people are not themselves but continue to play the role their families or social environment provided for them. Thus, they live with a restless need to attract attention to themselves, tirelessly seeking the protection of a mother and father united by a sublime love who are absolutely present, and who will treat them like exceptional beings.

In cultures where religion venerates a god as Father, this thirst to get perfect attention is more evident in women because the founder priests of social structures have belittled them. This is observed not only in the Judeo-Christian world ("Unto the woman he said, I will greatly multiply thy sorrow and thy conception; in sorrow thou shalt bring forth children; and thy desire shall be to thy husband, and he shall rule over thee"—Genesis 3:16), but also in Buddhist cultures. For the Buddha and his first disciples, no woman could illuminate; she had to die and reincarnate into a male form. The masculine tradition combined with the parents' narcissism induces the wish for a male firstborn. If the opposite occurs, the father can feel disappointed and the mother guilty. The little girl grows up making every effort to adapt to paternal demands by denying her body, hiding in her intellect (traditionally a male attribute such as the cultural limitations define it), and imitating masculine behavior.

The need to be seen, mixed with impotent despair, can follow a person all his life: "I am nothing. I know nothing. I can do nothing." Or he may experience a ceaseless effort to attain stardom whether in arts, sports, politics, or crime.

When a second child is born, an elder sibling may see her triad threatened: an invader has come to steal center stage. Even twins do not accept a quartet; each feels she is the only child in the Unconscious and each feels she deserves to be favored. Facing this rival (or these rivals), to maintain her privileged position, the child opts for an aggressive channel, or she unconsciously chooses to become seriously ill, or she behaves as if the newcomer does not exist, or contrarily, she demonstrates the height of care, making it essential and again becoming the center of attention with "sisterly love" and "kindness," which are, in fact, "strategies." When the firstborn is a girl, and a few years later a younger brother arrives, because she enjoys intellectual advancement due to her age it is not rare for her to bestow an intellectual inferiority complex upon the younger one.

The study of the anxiety and dissatisfaction at work in the triad, and the conflicts engendered among siblings caused by the struggle to be the center of attention, is an important step on the path of metagenealogical Consciousness. Conflicts between brothers and sisters are mainly caused by conflicts the consultant's mother and father experienced in childhood with their own brothers and sisters. Among the different dangers of the triad, we can cite as one of the most common tendencies that of parents to project more on the second child than the first (or on the eldest, the youngest, and so on, according to their own place among their own siblings).

I have had four sons by two mothers. At first, I lived with two of my sons and my Mexican wife, Valerie. One day, I read this sentence by the occultist Maitre Philippe of Lyon: "The debts you don't pay in this life, return to you for payment in the next." I realized that I was another boy's absent father. I decided to end this irresponsibility. I wrote to his mother, asking her to trust me, and by one of those miracles with no rational explanation, she consented. Valerie and I thus found ourselves with the duty of raising a group of three young males, with the fourth, Adan, soon to be added. Each of them had an explosive character. How to eliminate the arguments, competition, envious comparisons, or hatred that might arise between them, and awaken brotherly love?

After watching the Marx Brothers film *Duck Soup,* by Leo McCarey, we decided to use these actors as examples for raising our sons. The Marx Brothers, although members of the same family, were each very different from the other: Groucho, the aggressive materialist; Harpo, the poetic madman; Chico, the humble clown; Zeppo, the corny seducer.

I am always shocked to see couples surrounded by children all dressed identically. I understand that uniforms are required in the army, but they become monstrous if they are imposed on a family: they reveal an obligatory equality equivalent to castration. During my long life, I have lived in the company of cats and have never seen two with the same character. Each is born and develops a feline identity of its own. It's the same with humans. To standardize children puts their creativity in a mold that restricts them spiritually.

Valerie and I had accustomed our sons to receive a sum of money dedicated to buying clothes. "This is how much you have to get yourselves dressed, and for your underwear, and for your shoes." Each chose according to his own tastes, without prior instruction: Teo, for example, loved to wear a sock on the right foot that had nothing to do with the sock on the left foot; Brontis always chose his clothes in shades of gray; Cristobal, in bright colors; and Adan very quickly developed a taste for elegance. It is the same with their personalities. Each unfolded ideas and tastes of his own: one had a passion for sports, one for literature, one for magic, and one for music.

Even if our financial situation was not flourishing, we made sure that no one inherited the clothes of the older brother. Our desire to affirm their individuality, without providing incentive for selfishness, drove us also to buy the cutlery they liked. Each one chose the fork, the spoon, the knife, the plate, and the cup to their liking. Cristobal liked the black plates, Brontis the Japanese, Teo the metal, Adan the silver and plates decorated with the head of cats. Each could paint his own room the color of his choice, choose his own furniture, and hang anything on the walls he wanted. Raised in such freedom, they developed strong characters, and they fought a lot, mostly because of jealousy.

During dessert when we cut the cake my sons watched me distribute the pieces; whoever received the largest piece was obviously, in their eyes, the favored son. The solution we found when they quarreled was to have one cut the cake while another one would choose who would get each piece.

At one point in their growth Cristobal felt aggression toward Teo, so we created a puppet theater where one puppet represented Cristobal and the other represented Teo. I asked Cristobal to animate Teo's puppet, and vice versa. Each then developed an understanding from inside the other's character, and communication between them improved significantly.

Then one day Teo's insult of "mental midget" enraged Cristobal. When Cristobal, furious, came to tell me this, I welcomed these negative feelings instead of rejecting them. "Evidently, an insult like that had to make you furious." With a smile, he felt understood and replied, "Exactly."

Another time, Brontis, who very much wanted to watch a movie on television, brawled with Teo, who had taken command of the remote control. He was shaking with fury. I kindly interjected and asked him to let go of his brother, and rather than treat him "violently" or "meanly" I suggested the following exercise: "Instead of hitting your brother, why don't you focus your rage on this watermelon? I give you permission to crush it with your kicks. Then, you will write a letter to your brother to tell him that when he monopolizes the television that makes you very angry. He will understand your words better than your fists."

In general, above all, we avoided comparisons. "Look what you did to your shirt when you ate! Even your little brother didn't do that. He is cleaner than you . . ." This kind of commentary incites the child to think incorrect thoughts like, "They love my brother more than me." Instead, we say, "A little sauce fell on your shirt." The child hurried to clean it without falling into useless abandonment anxiety.

Children compete for affection and their parents' attention. When parents seem to prefer another, children can become filled with spite and engage in relentless competition for dominance. The presence of each brother and sister means "less" for them: less personal time with parents, less attention when they suffer a disappointment or hurt, less applause for their success.

Each gesture that is interpreted as preference leads them to believe, "He or she is best; I am worthless; they don't love me; I am in danger." The mother and father provide everything a child needs to survive and progress: food, living space, clothes, warmth, caresses, and essential teachings. However, as the child fears anything that may threaten his well-being, he becomes a prisoner of constant and agonizing comparisons. He competes to be the best, to be the one who receives the most, the one who receives everything . . . all the toys, all the food, all the space. He wants to feel safe and be the only one loved.

Understanding this, we did everything humanly possible to improve the relationships between our sons. In giving each one the opportunity to display a different personality and to create a personal environment, we were able to eliminate envy that pushed them to want the others' possessions. They learned to collaborate and to share, considering their brothers' existence to be a pleasure.

Neither Valerie nor I were given any such chance. In my case, having only an older sister, I was not treated like a clone of the ideal model but the behavior of our parents aggravated the hostility between us. She was the fruit of passion, whereas I, who was born later, was the product of intercourse carried out in total hatred. My parents then made Raquel the summit of the triad and treated me as if I were invisible. For my sister there was quality furniture, countless shoes and clothes, private lessons from swimming to piano, frequent outings with my father to the rink, little secrets shared with my mother when they locked themselves away. For my part, I receive one suit, one pair of shoes, one old chair, and a dilapidated bed. I never had the right to a walk with my parents, and never a caress. Searching for love, I could not seek refuge in my sister's arms because her deepest wish was to see me disappear. Her least cruel commentary was, "Take your toothbrush, and go far away from here. No one loves you."

To each of these insults, this scorn and these scribbles on my school notebook, I cried. She laughed. These harmful experiences conditioned my behavior, my thoughts, of how I saw myself. In spite of my artistic success, until I was forty years old I felt that everything I did was of little value. I plunged into endless quarrels and rivalries with all the women with whom I tried to have a relationship. I worked constantly to have more, but nothing could fill my emotional emptiness.

As a theater director I helped actresses succeed, but instead of congratulating myself, I felt envy. They were beautiful, loved by the public, talented, all the things I would never achieve.

My wife Valerie, the daughter of a virile woman, committed the "mistake" of being born female. Her father, a Mexican guitarist, approached the newborn's cradle, looked at her crotch with disgust, and exclaimed, "How ugly! If I must be a father, I want only boys!" With that, he left the home forever. Of course, Valerie's three older brothers (six, four, and two) were perpetually in conflict to determine who was the abandoned mother's favorite, and they made the little one their scapegoat. She was considered the "ugly" one, the "idiot," "stinking," the "intruder." Not a day passed without their mockery, assaults, and contempt.

My wife and I, incapable of being happy because of emotional wounds caused not only by parental conflicts but also by the rivalry between brothers and sisters, dedicated ourselves to making each son feel that he was an individual being who deserved special love. We strove to convince them that our hearts were large enough to love each of them in a unique way, different than any other person. And instead of worrying about their disabilities, we concentrated on their abilities. This is how we taught them the delights of collaboration, exchange, mutual support, and respect. They had the great privilege of knowing brotherly love.

At the same time, we had to work very hard to heal our own pasts. Our parents' misunderstanding, their deafness to our feelings, never allowed us to express fraternal hostility with creative acts. They never ceased making comparisons, which caused disunity. They used us as their audiences, and as accomplices in their disputes. In short, they forced us to be what they wanted us to be without ever taking into account our authentic Being. All of this transformed me into an adult consumed by the need to dominate others, leaving me exhausted from always trying to be he who triumphs. My wife, after childhood, became a woman who could not bear the slightest comparison to others because it gave her the impression of being a bad witch.

Countless are those who, because of the aggression of brothers and sisters, fail to find peace in adulthood.

With patience and perseverance we transformed the competition between our sons into a healthy collaboration, but the moment arrived to send them to school. We sometimes found it necessary to fight against education, which too often inculcates competition and the attainment of material benefits over seeking the truth.

To promote cohesion between the four brothers, I helped them to develop the feeling of being part of a sacred family. One day, exalting our family name, I showed them that the syllable *do,* shining like a diamond in Jodorowsky, means "path" in Japanese—like *karate-do, aikido, kendo.* Also in Japanese is the word *dojo,* a room devoted to spiritual exercises and martial arts; Jôdo, doctrine of the Pure Land, advises disciples to forget the personal name while reciting "Buddha" with sincerity and deep faith; *jo* is purity; *ky* turns into *chi,* which means "knowledge and wisdom." In some Shinto schools, where esoteric meanings are given to colors, the yellow *ki* recalls the sun's rays, which is thus the center of the center, unity, the Creator.

"Sky" is also in Jodorowsky. The "w" preceding "sky" in Western occultism is taken as a symbol for heavenly water. And if one turns it around, it becomes "m," the symbol for earthly water. If "v" represents the five, the double "v" ("w") represents ten, which joins male and female, spirit and matter.

Jod (pronounced "yod") is the tenth letter in the Hebrew alphabet. The number 10 (also the sum of the letters in our family name) fulfills the return to unity, $1 + 0 = 1$. However, there is a difference between 1 and 10. The 1 contains all of the generator polarities, inactive as long as they remain undifferentiated, which, when the unit breaks and they separate, creates the universe. It is precisely the 10, created from a masculine seed and a feminine seed, that represents the newly distinct polarities of the sperm and ovum, the phallus and vagina, fullness and emptiness, expansion and constriction. $1 + 2 + 3 + 4 = 10$. 1 and 3 are masculine, 2 and 4 are feminine. In Mayan civilization, the 10, *lahun* (that-which-is-two-and-one), should never be pronounced because of its extremely sacred character. To avoid even writing it, one writes 5 twice instead. In Indian Buddhism, the path of the Bodhisattva has 10 *bhumis,* or levels of spiritual attainment. With the tenth bhumi, when the wisdom gained produces nonidentification to the teachings, to the path, to the technique, the Bodhisattva ceases to identify with the path: he becomes the way, the path.

Jod is the first letter, and the most sacred, of the unpronounceable tetragrammaton, Yod-Hé-Vav-Hé, Yahweh (or Jehovah). It is the smallest of the four letters, compared to a point. An esoteric law says the more simple the symbol, the more spiritually powerful it is. Strength displaces form. The more form disappears, the more strength appears. If the intellect learns to be the receiver, the ego shrinks and achieves annihilation of the "me," which is a disregard for the Consciousness of one's own importance, dissolution of personal existence in the sacred impersonal.

In Arabic, as in Hebrew, the word *jod* means "hand." The right hand is considered a good omen, the left hand a bad omen. One is "light," the other is "dark." The "or" in Jodorowsky means "light" in Hebrew. The illuminated hand, the right hand, does not exclude the left. In the human body there is no organ that consists of only one part; even the brain has two hemispheres and the heart two ventricles. The human takes parts from left and right, which marks and impregnates him with the Consciousness of an ambivalent behavior. The hands, when the ten fingers are interlaced in prayer, have the ability to symbolically unite whatever is separated, lost, or dispersed. The majority of myths mention the loss of something precious that needs to be recovered, rebuilt, or replaced. This loss by destruction, disappearance, or neglect evokes a prior integrity that refers to a state of primordial perfection, which is primarily an original language shredded into a multiplicity of languages in which the unpronounceable sacred Name was a secret due to its supernatural virtues. Many esoteric schools allude to a supreme Name whose knowledge is the Secret among secrets; social cataclysms dispersed this Secret into a multitude of small pseudo-secrets.

All of the initiatory schools restore union with the sacred Name. In some Sufi schools of Islam the master takes the candidate's right hand between his two hands, with the right above and the left below, to reconnect to the original root. This "union of hands" is held while the blessed words are recited, providing for the transmission of the ineffable Secret from master to disciple. In the Zohar of Jewish Kabbalists it is written, "The holy right hand—Blessed be He—emanates all of light, blessings and freedoms. The left hand emanates rigor. In achieving their union, all rigor disappears." By the imposition of hands, Catholic priests perform the mystery of union and love—together; they do not oppose but complement one another, turning into only one hand of benediction and mercy that transmits the divine influx. In the book of Job (37:7), God "sealeth up the hand of every man; that all men may know his work." In symbology the left hand represents temporal and royal power, the right hand spiritual and priestly power—the former is the path of Earth, the latter the path of Sky. The two paths unite as the disciples advance simultaneously on one or the other; one is the spiritualization of matter, the other is the materialization of the spiritual. The left hand represents the past while the right represents the future; united in prayer they create the present: Jod, or the Hand of Light.

Having thus exalted our name, I explained to my sons that we had identified the stigma that my father had broken. Wanting to be considered Chilean at any cost, he joined the Communist party under the name Juan Araucano and hated the name "Jodorowsky," which he felt identified him as a foreigner. This experience was very useful to them. Each new concept they identified with changed their way of seeing the world, and their attitude toward others. Their name mutated. It was turned into a precious and secret object, which united them and made them feel that in spite of all its obstacles, life presented by society was worth living. Receiving the sacred meaning of their secret Name, they developed an unalterable confidence in themselves and a continual joy for living.

All names, without exception, can be exalted. Take one of the most common names in France, Dupont. One can break it down into "from the bridge" and explore the meaning from the perspective of the symbol of a union between the material and the immaterial worlds—with the ability to move from one bank to the other, from earth to heaven, from the human to the superhuman condition, from contingency to immortality. In Spanish, an equally common name like Sanchez begins with the root "san," which refers to holiness. "Che" is the first syllable of *chela*, which means "the disciple of a master" in Sanskrit. This syllable also has to do with alchemy. Chemi was the ancient name for the land of Egypt. And *cherio* in alchemy is the quintessence, the essential quality free from all impurity.

Although we may be internally released from neurotic identification with names that have not yet been exalted, we cannot consider ourselves freed from the genealogy trap. That is why this work is essential for all of us.

TWELVE

From the Triad to the Siblings

Being Unique and Living Together

The new family takes form after the first birth—after the first pregnancy, in fact, because even if the pregnancy is interrupted the expected child may subsequently occupy a special place in the family memory, and the two family trees unite with their respective traps and treasures. In fairy tales, the fairies and witches who lean on the child's cradle to recite blessings and curses represent the positive and negative influences of the two trees.

The appearance of a family begins our study of family relationships, first within the triad (mother-father-child), then among siblings in the broad sense. How do children share parental attention? And what are the consequences of the family dynamics from one generation to the next?

Here, we enter into a complex study that can include a multitude of individuals. A whole genealogy tree composed only of children already represents fifteen people of one bloodline over four generations, but if the siblings are numerous, this number can reach the hundreds.

We must first endeavor to understand the parent-child dynamic generation by generation. Initially, we will see what happens when the couple becomes a triad and all the possible variants thereof with their future effects. Then we will look at the way in which sibling conflict is born, where children's relationships are poisoned by the parents' inability to treat each of them as a unique being. We will discuss the phenomenon of projection and compensation, which causes people from one generation to focus on their own childhood conflicts in subsequent generations, consciously or not punishing their own children for unjust harm they received from brothers, sisters, or parents.

This chapter will be based on a series of case studies that will help us to understand more concretely typical situations to which we refer.

FROM THE COUPLE TO THE TRIAD

After the birth of a child, the couple becomes a family. For the man, the encounter with the newborn seals the reality of fatherhood, whereas for the woman the child had already become a reality during her pregnancy. The first moments with a child are critical, heavenly, and cause many anxieties. The woman's attachment to the baby is principally supported by the production of natural oxytocin, which begins during delivery and peaks at the moment of birth (as long as the woman is not exposed to cold, stress, or intense light, and her privacy is respected).

It has been proven that the injection of oxytocin into a mammal's brain produces decreased aggression and greater resistance to pain, with increased appetite and maternal behavior in females. These effects last two times longer for females than for males. This "maternal love" hormone is stimulated during breastfeeding.

Thus, in the best of cases, the mother is completely focused on her newborn baby. But all might not be rosy, and for the man who shares a life with her, this can be confusing: seeing his wife's attention turned entirely toward the baby may cause him to consider the child an obstacle or a rival. The resumption of the couple's sex life may also come into question. In a healthy and evolved couple, this situation finds an easy solution: for a while, the man accepts this loss of attention from the woman who is devoted to the new (and sexual) pleasure of breastfeeding. He patiently waits for her desire for him to return. With a less balanced couple, this can cause innumerable conflicts including rape and physical assault.

The moment at which the father and mother engage again in an intimate relationship marks the end of the fusion (which is nearly a second pregnancy) between mother and baby. By claiming on the one hand to be companion and lover to the woman, and father to the child on the other, one might say that the father implements a balanced triad or a balancing of the three relationships (father-mother, mother-child, child-father), each of equal importance.

But many things can disturb the constitution of this fragile trio. The parents may have conflicts, or they may feel the arrival of their child is a threat, an invasion, a source of fatigue and frustration rather than a gift that allows them to enter a new stage in adult life. From a transpersonal perspective, we have seen that the idea of creating an infant returns us to our own deaths because the child reminds us of the immortality of the species. But on the purely personal level, the little one's arrival can be a source of anxiety, especially if a parent unconsciously blames the child for having dethroned or expelled him from his own place as the eternal child, depriving him of his illusory immortality.

Parents unable to grow up will generally have toxic behavior toward their child and may make the child feel that he is an embarrassment; they may systematically entrust him to the grandparents, making him a kind of "youngest sibling"; or they may abandon and devalue the child in other ways to confirm their position as "infant-king."

The question of gender also plays a part. A healthy mother who gives birth to a son will have the pleasure of having created a human being different from her, but perfect for himself. If this woman's femininity was devalued, the son is seen either as a kind of trophy on which she projects her frustrated masculinity, or else as an honored one empowered with a perfection to which she had no access, which causes her to become jealous. Similarly, when the firstborn is a daughter, a healthy father is not narcissistically disappointed but celebrates his daughter's gender and allows her anima (the feminine part) to be projected onto him. But if he is neurotic, in his narcissism he may despise and wound this new arrival who is unlike him, and who has deprived him of the satisfaction of being identically reproduced.

Symmetrically, the healthy mother will love her daughter and a healthy father his son, as a full-fledged person and not a smaller copy of themselves. They will give everything they did not receive from their own parents and will accept that this child exceeds them altogether. However, a neurotic mother may deny the individual existence of the daughter and treat her as an extension of herself, a tentacle, or else as a spectator. She may be in competition with her daughter all her life, preventing her from growing up. The neurotic father will make his son an extension of his ego, "heir to the name," and dress up his miniature replica, doing everything in his power to castrate his son, including covering him in money and gifts until an advanced age to prove who is head of the household.

Neurotic parents are always infantile, even under the guise of authority, dignity, and respectability. Their actions go in two distinct directions to equally devastating effects. They behave immaturely and force the child to play a little adult, endangering the child and preventing him from enjoying his childhood. Or they force the child into an eternal childhood, creating a false family paradise that prevents the child from growing up and becoming autonomous, and that forbids the child's abandoning the family.

All of the suffering of the genealogical tree can be interpreted by the parents as the refusal of their individual deaths, and thus the immortality of the human species, which become small deaths imposed by the child as the parents bear the weight of parenting instead of playing the role of infantile parents at the cost of the child's true Self.

The challenge of becoming a parent includes this mutation: suddenly, one is no longer a "son of" or "daughter of" but is, above all, the "father of" or the "mother of." Parents are forced to sacrifice their infantile demands, to override their own acute wounds and unresolved aspirations, to devote themselves to a vulnerable and dependent being who expresses the imperative need to grow and to be loved. These issues manifest at the very onset of life in the mother's womb: the denial of death for the sake of individuality or the acceptance of death (or, rather, the transpersonal being).

If one continues to think like a child, becoming a parent means becoming a selfish adult who does not want to die. But becoming an adult by authentically becoming a parent means becoming a transpersonal being who accepts one's own disappearance as an element of the continuation of the species.

It helps then to ask, what is the purpose of life for each parent at the moment of the birth of a child? In terms of the ego and the Unconscious, the parents may consider the child as something preventing them from achieving their goals, which reflects a low level of maturity. The parents then have selfish purposes and the child will be considered a nuisance who interrupts their game or childish dream. In many cases, the child is known as the continuation of the family tree and only asked to be the heir (to serve the past). But regardless of the parents' level of Consciousness, in terms of the Supraconsciousness we can say the child always comes to fulfill the union between the two parents, and to encourage them to develop (whether they succeed or not) their true purpose. It is also common for a child to create, in his own way, a synthesis between the parents' respective goals.

Example No. 1: Both parents are fatherless. This fundamental absence initially united them, each seeing their own reflection in the other's distress, but it also had the effect of keeping them in an immature state. They both lacked the ethical and existential structure that a father may have provided.

Ana is the product of a cuddle between a woman and her fleeting lover: the father discredited the mother before she committed suicide. Ana is, therefore, a "bastard" despised by the family. In response to this devaluation, she feeds her delusions of grandeur and dreams of becoming a screen actor. Juan was orphaned at thirteen and worked to pay for the education of his brothers and sisters, who all succeeded in their intellectual professions while Juan remained low on the social ladder. His purpose, as he was unable to go to school, was to be respected just the same as a cultivated man, something that was obviously impossible.

Quickly, the couple found themselves immersed in dissatisfaction, since the purposes of their lives were impossible. They rejected their daughter, who had to grow up alone in what she describes as "a kind of benign schizophrenia between the child in me and the adult who took care of me."

The father, hungry for respectability, eventually pledged allegiance to the Communist party, while the mother hungry for recognition got drunk on Hollywood films. Each, locked in an egotistical goal, missed out on evolving toward a transpersonal perspective. But the daughter, overcoming the emotional pain of her childhood, nevertheless managed to unite her parents' goals by becoming a universally respected filmmaker.

Example No. 2: The young mother of twenty-three years dreamed of being a fashion stylist. The father, at twenty-four years, imagined himself a respected reporter. A son arrives "by accident." The two parents are forced to marry and establish a stable family to take care of this little being. She becomes a housewife, he an editor at an advertising company.

Throughout his childhood, they make their firstborn responsible for their artistic and professional disappointments. After many difficulties and long work on himself, their son becomes a sales manager for a major fashion label and is required to travel all over the world. While studying his family tree at forty-four years of age, he nevertheless has a major vocation crisis and questions this passion for fashion and travel, which didn't particularly correspond to his true self. He literally "absorbed" his parents' disappointed ideals, but in reality he dreamed of a more stable albeit more mundane professional position, which ultimately allows him to start a family. He also now feels the need to turn toward fair trade and sustainable development. One might say that the first part of his life was devoted to the exterior fulfillment of his parents' goals of fashion, luxury, and travel, and now with maturity he has a service and authenticity mission in the context of his profession closer to that which the genealogy tree actually needs.

FIRST AND LAST NAMES

Individual Identity and Familial Identity

Each of us receives at least a first and last name at birth, and most often a surname that is literally the "father's name." In patriarchal cultures the family name (like a tattoo) integrates the newborn into the clan, marks the belonging to the paternal branch of the genealogy tree. This family name is often derived from a distant paternal ancestor: Dominguez or Martinez (descendants of Domingo or Martin), Vassilievitch or Nikolic (descendants of Vassili or Nikola), Paoli or Franceschi (descendants of Paolo or Francesco), Adamson or Mendelssohn (sons of Adam or of Mendel). In most cases surnames eliminate filiation through the mother, just as the Bible only mentions the names of the firstborn sons.* Today some countries allow children to acquire the mother's family name rather than the father's, but even the name that modern mothers transmit to their children is the product of patriarchal cultures. One might dream of a revolution of the family names where the women would transmit a female cultural contribution through an invented matronymic (Racheditter, Natalivna, etc.).

However, the mother may indeed intervene in the choice of a name. This first "gift" offered to the newborn individualizes him within the family and, in a certain way, does exist regardless of the mother. However, **the first name carries the weight of narcissistic fantasies and parental projections.** The child gets used to the sound that continually draws his attention until it is finally incorporated into his existence like an extra organ. Most of the time, unfortunately, the name sums up the aspirations of the family trap, whether as a repetition, when one bestows the same name as a family member upon the child, which

---

*Genesis 5:1–32 for Adam's posterity; Matthew 1:1–16 for Jesus's genealogy.

is to say the same identity, or a refusal, in which case the name corresponds to a curse.

Thus, parents, having conceived of a child due to a defective condom, named the child Pépin, referring consciously to the name of Charlemagne's father, but unconsciously to the slang use of the word *pépin*, which means "problem" or "disagreeable accident." Similarly, the female name Manon can be deconstructed into "ma" (mother) attached to the negation "no," and under the pretext of evoking the heroine, Manon Lescaut, it masks a stubborn hatred for the mother archetype. If the daughter receives the name of the father's secret lover, or the son that of the mother's lost fiancé, this name will link the child for his or her whole life to the parents' emotional or sexual secret, even creating an incestuous link that the child is sometimes not aware of since he or she didn't know of the existence of the idealized person whose name he or she bears.

The allocation of names in the family tree very often conceals the desire to revive ancestors or replay relationships with still living parents. The first name then is an additional mark, visible or hidden, of membership in the clan instead of an indication that the person coming into the world is an individual. The familial Unconscious may manifest this repetition in a direct way, like in families where tradition has firstborn sons carry the names of the two grandfathers and daughters the mother's first name. Or the name may be a variation or an anagram, where Carole becomes Caroline, Coraline, or Cornelia; Elsa becomes Isabel or Elisa; Maria becomes Marlene, Marilyn, Mireille, even Mario; Roland corresponds to Arnold or Orlando; Noel to Joel or Leo; all the letters in Dorothee are in Theodore; all the letters in Julien (or Julian) are in Jacqueline. First names change between cultures but retain the blatant link: Marc is Marek, Paul is Pablo, Raymond is Roman. Sometimes the first name is nestled in another, like Ana found in Mariana, Anastasia, Nathanael, and so on. One also sees a number of repetitions in initials (Albina, Alberto, Antonio, Anais, etc.). Sometimes it is the first syllable that repeats (Jacob, Jacinto, Jaime) or, contrarily, the first names rhyme with one another (Brice, Fabrice, Patrice, Beatrice). The repetition of syllables can travel throughout the entire family tree (Samuel's mother is Teresa and his wife is Sandra; the grandfather was named Oswald, the father Alfonso, and the son Pascal).

Children who are designated a diminutive until adulthood (Bobby, Lola, Jeannot, Mimi) must remain children forever thanks to their family's desire for them to not grow up, and to not occupy too much space.

The first name can also be the mark of social, cultural, and religious ideas, with the child named after a movie star, a war hero, or a politician. First names can also be overwhelming, as with imperial or mythic first names like Caesar, Hercules, Hadrien, Napoleon, or Alexander, or a name that refers to more or less eternal feminine archetypes like Eve, Venus, Cassandra, or Marilyn. Above all these refer to delusions of grandeur in the family tree, and the child may feel required to be a genius or a celebrity, or to have other goals that are not in her nature. Inversely, ethereal first names like Angel, Raphael, Gabriel, or Celeste may produce a sexual taboo and the inability to self-actualize. In Christian culture, all of the names derived from the life of Christ (Pascal, Dominique, Christophe, Jesus, Emmanuel, Christian) can induce neurotic perfectionism and, frequently, the tendency to fall ill, have a serious accident, or die at thirty-three years of age.

It is also helpful to know who named the child. If it was not the mother and father it means they outsourced their parental authority to others, or it was stolen from them: the child is unwanted or else captured by voracious grandparents who won't let their own children grow up. Naming a child corresponds to symbolically appropriating him, and this symbolic filiation to the grandparents, godmother, godfather, uncle, or aunt can give the child the impression of being unloved or unwanted.

Assigning a hyphenated first name to a child can reveal an underlying ambiguity on the part of the parents, especially when the two names are of different genders as in Jean-Marie, Maria-José, Rosa-Alberto, Veronica-Jesus, or Marie-Pierre. This can produce identity problems for children, who intuitively feel their parents expected a child of the opposite sex. Sometimes the hyphenated name serves to reconcile two parents who fail to agree on a simple name. If the paternal grandfather is named Charles and the maternal grandfather Henri, the firstborn son is called Charles-Henri, apparently to unify the two branches of the genealogy tree. This can actually carry a power struggle between the two heads of household: the young girl named Marta-Luisa, based upon the two names of her grandmothers, integrates the parents' desire to revive the sanctified (or insufficient) mother in their daughter as well as the conflict between the women vying to prevail in her.

A certain name can also evoke a painful situation that parents seek to resolve through the child: Renee (or Renato) can evoke the memory of a disappeared one whom a family member wants to see reborn. In French, Sylvie can be understood as "s'il vit" (if he lives) and can make reference to an unborn or absent son. Genevieve is the namesake for "je ne vis Éve" (I did not live Eve) and may indicate a deprecation of the feminine in the genealogy tree. Without taking wordplay (otherwise known as "the language of birds") to excess, it is obvious that as a person speaks through each genealogy tree culture, some wordplay slips through.

Feminized male names are very common in patriarchal cultures and they all carry the seed of the father's (or mother's) disappointment of not having a male heir. Forced to identify with his daughter, at the price of his narcissism, the father gives a name that sounds like a regret, and the mother, notified by this choice of a name, is made aware that she failed to "give" her spouse (or even her own parents) a male heir. It is rare for a boy to be given a female or ambiguous name, but in some very Catholic cultures the addition of Marie, Maria, or Mario corresponds to a feminine projection.

Example: The poet Rilke had the birth name René Karl Wilhelm Johann Josef Maria. And his mother, devout and coquette and a narcissist without a doubt, habitually dressed him up like a girl before abandoning him altogether. At age twenty-two he fell madly in love with Lou Andreas-Salomé, thirteen years his elder, who was his mistress and first mentor. Considering the name René to be a bit effeminate, she advised him to adopt "Rainer" as a pen name. We can only smile at the poet for including Maria in his new name—Rainer Maria Rilke—the last link to the absent mother who wanted a little girl.

The practice of the pseudonym, thus becoming one's own father and mother by renaming oneself, probably contributed to the strength and consequently the glory of many artists, like Neftali Reyes, who became Pablo Neruda.

A number of sects, religious movements, and churches name or rename the followers they absorb. In addition to the ritual of baptism one can include the induction of Zen monks, who upon entering the monastery shave their heads, becoming bald like a newborn, and receive a new name. Benedictine monks wash the feet in addition to changing the name, which symbolizes the washing away of old footsteps, acts, and gestures (the family tree), allowing them to start a new life within the Mother Church. A number of Hindu masters baptize their disciples with Hindi or Sanskrit names, whatever their nationalities, putting them back in the position of a baby who does not yet fluently speak the language mastered by the symbolic parent.

All names given to children contain projections and identify them as part of a particular family. These names should be decoded in order to detach from them, and in some extreme cases one might want to consider changing one's name.

INTROJECTION AND PROJECTION

When studying the influence of family on the child it is important to redefine the symmetrical context of "projection" and "introjection," terms forged respectively by Sigmund Freud and Sandor Ferenczi and widely used since then by psychoanalysts and psychotherapists of all persuasions.

Introjection refers to the process by which parents and family members enter as archetypes into our Unconscious. Psychoanalysts define introjection as the ego's absorption of a characteristic or trait received from the outside. It is, therefore, an **appropriation.**

In infancy, the only reality that we know is that of our parents (biological or adoptive) and of our family. To grow up is to become them: we imitate their way of walking, their gestures, their feelings, and their way of thinking, in order to be recognized by and integrated into the clan. Without the love of those closest to us, we are nothing. We therefore do everything possible to satisfy them. Part of our psyche becomes a mirror. We thus imitate not only our relatives' agreeable traits but also their anger, sorrow, and depression, all of which provide so much distressing interference.*

The inevitable process of identification begins with an introjection that our parents project onto us. If they see us as "intelligent," "excited," "slow," or "awkward," these qualities, defects, and descriptions will be integrated into our repertoire and personality. We will refer to them as often as possible, playing the role that was presented to us in order to be recognized and, if possible, accepted. If this is the case, we continue to develop the qualities that our families expect of us: being good, not crying too loudly, cleaning up, being sweet, getting good grades, developing the preferred qualities of our parents (art if they are artists, sports if they are athletes, cruelty if they are cruel). If we continue to feel excluded in spite of this, we make superhuman efforts to become what the family would have liked us to be even at the cost of our own vocation or in contempt of our own sexual identity: a woman becomes a "tomboy," an excellent musician becomes an accountant.

A child accepts all labels imposed on him, using them to form his own image of himself, and if the parents are in conflict, he risks tearing

---

*A famous sculptor had achieved everything she desired in life—prosperity, success, a healthy family—suffered from inexplicable bouts of melancholy that made her want to commit suicide by a bullet to the head. In reality, the melancholy and the suicidal obsession did not belong to her but came from her mother, a woman whose artistic vocation had been thwarted. Once awareness of this fact was achieved, a psychomagic act allowed the sculptor to definitively free herself from her psychological inheritance. She sculpted a pistol in marble, painted it black, carried it in her handbag for one lunar month, and at the time of her menstrual cycle, sent it as a gift to her mother with a box of heart-shaped candies. Later we will see how Psychomagic allows us to mirror the feelings of the individual to whom they belong in an artistic, nonaggressive way.

himself apart to fulfill their contradictory wishes. If the parents with-hold their love, the child makes excuses. "They are angry because I dis-obeyed them, because I'm worthless. Anyway, even if I misbehave or am inherently bad, they are there and they protect me. I must preserve this defective identity, because if I change they will cease to recognize me as a member of the family and will abandon me."

It is thus by sacrificing the sovereignty of our authentic feelings that we shape our acquired personalities. If the subject we are forced to study does not interest us, we are "lazy" or "stupid"; if we repeat the opinions of our grandfather, patriarch of the family, like a parrot we are "intel-ligent"; if we repress our power and fold under the neurotic orders of a mother obsessed by her household, we are "sweet"; we are "pretty" if we look like our father's favorite actress.

The family expects us to take after one or more of the family mem-bers, and we are convinced it is better to be seen as a copy of what already exists than to look like ourselves. It is not uncommon to see the clan hover over a newborn, verbally dissecting her into a Frankenstein collage of body parts: "She has her grandmother's nose, her father's eyes, she coos like her grandmother the singer, she is brunette like her grand-father, she has her aunt's hands . . ."

It is also possible to introduce values from other situations and other imprints not previously experienced within the family of origin. One may look at the Hindu guru Amma's international success, where her *darshan* (blessing) consists of taking followers into her arms and rocking them, one by one, symbolically conveying the cosmic Mother's unconditional and absolute love to them. Many people who receive Amma's embrace are seeking to finally experience a sense of being unique among the multitudes, something that cannot often be lived among siblings. Amma, who behaves like a saint, embraces thousands of people every day.

Projection corresponds to **ascribing our own feelings onto oth-ers** to protect ourselves from an emotional situation we cannot han-dle. Projection invests another person with defects and qualities not his own, and he then mimes them in accordance with the preexisting family model. The reactive projections of our adulthood correspond to our experiences in the past. It is common to see a person who was not sufficiently heard in the family as a child accuse those close to him of talking too much, or of not hearing what he said. Or a person who had conflicts with a family member (father, mother, or sibling) attributes the same kind of aggression to a stranger.

Projection is not only a defense mechanism, it is an active energy, capable of transforming reality like a dye stains material onto which it is poured. Our attitude, our beliefs, and our actions significantly modify reality. If, for example, someone has a conflict with his brother, it will lead to the same kind of conflict with any significant relationship with any other man. Of course, one is not generally conscious of any identification because projection covers up an intolerable wound. The most recent neurological studies show us that the human brain always chooses the solution that appears best suited for survival within the competencies acquired, cognitive as well as motor and emotional. In other words, on the emotional level there is a tendency to react in the least evil manner. For the child abused by his father it is, for example, less painful to choose all male authority figures (professors, professional superiors, police officers) for inclusion in one group labeled "dishonest bastards," all the while dreaming of the perfection of inaccessible and idealized figures (Gandhi, Nelson Mandela, the Pope, or the Dalai Lama) who deal with suffering and the emptiness he experienced during childhood because of an unjust, absent, violent, or sadistic father.

Projecting the anger, rejection, and, at the root of it all, aggressiveness allows us to avoid the vast, irreparable pain of a past that cannot be changed. Like a cut tree branch that never grows back in the same place, the emptiness in the past can never be filled. On the other hand, continuing with the metaphor, the tree can continue to grow with countless new branches growing in all directions. Identifying our projections implies and allows us to mourn the repairs that will never take place, and to continue to grow in a multitude of directions that are accessible to us today.

THE TRIAD AND DESTINY

Now we will see how the initial relationship between parents and child models the child's destiny.

Ancient thought represented Fate as a blind deity who determined in advance, in a precise and irrevocable manner, the path of living beings. In Latin *destinare* means to "determine, compel." Mythology's three Fates (Moirai in Greek, Parcae in Roman) were relentless performers: Clotho was represented spinning the yarn of each individual's existence; Lachesis controlled the ups and downs of this destiny, guiding and measuring the length of Clotho's woven yarn; finally, when Lachesis signaled, Atropos cut the string. Nothing could change their course of action. Each person would receive his *moirai,* literally his "share" of life's happiness and tribulations, at the onset.

Examining our notion of fate from the metagenealogical perspective, we can say that an individual's fate has three aspects:

- First, **fate** develops without external intervention. An expert gardener can predict the "destiny" of a seedling or sapling: this species grows in so many years and needs this kind of soil. In the same way, each human has a number of biological and psychological predispositions.
- Second, corresponding to our **free will**, if we are protected from potential danger by hearing "If you drive the car at that speed in this weather you risk having a fatal accident," the course of our existence can be changed by our own will, or that of an outsider. To a certain extent Consciousness, whether our own or another person's, has the power to create a new destiny.
- The third is shaped **by the influence of exterior factors** (familial, social, cultural) on the individual's psychological and biological predisposition, which is based as much on family tradition as on experiences that may have occurred during conflicts, epidemics, and wars.

The results of all of these factors steer each person toward the life and death that corresponds to that individual. When facing adversity, a variety of reactions are always possible. Obstacles can annihilate us or move us forward: it is the quality of our reactions that partially determines the ways in which we live and die. In other words, fate depends largely on individual decisions and actions.

We have seen, in regard to birth, how intrauterine and delivery experiences can shape a person's life. Modern psychology tells us that the relationships we have with our parents during the first years of life shape our destiny. In our view, parents will create a positive destiny if they make it a priority to lead the child to discover his inner treasure, his own values, everything that makes him unique. But if the relationship is negative, if the parents are unwilling or unable to fully becoming parents, the fate of the child will become a caricature of the worst aspects of the genealogy tree and he will be prey to the trap of the past.

Regardless of the number of siblings, regardless of the quality of bonds between them, each person is primarily turned toward the parents, driven by the fundamental need to be linked to them. Consequently, even if he has brothers and sisters the child considers his parents as **his own,** and as those who led him to live in some way as an only child, a central character (hero or victim) in the family saga. In a Christian prayer the psalmist says "Our Father," and through these simple words accepts his membership into the human collective and the necessity of a transpersonal position; in daily life, when talking about parents, one usually says "my father" and "my mother."

We call this essential mother-child-father relationship a **triad.** Even when both parents have died after the birth of the child this triad exists as a baseline of the family construct. Each type of triad shapes a particular destiny. Let us remember that our personal self and our relational self form the seat of all our wounds, frustrations, and psychological disease. If our essential Being (Consciousness, love, life force) supports that which we are and can, more or less, be expressed through our personality, it is through our personal self that we relate with others.

Every individual must create an illusory personality in order to exist socially. This can lead the person to discover his essential Being if it responds to his call or, contrarily, to deny it if he rejects it, therefore building upon an ego doomed to repeat past models. Anguish and suffering result in neurotic knots that we weave with our fellows, with all living beings, and with the world in general. By approaching our essential Being we can cause anxieties to disappear and thus know the joy of life, which is our true nature. On the emotional level, the path to fulfillment steers us away from the anxiety of dying to the euphoria of living.

In order to study the triads in the genealogy tree we must begin by understanding our own tree's dynamics, then go back one generation after the other to visualize our parents and grandparents within their respective triad.

Triads organize themselves according to a series of links that we will discuss below, covering all the relational patterns with two extreme limits. The ideal, never reached, would be perfect and total union in the four energies (intellectual, emotional, creative-sexual, and material life) amongst the triad's three members, this "holy family" being the ultimate model that we can envisage as a future project for humanity. At the most painful level we meet a triad where disunity is total and no links exist between the father and mother, or between the child and his parents, although this complete disunity is unimaginable since someone, be it an anonymous institution or a person, ends up raising every child, which therefore establishes a link.

THE EIGHT TRIADS

From Perfect Union to Complete Disunity

Three Tarot cards might represent the triad of perfect union: the Moon (XVIII), Judgment (XX), the Sun (XVIIII). The card in the middle, Judgment, shows a being rising up from the depths of the earth: he who was in gestation is born. This push toward cosmic Consciousness, represented by the angel who calls from the heavens, can take place because

three characters are in tune at the same level. Father and mother share a complete agreement: intellectual, emotional, sexual, material. On the left side of the woman we have the Moon, cosmic mother archetype. On the right side of the man, who represents the father, we find the Sun, cosmic paternal archetype. Between these two stars, a new being is born who unites the complementary male and female in the psyche.

The other Tarot couples represent aspects of the necessary union so the Judgment triad can take place.

The Empress and the Emperor, images of the human and passionate couple, look at and understand one another, each ruling over their own domain. The father has awakened the femininity within him, which allows him to realign with his partner's masculinity: the Emperor is seated on a throne where a female eagle incubates an egg. Similarly the mother, with a male eagle on her crest, has awakened the masculinity within herself, which allows her to realign with her partner's femininity. The couple is united, but not closed in, and have a common goal of conscious love, which implies respect for the other, for oneself, and for the world. The child is therefore united with his parents in joy and interconnectedness, and the family, far from being a fortress defending itself against exterior forces, becomes a sacred and open place where all living beings are blessed.

In the next triad the mother and father also have an equally outward action: inhabited by a high spiritual purpose they know the family must open to the world, and each one does the work while maintaining complete solidarity with the family unit. The parents, represented by the High Priestess (with a book that may symbolize writing, education, or account management) and the Pope (flanked by two disciples who do not belong to his bloodline but may be students, employees, or subcontractors), do not face one another but solidly support one another, giving the child the impression of belonging to a supportive and active community that faces outward.

In any case, Judgment remains in the middle because the child who emerges between two parents does not change: he is born open to all possibilities, ready to receive the upbringing his parents provide. If this upbringing has an optimal effect on all the centers and has a high level of Consciousness, the triad will have created a fulfilled child and provided him with a full and positive fate. This is what every human being aspires to. This is rare, however, due to the intense inertia of the past and the forces of repetition acting on the familial, social, and cultural plane.

We can schematically represent this first triad of the perfect union in the following way.

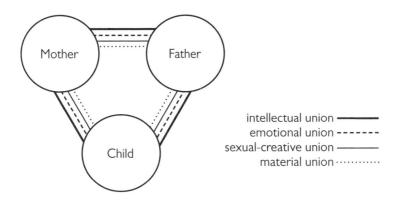

intellectual union ——————
emotional union - - - - - - -
sexual-creative union ——————
material union ············

Perfect Union

In this situation, the child is fully unified with the parents, who themselves have created a whole union. As we have already stated, this triad does not exist in reality but is a necessary reference for the kind of work we propose here. If one of the four possible relationships (intellectual, emotional, sexual-creative, or material) fails, the union cannot be considered perfect.

It may happen that a couple lacks in only one of these areas: the couple shares the same territory and the same budget, the partners understand one another sexually and they love one another deeply, but the two are incapable of aligning their ideas, their beliefs, and their visions of the world. Or else they share ideas in common and communicate in a satisfactory way, understand one another sexually and materially speaking, but are incapable of loving one another.

For other couples, two aspects work and the other two fail. For example, they love and desire one another, but they cannot stop fighting and ultimately pass on to their child the suffering that resulted from material problems. For still other couples three aspects lack agreement; there is only an intellectual, material, or sexual bond, and all of the rest of their interactions lack harmony.

Whatever the case may be, on one plane or another all couples suffer, and their children, raised in a defective union, inherit a negative fate against which they struggle for many years as they strive to fulfill their true purpose.

We will not venture here to give an exhaustive description of what would constitute a perfect triad. This concept can vary according to each triad, even if some elements are universal. In reality, it is up to each couple to imagine, according to their own criteria, what an ideal relationship could be in the four centers for the triad's three protagonists. We simply propose to accompany your reflection upon this domain. As with the exercise on the couple's union, your description of the triad relationship will depend on the specific mother-father couple, mother-child relationship, and father-child relationship. This means that your concept of the fulfilled triad can apply to yourself, your parents, and your entire genealogy tree.

This exercise is indispensible because it is the gap between the ideal relationship the partners can design and the actual imposed relationship that brings awareness to the failings in the genealogy tree. We could argue that it is only our experience with our real family, with all its failings, that can serve as a basis for imagining an ideal family. But this exercise consists precisely of going beyond the criteria of the family formation, to summon all of our adult experience, all the information available including mythological models, to reinvent the most perfect relationship we can imagine. It is through personal effort and the lengths to which we go that the elements of, and the blindness to, our genealogical formation can be discovered.

For example, we may postulate, "The ideal relationship between father and child assumes that the father takes the time to listen to the child, to explain that which the child doesn't understand, to talk of his own occupation in terms the child can integrate, to support the child with schoolwork, to help the child discover themes and theories of personal interest, while always respecting the child's freedom of opinion as the child grows. The father must guide his child without ever making him feel inferior, equally celebrating the child's reasoning and intuitive capacities, accompanying the child's studies while allowing the child to develop his own curiosity." Once this principle is established we can ask ourselves what intellectual father-child relationships really existed in our own genealogy tree, and with a new point of reference for considering whether these relationships were toxic, inadequate, or constructive—even if they had shortcomings.

Exercise: The triad of a perfect union

Here is a list to help you work on each of these relationships.

Ideal Relationship on the Intellectual Plane

- **Between mother and father.** Communication; ideological and moral agreement; languages spoken in the home; level of language; nonviolent communication; freedom of political opinion and of worship; capacity to listen; parents' culture and curiosity; sense of humor.
- **Between mother and child / between father and child.** For these two relationships we look at the way in which language acquisition occurs; how parents respond to the child's questions; how the parents instill and explain rules; what relationship the parents have with the child's academic learning; how the parents value the child intellectually; whether parents and child have a fun relationship; whether parents participate as a witness to their child's work and to

the child's main interests; whether the parents listen to what the child says and take it into account.

Ideal Relationship on the Emotional Plane

- **Between mother and father.** Marks of affection; resolution of conflict; absence of emotional blackmail; absence of jealousy and criticism; tenderness; capacity to forgive; hugs and kisses.

- **Between mother and child / between father and child.** Specific expression of paternal and maternal love (by words, gestures, attitudes); parents' ability to say no with love and to give the child reassuring limits; celebrations; birthdays; the family's emotional rituals; the manner in which the parents assist the child in organizing his negative emotions (grief, fear, disappointment); the ways in which friends and relatives are treated.

Ideal Relationship on the Sexual-Creative Plane

- **Between mother and father.** Imagine the ideal sexual relationship between two people involved in raising children together. How does each person express creativity? What would the parents' involvement be in this domain?

- **Between mother and child / between father and child.** One might ask how the parents accept their child's sexuality; the image of sexuality the parents provide; sexual education; limitations and freedoms; how the parents leave the child to explore his own sexuality; how they behave toward masturbation; if the parents encourage the child's creativity; how the parents let the child play; if the child is protected and given freedom for creative experiences; what image is given of art; what image is given of creativity in general.

Ideal Relationship on the Material Plane

- **Between mother and father.** How do the parents agree on all things concerning their needs and the family's (account management, food, sharing space); how do they share available money; what is their concept of comfort, money, body, and health; are the parents completely independent of toxic substances like tobacco, alcohol, drugs, medicines?

- **Between mother and child / between father and child.** Who earns the household's money; who takes care of the house, groceries, meals, and the child's needs; who provides physical security and how; what is each member's territory; how is the home organized; what is the level of the home's cleanliness; how are meals taken; how is the child introduced to money; what body image do the parents give the child; what relationship does the family have to sports, physical exercise, vacation?

It is advisable to do this work on the triad of ideal union before going on to the next seven triads, or it will cause divisions between one or more family members. These cuts can be total, for example a disappeared parent, or partial, as in the absence of concrete relationships, emotional silence, or refusal to speak. If the failure is made on the sexual-creative plane the mother or father may refuse the son's masculinity or the daughter's femininity. Referring back to the relationship diagrams mentioned in part 4, these links and cuts can take four distinct forms:

Union ●——●
Conflict →←
Separation ⊣⊢
Domination or (over)protection ●——◖●

Any relationship that is not healthy and does not encourage a child to grow corresponds to a toxic relationship. For example, if the father disappeared and the mother creates an exclusive bond and fusion with the child, the triad schematically becomes the following:

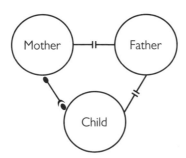

In this situation there is a cut between the child and the father and between the mother and the father, and a link between the mother and the child, but this link is painful.

Similarly, if the parents are so engrossed in their conflicts that they completely neglect their child, the link between the parents is expressed in a conflict style:

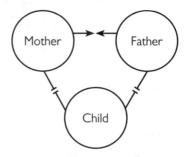

In addition to the child being abandoned, the child will learn to consider the relationship of a couple as something that is, above all else, confrontational.

The following seven triads describe situations ranging from psychological or emotional cuts with a replacement or substitute for the missing parent to serious cuts like mourning or denial of the absent, missing, or abandoned parent. Keep in mind that nothing can compensate for the absence of a father or mother. Replacing birth parents with grandparents, uncles, aunts, siblings, or adoptive parents—in spite of all the love the world—cannot prevent the injury that will become an obstacle to this person's fulfillment. Being deprived of the love of a father or mother induces a feeling of dissatisfaction and incompleteness, which the person must first recognize in order to fill.

We do not explain in detail whether the link or cut occurs as a kind of separation, conflict, overprotection, or domination; that would require more information than this book can contain. These triads represent situations taken in a broad sense, where the link is broken between just two members of the family. Each example, illustrated with two or more cases, makes no claim to offer a complete answer to the situation being discussed, but instead presents ideas of

how to study the triads of your own genealogy tree in terms of relationships and cuts.

The Child Bridge

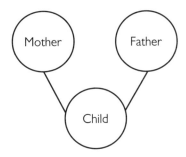

The father and mother are not united. The child, boy or girl, serves as
a point between them. Father and mother often stay together "for the
child." The parents communicate through the child, who is their only
point of union.

Example No. 1: The mother got pregnant on purpose, feigning a con-
traceptive pill oversight, to capture the father, who accepted a marriage in order to avoid being separated from his daughter, but he deeply
desires a wife he can constantly deceive. The only thing that prevents
them from separation is the child shared between them. Until the
daughter was three years old every effort made to reach an agreement
caused anger and misunderstanding. Gradually, they walled themselves
up in silence, united by duty and without any apparent violence. In
cases of dispute or disagreement each tried to win the girl's alliance,
so she felt mentally divided and always guilty for the love she carried
for her father or her mother. When she got close to either one the
other accused her of being a traitor. She lost the vitality of her childhood, attempting to force them make contact, to communicate, but all
attempts failed.

In the case of this young girl this impossible "mission" drove her to
attempt suicide in her teens by leaping from a window, the fall symbolically uniting the sky (paternal) and the earth (maternal). Fortunately

she survived this attempt, then began the work of psychotherapy in which study of the genealogy tree represented an important realization: all genealogy tree couples function more or less on the same model as that of the child bridge.

Example No. 2: In this family, the disunity between the parents turned to violent conflict. The consultant testified, "I was five years old, my parents quarreled more violently than usual. I saw my father raise his fist to punch my mother, who had insulted him. I remember clearly thinking that my mother should not insult my father, she made a mistake, but my father should not hit her either. I ran and got between them, my arms wide open toward my father, and I exclaimed, 'Do not hit her!' My mother took me in her arms, triumphant, and raised me up like a banner, shouting 'You see, you bastard, my child agrees with me!' My father threw 'traitor!' in my face with contempt. This event marked the beginning of a neurosis that lasted until I was forty years old."

The father cannot in any way convince the child that the mother is the enemy. Nor can the mother entirely train him for her camp. The conflicts provoke a tension that lasts for years. It will be hard for a man raised in these conditions to find a woman he respects, and he may develop a tyrannical and possessive character. His psyche will be divided into two opposing personalities. His decisions will lack unity. He will be indecisive, confused, and though he will want to do one thing, he will at the last moment decide to do something else. When he wants to act, a voice on the inside will say, "Hold on!" When he wants to abstain, a voice will say, "Action!"

By telling the child they stay together for him, and that they will separate when he is an adult, the parents impose a nonsensical responsibility on the child. If the parents divorce each will attempt to appropriate the child, without consideration of the child's emotional life. Neither could bear not possessing the child completely, and they will show him their disappointment. The father, in his desire to eliminate the mother, wants to play two roles, and the mother reacts the same way: they both want the mother-father role. They delude themselves: "My child does not have problems; I give him everything." Neither parent can bear to see the resemblance of "the other" (the enemy) in the child.

If the child is male, he risks feminizing and weakening himself in adulthood to become more like his mother in order to preserve her love by not looking too much like his father. If the child is female, she risks becoming a "phallic mother" in the same way.

The couple does not really stay together for the good of the child; rather they are using their own child to avenge what each of their parents subjected them to. The parents want to see their child not built up but destroyed. The neurotic scheme can include inducing very serious illness, and even the child's death. Faced with the trap that they themselves placed, the parents accuse one another without looking at their own relationship.

The Mother Bridge

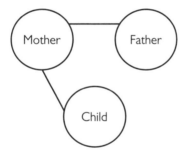

The father and the child are not united. The mother serves as the bridge. The father is either physically absent (abandonment) or psychologically absent.

Example No. 1: The father is physically present but, feeling unloved by his wife, cut ties with her a long time ago and lives apart. The mother poured all of her love into her son, with whom she has a very solid relationship (fusion even), which has driven the father even further away. The son grew up hating the absent, unfair father, whom he regarded as a scoundrel without completely considering the role of his father's wife—his mother, whom he places above everything else.

In response the father, feeling jealous and with his dignity stung, increases his aggression by making fun of the child, criticizing him endlessly, and doing everything possible to castrate and to crush him.

The son asks how his mother could have loved such a man, and how she ever could have even become involved with him. Little by little the child begins to fantasize his mother as an untouchable saint who, at best, will have passively dealt with her hated husband's assaults. He lives simultaneously as the son of the Virgin Mary and the product of marital rape. The mother constantly complains about her husband's absence and inadequacy, exacerbating her son's attitude and inflaming his hatred toward his father. The symbolic couple that she forms with her son allows him to feel eternally young and able to dominate a man. But, in adulthood, our consultant suffers from impotence: his manhood is unbearable because he rejects the part within him that corresponds to his father for fear of losing his mother's exclusive love. Studying the genealogy tree allows him to put the exclusive link attaching him to this woman back into perspective, and to discover that she was actively responsible for the cut with his father.

Example No. 2: Another consultant, in a similar situation, testifies, "Some years ago, a woman read my palm and asked me if I was an orphan. I told her no, and she explained to me that I was missing the line that corresponds to the father. I recalled that at the age of eight I rejected him, and have never spoken another word to him." Actually, the father rejected the daughter. If the child stops talking to the father it is because the father ceased communicating with the child. It is not possible for a child to reject a father if the father loves and treats the child tenderly.

Example No. 3: This woman's parents separated when she was very young. Her father completely bailed on her upbringing. Handed over to an exclusive relationship with her mother, who never remarried, the daughter grew up learning to hate men in general. Her mother's description of sexual relations discouraged her from even trying it.

She became frigid, the few relationships she tried to have with men resulted in sexual fiascos, and she experienced vaginismus, where penetration is painful, even impossible. At thirty years of age, she lived with her mother once again, and they formed a kind of emotional couple. She tried some homosexual experiences, which she says were unsatisfying mainly because the two women with whom she had relationships cheated on their husbands to be with her (as the mother had "cheated" with her father). Men also disappointed her, consciously or not. Feeling rejected by her father caused her to believe that she was not worthy of being loved. Work on the genealogy tree allowed her to reconnect with her father, at least enough to hear his side of the story. His description of what the long separation had done to him enabled her to better understand the genealogy tree's paternal branch, which belongs to her as much as the maternal branch (the only one she knew up to then).

The Father Bridge

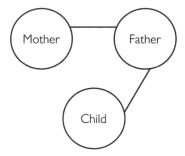

The mother and the child are in conflict, or are separated from one another psychologically or physically. The father serves as the bridge and embodies the principle of balance.

Example No. 1: The mother was nineteen years old when she got pregnant by accident. Her companion at the time, the son of a "good" family, could offer the child a stable environment, but the father's parents demanded the mother relinquish custody of the child. The father maintained a link with the mother, whom he financially supported under the condition that she never again contact the daughter. From time to time, the mother and father were again lovers. At home he reigns as patriarch and wins the naïve admiration and affection of the child, who considers him the tallest and most handsome man in the world. Under the pretext of protecting her, he forbids her from communicating with her mother, whom he considers "assisted" and "incapable." Basically, he is separated from her. The relationship with the parent of the same sex is the cornerstone of the construction of sexual identity. As an adolescent the daughter wishes to meet her mother, and in spite of all the evil said about her the daughter discovers a psychologically fragile woman who had never stopped loving her daughter, and whom the daughter took after physically. Also, on this occasion, she discovered that her mother did not choose to abandon her daughter but obeyed because she thought that was best for her daughter. In spite of the questionable nature of the choices her mother had made, these meetings relieved her and coincided with the "miraculous" healing of a stubborn eczema that she suffered from since childhood. The father, feeling betrayed, blamed and chastised her and withdrew his financial support in order to emerge from the emotional chaos. The young girl then began to study her genealogy tree to understand the neurotic motivations of her exclusive father and her resigning mother.

Example No. 2: The mother lives with her son and husband, but she is a depressed alcoholic. The father controls the family: he praises his son and treats him like a mirror of himself, sometimes using him as an accomplice to humiliate the mother. But he also uses the mother to debase the son. The narcissistic and basically debased father needs to feel dominant to reign over his wife and child. He separates them so that he is the only one whose value is recognized, the absolute center of the family. He feeds on that which he believes to be love of the subordinates, yet the child and mother feed on the hatred. He is the only one who feels loved, provided that his son looks like him.

It is also possible that the child cannot communicate with the mother because the father, an infantile patriarch, is jealous of the child and thus prevents it. Many men have this experience at the birth of their first son: that which was, until then, the man's "my woman" then becomes a mother who concentrates her affection on the newborn. Often, in their own infancy, they did not receive the necessary attention, and becoming adults, they compensate by assuming all the important decisions and plunge mother and child into silent obedience. One may also consider a mother's "disappearance," as in the case in which the father sexually abuses the child (son or daughter) and the mother silently complies with said abuse, pretending not to see anything, or in leaving allows the incestuous act to take place.

The Father-Child Couple

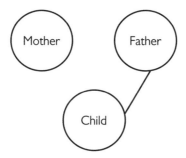

The father and the child communicate, while the mother is absent, expelled, gravely ill, dead, or incapable of establishing a relationship even with her child.

Example No. 1: The mother died when her son was three years old, and the child remained with the father. In the beginning they were united in mourning, but the father refused to remarry once the sorrow had passed, sanctifying the disappeared mother and decreeing that no one could be as good as her. The son, therefore, grew up in a purely masculine home; he submitted to the father and copied him. The absence of any female reference drove him to ignore his own receptivity and intuition. In his own words he became a "macho extremist" who reached adulthood collecting female conquests, but none who satisfied him emotionally. He is prideful, contemptuous, and independent, but pathologically jealous toward these women. His only deep affection is for male friends. In spite of having developed a very obvious virility, because he was separated from his mother he carries sadness and resentment for the maternal tenderness that was absent in his life. This anger pushes him to despise women (who are seen as inferior). He feels he has beaten them, forced them to prostitute themselves, and morally destroyed them. At the same time, under the superman disguise, these relationships are that of a child in search of a mother.

Genealogy tree work made him aware of the fact that his whole life revolved around the belief that "one cannot trust women." He finally realized that he had always searched for the affection of a mother but that this search was, at the same time, tainted with deep shame and a fundamental lack of belief. In order to repair, he must now detach from his father's exclusive example.

Example No. 2: The mother cheated on the father soon after the birth of the child. The father found out, and took the child with him to live in a foreign country. Throughout childhood the little girl heard insults about her mother; despised and considered dirty, the mother was symbolically removed. This negative view of the woman marked her. As the years passed she tended to masculinize herself, becoming first in her class (her father respects intellectual power, considered masculine, and calls the mother "stupid") and keeping her body androgynous, with short hair and masculine clothes. She acts like a tomboy, and a number of physical symptoms crystallize her conflict with femininity including painful menstruation, ovarian cysts, and cystic breasts: her body obeys an unconscious loyalty to the father. The incestuous attraction toward the father drove her to couple with a man much older than she. She hates pregnancy and childbirth is difficult. She develops a competitive character, is contemptuous of women, and specializes in logistics (a professional domain usually reserved for men). She comes to consult because she realized that in spite of her warrior facade she is seeking the impossible—attaining and living a satisfied life while believing that she does not belong anywhere.

If when the mother dies she is idealized and the father then remarries, it can be very difficult for the child to accept the stepmother, considered an intruder who has stolen the father, and the child suffers a "betrayal." A son raised under these conditions may have difficulty being a father because he will have internalized, and will repeat, the life of an adult who betrays.

The Mother-Child Couple

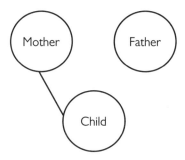

Taking care of the children often falls on the mother when the father disappears. The mother is united with the child but the father is absent, dead, sick, or completely absorbed in himself. He is incapable of transmitting the smallest directive or sharing the least bit of upbringing or affection, not even being present in daily life. When the father is removed, the child (son or daughter) learns to see the world through the eyes of the mother, which drives the child to reproduce the family failure.

Example No. 1: The mother got pregnant from a lover who was passing through and did not want to assume paternity of the son. The mother did not make a lasting link with the father, and the son grew up privately with the mother. This woman, exasperated by the fact that the father refused to have any connection with the son, concentrated her affection on "the little one," who came into puberty without any apparent body hair, and without gaining much weight, keeping his baby appearance until the age of seventeen. The mother, consciously or not, rejected men and did not want to see her son grow up. Nevertheless, she came to consult, worried about her "baby," whose depressive moods alternated with bursts of anger. The mother finally understood that her son was unable to find a male role model worthy of admiration and trust, a guide to fill the void left by the absent father: the son could not integrate the masculine energy he lacked. The mother finally realized that she receives a certain pleasure from his being submissive and dependent on her.

Motivated by a genuine love for her son, the mother accepts the need to undertake the necessary changes to allow him to grow up and become a man. She resumes contact with the father, who seems open; agrees to associate with other men, even if the first step is a simple friendship; fosters her son's stable male relationships (including with a martial arts instructor); and moves so that their bedrooms are no longer attached.

In many cases a son raised by a mother alone, a mother who has been deceived by men, will have all the trouble in the world assuming his manhood and will have to remain a child on the emotional, sexual, and/or mental plane(s). This can lead to him being disgusted by his sperm, to suffer from premature ejaculation, or to experience outbursts of anger or unexplained anxiety. He risks building relationships with women who despise or dominate him. He may also refuse to have children for fear of turning into an absent parent like his own father. It will cost him to cut ties with his mother, whom at the same time he loves (because she represents fundamental security) and hates (because she is invasive and castrating).

Example No. 2: The parents divorced when the daughter was barely one year old. The father moved far away, started a new life, and ceased all contact with his ex-wife and daughter. Finding herself in a situation of partnering with her mother, an actor who did not wish to begin again with a man because she "had her dose," the daughter can become the mother's manly "fiancé" (if the mother is infantile) or feminine "fiancée" (if the mother is phallic). In this case the little girl, who looks a lot like her mother, became her mother's double, locked in a symbolic relationship. The mother treated the daughter like a doll she plays with, made her a confidante, and asked her to be her audience, repeating her monologues in front of the daughter and asking her opinion. When the daughter reached adolescence the mother became her rival, getting plastic surgery and overtly flirting with the boys her daughter brought home. Terrified by the emergence of a young woman who could dethrone her, the mother criticized and devalued her daughter, forbidding the manifestation of her sexuality, and instilling the fear of men in her.

As an adult, the young girl was always a prisoner of this symbiosis. Anguished and living with the impression of "not finding herself," she complained of her own inexistence, continuously sought a vocation, and wondered what purpose she served. Our consultant constantly felt her mother's judgment and influence over her, seeing herself as a "lesser copy" of her mother. The daughter felt invaded by the mother's flesh, to the point of imagining that each time she gained a pound her mother's fat invaded her own body. Riddled by an obscure need to contact her father, she saw her sexuality overshadowed by genital and urinary disorders. The study of the genealogy tree, accompanied by psychotherapy, helped her break this symbiosis with her mother.

The mother-daughter couple can take on a sexual nature. In the case where a stepfather comes into the life of a girl who has a long symbiosis with her mother, it is not unusual that eventually there is "no difference" between mother and daughter, so the stepfather becomes the daughter's lover. Or else the daughter will marry a weak man who lacks character, have children with him, and "offer" her own children to her mother. After the birth(s) the daughter entrusts her child(ren) to her mother to care for and raise—so immature is the daughter that she will live as her own children's big sister, and they will be raised by their grandmother.

Example No. 3: In the case of a united family where the father dies, the son can idealize him beyond measure. It will be difficult for him to become an adult because he will feel the lack of a teacher, a guide who is stronger than he is. He will not be able to find his place and will feel condemned to disappear.

A Venezuelan photographer, whose father (a pilot in the army) crashed during a battle against guerrillas, made a series of self-portrait photographs through a skillful photomontage technique where he was dressed up as Simon Bolivar with a decapitated head floating three feet above his body. When he was a child his mother had idealized her heroic husband, decorating his portrait every day with a fresh rose. It became necessary for the photographer to be a hero in a portrait and—metaphorically dead and butchered like his father was in the accident—thereby receive his mother's love.

Example No. 4: A girl who finds herself separated from her father will suffer from his absence and, upon becoming a woman, will not have heard a father's tender and loving words telling her "You are beautiful" or "What a lovely voice you have," which would have helped to develop her femininity. When the father disappears, the daughter may tend to turn toward the "other life," the realm of the dead, to search for him. Instead of her father, the daughter will love a phantom. As an adult, she risks engaging in relationships with idealized, absent, or ill men who have difficulty fully incarnating.

A woman who had many accidents that forced her to stay in the hospital remembers that when she was a child her alcoholic father took her for walks, stopping in all the neighborhood bars for a drink, returning home only under the daughter's guidance, drunk and happy. The little girl, having become his guide, loved it and wouldn't think of criticizing. But her father fell very ill and had to go to the hospital, where he finally died. Entry to this establishment was off limits to children. Having never again seen her father, she felt the hospital had held him prisoner, stealing him from her. As an adult, she unconsciously caused accidents to be able to enter hospitals, where she searched for traces of her dear father.

Example No. 5: A mother kept hidden from her daughter the fact that the man who raised her was not her biological father. When the daughter became an adult, the mother admitted the truth. The daughter entered into a deep crisis because her supposed father, on whom she had projected a repressed incestuous desire, is revealed to be a man like all the others with whom she could, theoretically, conceive a child. The discovery of this lack of co-ancestry rocks the incest taboo. In the Unconscious of this young woman, the caresses that she received from him could have been traced to a lover. This ambiguity weighs on her emotional life.

The Exclusive Parent Couple

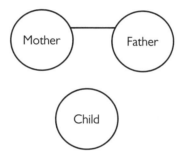

The father and mother enclose themselves in a relationship that excludes the child, unable to see the truth of what they are doing. Parents who behave this way are incapable of conscious love. Whether by wrapping themselves in a narcissistic relationship that satisfies them as they ignore their child, or by uniting against the child to abuse him, they will cause the child to lack confidence, which will contaminate all other aspects of his future life—especially as these parents, while concealing the conflicts in their own relationship, pretend to be perfect parents.

Example No. 1: "My parents loved one another enormously," explains the consultant, initially describing his parents as exclusively turned toward one another and apparently idealized by others—beautiful, envied by those around them, always bold in their opinions. As a child he adhered to the belief that his parents were wonderful and that the family was very close, which gave him a sense of security. But by deifying these toxic parents, he completely devalued himself. In reality his childhood was a collection of flagrant injustices: they deprived him of vacations; he was left in the care of a housekeeper while his parents gave themselves luxurious destinations; at the age of five he stayed alone in the house while the parents partied all night with their friends. He became imprisoned by a childish reasoning that caused him to believe that he deserved this kind of bad treatment. "I am to blame, my parents are perfect, and since I was wrong, they are right to not love me." The repetition of this kind of abuse can cause the child to habitually and automatically adopt a false personality each time similar circumstances occur. He may then embed this in his essential Being, which drives him to live in a self-destructive way. In our consultant's case he slashed his skin with razor blades, relieved each time by the physical pain, which recalled his own existence. The study of the genealogy tree allowed him to revise his version of the story, and he became aware that he was not the ugly duckling villain in a perfect family but the innocent victim of two immature egotists.

The son or daughter who was invisible on the psychological or emotional plane in childhood tends to live invisibly in adulthood as well. The parents of such a child are generally infantile, and by forcing their child into a parental role they rob him of his childhood. This negation of the child can lead to all kinds of abuse: verbal violence, insults, criticism, ridicule, emotional cruelty, blackmail, sexual abuse, and ill treatment concerning food, living space, or social relationships.

Example No. 2: A couple goes into a restaurant and leaves a one-year-old child in the car in the scorching heat. At the end of the meal, an hour later, they find the child unconscious and dehydrated. Furious, they run to the hospital, cursing the heat but not their own negligence.

Mother and father live their lives together, but the child does not belong and once out of childhood will have to make an enormous effort to accept that anyone can love him. As an adult he is constantly angry, depressed, or attracted to death. There is the tendency, when a child is not loved by parents who nevertheless love one another (and/or a sibling), for him to consider himself essentially defective, undeserving of life, even to the point of hating himself.

The couple can be alcoholics or drug addicts, objects of terror and shame for their child. Otherwise weakened, sick, or deeply depressed, they may force their child to take care of them or to work to support the family. This can also apply to obsessive perfectionists who require adult behavior and attitudes of their child in spite of his age. Under the mask of "parent buddy," these parents can cause their child to become an accomplice to their secrets, sexual or otherwise, reducing the parent-child relationship to a frightening bond.

This triad can drive a person to become involved in abusive relationships, as he may associate intimacy with suffering and abandonment. The person has a great deal of difficulty really knowing who he is, what he feels, or what he wants. He fears others will cease to love him if they discover his true personality.

The Total Cut

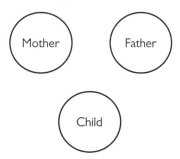

There is no communication between father, mother, and child. It is a household where each person is enclosed in him- or herself, in indifference or in hatred. This family does not know how to engage with the world either. This can also apply to an orphan who never knew his parents, and who has no idea about the relationship that exists between them. It is unusual for this triad to exist in its "pure state" because there is usually a relationship, even if negligible, between at least two of the protagonists. In the case of total isolation this triad can lead to tragic outcomes, like schizophrenia, cancers, heart disease, tuberculosis, suicide, and fatal accidents.

Example No. 1: "As far back as I can remember, our house was sad. My parents hardly spoke a word to one another as they lived together simply for lack of imagination. They were passive and thought that the only thing left to do was to wait to die. Later, in reading my mother's diary after her death, I discovered that she cherished a dream that some handsome stranger would take her out of the situation. After forty years, she still dreamed like a little girl. My parents dressed and fed me, but we had hardly any other relationship. At a very young age, I left the house and took to the street. From ashrams to hippie communes, I finally learned, and even if everything wasn't rosy, I can say that this human community taught me to live and to emerge from this pitiful childhood."

In this case, the child was begotten without any pleasure, without love, and without Consciousness. He was given nothing more than a roof, food, and certain material comforts. His relationships with others were cut off, the family being a kind of private club where strangers were not allowed. Unable to build a strong sense of self-esteem, he believed he had no value or ability, and he felt unworthy of being loved. A person raised this way may seek refuge in drugs, theft, or prostitution. A miraculous chance may put the person in contact with conscious and charitable beings who will allow him to open up, and in so doing learn to establish healthy bonds with the world and with himself.

Example No. 2: "Both of my parents died in a car accident when I was a baby. My paternal aunt took me in and brought me up in the cult of her brother (my father), whose photos adorned the whole house. She hardly ever spoke of my mother, and never about the relationship between my parents. It was a huge relief for me, in adulthood, to find one of my mother's childhood friends who told me the story of my parents' encounter and the love that united them. I finally had the impression that I came from somewhere, and I no longer floated above my own life."

A child orphaned by the loss of both parents due to illness or accident will tend to have a disproportionate idealization of them and may remain emotionally frozen at the age at which she lost them. If the deaths occurred during the child's adolescence, a sexual blockage can result from the parents' inability to help the child move through puberty and begin adulthood. It can lead to persistent immaturity, which may drive the orphan into an adulthood marked by childish, indecisive, or irresponsible behaviors, unless she chooses one or more figures to serve as her spiritual guardians.

An abandoned child in the care of a public agency has a missing genealogy tree. Sometimes he will find an institution that welcomes him, with people who play the roles of mother and father, but throughout life he will carry a hidden deficiency that will have an effect on his conduct. Often, an orphan invents an imaginary genealogy tree as well suited to study as a genetic tree. Occasionally this imaginary tree becomes immeasurably exalted, with dreams of grandeur, which contributes to a devaluing of his adoptive family.

An abandoned child fights to find her place, her personal territory. She constantly seeks the procreators who abandoned her with an overwhelming desire to forgive them, unconsciously believing that this forgiveness will make them give her the love they owe her. Even if the adoptive parents treat the abandoned child as well as possible, she can nourish an unconscious bitterness because the love and attention lavished on her by the adoptive parents may be a cruel reminder of what was missed from the biological parents. It is always advisable for an abandoned child to have as much information as possible about her biological tree, and to know (in due time) the reason why her parents abandoned her. Otherwise, it will be hard to accept the identity acquired from her adoptive parents.

Some Variations on the Triad

The triad can be more complex, depending on the life situation. For anyone who wants to set up the triads of a genealogy tree it helps to gradually learn how to make a drawing of the relationships in a more elaborate way.

Here are two examples of complex situations, and of their possible representations.

Example No. 1: The triad becomes a quartet when the father imposes a sexual partner onto the family, transforming the couple into a trio. Seeking balance, the mother compensates by strengthening her relationship with the child, and she attempts to renounce the "guilty" father, with whom she is nevertheless an accomplice.

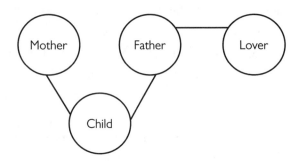

"My father and mother, since the beginning of their relationship, never agreed on anything. When I was little, my father recognized his homosexuality. He brought a man to the house and proposed to my mother that they make a trio. It pained me to see my father with this man and my mother immersed in solitude. But even if I took my mother's side, I never stopped loving my father. My mother took me as a confidante in hatred toward him, whom she saw as a 'degenerate.' As I deeply loved her, I began to see my father through her eyes. As I grew up, I doubted the virility of men: I never stopped falling in love with homosexual men, whom I ended up hating because they left me unsatisfied. Today, my father is dying of AIDS. I take care of him, which allows me to express my love for him, which allows me to finally look at men without hatred."

Example No. 2: Murder in the triad. While very rare, this type of situation illustrates the fact that an extremely confrontational relationship can lead to a definitive separation when a violent father kills the mother. And in this case the child was actually cut off from two parents: from the mother by death, and from the father by guilt.

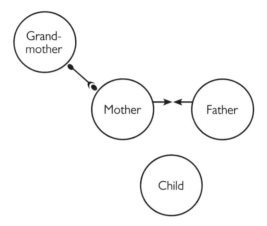

"Amédée and Joséphine, my parents, married against my maternal family's will. Josée, my maternal great-grandmother, opposed it when she saw Amédée, my mother's then fiancé, abusing her. The abuse never stopped. . . . When my mother realized she was pregnant, she felt a great sorrow because she was going to bring into the world a being destined to suffer in a home in a permanent state of civil war. However, she resigned herself to it. The first time I was aware of the ambivalence that prevailed in my family, I was four years old. My father, knife in hand, threatened my mother with death. That night I suffered a traumatic shock that resulted in infant epilepsy that lasted until I was twelve years old. From that moment on, I began to oppose my father and to defend my mother until he succeeded in killing her in one blow with a hammer. All my life I fought men. I found myself automatically in conflict with them. I know all of that has been programmed into my

Unconscious and I did not have the choice. But now that I am beginning to be conscious of it, I would like to change some aspects of my life
that are not useful and do not contribute to my nature."

THE GENEALOGY TREE
AS A WEB OF TRIADS

We have seen that the triad can take very elaborate shapes, marrying the infinite complexities of relationships to the interior of the
mother-father-child trio. Nevertheless, it is useful to begin with a diagram for the Metagenealogy of the tree. The inverse to what is done in
psychoanalysis and psychotherapy, Metagenealogy tremendously simplifies the relationships that preceded and formed us in order to better
enable us to demystify them.

Noting that "my mother did not have a satisfying relationship
with my father" or "my father was marked by absolute harmony with
his own mother" allows us to distance ourselves from these relationships, as if we attended the performance of a family that is not our own.
Understanding this "saga"—the eccentricities and the unspoken—is the
beginning of awareness, which places us as independent adults in opposition to the genealogy tree.

We saw that the past exerts its repetitive influence over a series of
more or less objective elements, like first names, birth dates, ages at
which the persons had their first child or met their spouses, deaths, and
professions. Identifying these repetitions allows us to disengage, little by
little, from the genealogy tree trap and to more or less consciously cease
to think according to these beliefs, to live following these laws, or to be
bound by loyalties to what came before, which we have seen are forms
of ownership.

The study of the tree allows us to acquire as much lucidity as is
possible toward our heritage. To do this, we must begin by "reducing,"
precisely because of the enormous influence our heritage exerts on us.

On the other hand, the whole complexity of our own person comes into play so that, faced with a legacy that has now become intelligible, we can determine the elements that weigh on us. While we may decide to conserve or leave some in place, that which we undertake to transform—using a variety of creative, symbolic, and ritual approaches—will allow us to integrate a new reality that is better aligned with our deep aspirations. It is a bit like deciding what to throw out, keep, or change when one inspects the furniture and objects of an old family home.

To accomplish this, the work on our own triad will extend to the whole genealogy tree. Indeed, the destiny of a child, forged and imposed by the parents, depends on what those parents inherited from their own parents and those who came before. The diagram of relationships in the genealogy tree, under the simplified version, will therefore take the aspect of a web of seven triads as shown below, where the bonds are represented by dotted lines. In each case, it should be noted if there is a union, a conflict, a separation, or a domination.

The Genealogy Tree as a Web of Triads

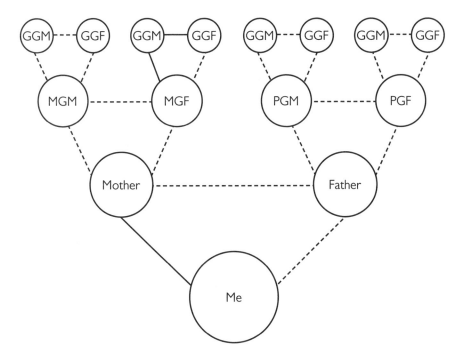

This first example of relationships in our tree is founded on the transmission of the direct line of every family member (me, my father, my mother, my grandparents); each member of the tree is seen as his or her parents' only child. Later we will diagram the tree's relationships taking all the members (brothers, sisters, aunts, uncles, people of decisive influence) into account, the goal being to learn how things like links, cuts, assaults, and injuries string together and repeat in our genealogy tree.

In general the triad concerns the first seven years of life. The triad does not, in fact, have a permanent character. Changes are produced by external events like war, catastrophe, ruin, grave illness, fantastic success, relocation, exile, divorce, or death of a parent; by parents' awareness; or by a child who disrupts the tree's relationships. The key here is to discover the **triad's first form,** which will mark our path for the rest of our lives. The parents' reception of a child in the first six or seven years of life is a link created during this critical period, and it determines a basic tone. This tone is what we must learn to recognize.

Exercise: The tree of triads

For each of the genealogy tree triads, establish the most exact relational diagram possible. The further back in time you go, in general the fewer elements you will have on a couple's relationship and on that of the parent-child relationship. And, due to an excess of information, you may also have more difficulty in establishing your own triad.

Based on the amount of information at your disposal, you can proceed with this in three successive stages.

- For the relationships that you know well (your own triad and, where appropriate, that of your father and mother), define the child-mother-father relationship in each of the four centers (emotional, intellectual, sexual-creative, material). For these twelve relationships, determine if their essential connection is through union, conflict, separation, or domination/protection. Define each triad in comparison with the dominating climate of childhood. For example, if the child was loved until the birth of a little brother, and the child then felt that the mother was distant, the dominant tone is separation from the mother. Similarly, and a well-loved parent dies during childhood, the mourning may set a more dominant tone than the separation. Conversely, if in adulthood one restores a bad relationship with the parents, but during childhood and adolescence the relationship was essentially conflicting, the dominant tone is conflict.

- Once you have determined the relational tone between the three protagonists in the four centers (intellectual, emotional, sexual-creative, material), it is necessary to summarize them into only one dominant tone. For example, if the mother-son relationship is lacking intellectually, sexually dominant, and emotionally and materially protective, the dominant tone will be domination/protection. If the father-mother relationship is united in a common ideology, conflicting in the material, and non-united sexually and emotionally, the dominant tone will be disunion.

For the triads that you know less about, try to note as precisely as possible the nature of the relationship between the three protagonists.

- Again reduce these relationships to a link—was it heavy, toxic, exclusive, conflicting? Or, in the absence of a link, was there separation, absence, ignorance, intermittent conflict without relationship continuity? Following this, reconnect the triads among them.

Each triad is now defined by the three relationships that summarize it. But the goal of this exercise is not to represent the genealogy tree with an absolute exactitude but more to begin visualizing the tree as a kind of piping system where according to a logic that links generations the love, attention, and communication flow, clog, or interrupt—sometimes for worse, sometimes for better.

SIBLINGS

Between Conflict and Collaboration

If every child tends to consider himself an only son or daughter, the family dreams it is a quartet. The most commonly held image of an ideal family is, in fact, composed of a father, a mother, an older brother, and a younger sister. This concept is highly linked, as we will see, to the patriarchal tradition of transferring the family legacy to the eldest son. If the family grows beyond two children, the parents unconsciously expect a new boy in the third position, then a girl in the fourth, and so on. (Of course, depending on family history, the basic scheme has exceptions.)

In the collective Unconscious, siblings are the primary representation of rivalry and, ultimately, of fratricide. A number of myths give us tragic history and rivalries between siblings that end in murder: Romulus killed his twin brother Remus, with whom he founded the city of Rome, because Remus challenged his brother by vaulting the sacred line drawn in the ground. The jealous brother Seth, who reigned over the barren lands, killed the Egyptian god Osiris.

Myths that concern siblings of larger numbers show factions organized by brothers and sisters where one or the other remain faithful to the parents. Therefore, in Aztec mythology, the pious mother-goddess Teteoinan, having created the stars and gods, gets pregnant by miracle while she is in prayer in the temple. Her daughter, Coyolxauhqui, believing her mother was dishonored, pushes the brothers Centzonhuitznahua (stars in the southern sky) to behead her. This barbaric act is narrowly prevented by the birth of Huitzilopochtli, god of sun and war, who emerges from his mother's belly fully armed, ready to massacre his sister and his weak brothers.

Siblings are the first model of all of society. Agitated by tensions, they can lead us to open warfare, torture, and murder. They are also the preeminent community, with an ideal of love, sharing, and successful collaboration.

The myth of Cain and Abel* can be interpreted in different ways. Some commentators even see traces of an old rivalry between sedentary tribes (like Cain) and nomads (like Abel, the shepherd). But if we read the text literally, we can isolate several interesting features.

Cain, born first, becomes the farmer, metaphorically taking possession of the land like the eldest in the family takes possession of all physical and psychic space available. One of the possible etymologies of his name in Hebrew is "I have acquired." Abel, the younger brother, whose etymology could be "precarious existence," arrives at already acquired terrain and becomes a shepherd. In other words, he plans to survive on that which is available, adopting and taking care of a living multitude.

It is Cain, the eldest, who takes the initiative to make God an offering. His younger brother, Abel, imitates him but with a twist: if Cain simply sacrifices "fruits of the earth," Abel will offer him "the flock's

---

*Genesis 4:1–15: "Adam made love to his wife Eve, and she became pregnant and gave birth to Cain. She said, 'With the help of the Lord I have brought forth a man.' Later she gave birth to his brother Abel. Now Abel kept flocks, and Cain worked the soil. In the course of time Cain brought some of the fruits of the soil as an offering to the Lord. And Abel also brought an offering—fat portions from some of the firstborn of his flock. The Lord looked with favor on Abel and his offering, but on Cain and his offering he did not look with favor. So Cain was very angry, and his face was downcast. Then the Lord said to Cain, 'Why are you angry? Why is your face downcast? If you do what is right, will you not be accepted? But if you do not do what is right, sin is crouching at your door; it desires to have you, but you must rule over it.' Now Cain said to his brother Abel, 'Let's go out to the field.' While they were in the field, Cain attacked his brother Abel and killed him. Then the Lord said to Cain, 'Where is your brother Abel?' He replied, 'I don't know. Am I my brother's keeper?' The Lord said, 'What have you done? Listen! Your brother's blood cries out to me from the ground. Now you are under a curse and driven from the ground, which opened its mouth to receive your brother's blood from your hand. When you work the ground, it will no longer yield its crops for you. You will be a restless wanderer on the earth.' Cain said to the Lord, 'My punishment is more than I can bear. Today you are driving me from the land, and I will be hidden from your presence; I will be a restless wanderer on the earth, and whoever finds me will kill me.' But the Lord said to him, 'Not so; anyone who kills Cain will suffer vengeance seven times over.' Then the Lord put a mark on Cain so that no one who found him would kill him. Then Cain went away from the presence of the Lord, and settled in the land of Nod, east of Eden."

firstborn." This can be interpreted in two ways: in sacrificing the first-born, Abel metaphorically sacrifices his brother, who is the firstborn and regarded as "the best." This returns us to the admiration felt by the younger brother toward the elder brother, mixed with the desire to eliminate him. Abel sacrifices that which is the best, while Cain, legitimately eldest in the land, is not ready to offer an authentic sacrifice, as sharing is already a lot for him.

God favors Abel's offering, those lives in which he shed blood fore-shadowing his own sacrifice, returning us to the fact that the favorite in the family is always paradoxically sacrificed because being the preferred child is a burden that reduces the amount of affection received from the brothers and sisters.

When Cain, agitated by his own jealousy, reveals a "downcast" expression, the Lord notices immediately, representing the attentive unconditional parent who does not ignore his child's feelings. God gives him the following choices: If you do well, shall you not be accepted? And if you do not well, sin lies at the door and you shall be its desire, and you must rule over it.

This fundamental choice is that which will govern war or peace: the first movement, the "sin" or "fault" (or the "lurking beast," according to other translations), is that of Cain's jealousy, which finally triumphs and drives him to murder. But the choice exists, and the care that is shown in how the Lord addresses Cain registers the choice for all of mankind. If Cain accepts the sacrifice of his ego—his desire to have everything, to be first in everything (as Abel did, sacrificing his lambs for it)—he will be distinguished, and upon abandoning the personal satisfaction of unlimited ownership he will discover the transpersonal joy of sharing. Moreover, once the murder has taken place and Cain's banishment is announced, his lineage will learn the lesson because all his descendants in the tribe will become nomadic farmers, like Abel was. Seth, Eve's third son, will begin the lineage that leads to David and Joseph, Jesus's adoptive father—once the fratricidal struggle happens, the third son (who has learned the lesson) will beget conscious humanity.

This creation myth from Judeo-Christian culture brings us back to the siblings as the **first place of otherness, and of complementarity, rivalry, and sharing.** Competition is at the heart of being siblings, with this fundamental issue: children learn to live among their peers in the privacy of their homes as much as in their early socialization experiences at school or day care. The attitude of adult educators (which is based on their own experiences toward their brothers, sisters, and friends) will be crucial in facilitating the child's adaption to life in society. The ideal would be for each person to ultimately live both as a sovereign individual and as a member of the community. It is very rare that one arrives at adulthood in a state of serenity toward others, which is to say, toward the person's own siblings.

Sibling conflicts ultimately lead to conflicts in everyday life. The problems of rivalry among siblings always bring us back to the same request: to be loved by one's parents—that is, to save one's life. A child's need for love, security, and attention is always thwarted by a multiplicity of challenges that face parents: everyday life stresses, accidents, and economic, emotional, or professional difficulties.

When parents bring up their children with an extreme lack of consciousness, or even maliciousness, they put their powerlessness, anger, and worn-out solutions from their pasts onto the siblings. Thus, fixed hierarchies are born. And, while apparently useful for keeping order, these hierarchies are devastating for children placed in dominating or subordinate positions. Whether in the form of comparisons, exposed preferences, or exclusions, they forever mark the fate of future adults. Each time parents fail to respond to a child's requests in an acceptable way, whether agreeing to or refusing to do something constructively, the child solidifies his failure as an element of his neurotic future identity.

Under the protective mechanisms discussed above, in adulthood these old sibling rivalries leading to conflict among peers are always oriented toward a higher authority that represents the parents: the boss at work who doesn't know how to "separate" the employees; parents or in-laws who oversee the couple's quarrels, making a brother or sister of the partner. There are also battles in the name of an abstract entity (God, justice, peace) or two rival factions, each with an honest belief in fighting for the sake of ideal parenting.

The following discussion will offer some ways to understand how suffering may be experienced among siblings through the genealogy tree for several generations.

RAISING SIBLINGS

The Challenge of Sharing

We have seen that siblings, strictly speaking, begin with the quartet (ideally a son and then a daughter). A sibling, at the same time, creates and threatens the triad. The first child made the couple parents for the first time. After the first child, parenting ripens: no parent is the same toward every child, and no parent is the same toward a household where little beings demand more and more attention and care. With each addition, a newcomer raises the increasingly more complex question of sharing. We have seen that for the first child balanced sharing leads to a balanced triad, where each is in a relationship with the other on the four planes: emotional, mental, sexual-creative, material. How time, space, needs, desires, feelings, and words are shared is important, not only among siblings, but also between parents and children.

If we return to the foundations of Judeo-Christian society, two examples of sharing illustrate the ideal of pooling an unlimited abundance rather than competing with each other. In Jewish thought, the Talmudic philosophy expresses sharing on the intellectual plane: the rabbis gather to comment on the Torah, each gives his interpretation, no one refutes it, the Lord decides in an unknowable way. Basically, he who is chosen by God will be the future reader of the Talmud, meaning that each individual's ethical, intellectual, and spiritual responsibility is respected. There is no competition between the various opinions. The process does not have to do with finding the correct interpretation that will make this one or that one the favored child, but with an abundance of virtually unlimited thought intended for what is most important, Spirit—which is wholly capable of accommodating all individual thought.

Similarly, at the Last Supper, Christ symbolically shares his flesh and blood with the twelve "sons" who are his apostles. During this meal, there is no competition because total love reigns there. But each one of the apostles has his own specificity in the eyes of Christ. The ritual of the mass reproduces this feast where dinner was shared in total love; each one of the faithful can will themselves to receive the body of Christ from the hand of the priest who represents him without feeling that his neighbor's wafer will deprive him of his share.

These two models, very different in appearance and very similar in principle, summarize the basic desire of each child who has siblings: he doesn't want less than total love, total attention, and total recognition. Because genuine sharing is not a division of a limited commodity into even more limited but equal parts. It is, contrarily, the fragmentation of the infinite into an infinity of equally unlimited pieces of which each piece is the totality. One can only share that which is limitless. **Sharing is the portion of the totality—of love, life energy, senses—and not its division.**

Every child's complaint or requirement comes from this request, whether for more cake, one minute of attention, a garment, a toy . . . the more urgent the appeal, the more it means the child does not feel loved. Faced with endless occurrences of this fundamental demand, the parents are called upon to act in terms of the family. In Consciousness, starting from the essential Being, parents find themselves in the same situation as a Zen practitioner placed in front of a koan, where riddles with no possible response cannot be resolved except by going beyond the mental and individual limitations.

This is not an easy task. With all the best intentions in the world, many parents who are anxious to do the right thing unwittingly adopt attitudes that they hope will free them of their own upbringing, but that are actually a reaction to it—and that unfortunately prove toxic. We have seen the tree's trap is not only by way of reproduction, but also by more devious forms of repetition, particularly compensation and opposition.

There are also parents who exhaust themselves, and their surroundings, trying to respond to every one of their child's demands, eager to give him everything they did not receive, leading to an infant-king who occupies the space of an adult, monopolizing conversations and multiplying whims, believing he deserves the attention. The parents live according to the infantile schedule, sacrificing their own. Caught in a trap, the parents' actions are in compensation and opposition to their own upbringing. Having been frustrated by strict rules and categorical refusals, they show themselves incapable of opposing their own child's desires, or of imposing prohibitions in a caring way by saying "no" with love. Children raised this way lack reference points and have trouble finding the kinds of limits that can reassure them. This can result, for example, in sleeping difficulties that betray a deep anxiety related to lack of structure.

Under the same mechanism, the parents who have suffered from a lack of communication in their own families spend their time explaining everything to their toddler, even to the point of asking him for advice. Therefore, we see some parents engaged in long parlays with a three-year-old child on whether he wants vanilla or strawberry ice cream, or they may embark on an endless conversation with a child to find out whether he is tired or not. Actually, there again, this lack of decisiveness on the parents' part is distressing for the child and can lead to attacks of rage that the clueless parents cannot explain.

The family situations where one child over another is preferred (for example, because he is the first male heir) are equally harmful, not only for the siblings who suffer the injustice but also for the favored child. As a general rule, a child who is not brought up with sharing will always want everything for himself. His siblings, members of his society, his colleagues, and fellow citizens will always be rivals. He will live in a world of rivalry and competition, endlessly comparing what he received with what others received. He will always need something more in order to feel "preferred" or "favored" and to feel that he exists. The consumer frenzy in which today's society is immersed is in large part based on a lack of sharing and a lack of justice.

Just as the solution to a Zen koan comes from a mental mutation obtained through meditation and nonidentification with personal thoughts, the solution to the paradox of sharing—everything is for me, and everything is for everyone else too—can only come from changing the level of Consciousness, which corresponds to a new birth. One must emerge from the level of Consciousness of one's own family to raise one's children to share.

Using a typical family meal as an example, when it is time for dessert the cake is divided into absolutely equal parts among parents, brothers, and sisters. Everything is seemingly perfect, until suddenly one of the children calls for more cake, but there is none left. Under duress, between the hard material limit and the request of the child (who wants limitlessness), many inappropriate reactions are possible (and frequent). To the annoyed parents, who are rivals with their own children, this demand can send them back to their own personal failings and they may respond like this:

- "Who do you think you are? There is no reason for you to get more than anyone else."
- "Oh well, there isn't any more. There! That's life! You can't always have what you want."
- "You never have enough! You are too fat anyway."

All aggressive reactions have a negative effect on the child's opinion of himself.

On another, parents who are well intentioned but incapable of solving any problems will feel guilty about their own parenting ability and may respond, for example, in the following ways:

- "I'm sorry. There's no more. I will make more just for you." (A reaction of goodwill, but the drawback is that it puts the parent at fault, which is distressing for the child.)
- "Everyone already took all of it." (This reduces sharing to material dissection, where each one receives the same thing, and is therefore a negation of personal identity.)
- "Here, take my piece. I'm not hungry anymore." (Obviously, the others will be jealous of this favor.)
- "You want some chocolate? A cookie?" (This ignores any underlying reasons for the child's request, reducing it to a desire for sweet food.)

The response of a parent in Consciousness is, actually, a process of listening. This begins with a question: Are you still hungry? The child is returned to his sovereignty, not to an all-powerful illusion, and can then express his needs.

The parent can ask him, if he really is hungry, "Since there is no more cake, what would you like to eat instead?" After feeding the child more (if needed), the parent should moreover assess the child's initial request, which was "one more piece of cake," this time approaching it figuratively to address an actual request for love. This additional piece could materialize as a type of coupon, "good for a slice of cake," that the child can exchange when he feels the need for more dessert, a hug, a toy, a half hour of cartoons, or some other activity of his choice—anything that requires his parents' consent.

In fact, the child who requests more cake is only further expressing the parents' unconscious dissatisfaction that drives them to hold back, in any given moment, something they could give to the child but they fail to acknowledge. For each child, this requested fragment of all that he claims will have a particular flavor: one will use his coupon "good for a slice of cake and more," the other will request a moment for dialogue, the third will even offer a drawing and will appreciate having it hung on the wall.

However, the desire to be loved more than anyone else may nest beneath a child's request. In fact, when the family fails to provide authentic sharing everyone is frustrated, and the resulting lack of strength develops a neurotic need to devour parental attention, which has nothing to do with "what we need," but rather with "having it all." If that is the case, it helps to teach the child a sense of sharing and community. Returning to the cake anecdote, it may be useful to propose the following: "Because there is no more cake, I am going to show you how to make one so, in the future, you can have more if you wish." The parent takes the time to do the necessary shopping with the child and then, in the kitchen with the siblings' participation as witnesses and assistants if they wish, the parent teaches the child to bake a cake that he will then proudly share with the whole family.

Here again the Tarot shows us the way with two great cosmic archetypes, the Sun and the Moon, which represent the cosmic Father and the cosmic Mother equally lighting the way. With endless generosity their "children" all receive the same attention and the same quality of listening—no one taking precedence over the other.

In the Sun, there are two brothers in a position of support. In the Moon, we see a landscape with three animals who look up to her with the same request, to which she replies without discrimination.

These different examples illustrate that it is not about presenting lessons to educate children, but understanding what the ideal situation would be that will offset the injuries and distortions that mark siblings in the family tree.

COMPARISONS, PREFERENCES, HIERARCHIES, PUNISHMENTS

Toxic Siblings

Lacking the tools required to achieve the ideal of sharing, parents who are prisoners of the genealogy tree trap employ actions that include these four principal strategies, intending to contain what they feel is the chaos of unmanageable individuality among the siblings:

- Establish hierarchies
- Affirm their preference
- Influence the children by comparing them
- Inflict corporal punishment on them

All of these strategies result in each person's richness and individuality becoming locked in a fixed role similar to a dungeon, which can lead to psychological wounds that lead to aggressive or self-destructive behavior in adulthood. Year after year family celebrations show how this playacting is repeated and, when played by adults, causes caricatures to develop. People outside the family are frightened witnesses of the rituals between the "favorite," the "rebel," the "sweetie," the "unloved," the "beautiful," the "sick," the "scapegoat," the "clone of dad," the "mom," and so forth. It is often easier to identify the family comedy of others ahead of our own, and is an excellent exercise in awareness that helps reveal the dysfunction of one's genealogy tree.

Also remember that all conflicts between parents will increase the likelihood of problems among siblings. The child, spontaneously loyal to both parents (unless forced to take sides with one or the other), is going to live with the parents' disagreements as an internal conflict. When it comes to two or more siblings, the conflict will reverberate between brothers and sisters, with some taking the mother's side, others taking the father's side.

Making the Hierarchy

The hierarchy allows the parents to confine each sibling to a precise place and function while delegating some authority to the "highest ranking" brother(s) and/or sister(s). The hierarchy is particularly practical in large families, where the eldest are required to take charge of younger siblings in order to relieve the parents of their childrearing tasks.

The immense disadvantage of this strategy is that it establishes the position of each brother and sister for life: "dominant" or "dominated," "nice" or "bad," "laborer" or "intellectual," "servant" or "served," they will probably grow up to be what they were ordered to be in the home. This concept of siblings as an army or internment camp can give rise to a lot of sexual abuse, as well as to physical and psychological torture, which the parents carefully avoid becoming aware of. A child, even an older child, is not mentally ready or capable of raising another child and may always feel ambivalent toward this request even if she appears satisfied with receiving the parents' love. Consequently, the child may exercise cruelty toward the younger siblings because she lacks the moral boundaries acquired in adulthood.

Standardization and Comparison

These two approaches go together, arising from the parents' incapacity to appreciate each child for who he is without trying to make him conform to a mold.

Standardization is a common, and very primitive, psychological method that overvalues similarities: common traits between parents and child, family resemblance, family culture, mannerisms. One frequently sees children all dressed the same, or each one forced to learn a given musical instrument to have his place in the family concert, and if the newcomer does not like the clarinet, too bad for him, the piano is already taken.

In standardization, as with comparison, the parents establish a model of perfection that corresponds to their own generally dissatisfying quests. Incapable of reaching their own ideals, they impose them on their children. Thus we frequently see a daughter whose mother is obsessed with her own weight become anorexic in order to comply with the mother's unreasonable standard of beauty.

Like standardization, comparison attaches an unchangeable objective that serves to convince a child that he must be something other than what he is by providing an outside model. This creation of abstract standards uproots individuality. Similarity to the rest of the family or to arbitrarily established models is valued, not difference.

Comparison, a tool of classic manipulation, allows parents to repress their own needs, feeling, desires, or ideas. By doing so they can evade the responsibility of taking charge in the relationship with their children, and avoid the risk of being contradicted or confronted with their own limitations.

The sentence, "Look at your brother, he is smart! He tidied up his room!" imposes the parents' wish (we want you to clean your room) on the children in the form of a conditional requirement for obtaining their appreciation, which is a limited commodity.

Similarly, instead of saying "I think you should eat less" or "Look how thin your sister is!" (meaning "she represents the norm to which you must comply"), the parent could establish a better relationship with the child on this point by understanding why he eats so much, accepting the possibility that it is because he is hungry, or that the way he eats is healthy for his morphology.

When delegating the child's own authority to an abstract, exterior model that becomes a standard or an ideal, the parent actually blackmails the child, implying that whomever adapts better to the model is going to receive a gratification from which the "deviant" child will be deprived. Thus, comparison leads to competition: the one who best complies with the parents' criteria will obtain his "piece of the cake."

Children raised in a permanent atmosphere of comparison will later become devalued, envious, competitive adults who will have a lot of difficulty accepting their own individuality and value. These individuals will also continue to apply the restrictive standards of their judgmental parents to themselves and to their surroundings.

Comparison leads not to excellence but to impotence: we must be the other person in order to do what the other person does, which is obviously impossible. This Zen story offers an excellent illustration: A monk, anxious to achieve enlightenment, watches his comrade meditate with a serenity that he himself fails to achieve. He shares his disappointment with his master, who leads him into the monastery's orchard and says, "Look, do you see this apple tree? Do you see this pear tree? Each one produces delicious fruit. And they do not compare."

Preference

Since we are not masters over affinities, it is absolutely normal to feel attracted to certain people, and children are no exception. On the other hand, endlessly manifesting preferences among siblings is toxic. Each child needs to feel loved as she is. A number of parents will unconsciously transfer the sufferings and failings of their own childhood onto their children, attempting to compensate for them to the detriment of a true relationship. We have already mentioned the fact that sibling rank is a critical factor.

Example: A father of three who was third among his siblings, raised by his big sister (the eldest of the three) and abused by his brother, transfers these same childhood feelings and the scenario in which he was raised onto his own children. His older sister is his first child's godmother, and he feels an inexplicable hostility toward his second son, whom he sees as a rival, the difference being that this time the "rival" is more vulnerable and weak because in his childhood the older brother was stronger. This vulnerability allows the father to take out unfettered revenge on his middle child for formerly suffered abuse perpetrated by his own brother. Finally, he ostensibly prefers the third child, on whom he projects all of his hopes and unrealized ambitions.

In the same vein, a mother who absolutely wants a son (probably because her parents hoped for a boy) may openly abuse her three daughters and worship her little boy. Children are often born by "accident," or born of sexual assault (which sometimes occurs even within a marriage), carrying the weight of a guilt that isn't theirs for the rest of their life. "You have deprived me of my freedom—because of you I had to get married," thinks the father, or "You were created out of rape, and I cannot look at your face," thinks the mother, while a brother or sister born years before or after can receive affection very well.

Whether treated better or worse, and having no way of understanding why, the child finds himself in great psychological distress and will do everything possible to make sense of this unfair treatment. If rejected by the parent, the child will feel fundamentally bad, exerting himself to deserve a love that will never come. If the parent shows preference toward a child, he can lose any notion of the other, or he can put his life in danger with heroic acts in order to merit the preference he feels guilty for receiving.

At times the notion of "preference" is related to abuse. For example, the father sexually approaches the eldest daughter, who sacrifices herself and accepts the abuse so he will leave the little sister alone. But the youngest, conscious of the situation and also living with the injury, mixes up the confusing idea that her father doesn't want her and blames her sister.

Corporal Punishment

This type of discipline is, again, related to a disguised admission of powerlessness by parents who are not capable of reaching their child's soul; of suggesting the solution the parents know to be the best to the child; of asserting their legitimate authority in an acceptable way; of imposing structural limits. Corporal punishment combines two obnoxious strategies of manipulation: physical pain and psychological humiliation. This has more to do with "taming" a child, as with an animal, than with raising a child; forcing the child to obey regardless of what he feels or thinks.

A parent resorts to corporal punishment because he is repeating the way in which he was raised, or because he is unable to persuade the child and has nothing left but physical strength with which to assert his position as parent. This approach reveals the parent's confusion between body and soul. One strikes the body hoping to revive the soul, but actually the punishment only wounds the soul. The parent has actually added a detour or twist that may lead the child to reject his own body, which he now sees as an obstacle, an enemy, a place where his vulnerability manifests in a belittling way.

Similarly, when parents let their child repeatedly hit another child they are guilty of failure to assist a person in danger. Even if these attacks take the form of teasing among siblings (deprecating bodily criticism), allowing a child to experience repeated physical attacks risks causing him to feel like a stranger in his own body when he reaches adulthood. One must be watchful, nevertheless, because punishment can also be administered by mistake. For example, the little sister cries and the father punishes the older brother, who usually behaves violently toward her. However, this time she is crying because she has fallen.

Physical violence must be distinguished from the occasional need for restraint where the mature parental body serves as a reference for the child. A parent's gesture of immobilizing the child by putting him in the bed or shower to interrupt a tantrum—imposing a "stake," or moment of stillness and silence—must always be imbued by a deep respect for the child's integrity and intended to bring respect for himself and his environment.

A huge variety of situations exist among siblings, but when they become pathological they most often fall into one of these four dysfunctions discussed above, or all four at the same time. There is also the terrible situation of parents who completely abandon their children, providing only shelter and food. The relationships then organize themselves among the brothers and sisters, like a herd without adult guides, where the strongest imposes his infantile will and abuse is born of his own despair. The parents' slightest gesture of interest will be taken as preference, and in such situations, it is certain that these parents lean on a hierarchy based on the law of the strongest.

SOME FAMILY DYNAMICS

Without claiming to exhaust all possible situations, we are going to study some typical configurations that will help you understand your genealogy tree's siblings. The goal is to see clearly, not only among brothers and sisters but also among aunts and uncles and great-aunts and great-uncles, in order to be able to represent the context in which each sibling group was raised. In various ways cultural, social, and historical constraints can obviously weigh heavily on family dynamics, but the quality and balance of emotional relationships within the home always play a leading role.

Throughout time, siblings have happily coexisted in poor families where everyone shares space and available food joyfully. Conversely, children from a bourgeois, twentieth-century marriage—perhaps materially satisfied, but raised by nannies—may have suffered from abuse and the absence of their parents, or were scarred by the social stigma of scandal, divorce, adultery, or psychiatric internment.

The purpose of the examples provided below is to allow everyone to imagine how the sharing behaviors of our parents and grandparents with their siblings determined, in large part, their future personalities. This allows for a better understanding of trans-generational links and illustrates how a child of one generation may pay for the suffering of parents from a previous generation.

The Case of the Only Child
At first glance, an only child will appear to be in an ideal situation because he has his parents to himself. But we must also know why the parents have only one child.

The only child is often the product of a situation where the parents are narcissists and consider children to be intruders. Sometimes a child is conceived simply to continue the lineage in order to pass down the family business or estate, for example. A common situation is that in which the parents did not agree, very quickly taking to separate rooms, and the child was then raised by a couple no longer able to share in anything but the material. In still other cases the child arrived too late, or inadvertently, in the life of parents who didn't really want any children.

An only child finds himself, in general, in one of these four situations:

- The adult child must raise his own immature parents, multiplying his own efforts in order to have his existence forgiven.
- The child of a broken couple forms an exclusive union with one of his parents to the detriment of the other, and the child suffers for having been the rival of his mother or father.
- The child is locked in an intimacy (which is, in reality, a great solitude of three) with the narcissistic or depressed parents.
- The child is responsible for fulfilling all of the parents' aspirations because he was conceived in order to be the child par excellence, sentenced to perfection and thus paralyzed by perfectionism.

The child will often feel incomplete, wondering what he would have become had he had a brother or a sister. Conscious parents will raise an only child by socializing him to the hilt, or by helping him to realize that he is not alone in the world of his generation. Cousins and friends who are the same age can constitute an important reference point.

Two Children

In French the expression *choix du roi* (king's choice) designates a family with a boy born first, then a girl. This tendency to favor the eldest boy crosses all the patriarchal families but is more or less affected by different societies and eras, and it arises from a need for organization. In Europe, this dates back to the Middle Ages when the transmission of patrimony to the first male heir was imposed as a model of economic and social stabilization to ensure that every father would have a legitimate son to whom to transmit his property. One of the only ways to ensure that was to get a virgin woman pregnant immediately following the wedding, and that she give birth to a boy. Subsequent pregnancies might be, theoretically, the product of adultery. This uncertainty as to the identity of the biological father also explains the stipulation that Jewishness be transferred through the mother. The long-term consequences are immeasurable, and the origin of much suffering, frustration, and injustice.

We will use couples with two children as the base model, with a focus on the relationship between the eldest and the youngest even in the cases where the two children are twins, since twins do not come at quite the same time.

The first thing to study is the difference in ages among the siblings, indicating the age of the eldest (hence his level of psychological maturity) when the youngest arrived. But it would be too simplistic to think that only two children close in age can suffer from rivalry between them. Jealousy has no age. If parents neglected their eldest child, he might become fiercely jealous of the younger sibling even if there is a twenty-year difference in their ages. This jealousy might be expressed directly (we often see small children candidly try to kill a newborn) or indirectly, as in the case of the little boy of seven years who returned systematically injured from walks taken with his nineteen-year-old brother. The elder, without even realizing it, would encourage the little one to take chances, which the young one did out of a desire to be loved and admired by the big brother. In reality, the "big" brother was raised by his grandparents, and having spent his whole childhood in their home he cannot bear to see his parents, who have become more mature, now taking care of his younger brother as he would have liked them to have taken care of him.

It is evident, but one often forgets, that the eldest is above all an only child who must integrate the arrival of the youngest child, whereas, for the younger child, the eldest child is already part of the family. This inequality must be compensated for through the wisdom of the parents, and ideally the new arrival must be presented as a contribution, a treasure whose presence doesn't generate competition or repetition, but rather contributes to the identity of each in all its splendor. The eldest can also become the younger child's guide somehow, albeit not as a replacement of the parents: he must conserve his identity, his world, and feel that nothing essential has been withdrawn.

The second fundamental aspect to the study of two siblings is in considering if each of the two children individually have their own place, or if the parents considered them to be two sides of the same entity. This often happens when they are given the same first name, names with the same first letter, or names containing the same letters, like Jean and Jeanne, Laura and Lorenzo, Albert and Berta, Marion and Roman, Dorothy and Theodore. It is very common in sibling pairs that there is, in fact, **only one space for two.** The two children must share their existence, which is a very common occurrence when they are the same gender but can also happen in cases of different gender: they are thus two sides of the same being. Everything one owns or represents, the other cannot be or have. One may become a great trader like his father, the other an artist, and the world is seen as a limited commodity that can only be divided into two halves. This situation is also observed in the case of twins when they are not playing the identity game.

Example: Sisters were born a year apart. The eldest, blonde, was named Simone. The youngest, brunette, was named Monique. They shared the same bedroom but differed in everything else. Simone was "beautiful." Monique was "intelligent." Simone was chubby. Monique was slender. One liked classical music, one liked pop. When Monique came to consult with us she was over forty, single, without children, and complained of living only "a half life." Then, around the birth of her first child, Monique twice attempted suicide, which she later understood to be an effort to "give my sister space." At the same time, Simone complained endlessly of having been unloved by their parents and asserted that Monique was "preferred" because she was a model child.

These two sisters illustrate the absurdity of a situation in which there is only one place for two: the common syllable in their names, "mon," means "my" in French, and each sister is convinced that she will never get what "belongs" to the other. Thanks to the genealogy tree trap confirmed by the parents, they continue into adulthood living with the belief that they must share reality like sharing cake.

Employing the metaphoric use of urine to mark one's territory in areas controlled by another, the first step toward healing this negative illusion will be to recover that which is thought to belong to the other by simply allowing oneself to practice a forbidden activity. It also means abandoning childish illusions that have become safe havens, like those defining attributes of quality and space that belong to the parents, which in Monique's case were "smart" and "intelligent."

When the roles are divided hierarchically between older and younger there is a **power struggle** between dominant and dominated, each person implements strategies to obtain the victory of receiving the parents' love. These situations can be aggravated by the attitude of those who divert their own contentious urges on their children, as spectators would do at a cock fight, often dividing the children as if betting on different teams.

Example: The parents, expecting a son, name their first child (a daughter) Alberta. When little Giovanni is born four years later, Alberta tries to suffocate him in the cradle, which shocks the very Christian parents. They punish her severely and they overprotect the son. Alberta grows to understand that violence leads nowhere, and so she chooses to overpower her brother by all other possible means. The family splits into two parts. One part, Alberta and her father, are absorbed in philosophical conversations, which excludes her mother and Giovanni. The other part, her mother and Giovanni, take their revenge on the material plane: her mother always gives Giovanni the best, the softest sheets, projecting her own dissatisfaction onto him by always referring to him as "the poor boy." In adulthood, Alberta comes to consult because she struggles with having conflicting relationships with the men who enter into her life. Those she understands well are intellectuals whom she does not desire and who remain as friends. But any passionate relationship with a man results in conflict. Little by little, she discovers the repressed love she felt toward her brother, as well as the original, locked-up family conflicts that were never discussed.

As we have seen, it is the parents alone who are responsible for managing the inevitable tensions that agitate the family during each transformation of the sibling group. When the family is not at peace and another child arrives, the desire of the eldest to "eliminate" the youngest can turn into outbursts and acts of violence. If the parents fail to establish the feeling of security and legitimacy for each child, this rivalry will only grow worse. The eldest and the youngest will use all means possible to destroy one another. The eldest may try to mentally annihilate the younger sibling by demoralization, destruction of toys, or the stealing of friends. In adulthood these battles occasionally cause guilt complexes in the eldest, while the youngest can become submerged in resentment, anger, confusion, and other psychophysical blocks.

The classic strategies of domination of the eldest over the youngest are:

- Taking the role of the mother or father, often with the parents' consent, turning at best into "a little mother" or "a little father" and, at worst, a torturer.
- Causing the youngest to be dependent on the eldest (speaking for him, systematically helping, etc.).
- Becoming overly helpful, and acting as intermediary between the parents and the younger sibling to the point of suffocating him (which is to say, replacing him).
- Giving the younger sibling psychological or physical complexes by having expectations of abilities beyond his age in order to develop a reputation of intelligence, skill, or superior strength for the elder child.
- Giving the younger sibling the silent treatment, ignoring him, which amounts to denying his existence.
- By using physical aggression, the eldest has the advantage of age

and of systematically winning battles during the younger sibling's first years, until the child learns to defend himself.

- If the younger sibling attracts too much attention to himself, the older sibling may have no other solution for living than to fail at everything or to fall ill.
- Sexual abuse may be part of the means by which the eldest triumphs over the youngest by imposing the emergence of his mature sexuality or by seducing him (and sometimes by attaching to him for a long time).

The younger sibling has "strategies" by default, which more directly appeal to the parents' power:

- Emotionally blackmailing the parents by complaining about the older sibling's apparent abuse, sometimes for no reason.
- "Angelism," sometimes real and sometimes simulated, which can turn the child's authentic personality into one of a model child, to his detriment.
- Becoming ill (psychosis, organic disease, epilepsy, etc.) to attract attention.
- Rebelling, escaping, running away.
- Outbursts of anger to monopolize attention.

Two brothers, especially if they are close in age, will frequently have a physically violent relationship. The battles generally last until the younger brother can regularly beat up the older brother, who becomes disinterested when physical violence becomes unsuccessful.

When a second child arrives, parents must refrain from projecting the pleasure or displeasure of having a younger sibling onto the eldest, whether the same gender or not. It is up to the parents to welcome the child, which is going to determine the firstborn's ability to love the younger sibling unconditionally. Unfortunately we once again witness a sexualizing of the relationship under the mechanism of projection, and social, cultural, and familial pressure may cause the parents to provide more physical contact and comforting to a girl than to a boy.

When the two children are different sexes it is not uncommon for parents to project their vision of the couple onto them, with the brother and sister reproducing the atmosphere between the parents; they may even quarrel like their parents quarrel. Or the siblings may be encouraged to form a relationship that can turn incestuous. This commonly held fantasy that brother and sister create a couple similar to that of the parents is actually a misrepresentation: a brother and sister are in no way a couple but rather two distinct individuals who coexist like two species of trees or two planets in a solar system.

If the relationship between the parents is cut off or combative, the brother-sister relationship becomes pathological. It may turn either into rivalry (each choosing a side or joining forces, for example, with the parent of the opposite sex) or incestuous because the parents are absent and the brother and sister transfer their affection onto one another.

Example: By all appearances the consultant, youngest of two, comes from a perfect family, united, harmonious. She did not speak about her unhappiness. She often spoke about her older brother of two years, whose perfection is overwhelming: handsome, tall, generous, brilliant . . . she presented him to us as a model person. He was named after the great paternal grandfather and was preparing to take over the family business. Her own father was the eldest of his siblings. She complained of having very little contact with her brother and says she missed him. Upon closer scrutiny of reality, we learned that the precious brother was raised like a prince, seemed to have developed an attitude of hostility toward the world, and had lost the capacity to interact with others. At thirty years of age he had virtually no love life and no friends. Our consultant, who spent her childhood at the service of her idealized brother, gradually ceased to see him as a hero and became conscious of the wounds they both carry from this hierarchical distribution of roles. She realized that they were somehow fated by the family to be a couple. Little by little, she was set free and met a man who suited her, while her brother put down his armor and, humanizing in turn, made a significant encounter.

It is common that, thanks to the male domination in force in society, the brother is considered wiser and more legitimate than the sister. Here, this distribution of socially accepted roles was clearly exaggerated, so the girl was inflicted by two factors of submission: the female gender and the role of the youngest. Rather than bringing them closer to one another, the seemingly idyllic situation created a great deal of havoc for both siblings, and they isolated from the rest of the world.

Three Children

In general, when there are three siblings one is sacrificed and will be forced to be a repeat, or else the child in the middle will not have the same prerogatives as the eldest or the youngest. That said, all configurations are possible in this triangle, and the impact of the children's gender on their positions in the family must be considered. If a son is in the middle of two daughters, due to the "quality of being male" he will likely be at risk for receiving all the attention, and the struggle to exist will "unfold" between the youngest and the eldest.

Example: In a sibling group composed of an older brother and two younger sisters, Irene, the youngest, is a clone of the older sister Beatrice. Irene spent her whole childhood dressed in her big sister's old clothes, while the eldest sister and brother regularly received new clothes. At the time of marriage she naturally chose her sister's husband's younger brother, with whom she had formed a childish relationship ten years prior to their engagement. Therapy coupled with the study of their genealogy trees allowed them to get out of their roles as shy shadows (her of the sister, him of the brother) and reveal their true personalities.

When the long-awaited "little one" is a boy it can increase the anger of the two older sisters, who may conspire against him.

Example: "When I was little, around four or five, I fell in love with all the girls no matter what age. I do not know if it is normal. I imagine it is normal, though I have my doubts. However, precisely because of this, one of my sisters, at nine years old, looked at me and made fun of me and tried to convince me that I was 'little,' 'ridiculous,' 'shabby.' Since I expressed my feelings for these girls, and said things like they made me want to 'declare my love to them,' my sister treated me with contempt. She said, 'You are crazy! No one cares about you! You'd better shut up! You're nothing but a snotty brat! Look at yourself in the mirror, look at that black, frizzy, ugly hair of yours! Our cousin is blond! He is beautiful, not you!' I don't even remember everything she said. These are just a few examples. But from that moment on, I totally lost confidence in myself. Every time I was face-to-face with a girl, I did not feel well. It was precisely my sister's keywords: she called into question my capacity to be 'good enough' to be loved. Today, thirty years later, I have still not recovered my self-esteem. I have never felt 'good enough' for anyone. I have had thousands of problems. For four years, I was addicted and at risk of contracting AIDS from prostitutes; I went to prison; I was assaulted. I thought I had overcome my addiction, but I never felt quite good enough about myself to find a life partner. Zero self-esteem. My parents were completely absent during this period; neither had the time or the desire to be in my life. Even when I was very young they only provided a roof over our heads, food, and education, and they left me in the hands of my older sisters, for whom I was a 'problem.' I loved them enormously, and I couldn't understand why they told me such horrors. Thus, whenever they spoke to me, I kept silent. Sometimes I cried and they laughed at and mocked my tears. I find it impossible to live a healthy and loving life because I still feel all of these things on the inside."

It is also possible that one of the three children finds himself completely isolated due to his age, or because the others form a coalition wherein there is a disparity and the child has no place.

In the case where the three children are of the same sex, diverse union strategies can take place. But as with two siblings, one may find a situation where available space is divided into three strictly limited territories.

Four or More Children

With more than four children, the configurations are numerous.

The first question is whether the large family was the parents' choice, and if the parents were able to give each child his own space, or if the children formed a kind of "mass" or "ball" where all were deprived of the essentials because they seemed too many to the parents. This can cause several problems, but in particular a constant aggression in defense of one's territory.

Relationships are usually organized in blocks: "the big kids," "the little kids," "the girls," "the boys." The gap in age between siblings must also be taken into consideration. Sometimes the relationships of preference, or the unions, make a kind of cross with first and third, second and fourth, or else eldest and youngest on one side, and the two middles on the other side. This all changes if the first three children are the same gender and the fourth is the opposite, or when the eldest is a different gender from the three youngest. In the Unconsciousness the odd places are for the boys and even places are for the girls.

A family of five children may very well be composed of a first trio (three children born very close in age), an isolated child four years later, and finally, ten years later, the youngest, who practically lives as an only child. Often, this child becomes a black sheep or a scapegoat.

Among large sibling groups, the roles often divide by increments after four years. For example, the first three are repeated in the following three.

It is common that the last of eight children feels almost nonexistent, as the mother and father, even the brothers and sisters, are overwhelmed by the immensity of the family. This child may feel like no one cares about her, and she can grow up feeling negligible. Frequently, the first son is also considered to be heir of the paternal genealogy tree (his physical resemblance with the grandfather and the paternal uncles is accompanied by the resulting responsibilities, preferences, or conflicts), so that the second is the male heir to the maternal genealogy tree.

The Dead, Abandoned,
or Missing Child among the Siblings

Dead children, stillbirths, or never-born (abortions or miscarriages) are considered members of the sibling group when collecting information necessary for the genealogy tree. In fact, even if the siblings are often in bitter battles they also have a **fellowship,** in the most sacred sense of the term, and bonds beyond human comprehension unite its members. In this sense, we cannot really have a "half brother" or "half sister"—children sharing parents are linked by the incest taboo even if they don't actually know one another. So, a missing child is always present in one way or another in the siblings' psyche. The ideal would be to be able to openly recall the missing without assigning him an excessive role, but without completely erasing him either. It is assumed that the mere fact that a deceased, abandoned, or missing child is a tragic event for the family in general, and for the parents in particular.

When siblings tally a significant number of deceased children, one must also seek the reason. Is it external to the family, a result of war or poverty? Or is it due to the mother's exhaustion, her body unable to support multiple births, for example in societies where birth control is unthinkable? But let us remember, the way in which a family experiences social misfortune has a psychological basis. We live through poverty, war, or famine according to family heritage, which has been received in a variety of ways including concept of money, level of Consciousness, and creative resources.

As a general rule, the early death of a member of the tree—whether during childhood, adolescence, or youth—causes trauma in the family. The familial Unconscious is going to seek the "guilty," or at least whatever is responsible for the death.

There are four kinds of responsible factors:

- **Outside of the family and impersonal.** An epidemic, a famine, war, poverty. One must then ask about the society in which this family is rooted, what the family's relationship to society is, what the family's resilience relative to the events that transpired is. In the families in which many men were killed in war, for example, one can ask what this family's concept of State is.

- **An individual who is external to the family.** This may be the person who is responsible for an accident, a doctor who committed an error, or a judge who condemns someone to death. In a symbolic way this responsible individual often represents a parental figure (often the paternal authority), and it is useful to reconnect the trauma of this premature death with the relationship had by those in mourning with said authority. For example, the child crushed by a train was actually crushed by the train's conductor, and it is not uncommon that one or both grandfathers were crushing father figures who metaphorically repeated the devastating influence of trauma.

- **Inherent to the family and impersonal.** As in the case of a genetic disease or an accident that is mysteriously repeated, this is where we seek the most direct transgenerational transmission systems. For example, was the dead child given the name of someone who disappeared before him?

- **Inherent in the family and personal.** In the case of an ill-fated gesture or someone's careless act, we must study this (sometimes) imaginary guilt. For example, a child of six years is given the little sister of two years to babysit, and in a moment of inattention, the younger one drowns in a tub the parents had left in the room and the older child actually becomes the scapegoat for the parents' fault. Conversely, for example, closely examine the paternal grandmother who "accidentally" killed a young son. What desire to murder, conscious or unconscious, did she fulfill with this gesture? Is it the repetition of an earlier death? Is it a fulfillment of a desire to kill her brother, or one of her kids? Is it a desire to eliminate her children's descendants? Is it a stubborn hatred toward her stepchildren?

The place of the dead child among siblings can be dominating. Conversely a child whose death was not successfully mourned, but rather erased, may still be present like a kind of shadow and weigh heavily on the rest of the living.

We must distinguish between several situations.

The Hidden Child

A death that no one talks about, that one or both parents never mention. This may be a stillbirth, miscarriage, abortion, or even a child considered to be "illegitimate" with whom all contact is lost and who is "dead" to the family. Silence may make mourning impossible, but shameful as well (to have lost a baby, to have aborted, to have given birth to a monster), so the personal Unconscious and the familial Unconscious are closely related. The other members of the sibling group will have a vague awareness of this child, whom they may sometimes evoke under the symbolic form of an illness or imaginary friend. A daughter who experiences a miscarriage, ectopic pregnancy, or delivery of a stillborn may be experiencing this "accident" of pregnancy at precisely the age her mother was when she had an abortion.

Example: A wealthy couple from North America conceived their first child after having taken all possible precautions, but on the day of the birth, the woman learned that the child has Down syndrome, which amniocentesis had not detected. Incapable of dealing with this, the mother abandoned the child to foster care and decided to never speak of the incident again. Two years later, the little brother developed a special relationship with an imaginary friend whose first name (which stupefied the parents) was the same as that of the older brother. The child's school psychologists regarded this relationship with alarm, and the couple eventually understood that the weight of the secret about the birth and abandonment of the older brother with Down syndrome likely destabilized the "normal" younger brother. After a lot of work, littered with resistance, the parents decided to introduce the two brothers to one another. The eldest brother's adoptive family, in this case, demonstrated wisdom and exceptional tolerance in allowing the biological family to resume regular contact with this once-hated child.

The Idealized Child

The idealized child is the disappeared child who, after dying in childhood or early youth, becomes a family hero who takes up all of the space, whom the parents place above everyone else, on whose absence the mother blames all of her dissatisfactions. The rest of the children receive the message that "Mom (and/or Dad) loves the dead more than the living, and I would be more loved if I were dead." In this case, it helps to go back to the reasons why the mother (and/or father) prevented any mourning, therefore creating the beginning of an endless depression and a break from the rest of the children. For someone who has no desire to be a mother, the dead child may become a pretext for resigning her maternal role and for refusing to give the living children the love she claims to carry for the idealized child.

Example: After studying her own genealogy tree, a consultant analyzed the reasons that drove her own mother to "remain a little girl," fearful and dependent, and saw her mother as having fulfilled her parental role poorly. "When my mother was three, my maternal grandmother lost a son to whooping cough or some kind of lung disease. From that day on she was in mourning and is still in mourning. Every Sunday she took her five children, dressed in their best clothes, to pray and cry at the grave of this little disappeared one. It was the only family outing they had throughout childhood. Before falling asleep each night my mother imagined herself dying, the whole village in tears and, with her mother first in line, following a white coffin. This idea comforted her. Her mother didn't so much speak to her as correct her, or ask her to perform some household duty. Photos of the deceased, whom my grandmother referred to as 'my angel,' were hung everywhere. When my mother met my father, she absolutely wanted to have a son. Fortunately, my father opposed her wanting to give me the deceased brother's name, and he also refused Gabriel without really knowing why. Today, I realize that my mother projected this 'angel' that absorbed all of her mother's attention onto me."

The idealized child constitutes an impossible model for his or her siblings to reach: a kind of divinity that cannot be attained except through death. It is actually a kind of passive aggression on the part of the parent, who unconsciously criticizes the living in order to remember that the deceased is no longer there.

The Replaced Child

Frequently a child born after an older sibling's death bears all or part of his personality and is even named after the dead child, with the name masculinized or feminized when necessary. The replacement child can also be called Rene or Renato ("re-né," reborn), Sylvie ("s'il vit," if he lives), or else Pascal (Christ risen, from Easter: Pâque). Carrying the identity of one who is deceased is a heavy and destructive task because the real identity of the living being is sacrificed in favor of resurrecting the dead. This may cause suicide, self-destructive behavior, and autoimmune disease, or it may push the person to feel "possessed" and constantly expelled from his authentic self by aspirations that do not correspond to his real nature. Further on in the book we will see how acts of Psychomagic allow for the materialization of the deceased, turning this burden over to us and therefore allowing a definitive separation.

Exercise: The tree of triads

Now include the brothers and sisters in the diagrams of the genealogy tree triads (see "The Genealogy Tree as a Web of Triads," page 298). You can begin to change the size of the circles to indicate the relative importance of the protagonists.

It is important to remember that each child feels like an only child and the center of the triad, even if there is a favorite sister or brother. In the depth of our souls, each of us is the hero or anti-hero of our lives. Each child will therefore establish a different genealogy tree in his Unconscious: his own personal story, and his vision of his parents. The tree is always a point of view that is dependent upon the way in which one experiences childhood events. Human beings are not born with the same "baggage"; we are more or less strong, more or less vulnerable, more or less sensitive, and we have more or less intellectual capabilities. It is possible that these differences depend in part on the pregnancy, on the way in which the parents treated one another, and perhaps on balances forged by nature. Science is still perplexed on this point; for example we know that some elements of DNA are inactive in certain individuals depending on whether or not they have been decoded by the body.

These psychological and existential differences between brothers and sisters imply that the events of childhood—experienced or missed, joys or sorrows—will be interpreted differently, and will produce different effects for each person. In the long run the behavior of the parents will also be dependent on the children's character; they will be more lenient and more generous with certain children than with others. The result of this wide array of attitudes and sensory perceptions is that different genealogy trees are born.

Exercise: In place of the other

You can establish the triads of each of your siblings with your parents. Or, where appropriate (if you were an only child), the triads of your aunts, uncles, and grandparents and the triads of great-aunts and great-uncles with great-grandparents. Again, this has to do with making an effort to represent family relationships from a variety of angles, not with a goal of achieving accuracy. Even for an aunt or uncle, a sister or brother, who is hated, you can see the situation from their point of view without criticizing. Keep in mind that we also have a goal of shedding light on the repetitions, and it is possible that you will view the triads in a nonegocentric way, discovering relational mechanisms that will provide you with insight to your genealogy tree.

PART SEVEN

From Bond to Knot

Psychomagic Rescues
Toxic Relationships

THIRTEEN

The Gordian Knot

By Alejandro Jodorowsky

In 1937, Tocopilla was a port in decay. The great rise of saltpeter (known as "white gold" and revered as a double-edged sword, powder of life and powder of death) had passed. It was on the one hand a valuable fertilizer for plants, and on the other a sneaky ingredient used in the manufacture of explosives. Synthetic saltpeter, invented by the Germans, had finally put an end to the prosperity of northern Chile, and from the docks of Tocopilla one no longer saw swarms of cargo ships at harbor. Busy Freire Street, filled with bars where exuberant, garishly made up, skeletal prostitutes nested and expertly exchanged their services for the pay of drunken sailors, had become an anemic snake. The locals, en masse, threw themselves hungrily at anyone who landed there by some unknown miracle. Fighting was not limited to catcalling; one would also see shining knife blades.

The so-called Lucho, one of these rare sailors, resided at a tavern named Loro Mudo, the Silent Parrot, a bar with walls, seats, tables, and bottles in uniform green and populated by matching anemic prostitutes, sad and silent like the gypsum bird at the entrance, stretching out a leg to call in unlikely lechers. Lucho was embedded there, positioned to protect Doña Ganga, the old madam. Lucho got up late, was served breakfast in bed, and washed and rinsed with a washcloth. He dressed in his sailor uniform and spent his time at the bar, where he served as a lure for the mythical sailors who were to dock, after their months of abstinence taking to the streets in search of relaxation. However, these awaited sailors did not arrive. The only customers were old misers and mutilated miners.

Lucho, dying of boredom, spent his days and nights making knots with two pieces of rope, something he had learned during endless voyages at sea. At dizzying speed he wove the two ropes into complex knots that no one could unravel. Just as swiftly, Lucho could undo them. Sometimes, to get some sun, he sat for an hour on a bench in the public square. Just as silently as the bird in the bar where he had ended up, he made five hundred knots one after the other, all complex, all different. The residents of Tocopilla looked askance at him, touching index finger to temple. With the curiosity of a lonely child, I loved to sit next to him with the hope of learning to do and undo such beautiful unions. Noticing my interest, he passed me the two cords from time to time, and invited me to imitate him. Every time, I clung forcefully to the ropes, making one rope out of two but never unraveling the unit. Lucho's knots were wise constructions. He knew how to do and undo them. I, however, could only create blind knots that required an agonizing effort to untie.

This childhood experience helped me to later understand the difference between a neurotic relationship and a healthy relationship. For the first, we suffer because of a situation that we have constructed and we cannot overcome: we feel possessed. For the latter, we unite with another without misgiving because we know we will have the courage to end the relationship and recover our freedom. Neurotic bonds are maintained by obligation and by impotence. Healthy bonds are held by desire and love.

The unions, which are the product of a community, reminded me of the marine knots. They must be solid but provide the opportunity to be undone in an emergency situation—a ship caught in a storm, for example. The psychological knot is also the product of a community. The purpose of its dissolution is to integrate into society, to be accepted by it, as a congregation accepts an initiate. As much as we keep the knot, we find ourselves separated from society. Every human being, in order to survive, needs to join others. The healthy knot achieves this purpose and deserves to be preserved as long as it is useful. The blind knot that we keep enclosed in our trauma must be untied so that we can move on to a more appropriate relationship—finding peace in the heart and, therefore, the joy of living.

Psychological knots, hidden in the obscure recesses of the Unconscious, arise continuously (even if we can identify them) and prevent us from being in the miracle of existence. Each is like a nail, lurking in the shadows, ruining the whole walk for the sole of a shoe.

Rafaela was a young Mexican consultant who managed to become aware of such psychological knots. She had attempted suicide by swallowing a bottle of pills prescribed for migraines. When she began to feel bad she called her mother, a widow of eleven years with no lover, and asked to be taken to the hospital. After undergoing gastric lavage she fell into a deep depression. She abandoned her artistic activities and locked herself in her mother's house. Unable to endure the deep sadness that prevented her from breathing, Rafaela asked me for a consultation. I asked her if she remembered when this sadness began and she told me a few months before, when she returned from the city in the United States where she had lived with her parents. It was this trip that had caused her to want to commit suicide.

Why?
Because I remembered that I had killed my father.
How?
It was when I was thirteen years old . . .
The age, also, at which you had your first period, I imagine . . .
Yes. That day, I finally thought I had become a woman. One week later, the misfortune took place. I was on the ground floor of the house playing the piano when my father came downstairs in a

crisis of fury provoked by the bottle . . . he insulted me. I yelled at him, "You are a monster! I do not love you! I wish you were dead!" Offended, he left the house. While driving his car, he had a heart attack, crashed into a tree, and died instantly.

How old was he?

Fifty-two. He had not ever had heart trouble. Returning to my hometown, I realized that since age thirteen, I lived with a terrible sense of guilt. This feeling still tortures me to this day.

Did your father always insult you this way?

No, even when he was drunk he behaved very affectionately with me. I loved him deeply. That fatal day was the first time he assaulted me.

And with your mother, how did he behave?

Horribly. He never ceased insulting her or threatening to hit or to kill her . . .

Rafaela, you feel guilty for an imaginary crime. No little girl has the power to kill someone with her words. You, the adult woman, do not suffer; it is the little girl you carry inside who suffers. Try to kill a dog or a cat by saying "I want you to die," and you will see that you do not possess this power. Today, I would like you to remember, with your twenty-four-year-old spirit, how you felt while playing the piano at thirteen years old on this, as you call it, fatal day.

I felt bad because my mother was next to me. She always wanted to be a pianist and singer but because of my birth she had to renounce her art and take care of me. Each time I played piano, she got sad and I felt guilty.

So you were not alone. What caused your father to come downstairs like that without warning?

While listening to me play, my mother started to cry. Then she said, "Your father has ruined my life, he is a monster, I hate him, I wish he would die!" Then, he came downstairs thinking it was me who said those things and he raised his hand, threatening to smack me. He yelled, "My daughter, how could you utter such idiocy? You

have never loved me. You are a bad daughter." At that moment I
said what I said.

That is to say that you repeated your mother's exact words.

Yes, that is right.

Did your mother try to rectify your father's mistake? Did she tell him
it was her and not you who thought that?

No, she stayed silent.

Somehow your mother possessed you. She had created a symbiosis
with you.

It is true. From the time I was very small, she told me the worst
things about my father and sealed our union against him.

I have found many cases in which people with heart problems were
not loved in childhood by their parents. I have also found that
the majority of alcoholics drink to compensate for the desire
to be breastfed by a mother who does not provide the necessary tenderness. What relationship did your father have with his
parents?

His mother never loved him. She treated him cruelly. His father left
the home quickly.

Why did your mother marry a man whom she hated?

Maybe because her divorced mother instilled hatred in her toward
her own father. My maternal grandfather was an alcoholic, too.

Rafaela's story is evidence of a genealogical repetition. Her father,
who was never loved in his childhood, married a woman (child of an
alcoholic) who remained in symbiosis with her mother, hating men
and incapable of loving them. He, attached to an incestuous knot,
enjoyed the dissatisfaction of being hated, which allowed him to keep
the sadomasochistic knot with his mother. If this knot came undone,
he would lose the only thing he ever had: a cruel mother.

Rafaela's mother was in a similar position. Accustomed since
childhood to seeing the world through the eyes of her mother, she
believed she hated her alcoholic father. So, she was basically united
with him in an incestuous knot. In order to not undo the knot she

married a man who was emotionally similar to her father, and her relationship would replicate all of the relationships in this genealogy tree where absent and unloved fathers partnered with possessive and invasive mothers who couple with their daughters, united by a lesbian knot.

Rafaela, by repeating the insults uttered by her mother, identified with her. She therefore revealed the incestuous knot with her father: she had her period, she became a woman, she could take the place of her mother.

I asked where her father was buried. Rafaela told me he had been cremated. I asked where the ashes had been dispersed. She said they were still in the urn, and she kept them in her bedroom closet at her mother's house.

Having understood the framework of the knots that acted on her depression and turned it into a parricide, I proposed a series of psychomagic acts to enable her to unwind those knots and redis-cover the taste of life.

Above all else, she would have to confront her mother and show her how she had contributed to her daughter's neurosis (even to cursing her father like a ventriloquist who makes the dummy talk). She would ask for a symbolic check for a trillion dollars in repairs— the price needed to pay for this kind of possession, and for having made her so ill. If the mother did not recognize the debt, Rafaela would cut ties with her for whatever time was necessary, a few months or years if need be. If she recognized the debt they would travel together to Teotihuacan and climb to the top of the Pyramid of the Sun, where her mother would serve as witness to the scatter-ing of the ashes, an act that would be undertaken with love by her daughter. If Rafaela cut ties with her mother, she would scatter her father's ashes accompanied by her boyfriend.

After having done that, she must buy her father's favorite rum and hang his picture above the bottle in her room next to a candle, a stick of incense, and a flower. Each night before sleeping, drinking a bit of this alcohol for blessing, she should rub the alcohol into her chest at heart level. Once the bottle was emptied, she will bury and plant flowers above it.

Rafaela, finally understanding the cause of her depression, told me, "Now I know where the tumor is and I know I must free myself from this, untie the knot as you say, but I cannot confront my mother. She will never understand. She will say I am insane. And if ever she may understand, it might kill her. Also, I cannot scatter my father's ashes because my mother expects me to keep them for the rest of my life." She defended her position, tooth, eye, and nail. She decided not to undo the knot even though it caused her continuous suffering and repeated failures in her artistic career because she could not allow herself to accomplish that which her mother could not.

I told her, "Rafaela, after having studied your genealogy tree and its repetitions, you know very well that your depression is the result of these psychological knots that distort your life and prevent you from being yourself, that obligate you to abide by what your mother and grandmother wanted you to be—the executant of their desire to assassinate a man." To give her courage to untie the knot, I told her a story of my youth.

My father, fervent communist and admirer of Stalin, believed his duty was to turn his son into a hero. His motto was "A hero is forged in battle against the world." He enrolled me in the Liceo de Aplicación, a school attended by the children of devotees of Nazism. At this time I didn't know I was Jewish because my father was pretending to be Russian and, as he was an atheist, I was not brought up in any religious tradition. From the first days of class, my school-mates avoided me like the plague. No one wanted to sit with me on the two-seater benches. Then, because of my nose, they began calling me "wandering Jew," "expatriate," "vulture." During recess, they refused to play with me. Then they organized passionate competitions, a kind of bowling played with three steel balls. I was dying to play, but I was systematically pushed away. One day when the ball fell into the mouth of a sewer full of disgusting rot and sputum they didn't want to get it; they remained paralyzed and incapable of playing their game. So I rolled my shirtsleeves to my elbows and plunged my arms into the sludge to recover their ball, thinking this act of courage would allow me to win the acceptance of my classmates. I only succeeded in becoming more despised, "Dirty Jew! We are not going to accept you just because you put your hands in shit! Get out of here!" They continued with their game without giving me a second look. I was ashamed of myself, and I hated them. Filled with resentment I said to myself, "It was a mistake to want to be accepted and to do humiliating acts for it. For them to accept me, I must dominate them and force them to admire me."

I studied relentlessly and became the best student. I founded an art academy, which was applauded by my professors, and I ended up being elected class president. Years later, during my psychoanalysis with Dr. Erich Fromm, I realized the hatred toward these students still lived in my heart. Once revised by my adult mind, however, this hatred became pity. These children were the victims of an upbringing that had transformed them into limited, egotistical, aggressive beings, incapable of "putting their hands in shit" to collect an iron ball, which was the symbol of the unalterable strength of the essential Being. To plunge one's naked arm into a sewer signifies consciously confronting suffering, making an effort to find oneself, and sacrificing the identification with the artificial ego created by family and society. The racist ideas they had been taught, the knots to which they remained attached, were this fetid sludge. Poor beings, incapable of freeing themselves and occupied by superficial games, they were condemned to waste their lives in a persistent infantilism, incapable of developing an adult soul that was not racist, cruel, or selfish. I, in spite of my emotional darkness, was capable of sacrificing my dignity and overcoming my disgust. They were furious because I did for the group what each of them was incapable of doing.

Tell me, Rafaela, will you one day be able to stop judging yourself and plunge your arm into the sewer in order to untie the knots and retrieve your luminous essential Being?

The psychomagic acts that you have given me will help me?

The nail hidden in the shoe, which ruins the whole walk, is very hard to extract. A psychological knot for someone like you who has suffered abuse in childhood becomes a necessity because it is the link that unites you to the family. You are afraid of undoing it, of no longer being recognized, of becoming a stranger, a renegade, a kind of orphan. You think that if you remove the nail, you will lose the shoe.

It is hard to be a good therapist. It is a task that one must choose as an altruistic vocation, without seeking the approval of others or without placing oneself on a higher plane. When I put my hand in the sludge, due to inexperience, I did not take into account the resistance of others. In order to successfully heal any illness one must first accept the remedy. Blind knots produce walls of insurmountable psychological resistance. The person who lives with these knots embedded in the psyche will protect them by using all strategies possible in order to maintain them in their current form.

For a long time, before beginning to read the Tarot, I attended karate-do classes. In essence, in addition to the goal of achieving self-control, the purpose of this art form is to learn to kill the opponent. Practicing the Tarot, I realized that the readings represented a similar struggle, though one intended not to kill the consultant but, on the contrary, to restore his real life. In these two arts one must learn to see the opponent's defenses with respect, not with hate.

In Mexico, the healer Carlos Said honored me with his friendship and allowed me many opportunities to observe his therapeutic magic. This excellent being, who died in 2009, did not work under his own name but under the name Doña Paz—I think he proceeded from there to overcome his personal ego. Doña Paz was an old invisible woman whom Said claimed was sitting on a gilded chair resting on the altar of a temple that he had constructed in the living room of his apartment. She would tell him, "This little box (the consultant) contains within it such-and-such evil (cancer, a heart in poor condition, etc.), and I advise this remedy."

This device recalls what Jacques Lacan said to his students: "You all can be Lacanian, I will remain Freudian." I learned from Carlos Said that a therapy cannot heal in its own name—in other words, by exalting the personal ego and trying to become a character greater than the consultant. The healer always works with allies. Said, before beginning a task, would put a thick noose around the patient's neck and explain, "This disease is yours—not mine, not anyone else's, it is yours alone. You must have the courage to befriend your suffering and soothe it without hatred so that it recedes of its own will, which is the will of God . . ."

I observed this same perspective in the XII Arcanum in the Tarot, the Hanged Man, where the character is attached upside down by one foot between two trees with cut branches.

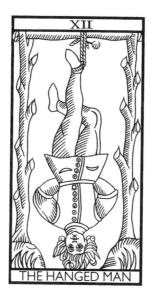

In essence the Hanged Man, willingly attached at equal distance between two genealogy trees, maternal and paternal, has sunk into himself and is heroically facing his knots. I understood that no person is capable of undoing the knots of another. At the very least we can help others to realize that they exist, and then help them to overcome their denials.

Said dramatized this struggle by feigning to cut the ill person's whole body with a knife some distance from the skin. Following this, he would rub the person with an egg (symbolic of the life force), establishing a feeling of the constant flow of energy that is the essential Being. For this "wizard," we were all healthy. He explained, "Doña Paz told me that there is no illness, nothing but invaded people. I don't cure, I expel evil by finding out who sent it." Then he put the patient on a seat and covered him with a sheet. Under the chair in a metal censer burned a large quantity of copalli, the popular Mexican incense. This was a spiritual purification, and maybe a way to erase the links between the patients and their childhood memories. In Zen meditation or in psychoanalysis, one wagers on the same results after years of effort.

Myself, after having consulted a good number of healers and *machis* in Mexico and Mapuche healers from Chile, meditating for five years with the Zen master Ejo Takata, and going through psychoanalysis with Dr. Fromm, I wondered how to overcome the defenses more quickly through this work on the genealogy tree—which takes less time because the tree trap is removed in the space of a few hours. I discovered that the quick solution, essential in convincing the consultant of the need to defeat his resistances, was to provide the means for him to be the actor of his destiny instead of leaving his role to his immediate family. I succeeded thanks to the use of Psychomagic, where the person turns into his own healer. Realizing that the Unconscious accepts metaphors, I began to suggest that my consultants employ actions in which knots were materialized in a symbolic way.

One example of this was of the Gordian knot of Alexander the Great. At the Phrygian capital Gordium, in Anatolia, priests presented to conquerors strings that were knotted in such a complicated way that it was impossible to disentangle them. According to tradition, whoever undid the knot would conquer the Orient. Alexander resolved the problem by cutting the knot with his sword: "To cut it off or to detach is the same."

If, for example, the consultant could not accept his cannibal knot,*
I would suggest this psychomagic act: take a white ball (the color of
mother's milk) and carry it in a backpack for seven days, taking it off
only to sleep and bathe. Then place it on your mother's tomb.

This act provides relief that would otherwise require a lot more
time in therapy. Thanks to Psychomagic it is possible to cut the link in
order to resolve the issue the person faces. By utilizing the fast action
of a psychomagic act his suffering is addressed, and he is assisted in
finding the courage to deactivate his defenses.

By performing the acts that I recommended, Rafaela freed herself from depression and began to fulfill herself as an artist.

---

*We will see what this knot corresponds to later.

FOURTEEN

Links and Knots

Unite in Consciousness

The family is a network of links. Some are very concrete, such as those that develop between members of a household, and others are more abstract, binding members of the genealogy tree that are two or three generations distant.

By studying this network of links, existing or broken, concrete or symbolic, we somehow enter into the **functional anatomy of the lineage.** A tree that develops harmoniously is a tree where the links between different members of the family are healthy, where the relationships unfold according to the material, emotional, and psychological needs of each. A "twisted" tree, where the links have become inextricable knots, creates stagnant situations in which one or more family members lose their lives, their time, or their creative capacity and remain locked in a system of deadly relationships. For example, a child who is given the name of a great-uncle who died very young in the war is going to be "pulled" toward the great-uncle, toward what he represents in the eyes of different family members, as in a human body where an inadvertent muscle contraction might immobilize the entire body.

To understand and resolve these transgenerational contractures, we must first delve deeply into the manner in which links are interwoven between children and those around them, and how thanks to the previously mentioned repetition process unresolved knots can impact several generations. In this chapter we will study the main knots present in most genealogy trees, their influence on individual lives, and the methods by which we free ourselves.

IDENTIFY RESISTANCE

First, let us recall the four kinds of repetition discussed in part 3:

- **Mere repetition** is a phenomenon of loyalty and identification with another where habit opposes creativity, and where difference is perceived as threatening in family matters: members of a lineage reproduce the same actions, the same dates, the same age, the same names, the same jobs, and so forth. It is a bond that involves repetition of the same, the unequivocal victory of the past over the present and the future.

- **Interpretation** operates with more subtlety, making it more challenging to flush out. It is the way in which a person uses his own system of references to translate information that the genealogy tree has bequeathed him, adjusting his life in a seemingly individualized and new manner. A son is abandoned by his mother, who dreams she is a character in a novel. In adulthood, using this process of interpretation he falls in love with a writer who represents the mother he never knew: a woman who animates fictional characters in his imagination.

- **Opposition** is well known. It is often an adolescent strategy that persists into adulthood and consists of losing the values of the genealogy tree, ostensibly to free oneself, but actually done in such a systematic way that the results are ultimately a repetition.

- **Compensation** is an attempt to get what the previous generation was not given. This is the process by which parents, in spite of the best intentions, make their children bear all the failures they suffered from their own parents (or from their spouses).

Example: The "psychology" column of a popular weekly magazine, recently recounted the story of a woman abandoned by her husband who decided to sleep with her four-year-old daughter so as, she said, "not to sleep alone." She wondered candidly if the little girl would urinate every night while asleep. The psychologist journalist's wary commentary was as follows: "The father's departure is also traumatic for the little girl so she must be given the choice to sleep in the bed." Very well. But, we add, by offsetting the absence of the father with the presence of the child, the mother imposes the impossible task of completing an irreconcilable conflict on the little girl: how to fix the grief that her mother feels, and how to replace the father? In other words, how to fulfill the need that was imposed on her, and how to stop being herself? The act of urination, which amounts to marking one's territory as mammals, is the only response that this little girl can give to her mother. She expresses with one gesture all that she cannot say: "You force me to play a role that does not correspond to me. You put chaos in my soul. My body can only say 'I exist. If I want to sleep with you it is because I love you. But to place me at your side to compensate for the absence of my father is truly murder. Grow up and take care of me as you should!'"

All eighteenth- and nineteenth-century philosophy teaches us that morality consists of treating the other as an end and not as a means. One can say that pathologies of genealogy trees have a common origin: the fact that adults, under various titles and in diverse ways, treat children in their care as a means (a solution, a compensation, an interpretation, etc.) and not as an end in itself. To accomplish this, the adults impose *orders* for children to not be who they are, and *prohibitions* that forbid them from being who they are.

These toxic repetitions can affect a child's four energies, causing debasement or intellectual vagueness, suffering and emotional blockage, disturbances of creativity or desire, physical or financial problems, trouble with appetite or sleeping, and so on. But no matter what type of suffering results, it is difficult to detach because this suffering is the vestige of a bond we had with parents or adult educators and family links become the inextricable knots.

The study of these knots requires great courage. Indeed, everything we missed becomes the source of a persistent infantilism in the corner of our being that hides under a series of resistances very familiar to professional therapists. The majority of therapeutic approaches have their own way of creating radical change by dissolving or bypassing the resistance of those who come for healing or for "treatment," which is actually an avoidance of change by putting oneself under the care of a substitute parent, hoping the therapist will bring about the expected mutation. Very similar natural resistance appears in spiritual work, and each one of the traditions has its own way of responding to it. There are also practices that interface with creative work, but in general in these cases the artist himself forges his own system, that allows him to overcome his own resistances. The best instructors in theater, singing, and all art know how to apply their previous discoveries to other strategic approaches when endeavoring to be independent of their heritage and upbringing—which is to say, their limits.

Similarly, many resistances oppose observation of repetition in the genealogy tree, which makes it necessary to face the stark vision of the shortcomings to which we have all been victim. We must also overcome a variety of fears (material, sexual and creative, emotional, intellectual), all of which have the same origin in the fundamental terror of being disowned by our parents and excluded from the clan, which corresponds (in the primitive mind) to a death sentence. This fear can create resistance that represents a **skill,** because it protects us and, at the same time, an **obstacle,** because it binds us to the past. From the metagenealogical perspective, we can say that **resistance is the specific way in which the past is embodied in an individual.** The difficulties posed will take shape thanks to one's own Consciousness, or, before any work can take place, through someone who patiently helps shed light on the family tree in order to identify these resistances.

The person who has not faced his own resistances can in no way be credible when he says to another, "It seems to me that you are resisting." Thus, in addition to identifying our own resistances toward the genealogy tree, we will also focus on all of life's situations that reawaken the painful situations we experienced in childhood.

The five main types of resistance correspond to behaviors that animals adopt when faced with danger in the natural world:

- **Flight:** if an animal feels the slightest weakness toward the danger that threatens
- **Attack:** if an animal feels the danger is stronger, or if escape is not possible
- **Withdrawal:** to protect himself, like a turtle or hedgehog
- **Camouflage:** in order to not be seen, like a chameleon
- **Self-destruction (in extreme cases):** like a scorpion committing suicide by planting its own sting in its body

These can manifest psychologically in the following ways:

- **Flight:** refusal to speak; becoming offended and leaving with a slam of the door; creating a diversion; being inattentive; daydreaming; falling asleep; crying; laughing for no reason
- **Attack:** creating anger; contradicting everything that is offered; physically or verbally attacking a person who is trying to help
- **Withdrawal:** overexplaining situations without really communicating; remaining firmly convinced of something in spite of conflicting evidence that explains the situation; staying silent; becoming immobilized; refraining from feeling
- **Camouflage:** adopting a false personality; substituting intellectual explanation for emotional feeling; lying to others and to oneself; trying to seduce the therapist; looking for theoretical explanations and applying them arbitrarily to a situation; hiding behind lines like "everyone else is doing it"
- **Self-destruction:** all forms of physical self-harm (cutting oneself, hitting oneself, pulling one's hair, biting one's fingernails, picking one's face); incessantly complaining; denigrating oneself; intoxicating oneself (drugs, alcohol, tobacco, dependence on work or sexuality); falling ill; attempting suicide

THE ROLE OF PSYCHOMAGIC
AND THE BENEFIT OF THE MALADY

In speaking of the "benefit" of the disease (described by Freud as attachment to neurotic symptoms in order to avoid an emotional breakdown or to get attention or appreciation), this "mutilation" of what is really being perceived is considered the lesser evil compared to any change that might cause unbearable tensions. We add that these mental or physical illnesses do not serve as recognition of the deficiencies from which we suffer: a child prefers to keep painful, even mutilating symptoms rather than admit that he was never loved. The pain of this absence exists in the Unconscious, but in order to avoid dealing with it one covers it with a persistent hope that the past is going to change, that things are going to get better due to a miraculous intervention by the parent, or by someone who represents the parent. We see mature, even elderly people persisting in this process, continuing to visit abusive parents with a constant thirst for recognition that will never come, desperately trying to establish a bond that will never exist. When the parent dies, a number of adults collapse, vaguely aware that the absent love will never henceforth manifest. And some have such a hard time with mourning that they will go so far as to consult spiritualists in hopes of finally hearing the words they have waited for all their lives: "My child, I love you, and I have always loved you."

It is, in fact, very difficult to face the knots that have shaped us. Faced with a father who disallows any outward sign of femininity, a young girl may unconsciously "choose" to reject her own body by taking refuge in the intellect, suffering painful menstruation, jeopardizing her chances of experiencing sexual pleasure, even hating herself and systematically failing every one of her undertakings in order to maintain the only bond with her father she has ever known. Rejected, with her femininity denied, she will nonetheless be identified and connected to her father by this disempowering relationship. Whoever dares enter into the convolutions of such knots must trace the link from end to end in order to be able to undo the maze of ties. But this process can seem hopeless. How many patients (considered "difficult" by therapists of all kinds) spend years roaming through the labyrinths of their suffering, reviewing each and every toxic order they received without ever finding a way out?

There again the metagenealogical approach is different from classical therapy. Facing these knots is a painful process that can legitimately discourage any determined person, unless one has been offered a solution for resolving and untangling the links in question. That is why we accompany the study of the knots with a series of proposals that will enable them to be resolved. The disease and the cure, the **strong resistance** and the **creative proposal**, go hand in hand.

It is here that Psychomagic intervenes. A healing art inspired by witchcraft, old magic, and also theater, this technique uses metaphorical actions and is based on the principle of reversed psychoanalysis. Instead of teaching the Unconscious to speak a language understood by the Conscious, one uses the language of the Unconscious itself—dreams, symbols and metaphors—consciously addressing it in an organized and deliberate way. Psychotherapists take the dream into account yet consciously explain it, interpret it, and question it, with rationality always overpowering irrationality. Inversely, with Psychomagic, conscious spirit learns to speak the language of intuition, renouncing its logical structure by virtue of more paradoxical, creative, organic, and dreamlike principles, agreeing to put into place the means to act in an analogical way. In this regard, primitive magic has long understood the power of analogy: when one wishes for rain, one executes a dance that imitates the sound of rain (the trampling of the dancers' feet on the earth); when one wants to kill someone, one destroys a statuette of his effigy.

When a person remains a prisoner of infantile decisions that make adult life impossible, metaphor becomes a favored tool for resolving conflicts between unconscious, imperious orders like "I am useless, and I should die so he will love me" or "I must remain attached to my parents forever" and the healthy inhibitions of a socialized, responsible, conscious adult who doesn't wish to kill, die, or transgress any major prohibition. When awareness, forgiveness, sublimation, and other reasonable alternatives are ineffective, metaphor and theatrical acts become preferred methods of achieving infantile desires without violating accepted norms, thus addressing fundamental taboos in a symbolic rather than a literal way.

So, **a psychomagical act is a theatrical and metaphorical scenario** that the consultant must implement by his own means (choosing appropriate location and assistants, making or buying accessories, etc.). It can have one conclusion, or several simultaneous endings:

- **Satisfying** a desire, need, order, or seemingly unattainable prohibition rooted in the Unconscious. This may be having a sexual relationship with a family member, dying, failing, killing someone, becoming a person of the opposite sex, obtaining impossible gratification, or appropriating a treasure in order to finally break free and move beyond, on to something else. For example, if a person struggles with the desire of coprophagia, it is not necessary for him to put his health in danger to literally fulfill this wish; he can instead place a bit of melted chocolate on his partner's thoroughly cleaned anus or on a clean chamber pot and metaphorically fulfill the act of devouring excrement.

- **Integrating** information whose absence has rendered a person unable to progress, like finally knowing what paternal or maternal love is, knowing that she can survive in a dangerous situation, reaching a state of grace or grandeur formerly prevented by the genealogy tree, mourning those who have departed without a proper funeral or death ritual, or being allowed to break apparently absolute rules. For example, a number of women have difficulty grieving an abortion or a miscarriage because the baby (or the egg) that was removed from them is generally thrown into the garbage or incinerator. In this case, a woman can put a piece of fruit on her abdomen (kept in place by flesh-colored tape), which symbolizes the fetus, and then with the help of an assistant who is dressed as a doctor reenact the original experience, expressing all that she could not at that time. Then, in a box decorated with care, she will bury the fruit of her womb and plant some flowers or a tree at the burial site to symbolize that life begins again.

- **Deactivating** negative programming, also injected via metaphor, which the child absorbed as a reality. This category includes imaginary crimes, like a child who wished for an adult's death being blamed because the person actually died, or an inadvertent and helpless witness of an accident that could not have been avoided feeling at fault nonetheless, as well as negative predictions ("you are going to die at such-and-such age," "you will never be a mother"), curses, spells, and other imaginary ideas. An example of this is a professional psychologist whose father told him many times during his childhood, "If you don't study science, you're going to become a bum. Other trades yield nothing." This psychologist, who felt limited in his practice because of this negative prediction, had few patients and thought that this curse had again bound him to his father. His act of Psychomagic consisted of dressing as a street urchin for an entire day while seeing clients. The theatrical fulfillment of this prediction freed him in the long term, and his practice expanded because he no longer allowed himself to limit the appropriate use of his skills and talents while doing his job.

In metagenealogical terms, we can say that **study of the knot corresponds to the work on the past, and Psychomagic to the work on the future.** These two aspects are inseparable. It is necessary to help the person understand that the way in which he lives today is nothing but the result of a series of traumas and concessions made to a pathological upbringing. At the same time, he must come to understand that facilitating the opening of his future by means of a metaphorical act is essential. The psychomagic act is a kind of trip to the future that allows us to have, here and now, an immediate experience of the kind of life possible when we are able to experience all that our past training prohibited. In other words, Psychomagic enables us to emerge from the artificial ego forged by our genealogy tree through unusual actions that are footprints of a broader dimension that return us to the genius, hero, saint, or champion we have the potential to become. The acquired personality is a collection of habits that the psychomagic act shatters by offering an unedited creative experience. In the dynamic between past and future, we finally have the means of **freely choosing our path in life.**

Throughout this work on the knots of abuse and the healing of the genealogy tree we mention a number of psychomagic acts that readers have the liberty to make use of if they wish. But if Psychomagic is attractive, we must also add that it is neither a game nor an easily mastered art form. A good psychomagic act looks like a top-flight artistic gesture, like a sublime picture, a pure and authentic song, an expressive dance that seems so easy and obvious that all people who attempt it feel something imminently familiar. However, not everyone is Michelangelo, Maria Callas, or Isadora Duncan. One must have solid training and enormous talent, courage, and experience to be capable of designing these truly lifesaving psychomagic acts, whether for oneself or for others.

In nontherapeutic art an invading ego can be an asset, the usage of drugs allowed, and a lack of talent immediately debunked by negative reaction of the public. For its part, the art of Psychomagic addresses people in distress and requires a transpersonal level of Consciousness and impeccable mental hygiene. Any overflow of the psychomagician's ego is an assault on the consultant's psyche, and the other's wound cannot, in any case, be a place of narcissistic delight for the apprentice psychomagician. And, unfortunately, all absence of talent or relevance risks going unnoticed if the consultant has such need for finding a solution that he naively applies an erroneous act of Psychomagic. Furthermore, the use of drugs is unacceptable when facing a person who is trying with all his might to attain clarity.

An imperfect psychomagic act is as dangerous as an improperly performed surgical procedure. One must not enter a person's psyche with impunity or use negative information that risks causing guilt, anguish, and grief.

For example, a number of psychomagic acts involve a burial ritual to symbolize that the deadly past can rest in peace, or that a disappeared person can at last find his remains. However, if we rationally accept death as an ending, the Unconscious considers it to be a season in a cycle called to regenerate endlessly. This is why we do not bury anything in Psychomagic without planting a flower or a tree over the gravesite. We can then be free of guilt and conclude that this is a peaceful act because life grows from that which was buried. Similarly, in certain extreme cases of staging one's own death—or, more precisely, the death of an old personality—a person can deliver his own eulogy before an assembly; lie in a hole and (except for the face) be covered with dirt; then, with eyes closed, let everything die that does not belong to him, being reborn into a new life by way of a name change.* This process is analogous to a snake shedding his skin, with this casting off manifested by an observed act. However, it is a big mistake if the budding psychomagician dares to "embellish" this act by proposing that the person burn his own tombstone and leave the burial place instead of planting a tree; that which is fertile ground for future life would become a cemetery instead, and the person would live with the feeling that part of him remains buried and enclosed in a given location.

We have chosen to provide the most general advice possible so that readers will be able to make use of it at their own discretion. If we are tempted to advise another person to use an act that worked for us, we should abstain. Although an apparently attractive and innocent process, Psyschomagic is a powerful tool that can cause damage when not used properly. It can be a quick way to resolve a fixation or trauma, but it should never replace the individual sovereignty of a person who is free to decide what is right for himself.

Psychomagic moves the human being's four energies, enabling him to get closer to the four principles of magic: desire (intellect), courage (the emotional center), power (sexual and creative energy), and silence, or "shutting up," and obeyance (living the act without

---

*This act will be described more in detail on p. 420.

exhibition or profit, peacefully welcoming the result without a goal).

As in Psychomagic, the four principles of magic are comprised of **aligning and uniting the four languages separated by a familial, social, and cultural upbringing** that force us to conform to a model of the past that embellishes a tradition and an already known identity to the detriment of our true selves.

- **Will:** A person who truly wants to change must be free of prejudices and family tyranny in order to be completely fulfilled and achieve her full potential, therefore obeying the higher will of universal Consciousness. Very often this means choosing between intellect and intuition, but once precedence has been given to intuition the intellect will eventually become its faithful servant.

- **Daring:** Daring is the decision to break away from the limitations of daily life and its emotional training in order to accept change and do different things by surpassing the fear of losing or failing in order to submit to new experiences, even voluntarily submitting to emotional pain in order to release the fear. This involves being able to enter into negative emotions with a level of attention and presence, which allows their full acceptance in order to move beyond them. And, as suggested by the Tarot Arcanum XV—the

Devil, full of eyes distributed about the body—the exploration of one's own depths suggests that the individual is losing the fear of being oneself. Indeed, with the radical act of seeing, the daily *me* will begin to immediately dissolve.

- **Power:** Proof of power is that one can be one's self, not who others want one to be, and do what one really desires. To do this, the path to the psychomagic act represents the triumph of an intention made to address powerlessness. One therefore frees oneself from the enjoyment of failure that comes from obedience to the orders and prohibitions of the genealogy tree. In traditional magic, the devil is despised because he is so good at being one who is unable, who fails, and who must resort to tricks to hide his failure. He is a loser before God. Psychologically, the devil represents the image we have of ourselves fighting against our own achievement, but the magician is capable of overcoming and ceasing to fight against himself. The psychomagic act, with its ritual and artistic dimension, represents a unique and unforgettable gesture that seals the victory over oneself, over the persistent child, over the inertia of the past.

- **Silence (shutting up) and obeyance:** This happens when we understand that words are not reality, and that thoughts are the enemy of the encounter with ourself. We decide to stop thinking in order to feel, to respect and thank life. Keeping quiet also means not discussing, stopping denial, and accepting receipt of the fruits of an act. It is a means to silence the ego that opposes change. The magician accepts the gifts that we have all received through inheritance—the whole universe that we share with all living beings. This is the meaning of "shutting up," going from *me* to *Nous*,* and becoming a sliver of the whole, that which we have already called the transpersonal being. Calming individual anxiety about a prohibited impulse, one stages an act and goes beyond the "me" (which is stopped in time at the age at which

---

*[The transpersonal identity. —*Ed.*]

the knot was formed during childhood) to the adult "me" (which incorporates the present, the collective, and the aspirations of the essential Being in the development of the future). On a practical level, if one decides to perform a psychomagic act it will be realized as such only if one does not fall prey to the temptation to babble, does not haggle or endlessly discuss it with one's entourage before, or instead of, proceeding with the action. On the other hand, once the act is fulfilled, one can retrospectively share the results with people of good faith whom this experience might interest.

THE CHILD AND THE CORE

There is not a family, a society, or any part of humanity that does not have connections. We are relational beings. But we must distinguish between a **healthy bond** that allows us to evolve and grow and a **blind bond** that chains us to a stagnant situation. The central concept to study in all relationships is that of freedom. The relationship cannot consist of a demand that the other be something he is not. Parents in particular must allow children to be themselves, with the freedom to think, love, create, live, move, and exist as masculine or feminine individuals.

It is the prohibition of being what we are, or the ordering to be that which we are not, that transforms the bond into a knot. Orders and prohibitions generally take the form of an imposed absence or excess on the child by those who raise him.

In order to understand the formation of a knot, we must first define the conception we have of the development of the child. We can say, in broad outline, that two trends oppose and complement each other in traditional psychotherapy: one considers the infantile unconscious as a receptacle of the primitive past (discussed below), and the other exalts the child as if infantile innocence were the greatest of human qualities (the "inner child" would allegedly be a resource of creativity, innocence, and endless energy).

Metagenealogy considers human childhood to be a step leading to various degrees of maturity in an effort to end at the highest level of the human being, which is old age. So, to conceive of the human as a **being in constant progress,** in transformation and with a purpose, testifies to the possibility of our evolution continuing until the moment of death—to the exact time of death, never too early, and in an intact state of Consciousness. We can also imagine that at the moment of our disappearance we continue with our development. Those who remain in a state of infantile discontent die unsatisfied, without the possibility of their final development, and a "good death" is impossible without having arrived at satisfaction. For this reason, the first cure that one must wish on a gravely ill person is spiritual healing. It is also the reason for occupying oneself with becoming who one truly is while there is still time, remaining vigilant (unexpected mortal accidents can happen), and trying not to be surprised by death while in a state of dissatisfaction. We will see in part 10 that acute awareness of death and the study thereof through the genealogy tree are the essential elements of this work.

Returning to the child, the psychoanalytic theory dominating the twentieth century is based on the notion of "perverse polymorphous," introduced by Freud. To briefly summarize this Freudian theory, we remember first of all that what Freud called "infantile sexuality" is not, strictly speaking, sexuality but covers all explorations made by a child in his search of pleasure (sensual, erotic, or otherwise), which will later reverberate through the adult personality and sexuality. The term "perverse polymorphous," which so shocked Freud's contemporaries, means that the child explores that which the psychologists call "partial drives"—functional elements of the body like sucking and control of the sphincters—which will unify in an adolescent to form adult sexuality. Freud used the term "perverse" based on the morality of his time to indicate that a child exerts this autoerotic activity without guilt.

But the assumption of this theory returns to define the Unconscious (and, in particular, the "It" conceived of by Groddeck and taken by Freud, which refers to the instinctual part of the human psyche, indifferent to any standard and any reality, governed by the sole principle of immediate satisfaction*) as the receptacle of humanity's "primitive" past. According to psychoanalysis, the "It"—or id, as it's more commonly known today—would be the primary authority of the newborn. Psychologists define the term "drive" (in German *trieb,* meaning both "instinct" and "thrust," and on which Freud based the concepts of his system of thought) as an interior or exterior movement whose aim is satisfaction.

Freud's heirs never imagined that the future could be active in a human being. Similarly, scientists postulated that man appeared on Earth by accident, and didn't imagine for even a moment that man could have a future intention: a need for the universe in order to create Consciousness.

However, if we allow the hypothesis that the universe has a precise plan and a purposeful goal, whatever it may be, and that in one instance this goal reflects that which we called the **collective Unconscious** (a part of the Unconscious as we see it, a union of past and future), we can no longer consider the child to be a "perverse polymorph." Instead, the child is a **being driven by the precise purpose** of participating in his own indispensible way in the formation of humanity through his evolution toward total Consciousness. Facing this purpose, the human being is not finished but is developing. All planetary accidents (ecological catastrophes, wars, economic problems) can then be considered to have occurred because of a lack of Consciousness on the part of humanity in the past and representative of necessary obstacles so that future humanity will have total fulfillment. Without obstacles, there is no growth.

In the inner world, which is analogous with the outer world, the major obstacle is the ego: the individuality produced by repetition of the past and shaped by family, society, and culture. This ego is absolutely

---

*"To the oldest of these psychical provinces or agencies we give the name of id. It contains everything that is inherited, that is present at birth, that is laid down in the constitution—above all, therefore, the instincts, which originate from the somatic organization and which find a first psychical expression here in forms unknown to us." (Freud, *An Outline of Psycho-Analysis*)

necessary, as essential as an egg to a bird's hatching. The ego is nothing but a fragment of the Being, and infantile impulses, far from being a repetition of past cruelties, are the womb of essential future qualities. For example, when a child practices masturbation he creates the conditions for a mature, fully blossomed sexuality that may even grow into sacred sexuality—the union of orgasm and ecstasy. Facing this practice, the sick society of the nineteenth century cauterized the clitoris of young girls, creating permanent mental and physical wounds, or, in the best of circumstances, threatened the punishment of hell or disabilities (like deafness) onto children for unacceptable behavior, a typical example of collective abuse due to a lack of generalized societal Consciousness.

Just as life and Consciousness are found in the explosive power of a galaxy, **the power of human Consciousness is contained in a child.** His "instincts," to use the psychological term, must be respected and accompanied as the seeds of future qualities of the accomplished human being. But every child born is affected by worthless ideas, feelings, desires, and needs acquired from deceased members of his genealogy tree. If the parents accompany their child's development with their highest level of Consciousness they will help him move beyond preset limitations with his own genius and, in this way, transform the transgenerational formation. However, when this process—which should be fulfilled in a happy and balanced atmosphere—is thwarted and prevented by interests, prejudices, repetitions, and abuse, the child remains a prisoner of all or part of the gangue of the tree and develops various neuroses.

For the word "drive" (which, as we have seen, means the child's relationship with the satisfaction of his needs and bodily pleasures), we can substitute the word **"core"** to designate a **still undifferentiated potentiality that speaks candidly and ungovernably**, which is to say, without self-censorship and with an imperious strength.

The study of hundreds of genealogy trees has allowed us to isolate six main knots from each of their corresponding cores. These six cores partially cover the drives described by Freud, and they go beyond the domain of material needs and erotic desires to affect the totality of the

human being in the power that is the child. These include his relationship with the senses; morality and language (the intellect); his emotional
relationship to his surrounding (feelings); the libidinal relationship to
the objects that surround him (sexuality and creativity during upbringing); and also, of course, his needs, body, and space (material life). Also
included are the stages of his spiritual development (his Consciousness)
and, for the social core, the way in which the family connects with society, projected very early with the child's entrance to nursery or elementary school.

A knot forms when a parent or other member of the family is incapable of supporting the growth of the child in a balanced way. The formation of the knots obeys the two main mechanisms of **deficiency and
excess.**

When the child is a victim of deficiency like lack, absence, abandonment, rejection, or deprivation, part of him tends to remain fixed at the
age at which this deficiency took place, waiting endlessly for someone to
give him that which he has not received; thus the knot is created by the
parent's flaw. When, on the other hand, the child is a victim of excess
like encroachment, enmeshed relationship, takeover, excessive demand,
sexual abuse, or overeating, this excess is also a trauma that will create a
fixation at the age at which it took place. The child, incapable of regu-
lating the excess imposed on him by the adult, remains fixated in the
core instead of evolving beyond it.

These deficiencies and excesses from adults can be provoked by circumstances independent of their will, as in illness, death, or exile, but as
a general rule they often obey the processes of **projection** and **compensation,** about which we have already spoken. In this case, as far as the
parents are concerned, the child represents some other character in the
tree with whom a previous knot was not resolved, and the adults unconsciously decides that the trauma this person inflicted on them will be
compensated for in their relationship with the child. The child may
thus find himself privy to a bond that he can legitimately claim or, to
the contrary, encumbered by a relationship that doesn't have anything
to do with him. For example, he frequently sees his mother—who has

no satisfying relationship with her own father—defer all emotional requests and disappointments of her own son. The child grows up in an imposed relational climate, which he literally "sculpts," and the paternal grandfather becomes, consciously or not, a kind of ideal model or repellent with which the child is endlessly confronted.

The majority of these relational deviations are performed in a completely unconscious way, and in spite of the adult's best intentions. They affect all generations, and it would be best if we could begin by identifying them in our own triads before adding to the genealogical tree. Indeed, an error (or a resistance) frequently consists of finding a hereditary gap four or five generations ago in the knot or injury and realigning the feeling of, for example, permanent abandonment felt from a great-great-grandmother orphaned by both parents, instead of clarifying the relational knots in the closer generations and analyzing their sequences, which would allow us to see that the lines of abandonment are there among parents and grandparents under the guise of a "normal" upbringing.

PERSISTENT CORES AND KNOTS
Manifestation and Resolution

We have seen that children's cores are potentialities rich in vital, libidinal, emotional, and intellectual energy, but are fragile as a young sprout. In the human being still in development, each functions and responds to a real necessity. If, instead of accompanying the development (and therefore the shattering) of this core, the adults establish a relational knot, the core persists beyond childhood in the form of stagnant or calcified vitality, which prevents them from fully living their adult destiny. The majority of these persistent cores are received directly from a knot formed with a close family member afflicted by an unresolved core.

Here are the six main infantile cores:

- **The incestuous core** relates to the necessity of the infant to form in the four centers, which is initially accomplished through an exclusive bond with family members because the family is the first intellectual, emotional, sexual-creative, and material reference.

- **The bisexual core** refers to our initial sexual nature, which drives the child to freely explore his relationship with the opposite sex while simultaneously exploring his relationship with the same sex in order to build his future sexual identity. As a persistent core, we will call it "homosexual."

- **The sadomasochistic core** connects with the essential exploration that all children undertake in order to recognize pain as a fundamental element of life. It deals concurrently with pain felt and pain inflicted, the two sources of intensity that the child is going to learn to healthily integrate into his existence.

- **The narcissistic core** concerns the stages of development where the child becomes his own privileged reference, thus building his capacity to differentiate (at first) from the mother or the caretaker by recognizing himself.

- **The cannibal core** represents all of the stages of development where the other (the parent, generally) is the source by which the child feeds himself—materially, creatively or sexually, emotionally, and intellectually—and is the child's legitimate appropriation of the physical and psychological energy of the other.

- **The social core** designates the process of assimilation of the child into the group, at first within the family itself, then by way of the family through all the stages of necessary socialization. As a persistent core, we will call it "social neurosis."

Ideally all of these cores are intended to open or melt into the blossoming of the fully adult person. This person is then freed of all incestuous, active attachments that were passively established in his sexual identity and erotic preferences. He is capable of experiencing pain without it becoming suffering; narcissistically stable, but conscious of the existence of others; capable of finding sources of energy without turning into a predator; capable of communicating with others in a true exchange; and ultimately socialized without losing contact with his essential identity.

In adulthood, the limiting action of the genealogy tree is generally aligned with the persistence of one or more cores in one or more of the four centers. One could say that the adult cores are the representations of the direct action of the genealogy tree on the psyche's interior. In general, the cores are so encrusted in the deepest formation of a person's identity that the person submits to them without protest, or without even noticing them. "This is just my personality," "I am just like this," "That's life," "This is just how the world works," "I am just doing what everyone else does," "This is just normal."

Work on the knots and the cores concerns four generations of the genealogy tree, and it is evident that the knots are transmitted from one generation to the next. For example, in the sense of multiple siblings, a strong incestuous bond may unite a brother and sister: they always count on one another more than on the rest of the family; they each get married but their children (his son and her daughter) are coupled in the next generation; these first cousins are married (legal in some countries/societies), which socially validates the incestuous brother/sister desire that could not be fulfilled in the previous generation.

To clarify the tree's knots, it is better to begin with one's own generation and go back gradually. This clarification has four aspects:

- **Understanding how the knot was formed:** With which family members, and for what reasons?
- **Recognizinge the persistent core:** If the knot is that of a parent or a grandparent, one must put oneself in that person's position. Being face-to-face with a persistent knot is often painful, because it sends one back to a lack or an excess experienced early in life. In order to accept it one can use this formula: "I was trained this way. It is a habit. I am not at fault but it has decisively influenced me all my life."

- **Learning to better know the core:** Facing it, whatever its nature, seeing it is a present trend in all of humanity, with all its nuances, as evidenced by contextual works of art and cultural practices. Understanding a toxic relationship can make it unravel; understanding a core can restore its vitality, replacing it in the dynamic of growth and thereby unlocking it. This stage is essential because in adulthood the persistent core will always give us a feeling of isolation, helplessness, and shame.
- **Embracing the core and acquiring the missing information:** What was not experienced during childhood? What freedom or fulfillment is possible beyond this persistent core? This is possible to achieve, as we shall see below, by means of a psychomagic act.

Of course, resolving knots is a question of evolving, and not of changing beyond recognition. The trace of the core will remain present more or less as an affirmed personality trait. One can then **exalt the old core**—that is, give it usefulness, or make it a strength rather than a weakness or a block. For example:

- Without the slight persistence of the sadomasochistic core, it is unthinkable that one could be a good surgeon, good butcher, or good practitioner of Vipassanā meditation.
- The narcissistic core is an asset for the stage arts and, in general, for all professions where one is seen.
- Trade in antiques, the preservation of patrimony, and all the activities geared toward the exaltation of the qualities of the past fall under an incestuous core.
- Learning, collections, and also some kinds of controlled nutrition fall under the exalted cannibal core.
- All organizations that collect human beings by gender (army, navy, football, convents) are derived from the homosexual core.
- The passion for political activity at the local or national level can be a positive fulfillment of going beyond the social neurosis core.

We are now going to study the six infantile cores, the knots that determine their persistence into adulthood, and some key psychomagic resolutions for each type of core in detail. For each we will see which of the child's psychic needs it responds to, how the core turned into a knot by absence or excess imposed by the familial or educative environment, and what the consequences are in adulthood of the persistent core.

It is impossible to exhaust the infinite shapes the genealogy tree's knots and cores can take by a series of examples, but we will present some practical cases that can assist the reader to better visualize the actions of the knots and cores, and the way to dissolve them. In some cases, a psychomagic act that has been invented specifically for the person will be necessary. Otherwise, awareness suffices to untie the knot and to blossom from the core, moving beyond childish attachments.

INCESTUOUS CORE AND KNOT

The Incestuous Infantile Core and Its Goal

A child is shaped to think, love, desire, and live in the immediate proximity of the family—parents, brothers and sisters, sometimes uncles and aunts or grandparents. The child's first movement in the four energies is to unite with the members of his family: he speaks a native language; loves those who take care of him first; learns to desire and know his first sensual satisfaction in the framework of the family; grows up, eats, sleeps, and lives among his own.

If this core is guided by mature parents, the child can **emerge from the family one day and take his place in the world:** because he has spoken his native language, he will be able to learn foreign languages; because he will have experienced a loving relationship with his parents, he will be able to love someone from outside the clan; because someone will have given him roots, a base territory, he will be able to explore the totality of the world; because he will have shaped his erotic and creative desires inside the family unit, he will be able to desire a person outside of the clan and create work, objects, and structures independent of the clan.

In summary, an incestuous core's goal of growth is **discovery of the world, and union with it**, and the woven ties with family members ultimately allow the child to leave the family.

The Incestuous Adult Knot and Core

This knot is very frequent because the relationship with the parents is the most fundamental and it is often disturbed in the genealogy tree.

Incest is both one of humanity's main taboos and, also, a universal impulse. Yet, as we saw with the triads, the child is absolutely dependent on the relationship with the parents. If they are absent or dead, or if they have difficulties in assuming their parental roles, an incestuous knot will be created, just the same as if one or both parents force a too narrow, too exclusive, dominant or fused relationship on the child. The person will thus retain partial or total fixation toward one or several members of the family when he becomes an adult.

The processes of emotional fulfillment might be schematically summarized as follows: first the baby is in harmony with the mother; then he discovers and identifies himself as a distinct being; then he discovers the existence of the other and ultimately of Nous (the transpersonal identity). Incestuous knots in the genealogy tree impede this process, and consequently a deprived member cannot access his essential Being and lives in a state of fundamental anger. Under the guise of unbounded love toward the family there is, in reality, an underlying hatred within the incestuous fixation because its foundation resides in the hate of not being able to become oneself.

All incestuous knots produce a confinement: if the goal of the incestuous infantile core is that of opening to the world, the effect of the incestuous adult core is confinement in the family and the inability to venture into the world.

The few testimonials that exist on the part of incestuous couples who openly overstep the mutually agreed-upon ban teach us that incest produces a feeling of immense superiority over the rest of humanity, paradoxically accompanied by a social stigma that cuts said couple off from the rest of society. Moreover, in extreme cases where violent and abusive (nonconsenting) incestuous acts occur, a situation of the victim's imprisonment* is nearly always found.

The incestuous knot may originate from **lack:**

- When parents die prematurely, they will often become an insurmountable ideal model onto which the child projects all possible and imaginable qualities.
- All prolonged relational lack begets an incestuous knot born of a deficiency. For example, a person who never had any intellectual relationship or any communication at all with the father can become a fanatical supporter of paternal ideas in adulthood, living according to his father's beliefs and ethics with the unconscious hope of attracting his attention (even if he is already dead). Similarly, a person who was not loved by his parents can compensate for this emotional deficiency by forming an extreme attachment to a family home, which then becomes the center of his world after their deaths. The emotional absence, "I was not loved," thus becomes an incestuous material core, "My parents' home replaces the love they didn't give me; I will destroy myself for this house if I have to."

The incestuous knot can also be the consequence of **excess:**

- An example is the frequent situation where the parent "couples" with the child: the husband lets the wife down, and the wife turns all of her affection toward her son. The child grows up with the weight of a relationship that does not fit him in age or status, making him the prisoner of a knot ("I cannot leave my mom, she would die"). It is the same process as in an actual sexual act, which also creates an incestuous knot.

---

*In April 2008 a seventy-three-year-old Austrian, Joseph Fritzl, was arrested for having held his daughter captive until she was forty-two years old. He kept her in a bunker under the house. His abuse begot six offspring, one of whom died. Some of the children were kept in captivity and Fritzl and his wife "freely" raised the others. The two hidden children had never seen the light of day.

- When parents make several children sleep in the same bed, one could say they encourage the development of an incestuous sexuality in which they symbolically participate by creating these conditions.

Here are some examples that can put you on the right track for recognizing an incestuous core according to the four centers:

- **Incestuous intellectual core.** Thinking like the father or mother. Defending the parents' ideas and speaking only the parents' language. Failing to shed an original accent by learning a foreign language. Studying subjects in order to gain the parents' recognition, or else failing these studies in order to get their attention. Adopting the parents' value system, voting as the parents vote. Systematically asking father or mother for advice before doing things. Being influenced by mom, dad, brother, sister, and their opinions. Systematically arguing with the parents in order to return to the infantile conflict relationship, the only one ever known.
- **Incestuous emotional core.** The main love object is mom, dad, a sister, or a brother. A sister marries her brother's best friend (incest by proxy). A man lets his mother separate him from all his friends. A girl marries a man whose first name is the same as her father, or else the man is her father's employee or friend. One only falls in love with those already in relationships, thus reproducing the Oedipal triangle where there is always a rival. The "heartache" of not having been loved by the father or the mother causes the person to remain unmarried throughout life, or to project idealized, emotional relationships onto unapproachable people (erotomanic delusion).
- **Incestuous sexual or creative core.** An incestuous relationship from the past remains the subject of fixation (secret, shame, phantom, or blockage, or a child may even be born out of incest in the family). A son remains a virgin or becomes impotent in order to

not "betray" his mother. A girl becomes a nymphomaniac and/or frigid after her father sexually contacted her, which was the only orgasm she ever had. On the creative plane, the son or daughter repeats and extends the mother or father's artistic work, copying the style, tapping into the parent's world, and incestuously uniting to the parent by way of this creation.

- **Incestuous material core.** In adulthood the child lives off the parents' money, sleeps in the parents' bed, wears other family members' clothing, lives to old age with the parents or other family members, can only eat food prepared by mother or father, works in the family business at a job that does not allow for blossoming or purpose.

Cultural and Religious Aspects

Many founding myths from diverse cultures are based on one or more incestuous relationships. This fundamental prohibition does not apply to the gods, and it makes sense that in ancient Egypt incest could be a royal prerogative reflecting the pharaohs' divine nature.

In the West, the Christian myth (understanding that by "myth" we mean an account on which religious beliefs are based) also presents us with the foundation of incest, experienced in a symbolic way: the young virgin girl, Mary, becomes pregnant by the Lord (the supreme Father). God the Father chose this pure woman, who never had sexual intercourse with anyone, joins her, and immediately becomes the son, while Mary's husband Joseph is only the adoptive parent. It can therefore be argued, if Mary is a virgin as stated in the Catholic religion, then her son deflowered her (as would a lover) during his birth. Once born, Mary accompanies him faithfully, one might say like a wife, until his crucifixion, as evidenced by the art of the West with sculpture (*The Pietà*) and hymn ("The Stabat Mater"). According to the Catholic and Orthodox versions of Christianity, Mary immediately rejoins Jesus in paradise after his death (the Assumption or Dormition of Mary).

Translated into the language of the genealogy tree, this founding story creates an order for women in the Christian cultures to beget a

perfect son through whom they are fulfilled, and whose father must symbolically be God himself (which is to say, for a little girl's psyche, her own father). If, in the genealogy tree, the first names Mary and Joseph repeat over several generations it is probably due to the tree being marked by this cultural influence. The perfect son is not necessarily named Jesus (this first name is only current in the Hispanic culture) but may be Emmanuel, Pascal, Christian or Christophe, Noel, Dominic, or else Salvatore, Salvador, or Slater.

The father of this child can be absent, unknown, dead, or disappeared. When the mother proclaims to have been impregnated by an "unknown" whose face does not appear in any family photographs, if she was abandoned during pregnancy or else if the man so disappointed the mother that she erased him, her unconscious desire is to have created a child with her own father—thus fulfilling the incestuous union that she dreamed of in childhood. If a son brought into the world is named after the mother's maiden name, the patrimony of her own father (this incestuous dream is fulfilled all the way to the state registrar), the offspring symbolically extends the maternal grandfather's lineage. Living past thirty-three will generally be crucial for a man born under such auspices.

In such a situation, the incestuous knot is doubled: between the mother and the maternal grandfather on one side, then between the mother and the son, who "incarnates" the grandfather in the same way Jesus incarnates God the Father.

Psychomagic Resolution

As mentioned, the incestuous core is one of the most frequent. Under different shapes this manifestation returns to the desire to have an intimate relationship with the father, the mother, and sometimes a brother or a sister. This infantile intention remains as an obstinate energy that developed a goal. To cite Oscar Wilde, "The only way to get rid of a temptation is to yield to it. Resist it, and your soul grows sick with longing for the things it has forbidden to itself."

For example, when parents and children (generally of the opposite sex) have not known one another, if the son or the daughter is an adult at the moment of reuniting the emergence of the incestuous desire is always of very high intensity. A number of daughters who did not know their fathers are disappointed when they are reunited to find him drunk, confused, or unyielding at the meeting, but these resistances actually cover the panic of facing the incestuous desire and its radical ban, which is one of humanity's founding continuums.

The central psychomagic act for this core can metaphorically **allow an intimate (sexual) relationship** with a member of family, something that must be accomplished without self-criticism: one is never responsible for the knot one carries; this persistence of the core was created by the parents. If my father made me his emotional or sexual partner, if one or both parents made me sleep in the same bed with my brothers or sisters, if I never knew the least manifestation of my parents' affection, it is absolutely legitimate that I would carry an incestuous core, and a liberator who can help me accept the need to face it metaphorically.

The act consists of dressing a consenting person (a prostitute if necessary) in clothes taken from the mother or father prior to the act. If this loan is impossible, one can print a T-shirt with a photo of the parent on it, and eventually write the parent's first name on the partner's forehead. Once the metaphorical father or mother is adorned in the clothing, the consultant delivers this introductory dialogue:

> "For this psychomagic act, do you accept to incarnate my mother/ my father, (parent's first name)."
> "For this psychomagic act, I accept to be (parent's first name)."

Then the "child" must propose to the "parent" the sensual, emotional, and sexual act that suits him. At any moment the consultant can modify or interrupt the course of this intimate rapport. If the core has an important sexual dimension (for example, if it produced a sexual inhibition), it is preferable to have a complete sexual experience accompanied by a real orgasm, or one very well imitated by each partner. It is permissible to use additives that facilitate the sexual experience (lubricants, medication, etc.) the key is anchoring into memory an act that disables and goes beyond the imposed limitations. In the case of a woman who is fixated on carrying her father's child, it is possible to have a round box of chocolates, a watermelon, or a cantaloupe waiting under the bed that will symbolize the "full" belly that results from the father's efforts. This belly can then be carried for twenty-four hours before sharing the chocolates or fruits with the father, or leaving them on the father's grave if he is deceased.

Once the "child" considers the act complete, the consultant undresses the partner and shows gratitude with this formulated ritual: "For this act of Psychomagic, thank you for having represented my father/my mother, (first name)." The partner is then let go. One can offer compensation in the form of money if it is a prostitute, or some kind of gift if it is a friend—or even a simple thank you on bended knee while holding their hands. The choice of partner is important. One should avoid suggesting such an act as a means of seduction, or moreover with the goal of winning back a partner with whom one has complex links. A life partner with whom one has confidence, or a person of good faith with whom the emotional or sexual relationship is very clear, would be ideal. If the act was performed with your life partner it is necessary to bathe together afterward, lathering one another, and in closing have the partner recite, "By this act of Psychomagic, I no longer incarnate your father/your mother."

The clothing used for the act, even if clean, must be washed before being returned to the parent with a little gift (honey, chocolates, wine), so that if the parent is surprised by the "gift," one can say, "Here, I had this at my house, but I think it belongs to you." In a case where the relationship with the parent is very conflictive, one can return the clothing without the parent's knowledge and send him or her white flowers anonymously. If the parent is deceased, the clothes will be brought to the grave (or to wherever he or she was cremated) along with a jar of honey.

If a condom was used, or if any other trace of the act remains, then it must be buried and a vegetable planted on top of it.

Cases

Case No. 1: The mother-son incestuous knot

Precociously widowed by her first husband, Salvador, who died of a heart attack, and without child, Marta remarried at thirty-three. From this union with Jose, brother of her deceased husband, a son was born who was named Salvador, like the deceased. Just after the birth, Marta began to sleep in a separate bedroom. Here the incestuous knot multiplied between the mother and the son, who represented the deceased spouse, but also between Jose (who found himself rejected) and his deceased brother, whose widow he married. It should also be noted that Marta's father is named Alvaro (all the letters of his first name are found in Salvador). The young Salvador grew up in his mother's incestuous emotional and material knots. At her death he experienced a deep identity crisis, and then he encountered Maria, whom he married. However, during the honeymoon, he lost the feeling of union with Maria and upon returning home replaced her with an attachment to his deceased uncle Salvador, an attachment of the same kind that his mother preciously guarded after her husband's death. Some months later, he had a heart attack from which he fortunately recovered, but which prompted him to begin work on his genealogy tree.

His first awareness concerned the incestuous knots in his genealogy tree, causing his identification with the deceased uncle. He performed a number of psychomagic acts of metaphorical incest with the mother, and he buried his uncle Salvador's wedding ring at his mother's grave, saying, "I bring you your beloved."

Case No. 2: An incestuous father

The mother of this little girl died when she was eleven years old. Actually, the mother took her own life, but the truth was hidden from the girl for a long time. The father, a doctor who until then had been very devoted to his depressed wife, sustained an absolute shock at the time of her death—which he had experienced as a personal failure. After the funeral, he summoned the little girl to the bedroom, and under the pretext of teaching her, showed her how to masturbate the masculine sex, his own. After this act there was no further incestuous connection between the father and daughter, but in adulthood she carried a strong incestuous core that was solidified by her father's gesture. The study of the genealogy tree allowed her to understand that it was not only sexual and emotional abuse from which she suffered, but also from the self-centered sense of the relationship that her father had imposed on her that particular day: he was only worried about his sex organs and his own orgasm.

The customized psychomagic act conceived for this consultant consisted in her masturbating with a little photograph of her father (now deceased) in her hand. Once the orgasm that he refused her was obtained (achieved by the same incestuous exchange, and fixed in the Unconscious as a goal), she placed a little bit of honey on the photo and attached it to an inflated helium balloon, metaphorically sending it to a superior dimension in the sky where the benevolent archetypical Father figure resides, allowing her to expel the past obsession from her psyche.

Case No. 3: The mother-father-child incestuous knot

A little girl, child of a soldier and a housewife, knocked one night at the parents' bedroom door with a bad stomachache. The parents, interrupted in the middle of a sexual exchange, strongly scolded her and instructed her not to bother them again. In adulthood she became a couple's mistress, without the power to exit her role as the third in the trio: the unimportant one.

In this person's case it was the loving parental attention that was lacking, and that set as a core the desire to sexually seduce them. Her psychomagic act consisted of finding a couple who agreed to reenact the scene but who, when she knocked on the door in the role of a child, gave her the care and attention she needed, massaging her stomach with essential oil. Sometimes the incestuous core deviates toward sexual fulfillment when it is actually an emotional need that remains unsatisfied.

Case No. 4: The brother-sister couple

These two children spent their lives in the same room, the brother two years older than the sister. There was no sexual act between them, but they grew up in an incestuous climate encouraged by the parents, who found their "little couple" so charming. In adulthood the brother married a woman who shared the same name as his sister—who became the godmother of his first child. At twenty-nine she had failed to find "the man she needed" since all the pressure of her genealogy tree had convinced her that her best partner was her brother.

The metaphoric fulfillment of incest with a partner who agreed to play the role of the brother allowed this young woman to free herself from her core. She placed two pairs of binoculars on the bed, which she later offered to her parents. These binoculars were the metaphoric tool used to help her see since the parents, because of their blindness, built the incestuous brother-sister couple. A "manly" pair of binoculars, used for hunting, went to the mother so she could understand the true needs of her son. Correspondingly, the other more "feminine" pair, adorned with pearls and used for the theater, was offered to the father so he could understand his daughter's real needs and desires. The binoculars were offered without commentary or explanation. The T-shirt with the image of the brother on it that was used to symbolize him during the sexual act, having been cleaned, was offered without commentary to the brother's wife.

Case No. 5: The incestuous family

There are many incestuous knots in this genealogy tree. The mother and sister lived together in a relationship with the father, who was the stepsister's lover; the grandparents were first cousins; the mother established an exclusive relationship with her son, and the father with his daughter. In the grandparents' generation there were probably incestuous acts between brothers and sisters, even between an uncle and a niece. In the third generation of this tree, which is very strongly marked by the incestuous core, the family appears as a true micro-society where all the members are interdependent: they work together, are mutually supportive, and live together in big households. When someone from the outside (friend, spouse) entered into this family, she was declared "adopted." Our consultant was smothered in this apparently happy clan and didn't understand why she had such a hard time fulfilling herself, suffering intolerable anxiety as soon as she left her city of birth or traveled alone. She was in a relationship with a man with the same first name as her brother and was employed by her father.

The awareness of the omnipresent incestuous knots in her tree enlightened her and allowed her to begin to trace her own path. A psychomagic act was added. She cut as many silhouettes out of white fabric as there were members of family, living or dead, to whom she felt attached by restrictive bonds (she chose fourteen). She then painted, as accurately as possible, each family member's face so each puppet had a well-defined identity. At night, she hung all of them in her room while she slept. During the day, she carried them everywhere with her, rolled up in a small suitcase. She gradually got rid of this entourage, beginning with the people to whom she was less closely related. Each time she freed a silhouette she painted seven gold dots on that figure's seven chakras.* Having thus symbolically blessed the person, while in an open space where she could see it floating far away from her she freed herself by sending the silhouette into the sky attached to one or more helium balloons.

BISEXUAL CORE, HOMOSEXUAL CORE, AND KNOT

The Bisexual Infantile Core and Its Goal

At the base, we are all bisexual. That is to say, our need for intimacy, for love, for identification is turned as much toward the father as toward the mother. The child needs to confront both sexual polarities in order to identify, little by little, the sexual identity that is his or her own.

---

*The chakras can be found at the top of the head, between the eyebrows (the "third eye"), at the base of the throat, at the heart, at the solar plexus, at the sacral center where *hara* (energy) enters the navel and the pubis, and at the base of the spine at the level of the perineum.

The Oedipus is bisexual; the basis of the child's development is to be attracted to both parents. Some consultants, male and female, have a very strong memory of desire for the father in which they wanted to be the wife, to be able make his children. In the same way, the desire can exist for both boys and girls to be able to make the mother's child. It is also absolutely healthy that in the course of development the child crosses into a phase of fleeing from the opposite sex, concentrating on the same-sex children and adults. This identification with the same gender group reinforces the masculine or feminine identity. It is the age where the boys refuse to play with girls, and where little girls decorate their rooms with posters of female movie stars or feminine heroines.

The masculine or feminine identity is thus established both on the basis of personality and according to assignments we are given. In adulthood one lives as a man or as a woman, but actually each of us is, in varying proportions, both masculine and feminine in the four centers. Moreover, we can have an inadequate, controlled, strong, or very strong attraction toward one or the other of the two sexes. All of these factors determine the sexual identity of everyone in society. Reproduction is assured by the heterosexual encounter. But **the essential Being is beyond gender.** One might say that the essential Being is androgynous in the sense that it unifies and goes beyond both polarities indiscriminately.

If the parents serenely live their own sexual identity, if they are capable of accepting the diverse degrees of masculinity and femininity present in everyone, the child can go beyond the bisexual core equipped with an organic identity (male or female) with access to his essential androgynous Being (part feminine, part masculine), no matter what his sexual orientation. The child will then be capable of functioning from his femininity or from his masculinity, while accepting the two sexual polarities in everyone. He can then serenely enter into relationships with all people, whatever their sexual identity or preference, and face the diversity of the world.

In summary, the goal of the bisexual core's growth is to peacefully accept of one's own gender and one's own sexuality, as well as that of others, and to experience the **Consciousness of the essential androgyny.**

The Homosexual Adult Knot and Core

Several factors can create the homosexual knot:

- A problem tied to homosexuality in the genealogy tree, like homosexual abuse, prohibition of homosexuality, secret liaison, or thwarted love.
- A monosexual attachment that proceeds according to outright elimination of one of the two polarities in one of the four centers. This can result from experiences like the emotional or total absence of the father for a son or of the mother for a daughter; a radical intellectual devaluing of women; hatred of men; or prolonged internment of a child in the single-sex environment.

While homosexuality is forbidden or considered a perversion by cultures bathed in a dominant heterosexual ideology, it is inversely true that fear and prohibition of sex between men and women in state or religious institutions has de facto approval of homosexual situations, which are often secret or abusive. In environments like the military, convents, residential schools, and prisons where mixing of the sexes is forbidden, the sexual energy has nonetheless propagated homosexual situations by expression or by force.

Our intention is obviously not to stigmatize homosexuality, but to clarify how many of our ancestors have lived their sexual identity and preference under duress. The masculine domination of most so-called evolved cultures, which share this point of view, has wreaked havoc on the feminine-masculine balance.

As soon as a generation is established in accordance with the homosexual knot by rejection, riddance, or devaluation of one of the two sexes, or by pushing back the homosexual drives in one or more of the four centers, the person concerned remains a prisoner of a core that we generally call "homosexual." Because of this core the freedom between man and woman, homosexual or heterosexual, is compromised and access to the essential androgyny is barred.

Due to **lack, rejection, or secret,** the homosexual knot causes:

- **Systematic devaluation of a gender.** If the infant born is not of the family's wished-for gender, she may mimic the other gender in order to be accepted, a very common knot for girls in our masculinist culture. Or a mother, disillusioned by men or a father who despises women, may instill hatred or contempt toward the opposite sex in her children.
- **Secret or repressed homosexuality.** This can put its whole weight on all of the tree's emotional relationships.
- **Uni-sex education.** If the father disappears and the child grows up in a community of women—or, inversely, only among men—the experience of growing up in a uni-sex residence can negatively condition relationships with the opposite sex in adulthood.

Due to **excess or abuse,** the homosexual knot causes:

- **Prohibitions placed on the child.** These will prevent him from openly living his developing sexuality and can include subjection to a series of abusive measures, surveillance of masturbation, guilt-tripping around his sexuality, and being prevented from going out to meet people of the opposite sex.
- **Homosexual abuse.** This can take place in the framework of educational, religious, and familial environments.
- **Oppression and confusion.** If the society or the family overtly favors one sex over the other, the children will have the tendency to either identify with this "preferred" sex or to refuse their own identity, which is synonymous with oppression. For example, in many cultures where the male is called "strong," he has the prerogative of money, freedom, work, and intelligence. In these instances the mother can be painfully masculinizing, passing down a confused vision of the feminine to her children.

The adult homosexual core manifests in the four centers in the following ways:

- **Homosexual intellectual core.** Misogyny; ultra-feminism; chauvinism; contempt of masculine or feminine thought; all theories and morals that exclude one gender at the other's expense; favoring the thought or expression of one sex to the detriment of the other. Likewise, devaluation or overvaluation of the rational or intuition falls under this core (it is the collaboration of these two authorities that completes the spirit).
- **Homosexual emotional core.** All of the exclusive and intense feelings toward a particular gender fall under this core. When fathers or mothers prefer their same-sex friends to their family, one can call this a homosexual core. Inversely, hatred toward the opposite sex is also a manifestation of this core.
- **Homosexual sexual-creative core.** Within this core we see manifestations of the repression of authentic desire, be it heterosexual, bisexual, or homosexual; a hated sexuality as with date rape, which is a manifestation of the homosexual core; homosexuality by proxy, which would include sleeping with the partner of one's best friend or boss; creativity that ignores or rejects the influence of one of the two polarities or that unduly exalts one sex over the other, which the case with westerns and war films from the male perspective and of television series like *Sex in the City*.
- **Homosexual material core.** All the situations in which one sex is excluded from a given territory fall under this core: clubs for men or women, sports teams, monasteries, residences for boys or for girls, military corps closed to women.

Cultural and Religious Aspects

As we have already mentioned, the masculinist, patriarchal culture was born of solid homosexual cores. Disgust for the "impure" female body, the horror of menstruation, the virginity imperative impregnating all of Judeo-Christianity—all contribute to this exclusion and **fear of the**

feminine, which justifies priests' celibacy and the prevention of women from achieving any of the highest official roles in the majority of monotheistic religions.

In synagogues and mosques women must pray in hidden places—much smaller and less decorated than those reserved for men—so the men will not be distracted from their piety by the presence of any women. These spiritual aberrations have been commonly accepted for centuries, creating a **separation of the sexes** that in reality makes room for lots of homosexual situations and for abuse perpetrated on children, and also, of course, for the development of an assumed homosexuality. Buddhism is not exempt from the exclusion of one gender at the expense of the other, as evidenced in the following comment by Léon Wieger in *Récit de l'apparition sur terre, du Buddha des Sakya:* "The sex change is a step toward deliverance. No woman is saved as a woman. The last stage is always male."*

Around the whole world men still essentially control the management of economies and money is considered a manly attribute in most genealogy trees; one must keep this in mind when analyzing the tree's relationship with money.

Psychomagic Resolution

The homosexual core is going to take on different shades depending upon whether the person is man or woman, homosexual or heterosexual. It is always difficult to show a world where the two genders coexist in a fulfilling way. In the genealogy tree, this persistent core also very often concerns a refusal or an expulsion of homosexuality as an expression of desire.

The Female Homosexual Core

The female homosexual core is very frequently aligned with a **devaluation of the feminine** in one way or other. If the parents (the father in particular) wanted a son, and the daughter is masculinized in order to merit attention, the first step for the consultant is to recognize the

---

*Chapter 59 of *Récit de l'apparition sur terre, du Buddha des Sakya* (compiled by the Chinese monk Pao-tch'eng in the time of Ming) in *Les vies Chinoises du Buddha.*

tendency to live as a "tomboy." For a woman this entails a profound lack of self-confidence that can take many forms:

- **Intellectual or social virilization.** "The only part of me that can manifest itself as totally male is my intelligence, my capacity to direct, to produce money, to dominate reality." The compensation is an enormous physical, sexual and creative, and/or emotional insecurity.
- **Rejection of the female body.** As if to obey the parents' orders, physical signs of femininity dwindle—among these are narrowing of hips, flattening of chest, vaginismus, frigidity, pathologies of reproductive organs, painful menstruation, and anal fixation in sexuality. The consultant lives in pain, like a mutilated androgynous being, all or part of her organic reality forbidden or experienced as a burden. She may also feel that she is only alive in her head, that her body is a stranger. This incomplete sense of self is painful and pathological.
- **Constant anger and frustration toward men, or toward women.** In reality these two attitudes fall under the same core, as if one of the genders were essentially "bad" or "guilty."

If a lesbian is the victim of one of these manifestations, one might consider her to carry a homosexual core in the same way as a heterosexual woman. In any case homosexual cores are likely already present in the genealogy tree in the preceding generations, and one must identify them. A number of fathers of women with homosexual cores hamper the femininity of their daughters by their misogynist attitude and emotional preference for sons or friends. Identifying these cores in the tree is the first step.

Psychomagic can therefore act on two planes: restoration of the female sexual identity (the body in which one lives cannot be inherently "bad") and expulsion of the artificial phallus—in other words, the projection imposed on the daughter that requires her to have something she cannot possibly have.

Exalting the Menstrual Blood to a Creative Medium

If the woman is still of the age of menstruation she will paint a portrait of herself nude, in a powerful setting with her menstrual blood visible, which she will then display in a silver frame in a room in her home or office without the need for justification. This psychomagic act restores the feminine to its creative capacity by allowing the woman to fulfill what is impossible without the vital function of her uterus. If she is already past menopause she can imitate her period for three months with fake blood, then on the third day of the third month she can make this said self-portrait. It is better to paint with one's fingers than with a paintbrush, but it is possible then to improve the details with the help of a lip pencil or other female accessory.

Valuing the Vagina as a Place of Power

Contrary to a widespread myth in phallic-centered culture, women are not "deprived" of an imaginary phallus but, to the contrary, endowed with internal sexual organs that have power and their own value.

"To have balls" is not the only way to assert oneself in the world. To restore value to the female genital organs, one can deposit three (or more) well-cleaned pieces of gold into the vagina in a little case made of sterile gauze, fitted and sewn together with a permanent string to allow maneuvering. Allow it to remain for minutes, hours, or days in a row based upon how comfortable you are. This symbolic "treasure" can support a creative activity, job interview, intimidating confrontation, and so forth. When the treasure has had its effect and is integrated into the personality, the woman can sell the gold pieces for a pleasant gift or turn them into jewelry. The gauze case will be buried, and blooming flowers or fruits will be planted on the grave.

If the devaluation of the female has religious or ideological origins, one can also copy an excerpt from a sacred text onto a piece of parchment, wrap it in plastic wrap, and carry it inside one's vagina during attendance at a religious ceremony.

Undoing the Artificial Phallus

If the family projects the desire that a daughter carry masculine sex organs, one must first materialize this projection in order to undo it. The consultant can buy an artificial phallus at a sex shop, weighing it down with lead balls if it's hollow or wrapping metal rings around it if it is solid. For seven to forty days (according to the intensity of the core), she will wear this appendage either in her handbag or on her pubis, and in each moment of anger or exasperation, she will take it out and hit it on the table, the ground, or the wall. Once this time period has passed, she will bury it and plant a flower above it.

Beyond these psychomagic acts, activities that exalt the female body (like oriental dance, for example) are strongly recommended.

The Male Homosexual Core

The male core is similar to the female core but is colored differently by cultural context. It is often a loyalty to the mother that produces this core: if she hates men there is a strong chance that she will project the desire of not growing up onto her "little boy" so that he will not become "like those bastards." The boy might grow up riddled with guilt over his sexual drives or secondary sexual characteristics if the exalted men in the family are priests or bachelors, and therefore theoretically "pure." Inversely, many men develop a homosexual core due to the absence of the father.* Abuse sustained by a man in childhood or adolescence can create a homosexual core and, at the same time, an attachment that

---

*It is interesting to note that two of the greatest homosexual French writers of the twentieth century, Henry de Montherlant and Marguerite Yourcenar, had a common history of having damaged (killed, in the case of Yourcenar) their mothers at birth. Montherlant's mother never recovered from a uterine hemorrhage. The father's insemination, thus the inseminator phallus, caused the mother's death. For Montherlant, one can speak of the homosexual core since he hid his homosexuality his whole life. The absence of the father is, without a doubt, a strong element in the homosexual core, as this quote testifies: "The tears poured into a stranger, as if he were my father, simply because this stranger was great—everything that is great is my father, uselessly."

re-creates this abusive sexuality and shame. Often the young boy cannot tell anyone about the abuse, and the secret maintains the core.

In every case, devaluation is physical or sexual. It can lead to problems with erection or ejaculation, the desire to be possessed anally or orally, and the accompaniment of shame with this desire. Or it may have psychological manifestations, like feelings of guilt, horror toward one's own sperm, or feelings of powerlessness or weakness. In our societies, where money is a manly prerogative, it is possible that this core comes from the tree's relationship with money, as in cases of bankruptcy, poverty, or "dirty" money.

Here again, the process of restoration comes from the personal exaltation of male identity and by directly confronting the core.

Restoring the Sperm's Dignity

If in the relationship with the mother sperm was considered dirty or devalued, the consultant—whatever the family's religious orientation—will take a votive candle from a church, bring it to his home, then deposit his sperm at its base. Finally, he will light this church candle in front of an image of the Virgin, preferably in a cathedral. This sperm, thus purified by an authority superior to the mother, will then be diluted in gouache (or watercolors) and used to paint a self-portrait, which he will then exhibit in a gold frame. For more power, the consultant can also smear his testicles and the soles of his feet with a red, edible and nontoxic, vegetable dye to symbolize life force and virility.

The Value of the Phallus

To deactivate the feeling of powerlessness or castration resulting from an exclusive relationship with the mother, absence of the father, or humiliation due to a rival or scornful father, the consultant will gather a significant sum of money (which can be counterfeit). The bills will be rolled vertically in order to produce a lengthy tube, the symbol of a phallus. Then, using fabric or a bit of leather, the consultant will sew a sack to hold the money phallus and two silver Chinese Baoding balls, the symbol of powerful testicles. He will wear this object of power in his pants against his own sex for three to seven days, according to need. Once the act is accomplished the money will be returned if it has been borrowed, and the balls and holster will be buried with a robust shrub planted above them.

To undo extreme cases where the father oppressed the child, the consultant might violently throw the Chinese balls against his father's office window. We do not venture to recommend such a conclusion for this act, but in one consultant's case this counteracted the tendency for suicide, thus saving his life.

To face the genealogy tree's female or male homosexual cores, the act will differ according to whether or not the person has a homosexual orientation in their desire.

For a Heterosexual Woman

Getting to know female homosexuality is necessary in this instance, possibly by spending a festive evening among lesbians. If a strong homosexual knot exists with a mother, sister, or grandmother, one can invite this "partner" to share in the evening, either in person by dancing at a lesbian club, or by carrying their photograph in a pocket—and perhaps after going out dancing sending the photo back to the partner with chocolates and this little message: "We had fun!"

For a Heterosexual Man

According to the consultant's level of real homosexual desire, he can go to a gay bar or gay sauna, knowing that the choice of place will determine a more or less greater possibility of being sexually solicited. The minimum is to go have a drink in a gay bar. If the consultant is very timid, he can cover his face under a mask made with a photograph of Oscar Wilde or some other famous homosexual artist, writer, or philosopher.

If the Parents Wanted a Child of the Opposite Sex

- **Living parents.** Carrying a pair of scissors in a pocket, pay them a visit dressed as the boy or girl they wanted. Tell them, "Here is the son (or daughter) you wanted, but it is not me!" Then, by shredding the clothing with the scissors, express all the pain felt, finally standing there nude before them and saying, "Look at me." According to their reaction, one might then (without getting dressed) share the cake bought beforehand for the occasion. Or, if the parents react badly, calmly go out to the street while still nude, where a person of good faith waits with a coat, and share the cake with this person. The shredded clothing will remain the property of the parents, who if possible will bury the pile, planting something above it.

- **Deceased parents.** The same act is valuable, but performed at the gravesite or wherever their ashes were dispersed. If neither is available, perform the act while facing a photo of the parents that will then be buried in the countryside, leaving the shredded clothing and cake with it as an offering of peace.

If Parents Do Not Accept Their Child's Homosexuality

In the genealogy tree one part of the family will always evidence a latent or pronounced homosexuality, which is important to acknowledge. The whole family, without exception, must be made aware of the consultant's homosexuality. To do this, one will draft a personal letter to each family member—including children and the deceased, whose letter will be placed atop the grave—and send it with a photo of the consultant in the arms of his beloved (or another partner) as a symbol of the fulfillment of the homosexual couple. "Coming out of the closet" is the fundamental process of affirming oneself.

Often, the homosexual member informs the family of his homosexuality but never introduces them to a life partner. Therefore it is suitable to do so, preferably in a formal setting like Christmas or a birthday. If there is not an established partner ask a friend to play the role. Presenting oneself in a stable partnership to the family is a lifesaving step. To reinforce the affirmation of the bond, if the two people are really a couple they can each write the other's first name on their chest.

Cases

Case No. 1: A double knot that is homosexual/incestuous

A consultant told of the misfortunes provoked by men during her life. The first got her pregnant and then disappeared, another cheated on her, the third stole money from her, and she came to detest men in general. Furthermore, her father was an alcoholic and repeatedly tried to sexually abuse her. She lived with a forty-year-old man, her son, who spoke and behaved with her as a child would. What happened? As a child he wanted his mother to love him, but she hated all the adult men she knew. In order not to lose her affection, he spent his whole life frozen in childhood. The distrust and hatred his mother expressed toward men, their violence, their polygamy, and so on, caused the son to have a "dirty sperm" complex. According to him, this "grime" gets women pregnant so they are then abandoned or produce many children, which condemns a woman to a life as a slave mother. The difficulties he had experienced with women were directly related to the knot attached to his mother. When he tried to have a homosexual relationship, he realized that it did not correspond to his real desire.

In this case, mother and son must both free themselves from their homosexual core—she by speaking her anger once and for all and recovering her power, and he by detaching from the maternal vision in order to become autonomous and live his life. They agreed to collaborate in a psychomagic ceremony.

Initially the son dressed up as his own father, whom he only knew from photographs, and the mother symbolically expressed all of her anger and despair by hitting a pillow. Then the son stripped off his disguise, stating: "I am not him. Wash his faults from me." With a black khol pencil, he had previously written his father's first name repeatedly on his skin. The mother washed him until all the writing was gone, then coated him with honey and licked it off like females of the animal kingdom do with their newborns. Then they left the house together, the son driving the mother to a lesbian club where her mission was to enjoy herself after saying to him, "My wish is that you find your happiness." He continued on his journey, going on a prearranged date with a sexual partner (friend or prostitute) who was waiting for him dressed from head to toe as a man. He carried an erectile dysfunction drug in his pocket, to use in case the maternal curse left him temporarily impotent. His semen was gathered in a condom, then diluted, mixed with gouache of many colors, and used to paint a self-portrait, which he gave to his mother.

Case No. 2: The influence of the maternal homosexual core on a daughter

Men have disappointed the consultant's mother, and she acted aggressively toward them. Her father left the home when she was eight years old and didn't take care of her. Henceforth, at twenty-five years she saw the world and men through her mother's eyes, she never had the opportunity to live her own experiences, and the little experience she was allowed was always stained by an imposed filter. The mother had a verbose sexuality with temporary lovers, and she made her daughter an accomplice to these sexual experiences by recounting them to her in detail. But in the emotional domain, the mother relied only on her daughter, who became her life partner of choice. In adulthood this young woman thought that only emotional relationships with her women friends were exempt from danger. She asked, "How do I free myself from my mother's vision?"

Her psychomagic act consisted of enlarging a photograph of her mother's face and making it into a mask with two holes at eye level, then going for a walk with it on while carrying a mirror in her pocket. On the street she looked at men, then immediately into the mirror. She realized that each time she saw a man the invading feeling was her mother's, which masked her own. After this experience she taped the mask to her mother's door at night and then immediately washed her eyes three times in a row with a sterile solution sold at the pharmacy. She then took a walk without the mask, looking at men again but this time from her own point of view, once more looking into the mirror each time. She then sent the mirror to her mother without commentary.

Case No. 3: The influence of the paternal homosexual core on the daughter

The father with a homosexual core feels heterosexual because he has no desire for men, but he prefers men mentally and emotionally and enjoys only their company. This man has a daughter to whom he candidly admits that he wanted her to be a boy. She was the firstborn, and they named her Frederica. He raised her by instilling in her his hatred toward everything feminine, along with his preference for values traditionally considered masculine: physical force, courage, competitive sports, and rational thought. To please her father, the girl masculinized herself and eliminated everything feminine from her body. She developed a flat chest and narrow and motionless hips, and from behind she could pass for a young man. But she was also very emotionally devalued, feeling endlessly imperfect. Her sexuality was oriented toward a desire to be anally penetrated, she had no feeling in her vagina, and she lived as a homosexual. Moreover, she had a lot of trouble negotiating her fees in an intellectual occupation where she must endlessly set the price on her presentations, and she constantly felt swindled.

In this case, the artificial phallus imposed by the father must also be seen as a source of abundance: the consultant spent seven days with a phallus made of bank notes as in a psychomagic act usually reserved for men, then followed that with the value-creating act on the female sex organs with pieces of gold in the vagina. She thus metaphorically satisfied her father's wish in taking on a phallus before recapturing the dignity of her own sex.

Case No. 4: The influence of the paternal homosexual core on the son

A man with a homosexual core has a son. This man was raised in misogynist complicity, degrading women. The young man, with a "good Catholic upbringing," had the tendency to punish whenever he had an emotional and sexual experience with a woman due to the fact that his father despised the object of the young man's pleasure. He went from one relationship to the next humiliating his partners.

The father had actually cursed the feminine. The consultant, in order to go beyond this curse, must contact admirable female figures in all domains. His psychomagic act consisted of finding four female masters: one in the intellectual domain, one in the emotional domain (for example Amma, the Indian saint), one in the sexual (a tantric practitioner or sexologist) or creative domain (an artist or art professor), and one in the physical/material domain (masseuse or coach). Once the initiation was completed he put a little Easter egg that symbolically blessed the female sex in the vagina of a consenting partner, and then he ate it.

SADOMASOCHISTIC CORE AND KNOT

The Sadomasochistic Infantile Core and Its Goal

In the framework of exploration of the world and himself, at a given moment a child encounters his capacity to suffer and inflict pain, along with all the physical and mental processes that accompany this discovery. He learns to go beyond the discomforts and "boo-boos," but he also confronts his position as a predator, understanding for example that the meat he eats comes from an animal that someone killed. Physical pain is fundamental to experiencing the dangers in the world, as well as the limits; thus the child who burns himself learns to avoid the fire. While lessons of renunciation and injustice constitute mental pain—he can never have everything he wants or everything he might need—limitations at the same time always build the self, provided they exist in reasonable measures.

Therefore, little by little a child integrates the fact that pain is inevitable. If the parents accompany this learning process with maturity, humor, and tenderness, the child learns to heal all the complex relationships that generate cruelty and restrictions: his own and his partner's. Initially, if the child hurts, it is in an innocent way; it is his own pain that teaches him that others suffer just like he does. Someone who has never experienced suffering would be someone of limitless cruelty. The sadomasochistic core, when well guided by the parents, leads to the ability to avoid transforming necessary and inevitable pain into suffering—which is uselessly prolonged and avoidable pain. So the mature adult discovers joy, and the capacity to focus on the life force in order to get through painful experiences.

The Sadomasochistic Adult Knot and Core

The familial environment can create sadomasochistic knots that accustom the child to living with suffering: corporal punishment, deprivation, humiliation, verbal and physical violence, as well as parental or sibling conflicts. The child, above all a victim, will tend to imitate what made him suffer and identify himself in turn as the persecutor.

Pain is a strong signal that keeps us alive. This intense experience, originating from the brain's desire to keep us safe, produces endorphins in stressful situations that offset the danger or pain with substances designed to help us survive. In the same way some become dependent on drugs, many people become dependent on the endorphins that are produced in response to the repetition of distressing situations that are a way of life.

Moreover, the sadomasochist is organized around **dominant-dominated** relationships that are reassuring because the complexity of human relationships is then reduced to a fixed hierarchy. Within this dynamic a persecutor's victim is never alone because the persecutor needs the victim, and at the same time the persecutor's ability to control the victim gives the persecutor a feeling of being all powerful, even immortal. These relationships are basically the same, since **each is at the service of the other.** As such, they are at great risk of perpetuity.

Excess can set the sadomasochistic core:

- Sadomasochism is imposed by use of physical or psychological violence; by huge demands like the requirement to make the best grades in class, or to never cry; by arbitrary hierarchies whereby the child is always in the lowest position, unless he finds someone smaller who will take what he is subjected to.
- Paradoxically an excess of precaution, or a lack of normal painful experiences, can also create a persistent sadomasochistic core. The child brought up with buffers, who does not have access to pain as a teacher, has no experience of limits to contradict his sense of omnipotence. Thus, if the parents overprotected him and put him in subordinate positions he might develop a

sadomasochistic core, which actually translates into a persistent lack of autonomy.

The sadomasochistic core can also be the result of **lack:**

- This core can arise out of a fundamental absence of information when neither play, humor, or tenderness was part of the child's upbringing, so he knows only painful relationships.
- An adult inflicted with a sadomasochistic core can only live in persecutor/victim relationships, passing from one role to the other without understanding why happiness and joy are never present. Incidentally, one can spot a tree where the sadomasochistic cores are very active when a person pronounces his goal is "to be happy" or "to find joy." These aspirations, which correspond to the expression of the essential Being, are held back in the sadomasochistic core.

In adulthood, the sadomasochistic core manifests in the following:

- **The intellectual sadomasochistic core.** This core is the result of continuous criticism, verbal aggression, snap judgments, humiliating jokes, and intellectual subjugation where the persecutor aggressively repeats what the other says. A person brought up with verbal violence generally repeats this model as a means of communication.
- **The emotional sadomasochistic core.** The best example for this core is the couple where one is the persecutor and the other is the victim. Sometimes in old age or due to accident, illness, or impairment the roles reverse, and the former victim subjects the other to everything he suffered. These couples are generally long lasting and very prolific, and work on the genealogy tree will show that such-and-such grandmother married a "monster" but nevertheless had eight children and spent her whole life with him, even following him shortly after his passing to the grave. It

is essential then to examine the contract, or even the complicity, between the persecutor and the victim. Relationships of domination inherent in this core establish each role, and from a distance we can see how they reflect the fear of change, and consequently the fear of death. This represents a neurotic advantage for both parties.

- **The sexual-creative sadomasochistic core.** The world of BDSM (bondage, domination, sadomasochism) overflows with more or less painful and sordid practices that are presented in a more or less artistic way. These may include visual and physical restrictions, shackles, flagellation, suspension, stimulation at the edge of pain, or gradations of torture. Sexual sadomasochism is an established genre that will be useful to reference if there are many sadomasochistic knots in the genealogy tree. In the artistic domain, one may cite body art—tattooing and all other forms that aim to transform the body—as well as artistic practices that require suffering and physical deformations like classical dance. The sadomasochistic core in art is associated with intense perfectionism because it establishes a difference between "superior" and "inferior," once again the dominant and the dominated.

- **The material sadomasochistic core.** The praise of sacrifice and deprivation falls under this core, accompanying it in the belief that "life is hard." Abuse inflicted on children anchors a physical sadomasochistic core, which as Freud amply described can become sexual. Imposed greed, rigidity, and deprivation all fall under material sadomasochism. Some parents exhibit high levels of creativity with their cruelty. Moreover, sports like jogging that emit massive amounts of endorphins fall under physical sadomasochism. The belief that money must be gained at the price of intense suffering also falls under this core, where pleasure is found in negatively judging professional success that is the result of talent and passion—and then stigmatized as "easy money."

Cultural and Religious Aspects

Heroic figures capable of withstanding torture, injury, and deprivation abound in history, particularly in the context of war. A fascination with extreme horror is a core component of the sadomasochistic core, as is all entertainment where the public delights in the suffering of the participants, like circus games in ancient Rome and the Christian Inquisition (albeit under the pretext of spiritual enlightenment).

On the religious plane, the biblical maxim "you give birth in pain and you will earn your bread by the sweat of your brow" has a highly sadomasochistic depth, and in spiritual practices in general we can cite many practices that consist of humiliating the body. We think, of course, of the veneration of the Christian martyrs and their self-flagellation and scarring, but we can also cite extreme meditation in certain branches of Zen and in the current embracing of Vipassanā, fasting, some excessive kinds of yoga, very advanced asceticism, and all paths where illumination is attained through experiencing and overcoming pain. All the "you must suffer to be beautiful" formulas common in the so-called developed societies also refer to sadomasochism.

Psychomagic Resolution

When someone discovers the sadomasochistic knot in the genealogy tree, it is often a relief to understand that what she suffered, what he witnessed, is not life but a game of violence and cruelty that was imposed through false catchphrases like "This is good for you" and "You deserve it."

The persistent sadomasochistic core creates a deep anger, generally controlled during childhood because the consultant was in fact in a subjugated position. The violence suffered will then be turned against oneself at the risk of becoming prone to depression, suffering autoimmune illnesses, and losing one's teeth, one's energy, the joy of life, and so forth. Extreme masochism can lead to suicide.

The first step then is to face this suppressed anger in order to revitalize the life force.

Identify and Express Anger

In the first place, one must identify the aggressor.

- There may have been several aggressors (father, mother, brother, sister, grandmother), so buy as many watermelons as you need to represent each one. Onto each melon glue a photo or portrait of the person, cover the floor with clean plastic, then in a loud voice express one's grief while destroying the watermelons with blows from a club, hammer, or baseball bat, or even by kicking them. Once the anger is released, pick up the flesh of the watermelon and cook it down to make jam. Bury the rinds with the seeds and photos, and plant a vegetable on the grave. Give the jam as a gift to the guilty parties or take it, where appropriate, to their graves.
- If the anger concerns a person in one's adult life, glue a photo onto a plastic ball, perhaps a soccer ball, and kick it until satisfied. Then coat the ball with honey and throw it into the river. In the 1950s, the celebrated Chilean singer Violetta Parra was at the Café do Brasil. Angry at a journalist who was bothering her with aggressive questions, in one movement she stood up, lifted her skirt, and urinated on him, then left with dignity.
- If the anger concerns an institution, go in the night and bombard the door of the institution with a dozen eggs. In the case of extreme anger, drop excrement at the door or send it in a hermetically sealed box. Animals show their anger by defecating, which is a very primitive method of expression that speaks deeply to the Unconscious.

Symbolically Fight Back

A person who did not have the power to call a sadomasochistic relationship into question as a child can nonetheless fight back and become free in adulthood.

- Get a whip, the symbol of corporal punishment, or a belt. If the parents (or other aggressor) are deceased, go to where they are buried and beat the grave, or go to the place where their ashes were dispersed and beat a photo, releasing all of one's anger and suffering. Then burn the whip, bury the ashes, defecate on top of it, and plant a vegetable. If the parents are alive, visit them and whip the earth to express all that one has felt. If one is very afraid, use people to represent the parents instead. Finally, have them bury the whip and plant a vegetable atop the grave.

- To symbolize a link that one wants to undo, one can give the parents, or the gravesite, a pair of handcuffs, rope, or chain with a great tenderness.

- If one was a victim of verbal violence, write all the insults or contemptuous catchphrases that one suffered on parchment paper, returning it to the person concerned along with a cake or a box of chocolates.

Face One's Own Violence

Learn to Kill to Learn to Live

Sadomasochistic cores frequently produce a denial of one's own capacity for violence. In this case the person may remain potentially aggressive but does not do harm because of impotence or repression. A tree of sadomasochistic cores makes one falsely "nice," so in order to restore one's authentic personality one must begin to recover one's capacity to kill. This can be accomplished by taking a shooting class, then bringing a bullet-riddled target home and hanging it in a frame for a time. Another option is learning a martial art, one that is also a combat technique (unlike the internal martial arts like qigong or t'ai chi), and achieving a level where it is possible to feel sure of one's self. When one feels capable of attacking another person, one will be able to finally refrain from harming others—and do so voluntarily from a place of Consciousness.

Learn to Recognize Sadomasochism

In order to face these sadomasochistic cores in the genealogy tree it is essential to document the rituals, practices, and sexual sadomasochistic games, and to do this without judgment or prejudice. It is very possible that some practices can be attractive to the consultant or allow him to free himself. A number of BDSM rituals fall under theatrical games and do not involve physical pain. Opening one's curiosity to these new practices allows habits to be broken in order to undo certain, once thought unsolvable, knots.

Cases

Case No. 1: The little girl and the little whip

The second-to-last of eight siblings, this woman was the scapegoat of a sadistic mother who hit her for arbitrary reasons while her father was passively complicit. In adulthood she lived for a long time as a "little mouse," silent and submissive. She studied her genealogy tree within the framework of a wider therapeutic work undertaken in her fifties due to a permanent and profound discontentment with life, as well as to a series of physical problems most notably affecting her teeth.

The work accomplished with this consultant allowed her to connect the loose teeth to her repressed aggression; having always been the victim of attacks she held a deep anger in herself. A carefully thought out exploration of sadomasochistic rituals (in particular having a woman who accepted the role of the mother receive blows from a whip) helped her come to terms with this core, and to explore a personal sadomasochistic desire that had actually been relatively underdeveloped. Her psychomagic act was to go to the mother's grave and whip it, expressing all of her anger, then leave a pair of handcuffs—the symbol of the link that she decided to undo—and a jar of rose jam, symbol of the love underlying all of the relationships perverted by sadomasochistic cores in the genealogy tree.

Case No. 2: The corseted child

The consultant was a tall, thin young man who spent all of his childhood and adolescence wearing a corset prescribed by an orthopedist because of serious scoliosis. His widowed father raised him and gave him only ten minutes or so per day out of the corset to go to the bathroom—

never massaging him, playing with him, or proposing any other activity that might compensate for the physical restraint. Today, an expert accountant, he tries to study theater and singing (his true vocation), but he suffers from the fact that each time he takes a deep breath or expresses an emotion a crying spell results, which really bothers him. Moreover, he complains of an orgasm-less sexuality and a strong, permanent, unclear anxiety that disables him in a number of ways. In working on his genealogy tree he realizes that sadomasochistic knots are present, including a "tough" upbringing, corporal punishment, conflict between couples, and family relationships marked by coldness and cruelty. He says he has a "very strong" relationship with his father, but when asked how his father treats him, he is unable to name one sign of affection: his father endlessly criticizes and corrects him.

His psychomagic act consisted of procuring an orthopedic device just like the one he wore as a child and scheduling a meeting with his father. After bringing a box of chocolates as a sign of filial affection, he asked his father to eat them while he proceeded to hit the corset with a baseball bat to express all of the suffering he had experienced as a child. Then, in the company of his father, he buried the corset that had previously been painted gold, planting a vegetable atop this grave.

Case No. 3: Incestuous sadomasochistic core

The consultant complained of a cold, severe mother who raised him without tenderness, and who refused to offer any protection from his father's corporal punishment. Even though he was forty years old the anger he felt toward his mother prevented him from having blossoming relationships with women, and he often experienced impotence.

His psychomagic act consisted of asking a woman of good faith to represent his mother and, nude and on her knees, to play along with a symbolic flagellation. The consultant hit a cushion with a belt while with each "blow" the woman playing his mother let out a groan of pain as if the belt had struck her. The consultant then traced lines of red lipstick on her back, simulating laceration of skin. Once the act was complete he kept the belt, which became the equivalent of a shamanic "power object," and buried the lipstick with a vegetable planted atop. Subsequently, the consultant married the young woman who had lent herself to this act.

NARCISSISTIC CORE AND KNOT

The Narcissistic Infantile Core and Its Goal

Narcissism is above everything else the **love of self** in that it constitutes a fundamental stage for the child who, little by little, through his narcissistic core, undoes his identification to his parents, particularly his mother. Gradually, he starts to recognize himself in the mirror, asserting (firstly by negation) his own ideas and desires, identifying himself, and making an autoerotic exploration of his body. This first drive consists of experimenting with the pleasure of touching himself, leading to masturbation, then adding an ambiguous duality—the body touches the hand that touches it, as the hand touches the body it is touching. With self-satisfaction the whole body becomes the other: if my hand satisfies my body and if my body satisfies me, the hand becomes the whole body that receives pleasure, and the body that the hand touches becomes the whole body that gives pleasure. So, one divides into two, the basis of narcissism. From that stems the pleasure of recognizing ourself in the mirror, then in others, since we desire that others look like us.

These stages are fundamental to eventually being able to **encounter the essential otherness of others** with total confidence, and to taste that which does not look like us but enriches us.

The Narcissistic Adult Knot and Core

The way in which parents have experienced their own narcissism determines their capacity to guide their child from **the love of self toward acceptance of the other**. If a narcissistic knot is created around him, as an adult the child will remain a partial prisoner of his narcissism, incapable of having a relationship with another or of sharing to enrich this otherness.

The narcissistic knot is created by excess narcissism or by a narcissistic wound. For example, the children of a great artist with a very nurtured narcissism frequently live as pale copies of their father or mother, suffering from a sense of nonexistence.

The deep root of narcissism originates when the child, in order to live, needs to be loved: if he is not loved the child will feel like he is withering away, and as his personality bursts he will destroy himself. If the mother or father (or both) did not love him, the child will separate and love himself. Based on two key feelings, hate toward the parent who did not love him and the pain of not being loved, he will become a mental fortress. Because of guilt over this hatred, and denial of the suffering, the child will close himself in the narcissism. In order to get out, he must detach from the fear of suffering and voluntarily decide to face and accept the negative feelings that create the basis of narcissism.

The narcissistic knot that results from **lack** has the following manifestations:

- The narcissistic knot is created when extreme anxiety from not having been loved is compensated for through an excess of love of oneself, as if the only person worthy of trust were oneself. It is often the case that in adulthood, very charismatic people who "do everything alone" recognize only their own reflections in the world.
- The narcissist is endlessly confronted with the nothingness of his authentic being. Others do not exist because all the energy of desire, love, and attention is concentrated on his self. The world becomes a reservoir of matter destined to "become me," to combine with the only person existing: himself. The narcissistic individual enters into the world in order to carry out the activities that represent him, that are characteristic of him. This, however, is accomplished with a deep contempt for humanity because no one can be superior to him. Basically, all narcissists are orphans.

The narcissistic knot that results from **excess** has the following manifestations:

- When two people who form a couple carry similar first names (Louise and Louis, Carla and Carlo), when one's first name is an anagram of the other's, or when the couple's names include letters in common (Dora and Aldo, Simon and Noemi), it is likely that this couple is united by narcissistic knots and unconsciously refuse any intrusion from the other. The narcissistic couple is united by a mirror effect: the first names, a similar consonance in the name, similar name meaning, identical professions, or a similar geographic origin.

- In the case where the narcissistic knot is very powerful, the children will be named in the image of their parents: Jean and Jeanne will raise Jean-Paul and Janine, Carlos and Rosa will raise Carlitos and Rosita. Faced with a couple like this, the children do not exist and are only a pale reproduction of their parents. Despised, they cannot grow up because if they become adults (as important as the parents), the parents will not be able to stand it. This makes it very difficult for the children to become themselves, to emerge from the preestablished role of the parents' mirror, be it flattering or negative.

- As we have already said, narcissism supposes that there is no one better than one's self, and the narcissist is always an orphan either because he could not be the parental model or because his parents only allowed him to be their reflection. When a narcissist encounters a person who is superior to him (in physical beauty or talent, for example), he considers this encounter an injustice and will be prey to an unbearable envy. He will make any effort to destroy whoever exceeds him. The history of art is full of these rivalries: Salieri against Mozart, Nicanor Parra against Pablo Neruda, Dali against Picasso.

The adult narcissistic knot manifests in the following ways in the four centers:

- **Intellectual narcissism.** The inability to listen; rejection or devaluation of new ideas; inability for dialogue or to change one's vocabulary to adapt to another's; indulgence in complaints like "I am useless, I don't know anything, I have a confused spirit"; absence of intellectual curiosity; the inability to understand a system of unfamiliar thought. Intellectual narcissism also includes monopolizing conversations without listening to others. Some hypercritical attitudes fall under narcissism, such as the narcissist demolishing others' thoughts in order to affirm his superiority.

- **Emotional narcissism.** One wants to be loved without loving because love of self takes precedence over love of others. One rejects feelings that one does not understand. One frantically seeks one's "soul mate," the person to be one's mirror love. In the framework of wounded narcissism, the person can also spend time complaining and enumerating his past, present, and future misfortunes. The narcissist wants to be able to emotionally absorb the other: "We love one another so you become me." Practicing charity in an ostentatious way in order to be admired also falls under this core. The narcissist projects an idealized image of himself, but at the same time, he is absent from himself and at the mercy of the image he created. In emotional relationships, he requires that the other see his flattering personality and not his authentic Being.

- **Sexual and creative narcissism.** These two forms of narcissism are founded in masturbation as a creative achievement or sexual maximum: masturbatory sexuality (exhibitionism, use of the other for one's own masturbation) or self-referential art (self-portrait, autofiction, celebration of the individual ego in art). Capturing the image of the other and imposing one's own suffering and narcissistic demands on it to overpower it is also frequent behavior of artistic narcissism (fashion photographers, filmmakers, theater directors). The narcissistic knot is generally very evident with certain artists who become their own spectators and begin to talk about themselves in the third person as if they had become a brand. They also equate the price of objects as evidence of their splendor.

- **Material narcissism.** In this case the person maintains an obsessive relationship with his own body, which must be perfect, and submits to precise aesthetic requirements. Bodybuilding, modeling, and most of the stage arts (theater, dance) will draw from the narcissistic core, as will the world of sports, where the stars become real icons. The public is then not considered an interlocutor but a mirror. Paying a very high price for a sculpture or painting of one's image, a magnificent tomb, or an impressive house falls under material narcissism. A narcissist can become obsessed by every detail of his interior, which he will view as his mirror. Financially, a narcissist spends his money to decorate himself, his own world, and so on.

Cultural and Religious Aspects

Guy Debord foresaw current society as "the society of the spectacle," and Andy Warhol, a big narcissist if ever there was one, prophesized that "in the future, everyone will be world-famous for fifteen minutes." Both Debord and Warhol were occupied by narcissistic mercantile cores that cause the emptiness of celebrating fame to return the spectator to his own insignificance and, at the same time, to his dream of being the target of all that renown. Celebrity magazines, reality television, and the ideal of increasingly more inaccessible perfection—caused by retouched fashion photography that creates impossible-to-achieve bodies—all accentuate the narcissistic core of occidental society. In the same way that *les mignons* of King Henry III dressed and made themselves up like their sovereign, the phenomenon of imitation still in full force today with jetsetters and the world of fashion is designed to flatter the narcissism of powerful people in order to receive favors from them. All the phenomena of this trend fall under this core.

From the religious point of view all practices founded in imitation, as well as the meditation mirror, also fall under this core: imitation of Christ, imitation of the Virgin, and tantric practices where the meditator becomes the divinity. Like the guru Osho, who made all of his disciples carry a medallion decorated with his photograph, the adulation of spiritual masters is based on the narcissistic core. The New Age that has placed the "me" at the center of the spiritual quest, meanwhile promoting by-products, falls under this core, particularly when an inspired practitioner flaunts a state of trance or ecstasy that could be mistaken for an orgasm.

Psychomagic Resolution

One must distinguish between two tendencies in this core. First, the gloating narcissist rarely wishes to heal because he is caught in a trap of satisfaction. Nevertheless if one's essential Being is called, whether by revelation or a hardship like illness, mutilation, or humiliation, the person may want to leave his core. Second, within the narcissistic wound a person may be eager to repair her image of herself, but she can also be imprisoned in the negative narcissistic trance of "I am worthless."

Becoming Independent of the Mirror, of the Idealized Me

- For the person who is too dependent on his physical appearance, it is a question of radically changing looks: shave the head, grow a beard, change the hair color, wear the mask of an ugly person for a while and go out on the street as "worse than I am" in order to face the hidden me.

- For someone very dependent on her position and its benefits, it will be a question of changing status: for a day, adopt a humble profession, make a pilgrimage on the knees to a sacred place, dare to present a deliberately shabby artistic creation to a benevolent public, or do something anonymously for someone (a financial gift for example) with the person never finding out who was responsible.

Restoring a Wounded Narcissism

- If the parents were very narcissistic, make a mask with a photo of the father or mother with holes for the eyes, and then, dressed as the parent, with the mask on, spend a day in town disguised as the parent. At the end of the day, pack up the disguise and send it to the parent (or to his or her grave).

- To emerge from a devalued image of oneself, do the exercise in part 5 to visualize the "perfect body." Using makeup, wigs, hairpieces, heels, and so forth, dress up as if you were that "perfect body" and go out with a group of seven friends also disguised as slightly imperfect and physically smaller/shorter imitations of your "perfect body." Go to the most popular street in the city to have a drink or dessert, like a member of royalty and her court. Certain elements of the disguise can then be used as one desires, with the other elements stored in a box, pink for a woman or blue for a man.

Cases

Case No. 1

A thirty-three-year-old man came to consult because he was conscious of his narcissism. The obsession he felt toward his own image prevented his progress. Very determined, he asked for a radical act and was instructed to break all the mirrors in the house, keeping only a very small one, one inch by ten inches, so that he could shave.

Later, he confirmed that breaking the mirrors annulled his obsession with his own reflection. One day while having lunch with a young *en vogue* actress he noticed that she looked everywhere for her reflection, even in the knife she used to cut her meat. He felt very relieved to have been set free from this trap.

Case No. 2

A young actor obsessed with success came to consult. He suffered from an excessive need to be seen, to exist in the eyes of others. The study of his genealogy tree revealed evidence of important narcissistic knots: the parents were in a mirror relationship, with the same name in male and female versions and, in their own words, they lived "like two halves of the same orange." There was no space for the children; they had not paid any attention to their identical twin sons and they sometimes had a hard time telling which one was which.

First the actor marked his territory by depositing drops of his urine, which he carried in a dropper bottle, everywhere he wanted to act or be seen and recognized: in the city's main theaters, the local television stations, the most important newspapers, certain scenes. He made a an Oscar statuette, had a professional makeup artist make him up as a sixty-year-old man, and rented a theater where the 108 people he invited attended a ceremony that mimicked his receiving an Oscar for lifetime achievements.

One year later, he confirmed in a letter that after those two acts his career took a decisive turn; he became fully involved not only as an actor but also as a director, and he now feels much more sure of himself.

CANNIBAL CORE AND KNOT

The Cannibal Infantile Core and Its Goal

The mother's uterus is both a place to live and a place of nourishment for the fetus. When the baby begins to breathe, he enters into the world of the father and paternal air symbolically fills the infant's lungs. Then, breastfeeding binds him to the supplier of love and nourishment, the mother. Thereafter all nourishment—mental, emotional, sexual-creative, material—will come from the family circle, until he no longer needs its active intervention to raise the level of his vital energy.

One might say that all human life emanates from the **process of feeding:** the sperm itself is "food" for the vagina, and the sperm is the egg's "food" when the egg absorbs it at the time of fertilization. Subsequently, in the search for maternal love, one finds traces of this **desire to devour.**

When well guided by the parents, the cannibal core leads to the child's full autonomy. If the parents are negligent due to absence or excess, the person will remain a prisoner of his cannibal core and will endlessly search for someone to symbolically devour. He will not know autonomy or satisfaction, and he will toss around without ever finding his own focus, prey to an insatiable hunger. In this sense, we can say that the full victory of the cannibal core consists of detaching from familial, social, and cultural identifications, ultimately **identifying one-**

self with the essential Being: **the part of oneself that never misses anything.**

The Cannibal Adult Knot and Core

The cannibal knot actually comes from parents who themselves are consuming, and who devour their child. Just as "the old sow eats her farrow," some toxic parents consider the child a source of energy, a reservoir from which to draw. They devour everything in the child that their own parents did not give them.

This devouring can manifest itself as an **excess:** the parents overfeed the child to buy his love; invade his space; steal his time; make the child their public, best friend, or confidant. All of these relational propositions have the goal of refilling the parents, not of satisfying the child's needs.

On the other hand, the cannibal knot by **deprivation** comes from the parents' refusal to devote themselves to the child. In extreme cases it is malnutrition and deprivation of all kinds, which lead to an insatiable hunger. A child whom no one ever listened to, for example, can develop a cannibal knot with his parents. In adulthood, he will require a great deal of consideration and will refuse to admit what he means: he wants attention. He will continue to demand more.

Some people reach adulthood deprived of all energy, empty, continuing nevertheless to remain at the service of parents who don't give them anything. They have absorbed the information of the knot at their own expense and have accepted, lacking any other choice, becoming their parents' source of energy. Therefore, we see sacrificed children in some genealogy trees who are never able to build their professional or emotional lives because they have always been used as the mother or father's "crutch."

Disputes about inheritance highlight the cannibal cores. Some heirs want everything for themselves and others consistently feel cheated. Bitter fighting over a house, furniture, or shares of the family business reveal old cannibal cores in children who want to be nourished, filled, satisfied, and loved.

This manifests in the following way in the four centers:

- **Intellectual cannibalism.** The insatiable and conflicting intellect is founded in the excessive need to be heard. The person needs justice and completely ceases to listen to the other because he has lost all receptivity. The persistent cannibal core also creates imitators or idea thieves who shamelessly appropriate the theories of others, who are insatiable searchers, bulimic readers hungry for knowledge. This core is also that of mental energy predators, people who talk for hours about themselves and are annoyed if anyone interrupts them. In the intellect, the adult cannibal core is the enemy of the exchange.

- **Emotional cannibalism.** The person is consuming, making endless demands for affection and energy, but is never filled. Alcoholism and drug addiction are derived from emotional cannibalism, because even if their results are also physical, they are primarily relational. The person who is dependent on a toxic substance devours his surrounding while letting himself be devoured by the substance he pretends to be nourished by. The person who spends his time complaining, attracting attention through grief, anger, fear, or negative feelings, also devours others.

- **Sexual-creative cannibalism.** Sexual cannibalism leads to devouring the other directly or in the form of his fluids and diverse excretions, like the act of swallowing semen during fellatio, for example, if it is an obsessive practice. Several languages use the verb "suck" or "eat" to mean fellatio or cunnilingus; in these cases the male and female secretions are metaphors for maternal milk. Swallowing the sperm also amounts to devouring future children. Addictive drives like insatiability, nymphomania, Don Juanism, and various sexual addictions also fall under the cannibal core. On the creative plane, the cannibal steals his inspiration from other artists and he becomes a critic and an imitator, replacing art with quotes and collages. One might say that a good forger is an artistic cannibal. Some actors or stage artists who are hungry for the public eye, which actually represents the parental gaze, may go to any extreme to be noticed.

- **Material cannibalism.** Bulimic and anorexic drives can be stored in this core. One has to do with devouring everything, the other has to do with forced deprivation, of devouring one's self. Hoarders are also cannibals, especially when they collect objects relating to a particular person. The pathological debtor falls under this core because he "gobbles up" his money until a superior structure (the state or a financial aid agency) ends up paying, and he returns to symbolically feed off the parent's energies. Gambling addiction also has a cannibal background, especially if the person puts his family in danger by losing all his money. All excesses of the capitalist society fall under cannibalism, as Émile Zola so aptly illustrated in *Germinal* when he spoke of the mine as the "man eater." All outrageous exploitations like fraud and financial speculation, as well as endless accumulation, are cannibalism. Behind the energy that is represented by money there is always life, time, or the body of others that one devours. The reference formula might be "eat or be eaten." Pirates, thieves, and crooks are also cannibals because they appropriate money that represents the energy of others. Cannibals of time devour the time of others; cannibals of space never have enough space.

Cultural and Religious Aspects

A recent news report in Mexico told of a crazy man who killed his mother and ate her whole body. Once this feast was finished, he died of hunger because he refused to ingest anything else. Devouring the mother brings us back to devouring a divinity, and one might venture to say that the Christian Eucharist (believed to provide the body of Christ for worshipers to absorb) is a sublime derivation of this kind of cannibalism. Conversely, the Greek myth of the god Cronos, who devoured his children in order to prevent them from superseding him, refers us back to the desire for eternal life: one eats one's children in order to become young again and to not disappear. In the 1980s, the cosmetics industry began making women's beauty creams with placenta; these said "fresh cells" were a huge success. Recent ethical questions of cloning also fall under the cannibal core.

On the religious plane the sect that devours its followers by appropriating wealth, or using sexual and emotional abuse or brainwashing, is symptomatic of this core; totalitarianism is as well, with its concentration camps where human life is under the regime's complete control. Worse still was the excess cannibalism of Hitler's regime that imagined the creation of soap and other objects using prisoner's remains.

Pyschomagic Resolution

This core has two main aspects: to eat and be eaten. The first aspect manifests through persistent dissatisfactions and often self-destructive modes of compensation (drug addiction, compulsiveness, self-punitive behavior). The second aspect refers us to anxiety and the unconscious desire to be eaten by the genealogy tree. Actually, all traditions of horror films that include zombies, vampires, and predators without scruples reflect this very real terror.

To Eat: Undo One's Own Cannibal Core

Depending on the importance of the needs that were not taken into account, the resolution of the knot can be a true therapeutic journey. It would be vain to pretend that one can heal a bulimic or an anorexic of several years by only one act of Psychomagic. Likewise, the dependence on toxic substances (alcohol, tobacco, drugs) cannot disappear in one day, and one must undertake a real withdrawal whereby additional help can be indispensable. But a psychomagic act can make the decision to undo oneself from an addiction complete, allowing one to face the roots of this dependence. We do not cite specific acts because in this domain each particular case must be taken into account, and the reasons and patterns of addiction will vary according to each person.

The following cases illustrate all the ways in which one can replace artificial and toxic need with a symbol that refers to Consciousness as a universal nutrition.

Drug Addiction

The consultant was a heroin addict who came to find a "good reason" to begin a difficult detox. His psychomagic act consisted of walking for a whole day with a huge timepiece on his back in order to become aware of the time allotted to us, and of the weight of life.

Alcoholism

This woman began drinking in the same way as her mother, who had died of cirrhosis of the liver. She could not quit drinking, but she wanted to decrease its hold on her and avoid falling into an excess of drink where she ends up mangled, putting herself in danger by falling unconscious. For her act of Psychomagic she devoted a bottle of excellent whiskey (her mother's drink) to the symbolic healing, without drinking a drop. She glued a photo of her mother on the bottle and used the whisky to give herself a massage each night before going to sleep, all actions undertaken while praying. Thus, she made an alliance with her mother by way of the alcohol, and without the need for episodes of extreme drunkenness.

Tobacco Addiction

This man wanted to stop smoking. A strong Catholic, he was not interested in the psychological reasons that pushed him toward tobacco; he simply wanted to end the dependence. His psychomagic act consisted of gathering some bamboo chopsticks and cutting them into the size of a cigarette. Each time he felt the desire to smoke he dipped one in a little bit of blessed water, then put it in his mouth. This ritual simply served to enable the smoker to become conscious of his act. The smoker can stop if, at the moment of smoking, he is in total Consciousness, meditating on how he removes the cigarette from the packet, how he lights it, the path of the smoke in the lungs.

For another compulsive smoker who wanted to quit smoking but who, in speaking about the cigarettes, greedily stated "I love this! I love this a lot! I could smoke two or four at a time!" the act was different in form, but the goal was the same—to make her aware of her actions. This consultant committed to lighting not one but six cigarettes at a time each time she had the desire to smoke.

Bulimia

In this case one must always ask this important background question: "What or who do I eat when I get fat?" Then one must eat that thing or person metaphorically. A consultant who clearly linked her bulimia to sexual dissatisfaction put a sample of the food she intended to eat in her vagina, obviously respecting the rules of elementary safety and using a condom where appropriate. Another consultant who was disgusted by "all this crap" she was swallowing and who, moreover, linked her bulimia to her family's nutritional habits disposed of all the plates, dishes, and cutlery she had inherited from the family, and then for twenty-one days she ate anything she wanted, provided she ate the food out of a clean chamber pot.

To Be Eaten: Escape the Genealogy Tree's Cannibalism

With the greatest certainty in the world, some parents "devour" their children like the Greek god Cronos, who feared that his sons would dethrone him. For a devoured child, deposed of his own place, recovery of the healthy "me" is accomplished through the symbolic expulsion of the phagocyte in adulthood—going from prey to predator.

Having Been a Replacement Child

When a child replaces a deceased family member, whether a brother or sister who died prior to one's birth or another member of the genealogy tree whose name (and thus destiny) one carries, that child is considered to be devoured by the tree. In effect, this deprivation of the individual identity symbolically corresponds to a human sacrifice. The replacement child is devoured by whomever he replaces, as well as by the family because they are using someone else to feed their "hunger" for the disappeared.

The psychomagic act in this case will consist of buying a large quantity of almond paste (five to seven pounds, the weight of a baby) that one spreads on one's body in the middle of the night, and lets it sit from midnight to 3:00 a.m. One allows the almond paste to symbolically absorb the identity of the deceased who has colonized one's body, as well as to absorb the suffering that this substitution has caused. It is okay to fall asleep. Afterward, sculpt the baby (or character) whom one has carried with the almond paste and give it to the parents to eat. It may also be left on their grave as appropriate, where their ashes were dispersed, or, if there is no grave, buried with a vegetable planted atop.

Invasive Parents

A number of consultants feel their parents' invasiveness prevents them from living, even in adulthood. This can be a tangible invasion through telephone calls, omnipresence, or incessant demands, or more abstract, as in the parents' opinions, acts, or attitudes that invade the consultant's thought processes. The solution consists of recognizing the invasiveness without seeking to undo it, restricting it to one place and to symbolic actions so it does not infuse one's whole life. When the father or mother takes up "all the space," one can grant them a real, but reduced, space.

The consultant buys a birdcage into which she places an effigy—either a photo or a little decorated doll with a photo—of one or both parents. The cage will be fixed up comfortably, and the parents will be treated as divinities. Every day, the consultant will use doll dishes to feed the "parents" some of the food they prepared for themselves. A candle, flowers, and incense may complete this locked altar. In a case where the parents are particularly invasive, she may cover the cage with chicken wire. When the consultant goes on a trip she must find someone to "feed" the parents in the cage, as if they were domestic animals or plants. This act lasts as long as is necessary for the consultant to feel autonomous and free from the invasiveness. Once this moment arrives, the consultant will bury the cage, parental effigies, dishes, and anything else that served the act. Then a vegetable plant is planted atop.

Cannibalism and Devaluation

A person who was devoured by his family circle all his life without ever receiving anything in return generally finds himself in a state of great devaluation, and feels himself deprived of his life force. We frequently encounter such consultants who are reduced to uninteresting work, deprived of a circle of friends, and often living very close to the parents—even in their own homes—still waiting to be considered, nourished, seen, recognized, and heard by them. This can last until the death of the parents and beyond. Rather than sacrifice the cannibalism core, one can courageously decide to leave behind the old personality, in the same way that a lizard sacrifices his tail to a predator. A psychoritual of a symbolic death and resurrection constitutes a radical and effective solution; thus one sacrifices one's old skin in order to return to life as the essential Being under a new identity.

For this psychoritual the consultant must recruit at least two allies, a man and a woman. He may have up to fourteen people, preferably keeping it to half men and half women, who will represent the seven main couples of the healthy genealogy tree. This act takes place in nature at the time of year in which it is sufficiently warm to be able to dig in the earth and lie down. The consultant arrives in old clothing, symbolizing his old personality that has been endlessly devoured by the genealogy tree. With the help of the assembled allies, the consultant digs a hole in the earth big enough to lie down in. Then he reads his own eulogy, describing all the sacrifices, failures, and sufferings of this person who is going to disappear. Once the eulogy is read, the consultant pretends to die a personally appropriate death and is buried in the hole with his old clothes for a blanket. The assistants cover the whole body with dirt except for the face, which has been covered with a lightweight black veil to block the sun but not the air.

The consultant remains there for at least twenty minutes, remaining long enough for everything that he no longer wants within him to die. The assistants, seated around the grave, look after him in silence. When the person feels that everything that needs to die has been absorbed into the earth, and that the moment to live has come, he pronounces his new name in a loud voice. It is the signal of the resurrection. The assistants help him to emerge from the earth, where he leaves his old clothes, and he will plant a tree above it. The assistants wash the newly resuscitated being with blessed water; the manner of benediction will be determined according to the consultant's religion, beliefs, or philosophy. Dressed from head to toe in new clothes, endowed with a new first name, the consultant then feasts with the witnesses of his resurrection. For the benefits of this act to be long lasting, he must no longer allow anyone to use the old name (except, of course, the administrative authorities). It is particularly imperative that family members use the consultant's new name.

Cases

Case No. 1: The dead tree

After studying his genealogy tree, the consultant became aware that nothing from the four preceding generations nourished him. The whole tree was "dead." There was no transmission of life, feeling, love, or creativity. For a moment, the consultant was overtaken by anxiety for having been part of such a dead group.

In order to deal with his own vitality, and to be "nourished" by forces beyond his genealogy tree, his psychomagic act consisted of finding a dead tree in nature and uprooting it by hand, or if necessary with a tool. Once the tree was out of the ground, he made a joyful fire that a group of invited friends sat around eating meat, grilled vegetables, potatoes cooked under the ashes, even roasted marshmallows. Afterward, in place of the dead tree, he planted a living tree with the ashes from the festivities serving as fertilizer.

Case No. 2: The telephone cord

In this apparently simple and banal case, the consultant's mother called her several times a day for endless conversations. Said daughter felt guilty over the idea of not responding or not listening to the conversation, but she also admitted that this invasive mother "fed on" her energy. The consultant, a professional psychologist and psychiatrist, also has had problems with her weight, which says a lot about the power of the cannibal knot with the mother.

She began by procuring a telephone with caller identification, as well as a box in the shape of a heart. Each time she resisted the impulse to pick up the mother's call, she slid a bill in the box (ten euro, for example). If she picked up but managed to shorten the conversation, she put in the box a coin whose value was inversely proportionate to the duration of the conversation. Once the box was full, she bought something she liked.

The consultant chose to buy dinner in a gourmet restaurant, which marked the beginning of a period of healthy slimming down. Furthermore, she succeeded in reducing the rhythm of the maternal solicitations to one call per week.

SOCIAL CORE AND SOCIAL NEUROSIS

The Social Infantile Core and Its Goal

Since the time of his birth the child enters into a family system, his first reference, whose mission it is to shape him into both a unique and social being. All of the individual's relationships in society first pertain to the clan, and the child's initial requirement is to integrate and differentiate. Ideally, the family should assist the child in being capable of fitting into their society while maintaining his mental, emotional, sexual-creative, and material sovereignty.

When the family circle manifests a fixed social neurosis—on the color of skin, family name and origins (aristocratic or not), political or religious membership—the child will absorb it as part of his upbringing. He will then lose the capacity to refer to his own truth as it relates to ideas, feelings, desires, and authentic needs, being rendered mute in even the most intimate situations by the concepts or social tensions inherited from the genealogy tree. He will substitute these concepts received via the tree, which therefore take precedence over individual sovereignty, for his authentic Being. We therefore speak of the social neurosis core.

Tradition tells that at the end his life the Chinese sage Lao-tzu was offered the position of prime minister, and according to all versions of this tale his response was to run to the river to wash his ears: wisdom was intended to elevate us above honors.

Social Neurosis as Knot

When the parents are racists or corporatists they are, in other words, horrified by difference—the "their" or "that" of a particular group—and they taint the family circle with their scorn, feelings of superiority, or humiliation. It can cause a child to identify only with his family or group at the exclusion of all other groups, which are considered to be dangerous, scornful enemies.

But the most powerful social neurosis knots are those that implicitly or obviously oppose some portion of the family because of racial, social, economic, cultural, religious, or intellectual differences between the maternal and the paternal tree. Often the in-laws do not accept the son-in-law (shabby, adventurer, good for nothing) or the daughter-in-law (idiot, social climber, peasant, divorcée, disgraced). Whenever a family refuses the choice to love one of its descendants, the social neurosis will probably result for this child of a "mixed" marriage.

Moreover, fathers or mothers who suffered from strong social injustices during childhood can implicitly transmit traces of this suffering to their children by anticipating that they will live through the same experience. Or this transmission can be more obvious, such as the survivor of a concentration camp who demanded that every night his children kiss a tattoo that he refused to have removed from his arm.

This knot is nearly always aligned with an emotional demand diverted toward social position—a job, engagement, skin color, or title—that someone feels qualifies him or her to be loved, accepted, or granted the right to exist.

Example: A daughter in a family of laborers becomes a very successful veterinarian, but her whole family considers her social evolution a betrayal, and they reproach her for "going to the bourgeois side." Exasperated by the clan's disapproval, the young woman abandons her career and her passion and becomes a supermarket cashier, causing the family to open their doors to her again.

This neurosis knot encloses the individual in her social definition and forbids her from behaving as she truly is: a human being.

The core can affect each person differently, according to the center in which there is persistent rejection. The social neurosis manifests in the four centers in the following ways:

- **Social intellectual neurosis.** This consists of defining oneself and others, by use of careful consideration or with the lack thereof, based on the level of linguistic education (grammar, vocabulary, spelling, language level); identifying oneself with a dialect or a particular slang; suffering all of one's life for not having succeeded in a particular competition, passed a certain exam, or obtained a specific diploma; disproportionately demonstrating pride or shame of one's family name; according either superiority or inferiority to a religion, race, or particular culture.
- **Social emotional neurosis.** Falling under this core are class hatred; historical resentment toward a particular power or country; a fear of or irresistible disgust toward a particular social class, race, or religious group; and all negative, irrational feelings related to social class. Inversely, all romantic notions related to nobility, jetsetters, or social positions considered to be "superior" also fall under this core. The extremes that fall under this core are compulsive worldliness and misanthropy: the person is either incapable of being alone or incapable of being in the company of others.
- **Social sexual-creative neurosis.** Sexual excitation or disgust related to the other person's "inferior" or "superior" social position, or his or her origin of birth or cultural and religious affiliation, fall under this core. One desires only the inferior or the superior. For the artist, there is social neurosis when the desire to succeed goes before the love of the work.
- **Social material neurosis.** This core manifests as a sense of being

incapable of earning a living due to loyalty to the genealogy tree (sustained impoverishment), or else in the feeling of being obligated to earn a lot of money for loyalty to the clan (working beyond one's strength). All ostentation like wearing brand-name clothing and accessories or their imitations, wanting to possess signs of external wealth, falls under this core. Frantic pushiness is also a sign of social neurosis, more or less marked by the so-called sacrifices one claims to make.

Cultural and Religious Aspects

By definition, all societies are unjust to some of their members. Therefore any society will induce suffering and, ultimately, social neurosis. As compensation society spreads more or less feasible ideals embodied by the "dominant" class, like the court of the kings of France, noble and bourgeois society as described by Proust, today's jetsetters, and the pantheon of Hollywood stars who are idealized references for some. Ancient or modern fairy tales and the lottery also fall under social neurosis, as these refer to the impossible dream of magically changing one's social status.

Immigration movements induce social neurosis insofar as being integrated requires that immigrants must initially accept living conditions that from all perspectives are harder than those of the native population.

Finally, all religions and spiritual practices that were bullied by a colonial invasion can reappear tainted by social neurosis, such as the ancient places of worship in South America on which the Christian conquerors built their churches. Some branches of shamanism today, where the "enlightened ones" make a lot of money by sharing the secrets of their tradition with Westerners, refer to a social revenge as much as to a sharing of knowledge.

Every human is actually a planetary being, something more and more people now realize as we collectively face the dangers of ecological catastrophe, which is a concern for all of us. A fulfilled being is not defined by nationality even if he recognizes certain connections due to having grown up in one geographic location, with a particular language or a specific type of education. This is why we can say the **essential Being is metasocial.**

Psychomagic Resolution

The unique psychomagic acts presented below are designed to serve as inspiration, as the faces of social neurosis vary according to culture, society, and age, but the spirit of these acts can be valuable to many people.

Studies

When one suffers beyond reason because one has not been able to obtain a diploma or pass an exam at a given moment during one's education, a psychomagic act can help to resolve this attachment by allowing one to metaphorically achieve the dreamed-of success.

First, one must borrow the desired certificate or diploma from a trusted person who has one, scan the document, insert one's name into it, and then make a copy twice as large as the original. Hang this in the living room of the home, or in one's workplace. This act, of course, has a goal of undoing the infantile fixation while not pretending that one officially possesses a diploma one does not have.

Fear of Poverty

Poverty is the starting point and the culmination of all social neuroses. A person in this situation is totally downgraded and disconnected from society, which is why the obsessive fear or threat of poverty is inherent in many social neurosis knots. It may be necessary to concretely confront this anxiety in order to understand that each human exists far beyond definitions and social constraints. Living a voluntary situation of "poverty" for a day can tap into deep reserves, like talent and courage, and those that the benevolence of the world can offer us like serendipity, the unexpected generosity of strangers, and charity organizations. This act consists of taking a one-way trip to an unknown town without money, credit cards, or phone and spending twenty-four hours in the position of a homeless person without any resources. One must get back home. This act does not entail putting oneself in danger; and one must take good, commonsense precautions. The purpose of the act is to achieve a feeling of vital security, regardless of money or the social norms in force.

Money

Social neurosis is often linked to a limited concept of money as "dirty," or "hard" to earn, or inaccessible. To restore this dimension of vital energy, and to metaphorically wash away all negative connotations that the genealogy tree impressed on its members, one can fulfill the act called "the money bath."

First, borrow a large sum of money, enough to live on for a year without working. One by one put some fragrance on the bills with a perfume that will be kept afterward. Take a shower. Afterward, while still naked, run the bills over the body so the skin will metaphorically absorb their strength. Then return the money that was "enriched" with this pleasant smell to the owner(s). As in practices used by shamans of the Caribbean, the perfume now possesses the power to remind the person of his or her potential worth. Olfactory messages have a strong impact on the Unconscious, and the person will always remember his or her inherent value upon smelling the fragrance.

Cases

Case No. I: Social neurosis and sexuality

The consultant was afflicted by a strong social neurosis and dreamed of being an aristocrat. The consultant's mother, born of the "decadent lineage" of a bourgeois family that had been impoverished for two generations, despised the consultant's father, who had been a worker who later became rich. The little girl grew up in this conflict and absorbed the mother's dreams of grandeur. She spoke with a refined accent characteristic of the social class she dreamt of being a part of, but she suffered from chronic frigidity. Her sexual partners were always delicate men from "good" families, but they did not satisfy her. In studying her tree it became evident that her deep desire was to make love with a man from a working-class background like her father. She asked for a psycho-magic act, and it must be noted that the consultant was very familiar with the psychomagic approach, which had also helped her good friend.

Her act assigned her the task of dressing as a janitor and cleaning toilets on the third floor, the number three representing the Oedipal triangle. Her partner, fifty years old and a masseuse by profession, entered this building at an appointed time wearing worker's overalls and rushed into the bathroom, theatrically simulating a rape. Of course the consultant was aware that he would arrive and had the option to stop it at will. The consultant, having decided to fulfill this sexual act to the end, experienced her first shared orgasm at age forty thanks to this staging.

Case No. 2: Reconciliation with one's roots

We have seen that when the tree's two parts are in conflict, or in an unequal social relationship, the child will internalize this conflict in his psyche and feel divided. In the case of a mixed-race child, the contradiction of physical projections can be experienced in a particularly painful way where neither of the tree's two parts recognizes the mixed race as their own. Such is the case with this young female whose mother is French and father Vietnamese. Born in France with very obvious Asian traits, she felt inadequate, her suffering originating from the fact that she did not look like her blonde, blue-eyed mother, whom she considered to be the incarnation of female beauty. She refused the culture of her paternal tree: didn't like Vietnamese food, didn't speak the language, ignored history and current events in Vietnam. She saw herself as useless and worthless. The study of her tree rendered her mixed-race condition in the postcolonial context, where France was the stable and dominant referent.

Her psychomagic act consisted of soaking a mango seed in water until it sprouted roots, which she then took with her on a visit to Vietnam (where she had never been) to meet her paternal family. Instructed to plant the mango seed in Vietnamese soil to symbolize her belonging to the paternal tree, she was amazed upon her arrival in Hanoi to learn that her Vietnamese cousins (who welcomed her with great affection) had an orchard where many mango trees grew. She planted hers there, had an excellent stay, and realized that in Vietnam everyone noticed her Western physical traits. She returned with a deep appreciation of the culture she discovered and accepted, which induced a greater appreciation of herself.

Case No. 3: Break free from the horrors of history

The consultant who requested this act is the descendent of two Ashkenazi Jewish families in which all the members, except the parents who left Europe in time, died in Hitler's concentration camps. The heaviness of this historic tragedy weighed on our consultant, who had brilliant social success in a field where he was suffering and bored. He worked seventy hours per week to be "free from want," but without ever feeling that his efforts sufficed to free him from the enormous drama that weighed on him. He came specifically to see Alejandro and told him, "Your Jewish origins reassure me. I can only tell you my problem: I would like to be rid the Holocaust."

The psychomagic act assigned was as extreme as the historic heaviness weighing on the consultant—he had to carry a bag containing between eighty-five and ninety pounds of butcher scraps (bones, skin, fat, and meat) on his back for two to three miles until he reached a clearing, where he set it ablaze. Then, coated with the ashes of this holocaust and dressed in striped pajamas, he visited his parents and told them, "I need to use your bathroom." He showered in the bathroom of the family home, dressed in clean new clothing, and asked his parents to join him in burying the pajamas, over which together they planted a fruit tree. Ten years later the consultant had reoriented his professional and personal lives in completely satisfying directions. Moreover, he became a licensed psychologist while remaining a strong supporter of Psychomagic and of work on the genealogy tree.

Case No. 4: Take on mixed-race status in a racist context

The consultant is the son of an African man and a French woman. His parents were friends for a brief amount of time, but family pressures separated them even before the birth of the child. The father, occupied with the African cause, returned to his country to become a politician. The mother, who was from a racist family, gave birth in secret in a neighboring town. She never introduced the child to her family, and her parents died never knowing they had a grandson. At thirty years of age the consultant experiences his mixed race as a pain, which refers to his tree's ideological and emotional conflicts. Throughout his childhood he suffered from racism at school, and he has a specific memory of an aggression that was particularly traumatizing: his classmates glued white confetti to his face.

His act consisted of first finding a mixed-race woman who suffered a similar problem, and a friend who could wait with a van to enable them to change costumes and makeup. The couple strolled the Champs-Élysées from the Obelisque to the Arc de Triomphe, he with face and hands painted completely white while dressed like a European, she with face and hands painted black and dressed like an African. Once the route was completed, they changed in the van to reverse roles and strolled the route once more. The van awaited them at Concorde, where they dressed as each most desired. Then, with faces wiped clean, they took a walk through the city and had a drink.

After the act the consultant finally found the courage to go to Africa to meet his, until then, unknown father. His collaborator set in motion a process of emotional healing that allowed her to find a stable companion with whom to have a child.

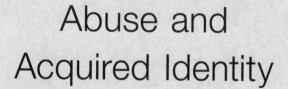

PART EIGHT

Abuse and Acquired Identity

"I Am Like That": The Tree's Final Trap

FIFTEEN

The Ghosts of Abuse and the Phantom Body

By Alejandro Jodorowsky

In Santiago, Chile, in 1947, when I was eighteen years old, I was relatively well known for my poetic work and my puppet theater. I organized friendly meetings in my studio where young artists showed their most recent creations, among them Jorge. He stood out not for his tales—a somewhat obtuse realism—but rather for his physical beauty. He was part of the upper class, *pitucos,* as they were called. He wore English-cut garments, silk shirts, and fine ties. His hair was thick, black, always well combed, and he had fine features: a well-formed nose, marble skin, a fit body, and feline movements. He was, without a doubt, the most beautiful boy of our generation. His resplendent beauty allowed him to conquer many girls.

One night, his throat burning from the liter of wine he had already consumed, he came to my studio and asked me for more alcohol. I offered him a bottle of *pisco.* After taking a big gulp, he stammered, "I am about to turn eighteen years old. I am a grown man. My childhood is over. Good riddance!" His drunkenness loosened his tongue. "I am going to tell you something I have never told another person. When I was seven years old, my parents put me in

432

a Catholic boarding school. The Jesuit father who gave me catechism classes, troubled by my beauty, forced me to lick his penis once a week and he would ejaculate in my face. Since then, I've hated my looks. So, punch me! Break my nose!" I refused to do it. He hit his face against the wall. I managed to calm him down. He cried for a long time—not from sadness, but from rage—then he fell asleep. The next day, he left for France to pursue his studies. Years later I saw him again, but I was unable to recognize him: alcoholic, carelessly dressed, thirty pounds overweight, he had lost his hair and his teeth, his skin was withered, and his face was deformed. He exhibited an aggressive ugliness. Nonetheless, he seemed much more satisfied with himself than in his youth.

I am convinced that the reason Jorge destroyed his beauty was because of the sexual abuse committed by the Jesuit priest. His face, which had excited the pedophile, was turned into his enemy. At the same time, the rape conditioned his Unconscious and incited homosexual ghosts, which reproduced the abuse. To some extent, as a child he was forced to be beautiful in order to satisfy his aggressor. The moment he reached what society recognized as adulthood, he felt relieved of this obligation. However, retaining the child's terror of being raped again, he did everything he could to make himself ugly. Once the goal was attained, he finally felt safe: no one wanted him, and he could overcome his homosexual desires.

Like Jorge, I was subjected to abuse, but not of a sexual nature: abuse can also be intellectual, emotional, or (as in my case) material. I have spent a large part of my life fighting against the consequences of that.

During childhood my parents favored my older sister Raquel. They did whatever they could to give her a "luxurious" life "befitting a lady": a white piano, Louis XV furniture, several pairs of shoes, costume jewelry, clothes. However, since I was "a man and not a fag," I only had the right to one vest, two pairs of pants, two shirts, a pair of shoes, a set of spare underwear, and nothing more. My classmates often made fun of my "potatoes" (my white heels emerging from a hole in my socks). When I dared ask my mother to mend them, she did it with a flesh-colored thread, which, needless to say, did not cut short the teasing. Until I was fifty years old, the thought of entering a clothing store caused me uncontrollable anxiety. I was able to use the same pair of shoes for years by religiously replacing the worn-out soles; I never had more than two shirts and two suits of the same color. I justified this by saying, "I am against ornaments and seduction: I must do as my Zen master who has only two monk suits, one for spring and summer and the other for autumn and winter." This psychological trickery intended to keep my childhood identity intact.

When I began to study genealogy trees, I discovered many abuses that my consultants refused to face. They asked me to make their suffering disappear in general, but not the deep cause of their discomforts: they clung to their pain because it conferred their identity. I, however, explained to them, "To heal is to become that which one is, not to become that which others want." Since childhood, orders and prohibitions were imposed on us. We had to do things we did not want to do, and not do what we desired. We sustained abuse that little by little became embedded in our spirits and in our behavior, which we took as our "identity." In adulthood we impose on ourselves what was previously imposed on us, and we reject what we were refused. And why? Because the clan does not accept us unless we correspond to the vision it has for us. Even if these knots inflict maiming, painful repressions, we consider them essential and something that binds us to the family. If we cut these blind knots, if we expel that which is artificial in order to develop our authentic being, we risk losing the pathological union that we confuse with love—a "love" for the child that is now alive, to nourish, shelter, and protect him. We think that if we change we will be expelled from the clan, that we will be condemned to solitude, and that we will be exposed to all dangers. And even more, we fear that our rebellion will cause the members of the family irreparable harm, even their deaths.

My speeches were hardly useful. A suffering person is afflicted with psychological deafness and filters the content of words, reducing them to sounds that the memory does not record. No oral language can help him. The only possible way of getting out of the emotional morass is to **deal directly with the body.**

I used this method with a man of forty-nine years from a "good" family who asked me to help him study his genealogy tree. We had hardly begun working when, without any apparent emotion, he told me his story as if speaking about someone else. He told me of the corporal punishment inflicted by his father, which he described with indifference, hiding in a playful superficiality by saying, "Oh! That was the custom of the times!" However, this methodical murder of his will by the stronger and overwhelming will of his father was precisely what kept him in a constant state of dissatisfaction: lack of authority (he complained of not being respected at work); limited creativity (he spoke with nostalgia of an old desire to paint, an activity that he abandoned under the pretext that he "didn't have any talent at all for it"); physical blocks and confinement in oneself (he had great difficulty expressing his affection and felt cut off from his children).

It became obvious to me that these restrictions were the consequences of the abuse and humiliation that he had repeatedly suffered in childhood, of still repressed anger, and of an intellectual and distant identity that he had forged in order to survive. How to heal? In classic psychology this person could face the trauma and be freed from the artificial identity after a lot of therapy where the variables of time invested, technique employed, level of intensity of the transference, and level of competence of the therapist all affect the success of a cure founded in language. Not being a psychiatrist, I chose to proceed as a sacred actor, adopting the role of the cruel father.

Without the consultant realizing it, so occupied as he was in talking of himself, I stepped back into the corner of the room and took off my belt. Then I started violently beating the ground and shouting orders, "Obey me! COME HERE! Bend over! Get on your knees!" The consultant started to shake and, seized with terror, collapsed on the sofa. I continued with my ferocious blows to the floor, then I approached him, took him in my arms, and rocked him with as much delicacy as possible so he could transmit the information he lacked: the father as a source of tenderness, protection, and understanding.

After this "comedy" we could continue to work in a far more useful way than when we were limited to the use of language, and we saved many years of therapy.

I was motivated to accomplish these acts by experiences attained through various healers and shamans. In Mexico I accompanied Pachita as she performed many magic "operations" where, using a hunting knife that she never bothered to disinfect, she cured cancers, diseased tumors, and all kinds of pathologies. Doña Magdalena, a mysterious saint who transmitted sublime spiritual states through her hands, massaged me. In Temuco in the south of Chile I participated in rituals where the Mapuche machis healed illnesses by strengthening their minds with solar energy. These primitive therapies allowed me to see that the body accepts metaphors and symbols as real elements.

Pachita's operations, considered by many people to be "miracles," were probably shams. A pinch allowed her to create the illusion of having opened the body with a knife. Flowing blood came not from the alleged injury, but from a flask hidden in her sleeve. The patient, lying on a table in flickering candlelight, saw an imposing woman dressed in a gothic cape who spoke with a man's voice while in a trance. All of that inspired a terror that made the patient regress to an infantile level, provoking in him the certitude of being operated on for his highest good.

When the machi asked the patient to lift his hands toward the sun and gather divine energy in them, and then rubbed the diseased part of the body, he had wisely used the moment when the person's arms were outstretched to establish a real link.

While shooting my film El Topo I spent eight weeks with two exceptional actors, one without legs, the other without arms. Both told me that for many years after losing their body parts, they still felt them. The legless person had endless pain in his "legs." The armless person's arms always itched. These testimonies convinced me that a whole **phantom body** exists in our brains, invisible but very real in feeling. Later, I learned that maimed or mutilated people can feel a phantom ear, a phantom nose, phantom breasts, and even a phantom penis.

The work of V. S. Ramachandran, director of the Center for Brain and Cognition at the University of California, San Diego, validated my conviction that the phantom body is not only a memory of the past and experienced in the body. In *Phantoms in the Brain,* he cites the case of a little girl born without arms who had phantom hands six inches from her stumps, and who used her "fingers" to calculate and solve math problems. My hypothesis is that in reality the phantom body is our subjective double, a receptacle of both past and potential experiences of the perfect body (which we talked about in part 5 of this book), similar to **the body of the essential Being.**

This phantom body is one that accepts symbols and metaphorical acts, identifying and transferring qualities from one element to another. All changes that are produced in the phantom body reproduce in the real organism, which is what allows shamans to achieve such surprising healing in their native, superstitious clients.

In the Mapuche language the word for "to practice medicine" is *ampin,* with *pin* meaning "to perform a healing" and *am* indicating a second body, subtle and ethereal, conceived of as an exact copy of the physical body. For the Mapuche, deterioration and imbalance, expressed as an illness or physical complaint, reside not in a sick organ but in a psychic double that is responsible for keeping the being alive.

To make it seem as if she was actually extracting a tumor with a knife, Pachita showed the person a piece of meat that had been soaked in the blood of a chicken. The machi would extract disease from the patient's stomach in the form of stones, thorns, tadpoles, and reptiles. I have already mentioned how the healer Carlos Said made some energetic cuttings a few inches above the patient's skin in order to clip the invisible links to the person who, according to him, had sent the disease.

It was in this way that I applied similar techniques to overcome the resistances of rational consultants while isolating them in their abuse, although by the use of nonsuperstitious methods.

I thus discovered that even if the intellect does not believe these "illusions," the body, which goes beyond all logic, trusts them. I had a lot of success with depressed people. I asked them to visualize all of their negative experiences and painful feelings as being glued to their body, forming a membrane that prevented them from communicating with the world. Then, with a letter opener made of bone or with a plastic knife, they shaved their skin, inch by inch—as if peeling this tightly amalgamated membrane from their bodies.

This total body scraping, carried out with an intense attention and conviction, could last for three hours. Whether the consultants were skeptical or not in the beginning, they felt a great release in the end.

Sometimes I used tattoos to resolve emotional, psychological, or physical knots. I proposed that a consultant who suffered from a painful scoliosis make a tattoo of a happy baby on his back. To a breast cancer survivor, I suggested a tattoo of a beautiful rose on the scar. For a convalescent who was terrified after having sustained a heart attack, I advised getting a dragon tattoo on his chest, a symbol of power, to help maintain good health.

During my conversations with the two actors from *El Topo* it did not surprise me to learn that (armless) Juan always felt his wristwatch, and that (legless) Pedro always felt the boots on his feet that he had worn on the day of his accident. I thus discovered that an object that remains tight against the body for a certain length of time will be absorbed by this psychic double, which considers the object to be part of itself.

I applied this hypothesis to create what I called psychoshamanic operations. Having found that what the eyes see might otherwise be perceived through touch, I got rid of all the conjuring that was intended to trick the sight and hearing and directly addressed the perceptions received by the skin. My consultant could clearly see that the gash I pretended to make in the body was nothing more than the pressure of a wooden knife, that what I presented as blood was nothing more than dyed water, and that the tumor I pretended to remove was actually a piece of beef that I pressed against his body for eight minutes. However, the consultant felt that I had actually cut something out of his flesh, he actually saw real blood appear, and he believed that I made a real tumor disappear.

A man came to consult with me who had witnessed his parents' assassination in Algeria. Since the incident he suffered from pain in his eyes that no treatment could cure. I proposed that he clean out the bad memory from his eyes. To accomplish this, after asking him to keep his eyes closed until I said to open them, I dipped two little sponges in warm rice water, placed them on his eyelids, and pressed on them for a few minutes. Then I told him that I was going to remove the eyeballs with a knife and wash them. Applying the spoon's handle to the sponges, with a bit of effort I made a digging gesture and inch by inch mimicked removal of the eyes from their sockets. I had a full glass of water near his ear in which I placed the sponges. I washed them and wrung them out, making as much noise as possible. I placed the clean, lighter sponges on his eyelids, pressing down on them as if replacing them in their sockets. Then I made them disappear into the palms of my hands. Finally, I asked him to open his eyes and told him that from now on they were washed of their painful memory. Upon raising his eyelids, he stated that the pain had disappeared. He burst into tears. When he calmed down, I asked him to bury the little sponges and plant a flowering plant on the grave.

For another consultant, I put pork in his anus in order to then extract the internal growths he feared were caused by cancer. The growths quickly disappeared.

Dramatic aspects enrich these fictitious operations that resolve problems in the genealogy tree. For example, a man suffered from a painful inflammation of the right knee for ten years. In studying his tree, I realized that he carried an unresolved conflict with his father. I asked him to buy bone marrow (to symbolize the inflamed knee) from the butcher. I had him lie down naked, and I pressed the bone marrow against his knee for eight minutes. I asked an assistant who was dressed in a T-shirt with the father's image printed on it to kneel before the consultant and touch his forehead to the ground. I used a serrated blade to mimic sawing the knee bone, removing it and replacing it as the consultant punched "his father's" back (protected by a cushion) while he screamed and shouted insults, the curses mingled with sobs. Once the operation was finished, the consultant took "his father" in his arms. The pain that had tortured him for ten years disappeared forever.

One may speak profusely of love for the father or the mother and yet avoid mentioning the other intense feeling that always accompanies love: terror. Jehovah is terrified in the Bible. Mexican people transformed the caring and loving Lady of Guadalupe into Santa Muerte (Saint Death), stripping her of flesh and turning her into a scary skeleton. Kali, Shiva's terrible and deadly wife who incites battles and destruction, is the other side of the soft, white Parvati, who is the obscure, black, supreme goddess of the Hindus. Jesus Christ was not a pacifist: he cursed a fig tree and caused it to wither; he put demons in pigs and caused them to commit suicide; at the synagogue he used great violence to admonish the unclean spirit possessed by a man and expelled it from his body.

It is possible that the creation of both gods that are both loving and terrifying is rooted in the love and terror inspired by the child's parents, who are the clan's main representatives. In Temuco, when I asked a renowned machi what the first step in healing was, she told me, "Before everything, I ask, who is the owner of the illness? It is generally someone in the family who must pay for this healing. If there is no owner, I can do nothing for them." The spirit frees itself from this family membership, but the body remains linked to the clan, sometimes for an entire lifetime. The machi added, "The first condition for healing is for the patient to want to heal." Similarly, in the Gospel of Saint John (part five), Jesus asks an invalid, "Do you want to be healed?" Once the sick man responds in the affirmative, Christ could produce the miracle: he said to the man, "Get up, pick up your mat, and walk." And the man was healed. What is the essential basis of the desire to not be healed? What role does terror play in your life?

I lived with a group of domesticated elephants during the filming of my movie *Tusk* in India. The young pachyderms destined for domestication stayed closely tied with their mothers for a minimum of four years and didn't let anyone get near them. At the time of weaning, they fought ferociously to not be separated from their mothers. All the same, when the breeders managed to separate the elephant calf from the mother, he became very sad and stopped eating. After a period of time, sometimes many weeks, he chose either to die or to accept the separation. If he decided to live, he began to work with the group of adult elephants.

We humans are terrified in childhood, not only of material needs and the existence of others but also by the mystery that represents the fact of being alive in an infinite world where everything is ephemeral. It is the parents who establish limits on the child's spirit: an absolutely necessary thing without which the child would go crazy, finding himself plunged into the unthinkable.

At the age of five I suffered abuse from my father when after I proudly brought him a Miraculous Medal given to me by a priest he took me by the hand, led me to the latrine, and threw the medal in the toilet bowl, saying harshly, "God does not exist! Or goddesses! One day you are going to die and you are going to rot! There is nothing else!" These words tore away my childhood, and sunk me into an anxiety that lasted until I was in my forties.

If it is true that the restrictions received by the infantile brain are necessary, they also correspond to the limited level of Consciousness offered by the clan. Hitler youth, imbued with Nazism from age six, committed major intellectual abuse much like certain so-called spiritual communities who in all good faith imbue their beliefs on children at a young age. This type of upbringing is so frequent that one can say that intellectual abuse begins at birth, continuing in day care, at preschool, and throughout the entire educational experience.

In adulthood we continue these infantile restrictions, which lead us to not love ourselves, to live unsatisfied lives without freedom, in restricted space, anxious about aging and falling into poverty. We become focused on competition; try to "appear" instead of "be"; consume unnecessary goods; accept wars, world hunger, and class differences as inevitable; waste energy; and poison the planet. We find a thousand ways to drug ourselves in order to forget that all of this is fleeting, space is infinite, time is eternal, and death is an inevitable mystery.

It is because of a terror of the world that the infantile adult clings to the principles inculcated by the family. Even if the clan subjected him to various abuse, it also fabricated an individuality that separates the deep Me, which binds with all the others, and is in isolation from the threatening and incomprehensible universe. This persistent child who is afraid to be what he is and not what his parents want him to be is occupied by an even bigger terror: the terror of himself. Recognizing that one is an adult means one does not identify with the intellect and thus ceases judgment, changing one's belief system to accept that nothing is personal, and that before being an individual, one is humanity.

It is this desire to live as a child without assuming responsibility and the cosmic Consciousness of the adult that provokes the resistance to healing. Accepting the deep Self, the transpersonal and essential Being—without patriotic fanaticism, sexual definition, age, name, or label, ridding oneself of submission to the family, and achieving freedom—is a frightening prospect.

The psychoshaman, a sacred actor free of sadism or the desire to dominate who is also without doubt or fear, incarnates the consultant's possible potentially superior Me, and like a terrible mother-father causes hidden infantile terror to surface from the depths of the Unconsciousness. The repressed pain resulting from family abuse emerges at the same time as this terror. The infantile identity suddenly presents itself its true form: a gathering of artificial restrictions. The metaphorical punishment gives this identity the possibility to express his rage, and the new awareness restores the real identity. The adult, devaluing the family's retaliation, ceases to do evil. In demolishing the shell of his prejudices, the infantile ego merges with the essential Being.

In the World, the XXI Arcanum of the Tarot of Marseille, we see four symbolic characters: three fitted with halos (an angel, an eagle, a lion) and one without a halo (a flesh-colored animal, identified traditionally as an ox, a bull, or a cow). The characters with the halos represent spiritual energies. The ruminant, an animal used for sacrifice, like the bovines that were the preferred sacrifice on the altars of antiquity, is the symbol of the ego whose role is to gradually fade away: a slow sacrifice that benefits the divine part, the vital source of our being.

In order to recover it, it is necessary to **free oneself from the infantile ego, but not to eliminate it,** as recommended by some therapist-gurus. This ego offers limits that prevent the psyche from losing itself in the vast mental ocean that contains a multitude of personalities. It is an abyss of unconscious impulses, angelic dreams and also nightmares, sublime feelings and destructive desires. When one does not give the ego the opportunity to transform, it fights to maintain itself, swelling immeasurably. Instead of letting the essential Being guide the ego, the ego imposes its restrictions on the essential Being. This produces confused desires, an incessant dissatisfaction, a cynical egoism, suffering, fear, envy, rage, and illness. The infantile ego is mystifying, and it keeps us on the surface of ourselves by making us believe we are that which we see of ourselves. When tamed, it eventually offers its energy to the essential Being. An indispensible instrument for us when developing our divine Consciousness is ceasing to live as victims.

Whereas for the Western man disease is a physical event, in shamanism it is considered **a wandering soul.** The shaman must find the wandering soul, bring it to the body, and proceed with the expulsion of demons. The recovery of physical strength depends closely on the restoration of the balance of spiritual forces. Selfishness transforms into generosity, gratitude toward the whole universe, compassion for all living beings, trust in oneself and humanity, and recognition of divine Consciousness.

SIXTEEN

From Error to Abuse

Emerging from the
Genealogy Tree's Conditioning

The concept of abuse is subject to both individual and cultural or societal interpretation; according to age, place, and customs what is considered abusive here will be common practice elsewhere. Child labor, sexual union between adults and adolescents or preadolescents, corporal punishment, retaliation imposed on political or civil prisoners, the female social and familial status, slavery or serfdom—all have varying degrees of acceptance that are dependent upon the culture in which they occur.

From the metagenealogical perspective, abuse and its consequences arise from any lack or excess in the upbringing of a child in which violence or repetition marks the personality in an apparent, insurmountable way.

Latin etymology of the word "abuse" refers to the verb *abutor*: "to use until the end, completely; disappear, exhaust, consume," "use freely," and "used to deflect the object from its original purpose."

Cicero used the term to designate an act of "hijacking a word of its meaning." Caesar used it in the sense of "serving oneself something until its destruction," abusing the life of his soldiers, sending them to massacre.

In modern language the term "abuse" still designates an excessive use or misuse of something, a disorder, a deviation. In French law abuse of power is the act of an official who oversteps his authority or breaches the public trust, but we must also consider the ancient usage of the verb "to abuse oneself," which is "to fail," and which is still in force in the French phrase "if I abuse myself." One can see that the notion of abuse implicitly refers to a moderate, fair, balanced, or relevant status, to everything that is neither error nor excess.

To determine the abuses suffered by the members of the genealogy tree, and even the abuse that affected us personally, it is necessary to establish just and pertinent relationships between members of a family in the four centers. It is that which we've done up to now in proposing to redefine what could ideally be the family lineage, and the conditions of a child's upbringing.

Using this logic, we will call everything that radically departs from an ideal relationship **abuse**; whether through lack or excess. In other words, we redefine abuse in the four centers as **the fact of not having received what we needed at one time, or (contrarily) to have been confronted too early or in exaggerated proportions by something we were not yet ready to receive.**

The field is vast because, in virtue of this definition, each of us has experienced abuse at one moment or another.

Some clarity for certain points:

- Abuse does not only concern acts inflicted on a vulnerable and nonautonomous child by the adults who are responsible. It also includes situations such as an older brother of ten years who repeatedly hits a younger brother of eight years. Of course, in this case the abuse is actually attributed to the parents, who did not manage the conflict between the two children. If one feels abused in adulthood by a friend, partner, colleague, boss, guru, or therapist, it is useful to seek out the abuse that preceded this recycled situation, because it is always the persistent child whom the adult abuses. As such, a relationship with a "person of power" is often an opportunity to relive and reproduce abuse experienced in childhood that one is not necessarily aware of.

- The level of responsibility of the parent or adult educator for the child determines his participation in the abuse, just like direct actions. Therefore, all silent complicity is abusive. An example of this is the mother who "closes her eyes" on sexual abuse perpetrated by her husband or her partner on the children. This is abuse by default, the same as not helping someone who is in danger. The same holds true for a parent who self-destructs through drugs, alcohol, or any means: as far as the child is concerned, this parent is abusive since he does not comply with parental responsibilities.

- Abuse concerns either a traumatizing act that occurred several times or an act that appears "innocent" but whose repetition when combined with other acts of the same nature eventually creates a well-determined, abusive climate. In the same way in which a drop of water that repeatedly hits the same place a thousand times can lead to death, aggressive jokes or daily humiliation continually directed at the same child represents a serious abuse that is just like a wound or a rape.

- Abuse is not necessarily voluntary or deliberate; error can have serious consequences, and the persistence of a mistake can constitute abuse. A parent who "doesn't know" something, or who blindly applies the lapsed and toxic rules of education with the best intentions in the world, is not any less abusive.

From the metagenealogical perspective one can say that **all abuse comes from a lack of Consciousness,** and that all education experienced in this way involves abuse. In this chapter we are going to provide a detailed description of how to recognize abuse that has been inflicted on us, and how abuse is embedded in us and becomes part of our identity. We will explain how to liberate oneself on the psychic plane as well as on the physical plane because the body keeps track of any unresolved abuse, and show how for this liberation to be sustainable it is necessary to recover the essential body: a living body where negative memories are replaced by pertinent information that serves as an anchor in the present.

ABUSE

The Basics

The notion of abuse in contemporary psychology mainly refers to sexual abuse, which is generally an act by which a physiologically mature individual seduces or forces a still immature person to have sexual relations with him. Sexual abuse is paradoxically easier to identify than other forms of abuse because the physiological gap between the mature aggressor and the immature child is readily apparent. However, the impact of psychological abuse—in intellectual, emotional, creative, or material form—is just as considerable, even if it is more difficult to prove a gap exists between the child's growing psyche and that of a stable parent who imposes a destructive relationship on the child. These impositions can include beatings or humiliating acts, or abusing the child's psychological dependence by imposing trust or conflict that the child is incapable of managing in an autonomous way.

All abuse creates a kind of **possession** in the mind of the child who suffered. This marks the victim and becomes an **obsession,** phobia, or fixation that the person, incapable of detaching from the sustained trauma, tends to directly reproduce either by repeatedly subjecting himself to what he previously experienced or by subjecting others to it. Or he may indirectly reproduce the experience by seeking to move away by all means possible, but still maintains the abuse as the center of all concerns.

As we have seen, we continuously reproduce the emotional atmosphere of our childhood: we treat ourselves as we were treated. The majority of apparently unsolvable problems we experience as adults can be interpreted as a repetition of childhood situations, where we project the familial archetypes of childhood on people in the present. As we did in childhood, we may find ourselves enmeshed in endless conflict, a couple that finds it impossible to be happy, tendencies to unite with absent people or those incapable of loving, and so on.

According to the process of repetition, a person who was treated harshly as a child will seek partners who will treat him with the same harshness and he employs all his strength to make them friendly. If he receives the desired results, however, his partner will fall from grace in his eyes and he will leave her. It is the same when one who is infatuated by a married man or woman—a projection of a parent of the opposite sex to whom that person is linked by an incestuous knot—loses interest if the married person separates from his or her spouse.

The infantile feelings, and the kinds of treatment that we preserve, are the basis for the formation of our individuality. Even if these experiences are painful, they are our link with our family. However terrible and dramatic the family life was, it offers us pleasure and the essential security of belonging to a tribe. Having a callous father, a dominating or destructive mother, toxic parents—all provide the pleasure of being attached, of being united. This unconscious and paradoxical pleasure models the infantile psyche, and consequently the construction of the individual. Once autonomous and mature, we are pushed to reproduce with others (particularly our children) what we experienced in childhood.

In summary:

- I am what you made me. I do not give what was not given to me. **Examples:** A sexually abused person masturbates compulsively to scenes recalling the abuse. A woman who had a violent, alcoholic father marries a violent, alcoholic man.

- I inflict on others what was inflicted on me. I am incapable of giving to others what was not given to me. **Examples:** A person who was sexually abused in childhood grows up plagued by a pedophiliac drive and acts out on the children in his family circle. A woman whom no one helped, or listened to, during the time she was being abused by her stepfather "does not realize" that her own daughter from her first marriage relived the exact same story twenty years later with her second husband. A man who had no relationship with his father, who disappeared the moment his mother conceived, becomes an absent father.

- I refuse to remember what reminds me of my experience, and I cut off others who remind me directly or indirectly of the abuse. **Examples:** A woman who was raped in a meeting for adolescents when she was twelve spends thirty years in therapy without succeeding in finding a way to achieve an orgasm. A person whose parents were alcoholics relentlessly forbids her partner and their children from drinking even a drop of alcohol.

Why these repetitions? Because in reality the abused child, a being thirsty for tenderness and attention, becomes an adult obsessed with a need to be acknowledged. Familial abuse becomes the only known link, the only way to connect with those whom one hopes to receive love from. The child, thinking he deserved all that was inflicted on him, integrates the abuse with his own identity since it is the only way he knows how to belong to the clan. If the abuse is the main relationship that he had with a parent or a loved one, it is both unbearable and oppressive—unbearable because Consciousness knows he was cheated, but oppressive because repetition of the abuse has provided it a lasting place in the parental archetypes, and it is indispensible to his psychic balance.

Our inner "father" or "mother" is this violence, trouble, rage, dissatisfaction, ban, pain, or invasiveness that we tend to repeat. Repetition is both reassuring (nothing changes, the childhood atmosphere is not disturbed by any agonizing innovation) and painful, because it is accompanied by feelings of guilt and shame. All abuse obeys more or less the same mechanism: what we did we continue to do, and what was prohibited to us we continue to prohibit. The errors and deficiencies that focus on the process of violation are all traps of the genealogy tree.

Immature Parents

Abuse can come from three sources:

- **Error due to a lack of Consciousness.** This error took place at a given moment but was never corrected, for example when a parent inflicts an unjust punishment on a child and forgets that he did, so the injustice remains in the child's mind.

- **Perseverance in the error.** Thinking they are helping, parents repeatedly impose abusive acts, beliefs, or modes of relationship, against which the child protests in his own way, or which the child is incapable of understanding. This perseverance of the error actually reveals the parents' inability to question their own heritage. One could say the parents choose repetition over originality and that they forbid themselves from trying other methods, but trying, even at the risk of failing, is a process that leads to maturity.

- **Deliberate abuse.** The parent is actually conscious of carrying out a harmful act on the child, but he "cannot do otherwise." Either he observes his powerlessness, as in the case of an addiction, or he justifies it with ready-made statements: "I also suffered from the same thing and I didn't die," "Children must put up with it," "It was his fault, he was unbearable." These abuses are always repetitions or derivations of an abuse the parent endured during his childhood that he has never taken the time or the trouble to deal with. The child becomes the solution to an unmanageable psychic conflict.

In reality, these abuses come from the inability of the parents to truly become adults. The majority of abuse is perpetrated in an unintentional or unconscious way. Sadistic parents who are deliberately cruel are relatively rare. All the same, we were all abused in one way or another. It helps to make a distinction between **deliberate abuse** (physical torture, child martyrs, succession of violence in the genealogy tree that creates a physically or sexually sadistic environment) and that which we call **"average" abuse,** which is committed in good conscience by parents subservient to their own genealogy and to the dictates of the society of their age. The parents who never questioned the abuse from which they themselves suffered, and which they merely relay without reconsidering what they transmit, might be underdeveloped in terms of Consciousness.

It is helpful to make a distinction between the **spirit of childhood,** full of innocence and potential creativity, and **infantilism.** All artistic ideologies and psychologies of the "inner child" can become toxic if they advocate a persistent or stagnant infantilism. That which Zen calls the "inner child" is a call to retain the primary impulse of the child's imagination while still developing. Childhood is a stage, just as a seed or a nut is called to become a tree. One cannot glorify this seed if one remembers that it is in no way superior to the tree.

Continuing immaturity into parenthood is the root of multiple abuses. There is nothing worse for a child than the duty of acting like an adult, and nothing more neurotic in a parent than to behave as a child toward one's own children. In general, when an adult remains infantile and neurotic, it is the result of a trauma or an abuse that the parent sustained from his genealogy tree. But we can postulate that each generation has the duty of completing its work in Consciousness and arriving at maturity.

When an infantile adult becomes a parent there is a tendency to unload the gaps that parent sustained on the child, and thus implicitly to require the child to behave as the parent throughout his childhood. But a child is not psychologically ready to assume such responsibilities. This always has to do with the **robbery of a childhood,** where the child is torn from his main activity of playing—which is physiologically and psychologically indispensable—to find himself projected into an overly complex world, forced to solve unsolvable problems or, more concretely in the case where a child is forced to work, to assume a load that is too heavy for his strengths.

This ultimate abuse stifles the development of the imagination. Failing to develop, the child thus abused will later become an adult incapable of using any other mental resource except his rational abilities, and he will lack confidence in the deep strengths of his Unconsciousness.

Parental immaturity can take many forms:

- **Infantile parents and adult children.** These are situations where parents—irresponsible, alcoholic, drug addicted, drifting—discharge their responsibilities, forcing children to assume all necessary tasks for physical and mental survival. This can also be parents obsessed by material livelihood who force their children to work from a very young age, or emotionally infantile parents who claim to be their child's "best friend" and impose out-of-proportion and age-inappropriate emotional conversations or responsibilities on them. All children living through this situation suffer from a robbery of their childhood. The trap in these cases is that the child is generally devoted to being "useful" to the adults who abused him.

- **Infantile parents and martyr children.** Here the immaturity of the parents moves into the realm of total irresponsibility. Children suffer directly from this abdication of responsibility when parents do not provide for the child's education, abandon the child, or entrust their child to other people, or because the parents attack the child with a more or less conscious cruelty, as in the case of physically abused children who are tortured, locked up, or systematically punished for errors they did not commit. In addition to the suffering endured the abused child grows up with a constant feeling of insecurity, and often a suppressed rage, as the parents who are irresponsible or not present shirk confrontation.

- **Hypernormative infantile parents.** These parents do not forge a vision of the world that is their own and merely transmit fossilized standards of education: sexual prohibitions, suspicion of creativity, inapplicable and lapsed ethics, spirit of sacrifice or excessive suspicion toward the unknown. None of these mutilating norms can serve to guide their offspring, and the result is that the children remain attached to the family home into advanced age. In some cases the norms are so harsh that separation is welcome and the children go out into the world expelled from the home as their parents were before them, although they remain psychologically dependent on the family's opinions, morality, religion, and beliefs, which they cannot evade even at a distance. In other cases, the parents require an unbroken loyalty to the familial clan and create links that are forbidden to be questioned, as with a certain number of phone calls or visits per day, per week, or per month.

- **Infantile parents and patronized children.** These parents create a fairy-tale home in the form of a cocoon where the only way to be an adult is to play "perfect parents." Apparently idyllic, this familial structure offers no other solution for the child to face the challenges of adult life but to leave the family. It is the syndrome of the "ideal home" to which the child can return, relieved after a day at school (which is an insurmountable anxiety for the child). The parents create hatred or fear of society and of adults in the psyche of their child with the unconscious goal of keeping the child close to them, as if the development of Consciousness were an aberration and that to remain a child is the only purpose. They forget that childhood is only one stage of human development. Attached to this kind of family, where the parents seem incapable of surviving the change inherent in the departure of their child, is a more or less declared blackmail: "If you leave, I'll die." They pressure their children with an insurmountable guilt, since growing up and leaving home is forbidden.

Institutional Abuse and Its Consequences

Just as the individual repeats the abuse of the tree, the tree repeats the abuse perpetrated by society and culture: social injustices, poverty, moral lapses, and totalitarian regimes directly influence the family, while the family doesn't have the power to interrupt the toxic flow of abuse. Inversely, a toxic tree full of abusive parents hurts not only its own children but a vast number of people and social groups through those children. Consider how many millions of people have paid for, and are paying for, the abuse Hitler and Stalin suffered during their childhoods.

Each generation retains trauma that is transferred, aggravated, onto generations that follow. A number of problems from which individuals suffer originate in **morality,** and some generations later this suffering will result in physical, sexual, creative, or emotional pain. Morality is the product of **religion,** a transcendent law expressed by commandments and prohibitions. The Ten Commandments for Christians and the 613 *mitzvot* for the Jewish religion specify rules to follow. Likewise, the Koran contains teachings that can be interpreted as commandments or prohibitions.

Most of the time, societies based in tradition impose merely on individuals and ignore the needs of the community. For example, individuals do not have the right to kill, but governments assume the right by way of war, the death penalty, and so on. It is forbidden for citizens to steal, but banks, big businesses, and other institutions (political parties among them) do not deny themselves the right to rob. Lying is stigmatized, but the media and political debates are founded in lies. A lawyer's skill or a complainant's financial means can influence the "truth" that emerges out of a lawsuit.

A huge abuse in Jewish tradition was in believing that study of the Torah was only for men, whereas women were forced to remain uncultivated, absorbed in housework, on the pretext that they carried the sacred texts in their flesh. Similarly, the Catholic religion banned women from officiating religious ceremonies. In many genealogy trees this produced **cultural abuse** that encouraged sons to turn toward studies in preparation for existing in the world, while offering beauty and submissiveness to daughters to prepare them (specifically or not) for doing household chores. On the sexual plane, many traditions demonize natural impulses, while the influential and powerful (the "rich and famous") dodge these prohibitions. Some religions stipulate that one must not use God's name in vain, although God's name is used thus to justify and bless terrorism.

Morality, with its religious and superstitious roots, opposes all individual healing. Having become a hollow shell, void of personal investment, it can turn into a defense of the opposite of what it promotes. By force of simplifying its commandments and prohibitions, it renders the consideration of individual complexity impossible. For example, as we have seen with the study of the cores and knots, it is not a sin or a crime to sexually desire a family member: it is a fact that should be accepted in order to solve it without it actually materializing. Also, after someone has been sexually abused, it is not a crime or a disgrace for that person to feel a compulsive desire to repeat the abuse in derivative ways: it is a sexual fixation that one must accept and solve. It is not wrong to wish for the disappearance, even the death, of a brother or sister who monopolizes a parent's attention. This is a feeling that is created in a toxic environment where the parents reign over the family and flagrantly express their preferences. Once again, it helps to recognize this, accept it, and solve it!

When priests or religious officials find themselves custodians of these complex situations they may be tempted to apply ready-made solutions by repeating the past rather than applying the salve of future creativity to unique problems. If during confession a priest deems a repressed desire to be a "sin," there is no other solution but to pretend to have it erased through absolution. But in most cases it stays in the person's mind as persistent shame, and the inability to accept the impulses as they are remains.

It is common for the holders of religious morality to themselves be perpetrators of sexual abuse. With so many cases of sexual abuse now identified in the Catholic Church there is every reason to believe that other religious traditions, to the extent that they impose ultra-strict sexual morality, promote similar acts. The abuse can be very subtle or indirect but still very devastating.

Example: A woman came to consult because she had shaken her head constantly, as if to say "no," since childhood. In reality, the tic began during confession when she was ten years old and she had confessed minor faults. The priest, much more interested in potentially deadly sins, questioned her with urgency about her "impure practices." She had started masturbating months before, but feeling unsure about talking with a priest about this—at the risk of being blamed—she said nothing. But she had learned that lying during confession was a serious act and carried the risk of being sent straight to hell. The priest, seeing that it was obvious she wasn't telling him everything, told her, "If you lie, you will lose eternal life!" The result of this abuse, which qualifies as both sexual and spiritual, was the tic: a compulsive gesture of negation as if her whole life should be spent opposing the unhealthy curiosity of a priest who was fond of sexual confessions. In the case of this consultant, the trauma was so anchored that becoming aware of the origin of this tic did not suffice to diffuse it. She had to stage a psychomagic act where, in front of an audience of witnesses, a man invested with moral authority (Alejandro Jodorowsky in this case) assumed the role of the priest. The consultant confessed to masturbating and consequently received this blessing: "That is perfect. I bless you of this healthy and natural act, which will allow you to have many orgasms." The tic disappeared and has never returned.

Having a group attend an act like this is crucial because a gathering of people of goodwill who bear witness to an establishment of a new morality is indispensible in counteracting the strength of the social group that is the power behind all religious morality.

In cases like this one might say that the priest and the incessant curiosity assumed by all religious authorities of the church was responsible for the abuse, but the parents were the relay for this abuse because they entrusted their child to a religious authority so they could be relieved of their own roles as educators.

Identify the Abuse

The main consequence of abuse is the lack of love of life. One might say that **abuse interrupts the spontaneous movement of life and Consciousness,** and to varying degrees it cuts us off from that which is our true nature.

However, it is often easier to discern past abuse in others than that which resides within ourselves. We have seen how abuse presents itself as a facet of our identity, that we repeat the abuse most of the time without even knowing it and without knowing that a different situation, a different life, can be experienced. In general, psychological growth ends when the abuse begins. Every part of the individual is blocked at the age of the trauma. Therefore, one may be forty years old but have the emotional response of a child, which also makes identifying abuse difficult.

We can initiate personal investigative work by asking ourselves, "How old am I in each of my centers?" In fact we have an intellectual age, an emotional age, a sexual age, a creative age, and a physical age, which are all independent of our official age. As an adult, we may keep the body image of a big baby. Intellectually, we can be younger or older than our age. We can also distinguish the age at which we function in everyday life from that which we fall into when confronted with a problem or stress, when angry or locked in a fearful situation, when we find ourselves in competition with others, and so forth.

But once this profile is established, at the moment of asking what abuse is still supported, anyone of goodwill will collide, more strongly than ever, with the tree's official ideology. In other words, the whole family such as we have inwardly integrated them will protest, "Who are you to call this abuse?" The abused child restores balance by imagining himself guilty of the abuse that the perpetrators inflicted on him. But if the abusive parents are not capable of seeing us as we are, as adults we will have all the trouble in the world in seeing ourselves. If you do not see me, I am incapable of seeing myself. If no one loved or accepted me, I am incapable of loving or accepting myself. Those who did not see or accept me are unable to see, love, or accept anyone.

In the domain of abuse, the tree practices denial and each one of us has integrated a certain number of denials.

Below is a list (though not an exhaustive one) of **denials** and **responses** that can oppose them in Consciousness:

- "That's just the way things were back then." But not in all families. What would we, in our souls and in Consciousness, do today in the same situation?
- "My parents meant well." Has anyone ever protested this? What was the reaction? How did they take into account the protestations?
- "They had no choice." Not even the choice to explain, alleviate, or communicate?
- "It's not their fault. Alcoholism, drug addiction, the substance

took over." And who was addicted to the stuff instead of devoting himself to his family? Who suffered from the yoke of this dictator, this boss, without searching for a solution?

- "My parents didn't have anything to do with that; they didn't know the abuse took place." If the parents' responsibility is to look after their children, how could they not know? What quality of dialogue took place in the family? Why didn't they talk with their children about what happened to them?

- "I was a difficult child." If we envision the child as an adult, how would he treat his own child, also "difficult," in the same situation? Would he react like his parents did then?

- "I don't remember anything." If we were to rewrite a fictional story about this age or era, what would we say?

- "I deserved it." Would we submit a child we love to the same punishment? We imagine the consequences that this punishment would have on the child's life.

In summary, all abuse manifests because of an inner stagnation: knot, fear, anxiety, shame, compulsion, or any element that gives us the impression of being cut off from ourselves, guilty, mutilated, incompetent. In general, any thwarted development corresponds to abuse. In order to find our potential and to be able to extend ourselves in all directions, it is thus necessary to understand the traces of abuse left in our four centers.

ABUSE IN THE FOUR CENTERS

As we have seen, the family is both the producer of abuse born of these internal conflicts and also the intimate relay of institutional abuse. We are now going to detail as much as possible how this abuse weakens the four energies. In fact, as with all other concepts, abuse can be better understood if we apply it to the human's four dimensions. Certainly sexual abuse is serious and recognized, but what about the others? We will give many examples to do our best to illustrate what the child's real rights and needs are in each center; what attitudes pathologically override these needs and neglect these rights; and the possible consequences abuse will have for the adult in later years.

In order to study the chain of abuse in the genealogy tree, it is necessary to consider that the abused person tends to repeat the abuse once he or she becomes an adult because that person is still unconsciously affected by the desire of the act or of abusive scenarios. But it so happens that an abuse in one center produces an abuse in another. For example, a person who was physically beaten and humiliated may perpetrate verbal violence and intellectual abuse on his children. Some fathers who sexually abuse their daughter never experienced sexual abuse themselves but were deprived of any kind of tenderness or love in their childhoods and never knew affection until becoming sexual in adulthood. This past emotional abuse went on to produce sexual abuse because these men, marked by deep emotional ignorance, react to the tenderness of a little child with an irresistible sexual craving.

Intellectual Abuse

Much intellectual abuse comes from the blind application of social and religious morality to which the clan is attached.

This abuse consists of instilling concepts in the child that were used in another time and situation by other people, and that became obsolete (like misogyny, religious morality, or racism) but are anchored in the clan's outdated prohibitions nonetheless. These concepts will clutter the child's mind without ever serving him in any way. The ideas received can remain active for a whole lifetime.

Any idea must be modified according to its time and place, and according to the person whose idea it was. For example, the concept of freedom represents two distinct truths for a government and for a slave. And concepts change according to their formation in regard to social class, social climate, gender, and sexual orientation, like the sacrament of marriage, which was established during the Middles Ages and concerned a population for whom it was rare to live past the age of forty-something. To maintain the moral dogma of strict monogamy in a society where one lives to be one hundred implies a whole other kind of social, familial, and psychological organization.

Some beliefs presented as "truth" refer to an ideology derived from a specific time. Colonialism and slavery generated accepted ideas like "people with darker skin than mine are less intelligent than me." A Jewish person's place in nineteenth- and twentieth-century Western society is that of a miser. Male chauvinism inherent in patriarchal political, economic, and social organization in the West generates the idea that women "are dependent and must take care of the home and the children."

Intellectual abuse can be compared to a label permanently glued to the brain that produces a **mental rigidity:** "If I am a man, I must think like a man; if I am white, I must think like a white." The basis of this identity abuse is to confuse a person with activities, status, or even an error he or she once committed: "So-and-so is a doctor," "So-and-so is an imbecile," "So-and-so is a thief."

Moreover, there are intellectual abuses that may be used by a particular family in the form of insults, criticism, verbal assaults, and any instance where speech is used to "strike." If blows hurt the body, words can hurt the spirit in a more long-lasting way.

Inversely, even when they have the best intentions in the world, parents who believe they are creating a genius or gifted child by prematurely imposing invasive lessons on him actually commit abuse. One sees parents waving illustrated cards before newborns to teach them vocabulary before they have even begun to speak, or imposing on a little one premature foreign language lessons. The child does not have time to play, to explore his own process of learning, and is literally invaded by his parents' intellectual training. This can cause either dyslexia or great intellectual agility coupled with a distressing lack of self-confidence.

On the other hand, it is essential that the child develop his curiosity for his mind to develop in a healthy way. Parents or elders may commit the frequent abuse of rejecting or judging questions posed by little ones: "You don't need to know that," "Leave me alone! Enough with the questions." This kind of response is as much an aggression as it is an attempt to hide bewilderment or lack of availability. It may also be the repetition of a kind of abuse the parent experienced.

Likewise, the child's current level of intellectual development should be respected and he should not be less loved, despised, treated like an "imbecile," or made fun of because, for example, his pronunciation or syntax is not yet on point. When older siblings are jealous of younger siblings they sometimes attempt to intellectually run them over. The parents must be vigilant to prevent this rivalry from turning into abuse.

Lies and promises not kept also fall into the category of intellectual abuse because they create a lack of trust in speaking.

Emotional Abuse

The worst emotional abuse concerns the **lack of love of parents toward their children.** When parents project hate, anger, jealousy, or other neg-ative feelings onto their children a kind of psychological short-circuit is produced. The child cannot accept or psychologically "metabolize" the fact that a parent whom the child loves without reservation is incapable of returning his love. The child will then build a psychological defense system founded in his own guilt: "My parent does not love me because I am fundamentally bad." The suffering resulting from this useless or incorrect knowledge is less unbearable than the fact of not being loved because the child can at least imagine that through effort or radical change, he will be able to one day obtain his parent's love.

Similarly, every situation where the parent deprives the child of his time by entrusting him to other people is abusive. Even when a loved one, grandparent, or nanny is very tender with the child, the result is pathological because the child seeks closeness with the parents.

Within the same realm we have seen a connection with traumatic birth where a child suckles not from her mother's breast but from a bottle or the breast of a woman other than her mother. The milk is not the same; the breasts are different. The baby's animal instinct requires the maternal breast, given with love.

Most emotional abuse in apparently "normal" families comes from parental preferences. When one child is pointedly preferred over others for reason of gender, affinity, or likeness to the parents themselves or because the child has an illness or is weaker or smaller, one risks causing emotional abuse. Obviously this does not mean standardizing the love that one has for one's children, but if a preference exists it is urgent that parents recognize it in order to consciously balance the manner in which their children are treated.

All emotional blackmail is also abuse. A child needs to be loved for who he is, not to reward his actions. Saying things like "I love you if you are nice, but I do not love you if you disobey" or "I love you because you are good in school" creates a situation where the parents are blackmailing the child and can drive him to feel that he must earn his parents' love.

Causing stress because of failure to share information with the child, by surprising her or refusing to communicate family changes like moving or a death, is also emotional abuse. It is essential to honestly communicate with the child from birth, and to listen to her feelings. Telling an orphan "Your mother went on a trip" is intellectual abuse because it is a lie, but above all it is emotional abuse because the child is forced to wait for the impossible—the return of the dead—experiencing loss while guessing what the reasons for the abandonment really are.

Parents' intervention into emotional relationships of the child during adolescence must be restricted. Forcing a son or daughter to unwillingly marry is obviously major emotional and sexual abuse, but continually criticizing the child's friends or amorous relationships is also abusive.

Hiding the fact that his father is not his biological parent from a child, or that his parents adopted him, refers as much to emotional abuse as to sexual abuse. In fact, one touches the incest taboo when the child discovers the truth in adulthood. All the gestures of tenderness, all the surges of love that he felt toward those he thought linked by blood, can in the strict procreative sense actually feel like an expression of incest, which otherwise had no reason to be there. That can create a lasting confusion between love and sexuality.

Asking a child to take responsibility for a parent's emotional stability, as if the child were an adult capable of containing his parent's distress, mourning, or feeling of abandonment, is also a serious abuse. In the case of divorce, for example, abuse exists when a parent confers both rage against his partner and the need to be loved onto his child.

Forcing a child to take part in the couple's quarrels is a grave emotional abuse. As a general rule, for a parent to place the anger she experiences toward her partner onto a child is abusive. This may occur when a child was conceived during a marital rape, or born into a marriage between two people who simply do not love each other.

Finally, the absence of emotional communication—whether motivated by indifference or by an unresolved block on the part of the parent—is grave abuse, albeit through silence.

Sexual Abuse and Abuse of the Creative

Sexual abuse is currently a subject of study in psychology, though for a long time it was for the most part not spoken of. We must obviously consider the possibility that this study will be helpful, but without seeking to flush out emotional, intellectual, or creative wounds that exist on the genealogy tree the use of psychology alone may be insufficient.

Sexual abuse occurs when an **adult or adolescent forces a child into a sexual experience before an appropriate age and/or impedes the child from knowing about this experience at an appropriate time.** In any case, abuse exists when parents or adults see the child or the adolescent as a sex object with or without acting out. The definition of sexual abuse is vast; it can be any action or behavior that might impair the person's development.

Sexual abuse then can consist of a rape or seduction with or without pain or pleasure. It is also perpetrated by actions that are seemingly harmless, like entering the bathroom when the child is bathing, spying on him, and showing him pornographic images, or by speech, as when sexual secrets are imposed on the child. However, banning sexuality and causing the child to feel guilty about it also constitute abuse—parents who oversee and punish masturbation are abusive. These kinds of sexual abuse reveal that the adult sees the child as a sex object, and not as a **sexual subject.**

One must note that sexual abuse within the framework of the family is often devoid of violence, and thus is more comparable to seduction. The child, lacking attention and love, clings to this exchange because it is often the only close relationship that he has with the adults of his family circle. This could cause him feel like an accomplice, and he may feel guilty about the abuse or the secret that weighs on him. Moreover, all sexual abuse causes lasting dissatisfaction: children subjected to this kind of relationship will always wait for the love the adult did not provide, which will cause them to risk their future life as they reproduce the same circumstances of abuse, waiting endlessly for the love that they never received in childhood.

In the mother-daughter relationship sexual abuse can arise from an absence of the father because it is his role to establish the difference between genders, to cut the symbolic ties between mother and child, and to inform the daughter that she is not her mother's mirror. When the father is missing due to absence, divorce, or death the daughter tends to feel symbiotic with the mother, and frequently the mother's lover is tempted to become his lover's daughter's lover. In this case it is as if mother and child share one body, one sexuality. In this case there are actually three people responsible for the abuse: the adult lover who seduces the child, the mother due to lack of vigilance and implied acceptance of the symbiosis, and the father because of his absence.

Likewise, when a parent uses his child as a confidant for his sex life, an incestuous link is established.

Overtly devaluing females in front of a little girl, or males in front of a little boy, also falls under sexual abuse. Here one is imposing a negative vision of sexual identity on the child, which will cause the child to repress the expression of her femininity or his masculinity.

In summary, when we speak of sexual abuse it helps to determine what parts of the body are concerned, in what situation the abuse took place, and what words and actions accompanied the abuse. And finally, the means used by those responsible for subjugating the victim must be established: threats, ruse, force, physical or verbal violence, seduction, "prostitution," offering of sweets or entertainment in exchange for the relationship.

One speaks very little about **creative abuse,** which consists of **forbidding the child from dreaming or developing his talent, or otherwise imposing a rigid artistic practice on the child and subjecting him to endless criticism.**

In other words, it goes back to preventing a person from expanding his own capabilities, directing the child toward projects or a destiny dictated by the genealogy tree's limited level of Consciousness.

Human beings have a variety of talents. People often make the mistake of thinking everyone in the family must have the same talents. When a child is different, the family often treats her as if she is "off her rocker" or a "traitor" and excludes her from the clan.

Inversely, imposing the study of a type of art, a particular musical instrument, or one musical genre on a child is also an abuse and may bring the child face-to-face with a normative model of excellence without allowing the child to develop his own taste for beauty. When a parent seeks to extract talent or genius from a child it very often serves to above all nourish the parent's thirst for attention, even if the child is in fact a small prodigy. No child can behave like an accomplished artist before having attained his psychological maturity.

Lack of attention, and a lack of someone to listen, can also lead to a creative abuse. Each child is an individual who must go through his own process of learning and discovering at the risk of failing. Forcing the child's rhythm—pressuring him or slowing him down—always constitutes an intrusion into the evolution of the child's own spirit.

It is equally important to let the child develop her own taste without criticism, allowing her to choose whenever possible in matters like dressing herself or decorating her room the way she wants. The relationship to beauty is personal, and impositions on the child's own aesthetic sense is an error that can become an abuse.

Physical and Material Abuse

Hitting a child and instilling a fear of punches, raising him by the use of terror, creates lasting damage to the child's relationship with his body. Similarly, mockeries concerning the child's physical appearance, weight, skin color, or personal traits is abuse. Loving or hating a child because he looks like other members of the family causes him to deny the unique and precious character of his embodied existence. A seemingly innocuous act like cutting his hair against his will, or forcing him to wear uncomfortable clothing, may represent abuse.

On the plane of nutrition, undernourishing or overfeeding a child is an abusive behavior, the same as forcing a child to eat food he hates with threats or punishment.

Every child has the right to have space and time to himself, and it can be as little as a protected corner. Having a feeling of being constantly invaded because all space must be shared with others represents abuse. Locking a child up, preventing him from knowing the world, or, contrarily, always carting him around from one place to another, is abusive behavior in the sense that neither respects that every person needs a territory of reference while being able to open himself up to the world.

Parents whose toxic and self-destructive behaviors are pursued in front of a child, like smoking, using drugs, or drinking excessively, are actually abusing their children.

When a child is ill or needs care, a parent who exposes the child to excessive pain or anxiety is an abusive parent: the child must feel as though she can recover her health in a protected atmosphere.

As a general rule, physical abuse also depends on the way in which sharing takes place in the household: the child need not be treated like a king **but should be treated fairly in relation to the others living in the home.** If one takes advantage of the child's weakness and appears to treat him less well than older or younger siblings, no matter the living conditions, the child will feel abused or cheated. Many arguments about inheritance in big, wealthy families are based on these infantile inequalities and preferences; even the collapse of a financial empire can occur because of past abuse that marked the siblings.

OUT OF ABUSE

Summary and Confrontation

We have seen that abuse, the last trap of the genealogy tree, is a kind of psychic tattoo that forces us to repeat behavior that is radically opposed to our authentic Being.

We must adopt a dual position when facing the multiplicity of abuse in our own history and in that of our ancestors: that of the **defender** of ourself and of **witness** for the abuse detected in the genealogy tree. As such it is important to understand how from the outside we can help, hear, and understand a victim of abuse without the goal of being a therapist, and to be able to view the abuse that our own parents and grandparents were subjected to without anxiety.

Like a meditation practice, where it is useful to understand the function of the human spirit and the need to clear our incessant "internal dialogue" when we sit quietly, we must understand the universal process of abuse that is present in every genealogy tree to be able to flush it out and move beyond it in our own history.

The Abused: A Full-Fledged Role

Anyone who has witnessed abuse tends to react from one's own fears and one's own boundaries: it is difficult to hear an account of abuse, especially when it concerns torture or sexual violence, because one tends to identify both with the victim and with the abuser. One is fascinated and horrified; shameful of one's own curiosity, one tends to deny facts or show unqualified solidarity with the victim. It is one of the reasons it is very difficult for a person who has suffered from hidden abuse to open up to relatives, as most people do not know how to listen or receive such an account.

And so the first thing to do, for oneself and for others, is to be capable of **facing an account of abuse** in all of its details.

Being heard by a compassionate listener, whether one is listening for oneself or for another, allows the abused person to conquer his shame. The quality of listening, which must be devoid of all morbid curiosity and judgment while remaining attentive to the details of what happened, enables the person to unroll his memories and emerge from the secret linked to the abuse. Very often the abused person minimizes what happened to him ("It wasn't so bad") or simplifies it in a way that prevents any memory of the details. The initial statement "He raped me" is insufficient. What were the circumstances? The pain or negative feelings produced by the abuse must be part of the story because they are essential to its recognition.

Once the victim's facts and feelings are clearly taken into account he can finally enter the most hidden dimension of the abuse, recognizing that it may have given him pleasure (infatuation, pride, feeling of grandeur), and learning how and why he feels urged to repeat the abuse in order to experience the agitation again and again. It is common for the scenario of abuse to return while asleep, or as a fantasy that may accompany masturbation in the case of sexual abuse. We have talked about pleasure in the victim's case, and if this term seems shocking we must understand how the **manifestation of pleasure inside us seeks life and its meaning at all costs.** Once healing has taken place we will return to this faraway echo of the essential Being: the unalterable love of life. As such the child, abused by an adult and incapable of establishing a relationship of true love, participates in any relationship offered to him in order to draw comfort, no matter how little.

For a writer or an artist in general, abuse can be a source of inspiration to which he adds personal imagery. For a fashionable, sociable person this may result in recurring jokes evoking situations similar to those experienced, or contrarily as statements of hatred toward people who carry out abuse. An example of this is intense homophobia, whose root is homosexual abuse.

In the case of sexual abuse in particular, it is essential that the person tells someone close to her, even a therapist, in order to clarify the exact circumstances of the act (or acts) the victim was subjected to, as well as in what way she feels she may have participated. Healing, that is to say allowing the abuse to be put behind us, depends upon achieving this awareness.

We have seen that all sexual abuse produces the unconscious desire to reproduce it, to replay it, or in the case of violent abuse the desire to be able to inflict revenge on the aggressor. The victimization of those who have been subjected to sexual abuse is a double-edged sword. By being limited to the position of pure victim, generally under the auspices of a timid or ashamed therapist who errs on the side of morality and cannot consider **the victim's involuntary participation in the act of his aggressor**, they risk not having access to the key that can finally free them and allow them to interrupt the scenario of repetition. Victimization can occur either in their relationship with people who metaphorically represent the abuser, or in the pure and simple invalidation of their sexuality.

From this point of view, all forms of abuse must be treated according to the model of sexual abuse: **to get out of the trauma, the victim must embrace the role he/she played** and the psychic, emotional, and physical pleasure he/she felt.

Confrontation in Order to Begin Work on the Abuse

All branches of modern psychology, particular those based in group sessions and support, take an interest in repairing abuse. We will mention here the excellent work of American psychologist Susan Forward, author of *Toxic Parents,* in which she popularized the principal of **confrontation.** Confronting the person who committed the abuse either physically or by letter is, in fact, an indispensible stage. By this act the person who was abused during childhood defends himself as an adult, and as an equal of the parent or other adult who was formerly superior in age, strength, or influence.

The confrontation recommended in Metagenealogy is always, above all, **aimed at parents.** If someone else in the family circle abused us—an uncle or aunt, brother or sister, grandparents or other kin—there will also be time to confront those people once confrontation with the parents, who are initially responsible, has taken place.

The confrontation takes place on neutral ground, not at the parents' home or in one's own home, and is done face-to-face with the abuser. Even if the parents are inseparable, one must find a way to hold off the one while meeting with the other. If one feels very nervous, one might take a mild sedative. If one is afraid of the person who will be confronted, one might have friends or allies stationed close by, ready to intervene and help.

If the parents are deceased, the confrontation might occur at the gravesite or the place where the ashes were spread. Or if a family member kept the ashes and refuses to hand them over, the confrontation can take place in front of the parent's photograph. The five stages that we detail below must always be respected.

Finally, if one is truly very afraid of a confrontation because the parent is considered scary and dangerous or is old, ill, or weak, one might begin by doing it by letter, with the aid of a therapist, or with someone playing the role of a parent. Nevertheless, it is always ultimately most effective when a real confrontation is possible. Even if the parent is sick or suffering from degeneration of his cognitive faculties, the confrontation can take place without violence and with a firm calmness that aims for the highest level of Consciousness one is capable of achieving. One therefore will not risk causing the person's death or suffering of harm in any way.

One might begin by warning the person by telling him, "I am going to speak with you in an unusual manner, but it is important for me. At the end, I will give you the opportunity to respond." Then one explains the abuse suffered, the feelings the abuse caused, the consequences that resulted, the suffering one still experiences, and finally the repair due to one. Appearing simple, it is a process that demands clarity, firmness, and Consciousness. One might compare it to a process where one is both the complainant and the lawyer, and in which the ultimate goal is that the accused leave freed and washed of his errors after being fined.

We begin by detailing each stage, accompanied by two situations where the now-adult son confronts the father: in the first case for intellectual, emotional, and creative abuse; in the second case for sexual abuse.

1. "This Is What You Did to Me (and What You Did Not Do)."

Like an attorney taking the case of the past child, the person who was abused recapitulates the **facts** and exhaustively identifies all the circumstances of the abuse. Whether it was a single abuse (sexual, emotional, etc.) or a series of abuses that peppered one's childhood, this has to do with having the responsible party face what he did or neglected to do.

- **Intellectual, creative, emotional abuse.** "You always criticized me, my actions were never excellent enough for you, you did not listen to me or speak to me except to correct my homework, you were absent from the house most of the time, and when you came back, you showed me no affection. I studied drawing but you were never interested in my art. I never received any praise from you."
- **Sexual abuse.** "When I was eight, you closed your eyes on the fact that the neighbor forced me to have oral sex with him. I tried to speak to you about it but you never wanted to hear it. That went on for four years until I finally found the courage to threaten to tell everything. He intimidated me by saying that if I told, the shame would fall on me, but he never again forced me into fellatio. You never wanted to hear what happened to me, though you were responsible for me."

2. "This Is How I Felt"

The expression of **feeling** is extremely important and requires a bit of preliminary work where the person should get back in touch with the feelings he felt at the time and those that remain with him today. In fact, all abuse involves the abuser denying all or part of the feelings felt by the abused, without which the relationship would again become fair and the abuse would not be possible. The victim then finds himself forced to repress his anxiety, pain, anger, or fascination or pleasure.

This suppression continues into adulthood and cuts the victim off from himself. In the confrontation it is essential to **restore the subjectivity of abuse,** and to put the responsible person in front of the feelings he would not take into account at the time of the abuse.

- **Intellectual, creative and emotional abuse.** "I always felt worthless. Every time I speak with you it is with great anxiety. I was very sad that you did not love me. Each time you spoke to me, however, even if it was to criticize me, I felt like I existed, so I came to expect your criticism. I had and still have the feeling of being a bad person without value, and that no one can love me. I carry within me a deep despair."
- **Sexual abuse.** "I was afraid. I was disgusted, and I have often felt like I am suffocating. At first, I was above all extremely angry but that did nothing for me; I ended up not feeling anything. At the same time, I was somehow fascinated by this secret that was imposed on me. I felt ashamed toward you and the rest of the family, and I felt especially cut off from all of you."

3. "This Is What the Abuse Caused in My Life"

Paradoxically, long-term consequences of abuse can be negative or positive. One part of each individual is always resilient, and it is possible following abuse to become the first person in the family to initiate therapy, to authentically express one's creativity, or to devote oneself to a charitable activity. But this resilience is also accompanied by obstacles, personal suffering, or blocks directly caused by the abuse, and this step is about putting the person responsible in front of **all that the abuse caused** in the victim's life.

- **Intellectual, creative, emotional abuse.** "I have become a cold, distant father in your image. I turned away from my creativity. I put everything into my profession and into excellence. One day I felt that I was going to die if I continued to deny myself this way and I dared initiate work on myself. It is in this way that I discovered the extent of damage and the lack of confidence I had in myself, which you instilled in me."

- **Sexual abuse.** "For a long time, my sexuality was based in masturbation. I fell into drug use and then I quit. I was very angry at all authority figures until I realized they represented both this neighbor, who was stronger than me, and you, my father who did not protect me. I dealt with part of my rage by becoming a black belt in karate, but I am still deeply affected by what I experienced as I child."

4. "I Still Suffer Today"

On the day of the confrontation, the individual who had been abused must be very sure of himself. He must be as strong and mature as possible in order to provide a complete **accounting** of what he was subjected to when he confronts the person responsible for the abuse. Even if this encounter is accomplished, there will be knots, obstacles, suffering, and obsessions that remain in the psyche that cannot be resolved by this initial confrontation. The person responsible must face **that which his victim still suffers today.**

- **Intellectual, creative, emotional abuse.** "I was to going change careers and be better able to love my children, but your example stands between me and my desire like a wall. I suffer from this every day."
- **Sexual abuse.** "At thirty-six, I have never had a lasting romantic relationship. I feel major violence. I do not want to live like this."

5. "Here Is the Repair You Owe Me"

There can be no forgiveness if the person responsible for the abuse is not aware of what he did and does not recognize his **obligation.** Any unilateral forgiveness by the victim has no value from the point of view of the Unconscious. Either it was abuse, this abuse is recognized, and the repair allows the abuse to dissipate, or the guilty continues in the abuse by refusing to recognize responsibility, and ample forgiveness is impossible. One must cut ties then until the pain of the abuse is completely dissipated, which is to say, until the person responsible for the abuse makes absolutely no difference to one at all.

If the parent possesses an adult, altruistic Consciousness, at this point of the confrontation his only wish will be to repair the abuse and to be able to retrospectively transcend his error. The abused person must then suppose that Consciousness exists in the interlocutor, in truth or in power, by providing whatever repair can settle the debt in this regard. Even if the abuser is caught in denial and totally rejects all allegations made against him (which is possible), the fact of enunciating the price of the repair will be beneficial for the abused person. Whether in the form of a sum of money, a public apology, or any other act or object, it is essential **to give the repair a concrete value** in order to move beyond the abuse. If the parent refuses to grant the repair, life will do it another way, as we will see later.

- **Intellectual, creative, emotional abuse.** "I know you are not going to change, but you owe me two things: Buy from me, for a sum that I will decide, a canvas that I painted on during my adolescence and hang it in your living room. And one day come with me to an amusement park. We will take my children and give them the most beautiful day children could dream of. I will be there to make sure you act like a good grandfather."
- **Sexual abuse.** "You owe me apologies for failure to assist a person in danger, and a million dollars in symbolic repair for the evil you have caused me."

How to Make the Repair Right, and Is It Essential to Obtain?

The work on reparation is without a doubt the most delicate point of the process: **repairing a past action does not change the past.** It serves nothing at all to say to an alcoholic mother or violent father, "From now on, this is what I expect from you." This is the same as asking the parent to change into the parent we needed. As such, this miracle will not take place! The past is irreversible and all healthy relationships imply that one does not wait for the other to change.

The confrontation pushes us to realize that **we must mourn our infantile demand for love in order to be able to live in adult love.** Wishing for our parents to change means we continue to want to obtain what we did not have. As such, if the parents behaved in this way, it is because of their own knots, neuroses, and inability to function at an elevated level of Consciousness. If they had worked on themselves, they would have found out how to mend.

Other than offering them an accelerated understanding, the only thing one can then do is to require a repair that consists not of good-feeling promises but concrete acts, the same way a humane justice system condemns a person to a fine, public service, or prison sentence.

The whole question then concerns our figuring out **an act that can repair the abuse** and leaves us with the feeling of having been compensated. This act must be short, clear, and decisive, or else one exposes oneself to disappointments. Such was the case of the consultant who, at the end of the confrontation with the mother who abandoned her in infancy, concluded, "So you will call me every Sunday to ask about my life, my news." The mother agreed, promised, cried, but on Sunday, totally "forgot" to call her daughter. Such a demand puts the consultant in the infantile position of waiting for signs of love or of attention that don't come. Under no circumstance does the repair consist of trapping oneself like that. The repair must stand for a unique, symbolic concrete act where the responsible person accepts the request to charge the abuse **to his account,** recognizing his past responsibility as an adult and freeing the child of the guilt of having taken part.

The debt can be assessed in money. If the number is huge, "thousands of millions of dollars," the payment can be metaphorical, by means of a check or contractual letter that has no banking value, but which symbolizes recognition of the debt. One can then say to the person, "In compensation, you sign a check for ten million dollars," and receive the check right away in order to be able to "touch" the repair. One can even hang it on the wall in a frame.

But the compensation can be a gesture, an act, or a gift. One consultant, having declared, "In compensation, you must accept that I smack you," was surprised by his father's response, "I deserve two," as he turned the other cheek. Another, a young girl whose mother closed her eyes on the repeated sexual abuse that her father subjected her to, asked her mother for a convertible and the mother, in spite of her humble salary, immediately agreed in order to satisfy her daughter's need.

Once the compensation is granted, the concerned parent has the right to stay exactly as he was before (only an "adult" is required to change for the sake of the family). Because of the fact that the parent has accepted the principle of the repair, it is the **relationship that changes**: it is no longer obscured by abuse, and it becomes an equitable relationship between two consenting adults, child and parent, free to be who they are.

On the other hand, in the case of a refusal more distance will be necessary in order to permit the relationship to change. By affirming the necessity of distancing himself from an abusive relationship, and having justified the necessity for the confrontation, the abused person will manage to emerge from the toxic relationship. To continue the metaphor of the process, if the "accused" refuses to pay his "fine," or if the accused is not "creditworthy," the solution remains of inflicting a "punishment" on him. This may consist of cutting off all communication with the parent, prohibiting him from coming close, from telephoning, or even from sending messages for a period of time.

The Refusal of Compensation and Familial Fast

Children who were loved and well treated have no difficulty leaving the home of their parents, while people who were badly treated in childhood have all the difficulty in the world cutting ties. As mentioned this apparent paradox is due to the fact that we all tend to hope the failings of childhood will one day be resolved in adulthood, so we reproduce an infantile situation in a hopeless attempt to see the past change.

The solution to a number of neuroses will consist of breaking off the relationship with the parents, but few people are capable of choosing to do that. If they are aware of the wrongdoing, they continue to subject both their own projections and the pursuit of a relationship based on non-recognition of abuse because part of themselves remains in childhood. They wait, without admitting it, for their parents' deaths so they can become adults because they can't imagine cutting ties with them.

This difficulty has historic roots. It is the product of both Eastern and Western religious mentalities in which morality requires total respect for the parents and the ancestors: no matter what errors they committed, we are supposed to forgive them "because they gave us life." However, parents do not actually give life to their children; they transmit it to them. The being that incarnates was not created by them but by **humanity's need to reproduce.** No one created life; we all received it. Parents do not bring children into the world for themselves but for the world. Nor do they beget their children, but rather future adults. And this does not have anything to do with imprisoning them in the framework of a home, but requires leaving them free to build other homes even if this must be very far from the family roots.

To free oneself from a neurosis, from an infantile fixation, and to recover all mental health it is sometimes necessary to dynamite imposed traditional morality. Cutting the sick branches of the genealogy tree is an extreme solution, but it is sometimes necessary. If, even after a confrontation with the parents, they do not accept and acknowledge their error, it may be time to break ties with them or to at least get away from them for a while in order to follow one's path toward health and fulfillment.

At the moment of performing this cut, or this **familial fast,** all of the infantile resistances are going to mobilize. The first, as we have seen, consists of minimizing the abuse with the tendency to think one deserved what happened. Moreover, one who decides to cut ties is going to have to fight against the persistent desire to obtain that which the parents refused one in childhood. The confrontation provides the realization that one will never obtain this "treasure" since it is too late to change one's mental formation, but that one does not want to get it, anyway, since the link itself is based on the abuse and the pleasure of suffering. In this case one behaves like a drug addict because even while knowing it is destructive, one continues to desire the same stimulus to which all known intensity relates.

This is why it is useful to use the same approach as a detoxification process by cutting the familial ties, at least for a given period of time, as some alcohol treatment centers do. In this period of "abstinence," the rule of the game consists of not communicating by letter, telephone, or even the smallest gift. In short, it means refusing all attempts made by parents who request contact.

Other steps are also possible:

- No longer going to places where they go
- Placing their photographs and other documents in a box covered with black paper
- Writing breakup letters, and sending them through the mail to a metaphorical address in an envelope carrying their real first names and a symbolic address, like "Center of the Universe," "Consciousness of God," or "Temple of the Past," but without a return address

This period of distance will allow one to take as much time as is necessary to live as an individual, independent from a familial group, and to **focus on the relationship with oneself.**

PSYCHOMAGIC OF ABUSE

Violent or traumatic abuse imprints a continually repeating scenario in the memory, like a kind of interior ceremony. A psychomagic act that accompanies the confrontation can be beneficial in dissolving this obsession by restaging the known scenario and creating a different conclusion from what really took place.

The goal of this work on abuse is to **end the repetition**, ceasing to inflict on oneself that which one was subjected to, finally allowing in that which was denied to one. But further, this healing allows one to

open oneself to the world, and to begin giving the world what one did not receive.

Many of the psychomagic acts evoked for the resolution of knots can be found here because a number of knots come from abuse, and inversely an abuse that one has not resolved tends to create a knot in the following generation. The cannibal knots in particular are generally linked to abuse.

Bury the Parents of the Past

Choose statuettes that represent a masculine and feminine divinity, or a male and a female saint, according to the culture in which one was raised. Write the word "mama" on the female statuette, paint it silver, and glue a photo of the mother on it; paint the masculine statuette gold, write the word "papa" on it, and glue a photo of the father on it. Then bury them and plant a vegetable on top. It is not the real parents, who may even still be alive, that one buries, but the infantile concept of the all-powerful "papa" and "mama."

This pyschomagic act provides a space in which to transform the personality.

Free Oneself from Verbal Violence

Repeated criticism, curses, insults, sarcasm, and other toxic speech represent long-lasting intellectual and emotional abuse. Hurtful words remain encrusted in the memory, and symbolically in the ears: a person who was often insulted or criticized tends to filter all that we say into the negative sense, as if the ears only hear toxic words spoken by the family.

The psychomagic act consists of gathering all the contemptuous or insulting aggressive phrases that last in the memory, and reemerge at every instance, onto different colored pieces of paper. Once this collection is finished, once there are no phrases left in the head that have not been noted, it is time to confront the responsible parents. Put these papers in a box and, accompanied by sweets, bring them to the parents and say, "These words belong to you. I give them back to you."

Then ask the parents—or two people who have consented to represent them—to tenderly wash their ears with spiritually purified water. No matter what the religion of origin is, the water can be sanctified: it may be blessed water, water from a *puja* ritual, water that has been set before the portrait of a saint or other divinity, or water that has been exposed to the moonbeams and the the sun's rays. Finally, the real or metaphorical parents must coat the consultant's ears with honey—the mother the left ear, and the father the right ear—while murmuring positive words and, where appropriate, reading a text written in advance by the consultant.

Shed the Roles That Do Not Belong to Us

Quite frequently abuse occurs when the child is not seen as he is and he ends up gluing a persistently projected character or role onto himself, preventing him from living his own destiny in adulthood. To fulfill this act, one must have identified the personage or the role to which one has been assigned. This may have to do with another member of the tree, the parents having wanted a child of the opposite sex, or perhaps the child having been considered a "demon" or an "angel" (a "perfect child," Christ, or a saint).

The act consists of visiting the parents (or going to their gravesite), disguised as this foreign character, and saying to them, "Here is the child you wanted me to be; here is the role you projected onto me." On this occasion one may make a mini-confrontation, at the end of which one sheds the disguise to show oneself nude (or, if one is very modest, in flesh-colored underwear), telling the parents, "Here is the authentic being that I am," then getting dressed in new, becoming clothes. One quits the place of the meeting, leaving the costume of the old character with the parents to whom it belongs: the burden is on them to bury the costume and to plant a vegetable on top. If the parents are deceased, one leaves the disguise on the grave.

Example: Right before turning thirty-three Christian Joseph felt dread and was depressed. The study of his genealogy tree confirmed what his first name suggests: he is his parents' only son, a "Christ-like child." His mother, Mary White, worships her own father, who was considered a superman; his father, a weak and silent man, was absorbed in his work and often absent. The mother is therefore invasive. Christian's psychomagic act consisted of making a plaster Christ the size of a seven-year-old child and pushing it around in a supermarket basket for twelve days. On the night of the twelfth day he broke it with rage against a church close to his mother's home, then brought the pieces to her accompanied by a piece of heart-shaped chocolate.

Discard the Identity of a Ghost

One frequent abuse innocently perpetrated by parents and the rest of the family consists of giving a child the same first name as a child who died before him, or the name of a family member who died prematurely from tragic circumstances. This is an absolute abuse in the sense that it deprives a child of his identity, reducing the being to an empty shell where the soul of the deceased nests. The neurotic benefit of the abuse for the parents consisted in not having to mourn or—on top of their pain—welcome a totally new, different being to which they would have to make an effort to adapt. "Copying" the death is more comfortable both in order to deny the absence and to avoid changing any already established relationship habits, all of which is at the cost of the child, who will see his life energy, creativity, emotions, thoughts—his entire existence—encumbered by this inner corpse of which he is metaphorically a captive. A number of people in this situation spend years seeking their individuality in vain, feeling unloved and even persecuted by an invisible presence similar to a vampire. Some even lose their lives trying to console inconsolable people, trying to save those who do not want to be saved. It is here that one finds many who are codependent on alcoholic or addicted partners.

In this case we refer to the psychomagic act described in part 7 (page 418). If one carries a particularly tragic story that is linked to someone who is deceased, or if the death was violent, one can use the corpse of a small, edible animal, or a particular organ like a calf heart, as a symbol. One will place these "remains of the deceased" in a plastic bag on which one has written the name of the person who died and then carry it around for three days inside a black backpack. At the end of three days, one will bury this symbol of the deceased and plant a vegetable on top of the grave. Finally, throw the backpack symbolizing the part of the individual that "carried" this other for years into a river in the direction of the current, pouring a jar of honey into its wake. For optimal results and planetary awareness, the backpack can be handmade of biodegradable material.

Childhood Theft

We have seen how infantile parents who force their child to become an adult too early deprive him of his childhood, and of the time spent at play where his imagination and creativity would have developed.

If one feels that one was robbed of one's childhood and deprived of the free pleasure of play, after a confrontation one gathers a respectable sum of money (dependent upon resources) and then goes to a casino, exchanges the money for low-value chips, and plays until everything is lost. This has nothing to do with playing to win but entails playing purely for the pleasure of playing. If one accumulates a fortune, one will remain in the casino until all of it is lost, in this way discovering the pleasure of acting without utilitarian purpose.

Two Individual Cases of Sexual Abuse

It would be very difficult to provide a generic act that would heal this kind of abuse due to a countless number of scenarios and how they may come to take root in various levels of the psyche. Nonetheless, the following examples illustrate a general principle: when sexual abuse took place one may restage the scene and then deviate toward a positive resolution where the victim takes power of the situation and obtains what she wants, like satisfaction, compensation, or love.

Example No. 1: Abused by her father from the age of four this consultant chose a man she trusted, a therapist who was aware of her condition, to play the role of her father. She then stole some clothes from her father (who was still alive) for the therapist to wear. She herself dressed as a little girl. The "father" repeated the sexual abuse scenario by entering the "little girl's" bedroom and proposing the same acts that had been imposed on her in childhood (in this case, fellatio). The consultant began to repeat the action, but at the moment where she was about to uncover the man's penis she told him: "I would prefer that you take me to walk in the zoo garden, that you take care of me, and that you buy me cotton candy." The "father" then renounced his sexual drive, and the two went out walking to fulfill the scenario exactly as the consultant had proposed. Afterward she buried the child's clothes, planting a vegetable atop. She sent the father's clothes to the dry cleaner and then returned them to him. (If the parent is deceased one could put the clothes on his grave.)

Example No. 2: A man was sexually abused virtually under the father's accommodating eye by a cousin who was seven years older—he had been forced to sleep with his cousin each time he visited his cousin's family. The consultant bought two bull testicles and a sausage that he cut through lengthwise, creating a channel that he then filled with condensed milk. He scheduled a meeting with his father for the confrontation, and at the moment of compensation he substituted a kind of psychomagic act when he placed the sausage together with the two testicles on a table and crushed them with a hammer. Then he left his father in front of the undeniable significance of the object placed before him. The father had to throw away or bury the metaphorical phallus that symbolized what he wanted to ignore at the time of the abuse.

Abuse is the last form of accumulated trauma that causes transmission and repetition in the tree. Only the ego can be abused because the essential Being is inviolable. We will see how awareness of abuse can serve as a basis for repairing one's essential identity, as well as helping to repair one's love of life, in the following two parts devoted to healing the genealogy tree.

PART NINE

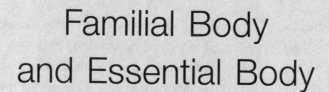

Familial Body
and Essential Body

The Genealogy Tree and Body Memory

SEVENTEEN

From Body to Soul

By Alejandro Jodorowsky

From the time of my birth until the age of forty I remembered only this: I was a little boy with long golden ringlets. The rest drowned in a black lake. My first vivid memory echoed in my mind, the rattle of the "lawn mower" of a Japanese hairdresser who transformed my long blond mane into a sad, shaved head and my father, Jaime, exclaiming, "The end of the feminine curls, you are neither a girl nor a fag!" I returned home with Jaime, who definitively presented me to my mother. She let out a cry of despair and immediately erased me from her own illusions: in her personal legend she was the posthumous child of a beautiful Russian dancer bestowed with long, golden hair who had died in an absurd accident. In a certain way, by the color and the curls of my hair, I was the reincarnation of her father. The view of my bare scalp destroyed her dreams. Without hiding her emotions she renounced me, expelling me to the world of vulgar males, and when she realized that my hair was growing back a deep, chestnut brown, she never touched me again. I grew up without ever knowing her caresses or her maternal kisses again, much less the paternal: my progenitor's favorite quote was, "Men do not cry and do not touch."

Through the years, having been deprived of this necessary tenderness, my skin seemed to harden. My intimate relationships with the women I chose, whom I was incapable of loving, consisted only of athletic prowess and relentless acts of domination that did not contain any sensitivity: "You don't love me but I make you bend." In spite of my sexual satisfaction, which remained localized in my member, the rest of my body eagerly sought caresses. For my father, an ex-boxer and circus trapeze artist, any demonstration of sensitivity on the part of a man revealed a homosexual nature. Accepting caresses, speaking delicately, or eating correctly was all out of the question. He also considered dancers, painters, actors, and poets to be "fags." The body was only an instrument for work, a weapon of conquest, a self-driven organism heroically mastering the ability to become accustomed to enduring pain.

To please him, I took refuge in my mind and used my "rhinoceros skin"–covered body as an instrument. I loved to show that I could resist punches as well as I could resist tickling. I felt guilty for writing poems and for dancing, playing, singing, or drawing, although I was very good at all these activities. When I tried to express myself in any art form, in my mind a gigantic vision of Jaime appeared and screamed "Faggot!" at me with scorn. With the helpless desire to be myself, and not what my father wanted me to be, I plunged into the "normal" world, transforming my organism into a puppet that was devoid of feeling.

My encounter in Mexico with the healer Doña Magdalena was essential.* Thanks to her massages, I discovered a sublime universe from which I had been banned since childhood.

This woman of great wisdom, an initiate of the Mazateco Indians of Oaxaca, made massage a true art. It was not only the sense of wellbeing in the body that she brought about with her hands; she also transmitted profound spiritual wisdom. At the beginning of our relationship Doña Magdalena told me a paste she used composed of petroleum jelly and powdered psychotropic plants was like

---

*This encounter is narrated in detail in my book, *Mu: Le maître et les magiciennes,* later published as *The Spiritual Journey of Alejandro Jodorowsky* (Rochester, Vt.: Inner Traditions, 2008).

marijuana, but some time later she confessed to using *Salvia divinorum*, a sacred plant called *ska pastora* in the Mazatecan language and *hojas de la Virgen* (the Virgin's leaves) in Spanish. "They are hard to find," she told me. "They have no seed and they only grow in the Sierra Mazateca. It is there I must go to find them. It is a divine plant, born of the menstrual blood that the Indians pour onto the earth. Before cutting them, I kneel and pray. If I do not do this, the leaves lose their power."

When she rubbed my body for the first time with this mysterious cream, running her hands lightly over my skin in a continuous motion as if sliding on an infinite path, I discovered corporal sensitivity. Before this experience I was not a conscious body but an intellect that lived on the interior of an enemy organism, terrorized by threats of disease, old age, and death.

"Let the memories that absorb your life come. They are crouching in every corner of your body, darling child of the soul," Magdalena murmured to me.

I don't know if it was the continual caress, the velvety tone of her voice, or the psychotropic effects of the *Salvia divinorum,* but the feelings from deep in time began to emerge in my flesh. My mother's nipple formed as large as a little finger in my mouth, robust, generous, pouring out thick, warm milk so delicious it made me tremble from head to toe. My arms suddenly had the impulse to hug the maternal body and never let go. The dark veil that had kept my first four years in oblivion was torn away, and I remembered a happy time when I had received endless tenderness, sucking every day from the milky nectar of the gods, when I was bathed, caressed, perfumed by a loving woman who embraced my golden curls, wetting them with her tears. And suddenly, the cruel cut, the expulsion from paradise: I felt on my scalp the cold metal mower that had robbed me without pity. I began to cry out in a child's voice with a rage and powerlessness I carried in the soles of my feet, which felt like a nest for the ghosts of my grandparents who had been savagely expelled from their Russian village, condemned to go to the unknown land of Chile, all roots cut. I felt Jaime's mocking and spiteful face glued to my own: a mask where grimace followed grimace without end, expressing his hatred toward the world. In my neck I felt the weight of the humiliation sustained by my mother, an orphan despised by her stepbrother and by her husband, who mistook her political ignorance for stupidity. I began to have pain in my legs that was the accumulated suffering of generations of emigrants, expelled from one country after another without ever finding a place about which to say, "Here is the earth in which I want to be buried." Suddenly the pain of a great-grandmother who died during childbirth burst in my stomach. My whole body was a nest where my many ancestors were clinging to life, to my life. Wherever I would go, I carried a suffering genealogy tree encrusted in my flesh.

Doña Magdalena continued her infinite caresses.

My body began to make the suffering that once gripped me, that I had avoided facing by burying it in a dense oblivion, finally emerge.

In my penis, I carried the shame of the time at school when in the showers after my first gymnastics class my classmates mocked me because I had no foreskin. In my ears, the resounding sound still echoed of the revolver with which my father blew the head off Pepe, my dear gray cat, right before my eyes when I was three to punish him for having slept with me. "These dirty beasts give people tuberculosis!" In my hands waved two little fists wanting to punch him in the mouth, breaking his cynical teeth that made fun of my tears. In my chest I felt a dark and bottomless hole, the same kind that had perforated my heart the day I was suddenly ripped from Tocopilla without warning and brought to Santiago, forced to leave behind forever my friends, my municipal library, my ocean, my hills, my magic world.

Doña Magdalena stopped massaging me and took me in her arms with an immense tenderness, the primordial caress of the mother that all my life—without admitting it—I had wanted to receive. I felt like I had become very small. "It is the unsatisfied child that still lives inside you. Those who bury the pain in oblivion stop growing, and under the carpet of amnesia and pain, anger accumulates. Trust me, dear child of the soul, let out your grief."

I was trembling, waving my arms and legs. A flood of cries poured from my mouth: I proclaimed insults, I wanted to break the walls, destroy the world, and a paralyzing terror invaded me. I whispered, "This is everything I have accumulated over the course of my life, like a poison. How can I be myself if I am possessed by this clan of phantoms?"

Her voice descended upon me like an avalanche and went straight to my heart: "Do not confuse what you contain with what you are. You contain your family, but you are not your family. Think of yourself as a book filled with white pages: many people have written in it, but these letters are not reality. Reality is the blank pages. Just like your body. Become aware of the language that covers you and prevents you from being who you truly are."

Doña Magdalena explained that events relative to the paternal branch of the genealogy tree sometimes manifest in the right side of the body in the form of pain, illness, and accidents, while the left side is where relatives from the maternal branches appear. The head is the symbol of the father, the stomach the symbol of the mother. On the right side are the brothers and uncles; the sisters and aunts are on the left. The joints may be considered as points between two ages. The problems of childhood, including lack of love, nursing, abuse, loss of space/territory, divorce, absences, and mourning, appear at the level of the feet. Anxiety about change and the refusal to grow up remain in the ankles. Childhood up to puberty resides from the ankles to the knees. The knees manifest problems inherent in the development of sexuality, and from there to the groin reside the conflicts from adolescence into adulthood. At the level of the stomach, united with the lumbar vertebrae, anger toward others and oneself accumulates out of failure to express it. In the chest region, together with the dorsal vertebrae (also the lungs and heart), a lack of love and the feeling of not having the right to exist manifest accordingly.

"A back that was not caressed by the parents wastes away, hard and dry. Shoulders raise uncontrollably to reveal a devaluation and a tendency toward failure. The neck bends under the weight of guilt and excessive responsibility. Eruptions on the skin denounce conflicts with adverse people. Difficulty breathing, the rejection of a crushing father. Difficulty swallowing, the rejection of an invasive mother. When the voice resonates in the nose, the father is absent. Chronic hoarseness signals an absent mother. Problems with the left breast, a negation of motherhood. Tumors in the testicles, punishment for forbidden desires. Pain in the big toe, the desire to flee a scary relationship. Pain in the thumbs, one thinks one does not deserve to live. Problems in the knees and elbows, difficulty with social integration. Eczema on the hands, to have chosen badly. Stomach pain, conflict in daily life and 'undigested' emotions. The humiliation that we cannot integrate affects the liver. The inability to let go of situations that weigh on us causes constipation.

But do not make a methodology of what I teach you, dear child of the soul. Never fabricate wholesale recipes. Pay attention. What I am telling you does not apply to everyone. We are all similar but never absolutely identical to others. Illnesses and pain from which we suffer carry a personal seal. 'The' flu does not exist, there is only 'my' flu, 'your' flu, or 'his' flu, each with distinct expressions and consequences. The same goes for the symbolic language. What I have revealed to you will not have the same meaning to the person who is suffering if he is left-handed, if his parents have a confused sexual identity (masculine mother, feminine father), or if he was raised in childhood by his grandparents or by guardians.

It is useless for me to tell you that a tumor is the realization of something unspoken if you will not then look into the lives of your parents and other members of your family, living and dead, for the secret that fights to emerge into full light. The body, in addition to its organic functions, is a cellular memory: in the flesh and in the bones we carry the memory of our tribe. The positive memories are venerated in the form of family legends and carry vital energy, but the negative memories that were repressed for generations in order to avoid facing moral and emotional suffering manifest in the form of illness and pain. These afflictions, like a pebble in the shoe, prevent you from progressing toward your fulfillment with joy and push you to constantly refuse to meet yourself."

Doña Magdalena, waving her arms like the wings of a bird and breathing to mimic a strong wind, began to "sweep" my skin. "The wind, which no one knows from where it comes or to where it goes, helps me to clean away this persistent memory that sticks to you like body armor. Be brave, my child, accept the change. How do your feet feel now? Concentrate all of your attention on them."

I felt like my heels were fragile, incapable of supporting me firmly on the ground. The foot's arch and the instep mingled in an archaic mass, locked in time that did not pass. And my toes, rigidly curled up as if to prevent progress like a steel wall, were impregnated with fear of the world.

"Do not twist the present into the layers of the past. You are no longer a child, let alone a fetus. You are released from the terror that you carried, glued to your flesh from the moment your mother wanted to abort you: you have the right to live, therefore advance! It is you yourself, just as you are in reality, who awaits you at the end of the path."

Released in this way, I immediately felt the power of my heels: two strong and sacred bone centers that offered a reliable fulcrum to show me that I was master of the earth. Supported in this way by the ground, the arch of my foot felt heat from the earth as my instep transmitted energy from the sky to me. My toes began to stretch out, accepting without anxiety and with delight that the path is infinite. With each step, my feet opened the route toward the immortality of the spirit. The wall that separated me from the world began to dissolve and reveal itself just as it was: an old illusion.

"Concentrate on your legs!"

I have never known the animal energy of these extremities as I did in that instant. I understood the origin of the myth of the centaur, symbol of the dual nature of man, the one bestial and subject to savage instincts, the other divine, a rider taming these elementary forces. My head, neck, arms, and the trunk of my body, each in its own way, gave orders to my legs: "Bring me over there where I can quench my thirst and appease my hunger, satisfy my sex, breathe pure air at a suitable temperature, far from any enemy." At the same time, my soul told them, "At the end of the day, take me to the temple where you will become roots, so being vanquished from desires you will find the rest of absolute emptiness." My trunk breathed, digested, produced sperm, torrential blood circulation, colossal beats, nerve stimuli, glandular input, holding up the chest from which my brain endlessly dreamed.

"This is the first time you're feeling, is it not? I cleaned your body of these parasites. You have ceased as the territory manifested by your parents. From now on your body is the expression of no one else but you. Concentrate on it. You will discover the miracle of life."

How to describe in words what I then felt? There was a monumental thirst of paths, the hope to move forward until the end of time in my vibrating feet. My legs were two powerful animals full of fidelity and obedience; my sex a sacred chalice that transported the elixir of immortality; my viscera functioning to transmit infinite love; my brain, keen receiver, giving itself to knowing the whole cosmos; and in my skeleton's bones incessant waves of bliss circulated. Invaded by these sublime feelings, I opened my arms and stretched out in a burst of laughter, as if I had been liberated from an enormous weight. Then I cried.

"You are not familiar with happiness. This child who cries, this is no longer you. Let him go."

The blind knots had come undone. There was almost nothing left of the pain bequeathed to me by my genealogy tree: finally, I let my dead die. What was left? A limitless gratitude remained. They gave me life and now, finally, I could live.

EIGHTEEN

From Familial Body to Essential Body

Initiatic Massage, Psychoritual, and Psychoshamanism

The work on and through the body is an indispensible element in healing the genealogy tree. For each one of us individual history, familial transmissions, prohibitions and ghosts from the lineage all live in an incarnated way and ultimately fit into our daily physical existence. All of these representations of our individual and genealogical pasts constitute what we call the **familial body** because of the way in which they incorporate our acquired and limited individual personalities: muscle tension, eating habits, addictions, organic "weaknesses" with predisposition to sorrow or illness, self-image, and the level of confidence in our physical strength or energy.

Our body, the short-lived part of us that eventually disappears, is granted to us for the duration of this life, yet it is also the agent of immemorial wisdom of the universe and holds the still unfathomable mysteries. Contemporary science explores these unsolvable questions: Why do we age? Why do we die? How do we get sick? Old age, illness, and death were the three great shocks that confronted Gautama, the future Buddha, after his escape from the secluded garden where his father had held him in an attempt to prevent him from knowing human suffering. Gautama founded Buddhism by going beyond these three great tragedies, but it behooves us to think that even these concepts are temporary and that, in the more or less distant future, humanity will be capable of conquering old age, illness, and maybe death.

From the metagenealogical perspective, the goal in bodywork is to wake up the feeling of absolute health, eternal youth, and immortality, which are attributes of the spirit but not yet of the body as experienced in our daily lives and our familial and social pasts. The body can, in fact, learn these inherent qualities of the spirit while the spirit, simultaneously, learns to disappear (die); learns to recognize its ego and its individuality as an illness (limited, neurotic upbringing); and attempts being in perpetual change (aging, which is to say, evolving).

Work on the body takes us to the point where **individual healing** and the **therapeutic relationship** meet. At a given moment individual work will always encounter a blind spot, a deadlock where the other becomes necessary. Inversely a healed person, one who has become an authentic individual, is often tempted to share what he has discovered and becomes a kind of guide, therapist, or teacher devoted to helping others.

As such, it is ideal that every person who takes responsibility for another's psyche—whether a parent, guide, teacher, therapist, or spiritual official—should be freed of his own abuse and not be capable of committing any. Whether intellectual, emotional, sexual and creative, or material, all dissatisfaction can move toward abuse because one tends then to use another as a means of living one's own life.

The dynamics of abuse creates a circumstance where getting out of the trap requires that the abused person receive help or intervention from another whose transpersonal qualities of being able to listen and hear, to give attention and unconditional love, are sufficiently solid for a therapeutic relationship to result that will allow the individual to go beyond the abuse and integrate positive information. This is why great therapists say, "Never **heal** others, but allow them to **heal**

themselves." The best therapist is one who is only a mirror or a catalyst for another's self-healing capacities because they bring the person back to the origin of his true self. The majority of therapeutic and spiritual paths, each with their own vocabulary and their own techniques, are based on this **return to self,** which is the basis of any fulfillment, of any healing.

But how can one be sure that this therapist, this guide, the person to whom we confide, is himself freed from any abusive compulsions? The field of ethics and code of conduct is based on this question. Nothing is easier for a therapist, teacher, or guide than to repeat the abuse that he or she was subjected to and which, as you have seen, tends to repeat.

The same question is posed when one wants to begin to heal the genealogy tree and to some extent become one's own therapist: how does one accept the healing and live in the present in a body freed from the abuse of the genealogy tree?

The first key is the radical freedom of the spirit, an **amorality** that is not immoral but is based on the **radical acceptance of what is,** without discrimination. This attitude is as valuable in a relationship with oneself as with another and has to do with accepting the knots present in this person (myself or my consultant) just as they are. This means not judging them as "perversions" but understanding them as **deviations from a natural drive** due to adapting oneself to the family environment where, in order to survive, there was no other choice. We have seen that once a knot has formed there is no way to sublimate it, and one must carry it out in a theatrical or figurative way as if staging a dream in reality. The knot will undo itself through the creation of a ritual act, sanctified by having been given a symbolic value and then engraved in time and space, which will ultimately allow for the being's deep transformation.

This ritual can take the form of psychomagic acts, but just as with the rest of our history any abuse we were subjected to remains inscribed in the body's memory and contributes to solidifying the limited conception of the self. The familial body is the body of the past, subjected to repetitive forces of the clan, which lives only fleetingly in the present. Bodywork and initiatic or spiritual massage in particular, for which we will now outline the main points, form a method of freeing oneself from limitations in order to fully live one's present incarnation, which will then become the vehicle of the essential Being. The person who lives in the **essential body** is, at the same time, less vulnerable to abuse and less susceptible to abusing others.

Methods like yoga, internal martial arts, and various tantric disciplines share a goal of freeing the body from its limitations and neurotic heritage, as well as fulfilling a union of the body with the universe. All these disciplines consider the body to be the key on the path to Consciousness.

Only the individual ego can commit or suffer from abuse: the transpersonal being is incapable of abusing anyone and cannot be affected by abuse. All abuse implies the seizure of power of one person over the other, and works in the personal dimension of the relationship. Once we are in transpersonal Consciousness, it is possible to stop any hint of abuse in oneself or in the other.

At every moment life continues to offer us its seemingly accidental dynamic, placing not only allies and enrichment factors along our path but also accidents, catastrophes, and obstacles. Like the family, society creates abusive relationships that are meant not to provide for a being but to uncoil power games, blackmail, oppression, or various forms of violence. Once work on the tree is complete the path continues; we can choose to repeat the genealogy tree's traps and impure solutions or we can establish a relationship with ourselves and others, counterbalancing the abuse and violence with essential contributions.

Once again, this enlightened relationship to oneself and to the other cannot be theoretical or abstract. It is passed through the body by means of touch and concrete acceptance of our presence here and now.

We have chosen to elaborate on initiatic massage not with the goal of providing academic explanations for body therapy professionals, but to propose a tangible path that will allow each person to develop enriching relationships in order to interact with others as a positive support, like the old sage or the good witch in fairy tales. **Each person can, at every instant, decide to be a source of Consciousness.**

IDENTIFYING THE FAMILIAL BODY AND REINTEGRATING THE ESSENTIAL BODY

Just as societies create negative physical experiences by overmedicalized birth and institutionalized illnesses linked to harsh working conditions or widespread pollution, the genealogy tree passes on real and symbolic family illnesses. Generations of smokers can cause poor respiratory systems, some dietary habits cause ulcers and liver or pancreatic dysfunction, one can "have nerves" like a grandmother's, or a heart like the rest of the genealogy tree's paternal branch. These transmissions are both from abuse (a child does not choose the air he breathes or the food he eats) and from the clan's trademarks. Illnesses unite us to our ancestors as surely as do career choice and following certain religious traditions.

Additionally, we received body concepts in childhood: "beautiful," "ugly," "strong," "weak," "slow," "quick," "fat," "skinny." Our physical identity was the object of commentary and criticism that we tended to absorb as if they were an integral part of our identity. As such, the body reacts according to the concepts and perceptions of others to a large degree, and the assumption can even be made that the organs function according to the Consciousness of others as well.

All aspects of the genealogy tree and society have a decisive influence on our health and our being in the world. The techniques of focus, imagination, and mindfulness, which assist us in overcoming the effects of these factors, will now be discussed in more depth.

The Voluntary Sense of Self

We can defuse the ideas we received about our body, abilities, and appearance by focusing our efforts on voluntary feelings and disconnecting from the opinions of others, arriving at a personal view of ourself by being able to capture the Unconsious and Supraconscious through the body. This personal view is not the same as the reflection we get from a mirror; it has to do with ridding ourselves of the *feeling* of these past messages, then spiritualizing the messages. This allows us to transform our experience of our body and our sense of self through intentionally induced experiences, thus discovering our unsuspected potentials. We tend to judge ourselves through the arbitrary qualities that must be attained in order to compete with the ideals of society or the genealogy tree, but it is possible to get out of this trap and **become free of our habitual feelings**. A whole universe of feelings exist that most people do not cultivate. Instead of defining them from the exterior, we can feel them: strong or tender, young or old, nimble or awkward, light or heavy, pretty or ugly, quick or slow, and so forth.

Moreover, we tend to translate the opinions others have of us—not only the way in which they see us but also the way in which they want us to be—into our own feelings. In other words, we integrate everything our family circle projected onto us when we were children as physical feelings and a sense of self.

The following exercise is done in two stages:

- Identify the acquired feelings, close your eyes, and decide, "I am (mother, father, or other character in the genealogy tree). I feel you in this way." Now feel how the judgment of this family member has influenced your physical sensations.
- Next, define a feeling that you seek, then close your eyes and say, "I am strong. My whole body is saturated with this force. I am capable of carrying any weight, of pushing no matter what object, of succeeding no matter what happens." Walk around the room with your eyes opened or half closed while concentrating on this feeling, experiencing your body as you have chosen to feel. If you are pursued by negative feelings like heaviness, ugliness, or weakness, begin by exaggerating this feeling, and then, when you arrive at the extreme of the negative feeling, begin to feel the opposite: lightness, beauty, strength.

The Feeling of the "Perfect Body"

At this stage you can deepen the exercise proposed in part 5. When you concentrate on the feeling of the perfect body, what do you visualize? Are certain parts of your body involved? Do you have more ease than before in feeling the perfect body? What limitations do you still feel with regard to accepting yourself in your perfection?

This exercise can continually progress, and it is possible that your perfect body will change every time you come back to concentrate on the feeling, as the Unconscious will use different images and different feelings to call upon the memory of this potential. If you are sick, imagine in the exercise that the affected organ functions in an optimal way: a perfectly healthy liver, lungs full of energy, flexible joints capable of dancing.

Who Lives in My Body?

Our focus now turns to more detailed work on the familial body we have received.

Stretch out on your back. If necessary you can have a copy of your genealogy tree with all the first and last names of your ancestors at your side to help you feel like you are symbolically accompanied by the work you have accomplished up to now. Mentally browse the regions of the body: your arms and legs, musculature, organs, the bones of your skeleton. At each stage, take a moment to ask yourself, "Who still lives here?" and let the response come. It is possible that several ancestors or fragmentary images of your genealogy tree reside in several places in your body.

From this point on, when you enter into contact with a character, phrase, feeling, or episode as you sacn your body, stay anchored in the feeling of the body and ask, "What are you saying to me? What are you showing me?" It is probable that this region of the body, or the character living there, will suggest an image, a phrase, or a word to you. You can let this image or phrase float before you for a moment, transform it or nurture it, then dissolve it.

If you feel that a particular region of the body demands more of your attention, and that a memory manifesting there cannot be resolved for the moment, say, "Thank you for showing yourself to me. I will be back." You can then begin the exercise again the next day or even days later.

TOUCH

A Taboo in Western Culture

Individual work on the body has its limits. In fact, from birth we learn to feel ourselves not only alone but in the way in which we are touched, caressed, or punished: the baby depends on those who are raising him for his survival, forming a part of his physical feeling from touch given and received. The first thing a child touches during breastfeeding is the maternal breast or, at least, the skin of the caretaker. One can imagine that our greatest desire is that the world would consist of this maternal skin.

As such, the region of the body that evokes this interdependence of human beings is a little zone in the back situated between the shoulder blades that one cannot caress (unless exceptionally flexible) by oneself. In Nordic mythology it is the only vulnerable point on the body of the hero Sigurd, killer of the dragon Fafnir, whose blood had the power to make one omnipotent and invulnerable. Sigurd bathed in the blood, but a leaf from a lime tree fell between his shoulder blades, leaving this zone vulnerable to the spear that killed him. "Sigurd's leaf" is both the region where the maternal hand supports the baby from the first instant of life and, for the adult, a point of blindness: for each of us that part of our body is invisible, and rare is the person who has a clear concept of his own back. The region of the upper thoracic vertebrae is, to most people, the least mobile even though it is crucial for the quality of one's posture. It is by far the most unconscious place on our body, but also the one where emotional reception of a comforting gesture directly affects us.

Every relationship involving touch brings us back to this external action, to the part of us that depends on others to know ourselves. We think it indispensable to refine our relationships with others as an element of healing the tree, to help as well as to be helped. Learning to connect with another person without it resulting in a relationship with the waste and abuse of our genealogy tree is an integral part of our evolution.

Improving the quality of touch in our lives is not only a matter of delicacy and precision. As we have seen, all abuse comes from being unfulfilled in one of the four centers. Our experience of touch—with ourselves and with others—grounds our identity not just in the physical body (the material center) but in our sexuality and creativity, our feelings, and our ideas. When we make contact, when we touch, we summon all that we are, consciously and unconsciously.

Touch is equally affected by the a priori culture and society. In the West this sense has been demonized as "sexual" and globally repressed. A hierarchy of senses was created: sight and hearing, considered indispensible, have the freedom of the city; taste and smell are accepted under certain circumstances; but touch triggers a suspicion of sexual intrusion, aggression, even a fear of being dirtied or contaminated.

Physical contact frequently has sexual connotations or is perceived as an interference or aggression. But tender and attentive tactile contact does exist, above all in couple relationships, in the interior of a family circle, even between friends. However, outside of the intimate sphere the only place where touch is usually culturally accepted is when it is used for the purpose of medicine, treating the body as a "soulless machine" that is cold and intellectual, intended only to diagnose disease. A majority of psychologists and psychiatrists avoid touching their patients, carrying out their treatment exclusively with words. In certain niches one finds different categories of massage intended to be either "medical" or for "relaxation."

But touch is very rarely used for the purpose of **soul-to-soul or spirit-to-spirit transmission.** Nevertheless, a person's level of Consciousness can easily be detected by his own way of touching objects and people. The Evangelists have presented us with "laying on of the hands" as the favored method of transmission of the Spirit: touch can communicate a truth that speech is incapable of conveying, putting the person being touched in direct contact with the level of Consciousness of the person who touches. In shamanism and other spiritual transmissions a priest or a shaman in trance can even guess the channel by which to practice contact with the divinity. Similarly, when a serene and loving mother touches a child she transmits to him a love that goes beyond her to maternal love to its universal form.

There is a huge gap between the touch for which we thirst and that which we practice in daily life. For example, we can easily approach a stranger to talk to him, but it is much more difficult in our culture to immediately touch him.

The following exercises will assist you in developing the quality of your essential touch and should preferably be carried out with someone you would like to share the experience with. The goal will be to **develop the Consciousness of touch,** listening, subtlety, and the ability to feel and incur touch.

- **Touch strangers.** You may also undertake this with people with whom tactile contact is socially "inappropriate," like colleagues. The other person must not perceive this contact as an invasion, accident, aggression, seduction attempt, or assumption of power. Your touch must be as natural as a kind word.
- **Listen to the sound of the heart.** This exercise consists of making your own heart listen to the heart of another, with your ear pressed directly to his or her chest (the first rhythm we hear is that of our mother's heart). When you offer your heart to the other in turn, how do you touch? What is a good-quality embrace for you: close or long, tight or loose, urgent or light? While you listen to the heart of the other, how would you like to be held or touched?
- **Utilize an "assortment of touches."** Practice touch from skin to skin, from muscle structure to muscle structure, from skeleton to skeleton, even from Consciousness to Consciousness. From where do you touch? What do you touch in the other? This exercise

requires a calm, nonviolent communication and the capacity to objectively express one's eventual remarks or suggestions with the goal of helping each other refine the quality of your touch.

- **Touch from each of the four centers.** Observe your movements and the quality of your touch with a partner while you successively anchor your hands in the intellect, heart, and sexual centers. Then anchor your feet as if they contained roots so your touch can be the product of the whole body.

THE INITIATIC MASSAGE

We have already mentioned the fact that familial and social education limits a child's physical movements by, among other things, establishing movement stereotypes that are considered to be "masculine" or "feminine," or by imposing very early immobility by means of the seated position and various physical constraints of the education system. The child who was subjected to this "training" will lose the capacity to use his body to its full potential in adulthood, forced to live locked in a kind of somatic corset composed of some twenty habitual movements repeated throughout life.

We can add to that the tendency to imitate the physical movements of other family members. It can then be difficult to determine what is genetic and what is mimicked, though the mimicry is usually observable in most cases.

Certainly some experiences, particularly in youth, can assist us in regaining freedom of movement, but this is often due to learning something for a specific purpose. Dance can wake up sensual pleasure, sport is generally oriented toward excellence, and in most such cases physical technique—a repertoire of normative movements that are considered "correct" or "beautiful"—is emphasized. Occasionally in adolescence a young boy or a young girl will imitate the movements or manner of speaking of a friend with a strong personality in order to emerge from the familial body, but this only represents absorption into another genealogy tree.

We must go further in search of a link between movement and spirit in order to encounter disciplines that aspire to wake up the larger cognitive zones. These may include different kinds of yoga, internal martial arts like qigong or t'ai chi, the Alexander technique, the Feldenkrais method, sacred dances of the Gurdjieff movements, Carlos Castaneda's Tensegrity, the spiritual massages of Doña Magdalena, the secret *mudras* of the Chinese Taoists, or even the ritual gestures of the magicians Eliphas Levi and Aleister Crowley.

Initiatic massage is a discipline that uses body contact to assist the consultant in discovering aspects of his spirit that he was not previously aware of. The **conscious touch** of the initiatic masseuse (we will describe the components below) must allow the stubborn illusion of "the world is how I feel it" to dissolve because our feeling of ourselves determines our conception of everything around us. Contact with the hands of the initiatic masseuse reveals to us that others do not perceive our bodies as we imagine them to be. In other words, conscious touch allows the consultant to become unidentified with his habitual feelings and thus **emerge from his acquired personality.**

As long as we live in the familial and/or social body, our touch will transmit not only the values but also the violence and various refuse of the milieu of our origins. Whether we are conscious of this or not, we will be the channels of our genealogy trees and culture. Just as there are levels of Consciousness, there are degrees of Consciousness in touch. We call the body at the highest level of Consciousness **the fulfilled essential body,** which is capable of transmitting this level of Consciousness by touch.

In effect, **two beings touching form one unit.** We can see this by observing animals' behavior. We can use the example of a woman who feeds birds in the park: the sparrows trust her and eat from her hands. If this woman holds the hand of a child or another adult in her own, the birds will also eat from their palm without feeling the least bit threatened. Once the woman releases the hand of this stranger, the birds feel differently about that person and continue to accept him or her. Similarly, when someone enters into a home guarded by a dog, the reaction of this Cerberus completely changes if the man or woman of the house welcomes the guest by taking him by the hand.

The goal of this chapter is not to be a manual for massage; a physical method can only be learned by practice. However, we had to detail some indispensable stages in order to prepare the groundwork for conscious touch and elements of initiatic massage, both of which can complement the genealogy tree work.

Preparing for the Initiatic Massage

As with all kinds of massage or physical contact, the masseuse must be scrupulously clean to ensure that no body odor will bother the consultant, having fresh breath, clean hair, well-trimmed nails, and skin and hands free from roughness and calluses. The place where the massage takes place must be calm, clean, neutral, and of a comfortable temperature in a space that offers a feeling of security, where no interruptions or loud noises are experienced during the sessions.

Moreover, in order not to fall into any sexual ambiguity, which would be catastrophic given the cultural prohibitions related to touch, it is essential to begin in an androgynous, meta-sexual way, excluding all ambition for power, individual desire, frustration, or insinuation. **The only role of the initiatic masseuse is to touch the consultant in order to reveal the body to that person.**

The masseuse will perform the exercise of the perfect body suggested in part 5. One can further prepare through use of the following exercises.

What to Do with the Hands

It is important to understand the symbolism of shapes made by the fingers, much like in the practice of mudras, symbolic gestures that often accompany meditation. But the great difference is that in the mudra one seeks contact with the essential Being while isolated from another, whereas in the massage these same hands are used to communicate a level of Consciousness.

On the symbolic plane, the left hand represents the receptive feminine and the right hand the active masculine. The thumb, connected with the other fingers and therefore capable of communicating with all of them, symbolizes Consciousness. The index finger, which indicates, designates, and understands, symbolizes the intellect. The middle finger, the center, symbolizes the heart. The fourth finger, the one that wears the wedding ring, symbolizes the sexual-creative center. The pinkie finger on the exterior, which joins the edge of the hand, symbolizes the body and all of material life. The palm, the part with which we can give and receive, communicates with the viscera and the interior of the body. The initiatic masseuse must work with the palm's flexibility and sensitivity, but also with the back of the hand, which is sensitive enough to use to massage oneself as well as others. The back of the hand symbolically represents the back, where the spine, the least conscious part of the body, is in effect an integral part of the hand, in the same way that the palm and fingers ultimately join with the totality thereof. Just as the skeleton is at the same time solid and articulated, being movable like a serpent at the level of the spinal column, the back of the hand must become a fluid structure capable of communication.

One obtains different effects according to the way in which the hand is used.

- When massaging with the fingertips one enters into the other's body, stimulates it, and wakes it up.
- The hand held flat constitutes support, care, and recognition of the other.
- The hand that slides over the body of the consultant recalls initial caresses, paternal or maternal.

One can also massage with the fist. The fist represents an egg if the thumb is on the inside, vulnerable, living in the fist like an embryo. It represents a stone if the thumb closes the fist to the outside, like in martial arts, thus making it invulnerable.

- A massage with the "fist egg" can be a massage of purification, the same way the Mexican shamans use an egg or lemon to create a *limpia,* an energetic or emotional cleansing of the body of another. In the same way the *curandero* (healer) breaks the egg or throws it once the cleansing has been completed, one must shake the opened hand and wash it to symbolize that the work with the egg is finished.
- When the fist is closed and hard like a rock, it allows communication with the consultant's bones: the solid part of the body, equal to the mineral element in nature. The closed fist communicates strength and represents an enemy for Unconsciousness, so massaging in a benevolent way with a closed fist offers an immense solace because as the potential enemy becomes an ally there is no longer any sense of danger. This can serve to erase the memory of punches received in the past.
- The nails are survival claws in the savage world of nature. The masseuse cannot have long nails; he must have filed down his aggression and tamed the beast. But he can use the nails while massaging in order to take the consultant back to his own savage nature. The nail scratch can create centers of concentration and attention. Wherever one concentrates attention, Consciousness can appear. For that, the five fingers come together at a point like a bird's beak, and the five nails press on an area of the body all at the same time. It is important that the nails be united and not separated; otherwise we have the symbol of a scratching claw once again.

Here are two exercises to refine touch:

- **Connect the hand to the whole body.** Extend the fingers one by one to your hara, the center of gravity located about two fingers below the navel, alone or with a partner. This extension of the fingers can be accomplished by touch on the skin, or by envisioning the touch then passing through the skin and into the interior of the stomach.

- **Feel the hands.** The goal of this meditation is to prepare the hands for the massage. Feel your hands with your eyes opened or closed, according to your preference. Look at or feel them just as they are. Then imagine them small, like the hands of a child, and feel them that way. Then feel them as the small hands of a fetus, and further still to the hands of a primate. See your hands in the past as far back as you can. What animal with claws do you see? Even go as far as seeing yourself as a piece of mineral matter. Then return gradually to the fetal hands, the child's hands, the adult's hands, ultimately making your hands old, beyond the duration of human life, as they dissolve into two emanations of benevolent energy. Close them into a fist and see all that the hands now contain.

Now, if your eyes are closed, open them, and see everything that you are capable of giving: a whole universe, the joy of childhood, sublime feelings, the history of the planet, cosmic energy . . .

The Masseuse and the Space

Once the sensitivity of the hands is developed, it helps to work on our relationship with space. In fact, all massage is done in three dimensions: in an environment, in space, and with movement. The person being massaged is not inert but is a sum of actions created by means of shared power. Likewise, the masseuse is not an inert body from which two arms emerge. The massage is an offer to dance, a union in movement between the consultant and the masseuse.

- **Bring the hands together with eyes closed.** This has to do with verifying that the tactile sense and the visual sense are in agreement with one another. During the massage, one endlessly passes from contact information to visual information. Once the two hands are joined, they mutually massage and caress, masculine and feminine, reception and action in agreement by the touch that joins the masseuse to himself.

- **Move beyond fear of the dark.** We have two main reasons for desiring birth when we are in the maternal abdomen: to see the light and to breathe. When gestation and delivery were not experienced in an optimal way, we can have a residual fear of the dark. This can influence the proper function of a massage.

  In order to move beyond this fear, and reconcile herself with sensing and trusting space even when it is dark, the aspiring masseuse can voluntarily place herself in a place without light and perform a self-massage designed to help her become aware of the fact that she is a benevolent and allied being. The naked body rubs against the darkness, feeling its caresses. As in a dance the arms penetrate the darkness, the whole body undulates, and this night massage allows her to move beyond fetal anxieties.

- **Shapes in the air.** Initiatic massage not only consists of discovering that which already exists through touch, but it proposes to create shapes as well. Take the time to make invisible sculptures that you define by massaging the air with your hands. Conscious of each shape that only you are aware of, touch them with tenderness and love, and through them convey their life, a pulse. Once a shape has been fully massaged, leave it behind you like an invisible reality, one with which you have created a union.

Enrich the Hands and Charge Them with Energy

Your hands are called to become the tools destined to wake up the Consciousness of others, and it is useful to confer upon them a power that you do not yet have: without falling into superstition, you can increase the healing ability of your hands by imagining capabilities that exceed those that you have had up to this point.

- **Massage of sacred places.** Over time many statues, rocks, and shrines have received complaints, prayers, and requests from the public. Choose an object or a place where these requests have accumulated and set an intention to give it solace, presence, and

Consciousness by providing it with a massage rather than asking for anything. You can also massage a tree.

This exercise supports the idea that we are in the world to help the universe engender more Consciousness, not to consume endlessly like insatiable children. After this massage your hands are charged with the energy of the sacred place from which you have asked nothing, but to which you will be joined at the most elevated level because of having offered it your massage.

- **Positively charge the hands.** Take precious stones, minerals, vegetables, or other powerful objects and massage them while imagining that your hands are absorbing and accumulating their energy. If such objects are not available you can imagine yourself to be massaging them, or else put a photo of them in your hands: for the Unconsciousness, the image of the object is the object itself.

- **Play with temperatures.** This has to do with feeling that the hands emanate a thermal energy that can voluntarily move from extreme cold to extreme heat. Each degree of temperature represents an aspect of love: certain bodies require being reheated, and others need to be cooled. Heat can energize while cold can refresh or calm.

- **Play with the sensation of hand size.** Imagine your hands shrinking, and then imagine that they grow enough to be able to touch the moon, the stars, or the center of the sun. This will help you later to visualize and "touch" the organs while massaging the body's surface.

Massage Exercises

This repertoire of exercises can be practiced with a willing partner in order to refine your capacity for achieving connection. Once again, we have no pretention of drafting a manual for massage here or of training inexperienced therapists. This has more to do with consciously increasing an awareness of touch in the framework of a friendly relationship.

Care

The masseuse first places a hand on the partner's heart to feel the beating and the rhythm of respiration. Then gradually, with both hands flat on the partner's body, he recognizes it as a sound, from right to left, front to back.

The person can be seated while the masseuse is working on the trunk and the head. The masseuse takes the head in his hands and for a few seconds, using deliberate movement, simultaneously touches the forehead and the occiput, then the right ear and the left, then the front and back of the chest, the front and back of the belly, and finally the right and left sides of the rib cage.

For the limbs, the person reclines on a massage table while the partner supports the right arm and the left arm simultaneously, then does the same for the right leg and the left leg.

Connect the Body to the Environment

This massage consists of expanding the sense of the body. The consultant lies on a soft surface, perhaps a thick carpet, and his partner massages his whole body by extending his chest toward the exterior as if the arms, body, and legs must reach the ground.

Stretch the Skin

The skin is considered to be a frontier, the extreme limit of the body. One might say, "I feel good (or bad) in my skin," and timid people lock themselves "inside" their skin. Yet, all organisms isolated from their environment decay: one essential aspect of life is our capacity to unite with everything.

The massage consists of lifting the partner's skin, pulling it up with all your fingers together in a delicate yet firm way that respects the direction of the skin's fibers and the sensitivity of each area. It is particularly useful to stretch the skin around the orifices, and you can practice the massage on yourself through these particularly intimate zones: eyelids (with complete delicateness), the skin on the testicles (of remarkable elasticity), and the lips of the female sex.

Once you feel the skin's elasticity, you can practice long "windings" along the whole body by rolling the skin in a circular motion between the fingers. This begins, for example, at the nape of the neck and ends with one foot, then the other.

This massage allows your partner to feel united with the skin as a single body and to go beyond the body's fragmented feeling.

Muscle Massage

The muscles' function is to move the body, particularly the skeletal structure. In this massage we are going to consider the muscles to be receptors of old emotions that are held and expressed by repeated, unchanging contractions. Thus, for us, this massage has the purpose of opening the muscles. Our focus here is on the strong and bulky muscles in the biceps, quadriceps, gluteus, loins, and abdominals, as well as the smaller zones of muscle that govern facial expressions in the forehead, along the contours of the mouth, as well as the fingers, the palms of the hands, and the soles of the feet.

- Place the fingers of both hands in the center of the muscle. Spread one and then the other hand toward the right and the left to symbolically "open" the muscle fibers.
- Using a similar movement, gently stretch the muscles by pulling one hand upward and the other downward.
- Covering an entire zone using the whole palm or flat fingers, depending on the size of the area, use a gentle clockwise and counterclockwise muscle rotation around the bone to which it is attached.
- Complete the massage by putting pressure on the zones that were worked, one after the other, as if to concentrate and tighten the body's muscular sheath. Depending on the zone, you may go so far as to add the pressure of your body weight. This moment of the massage serves to restore the body's compact feeling and to join the muscle (dynamic and emotional) with the bone's concrete matter (essential).

- End this massage by defining the skin that covers the muscles. As one hand follows the other, use an uninterrupted motion to slide over the skin while the person being massaged rolls from back to side to abdomen, like one long endless caress. This phase of the massage can last for up to a half hour.

Massage the Bones

One usually avoids the skeleton during a massage either because it brings up a terrifying image (death) or because it is considered to be an impersonal part of the body. Nevertheless, the skeleton is unique and alive: the bone marrow produces cells for our blood. Moreover, the feeling of the skeleton is very important because, as a general rule, the artificial ego flees from structure and prefers to coat the body with a shell (muscular, emotional, even clothing), living as a mollusk. Reconnecting with the skeleton allows us to once again meet with the essential path.

In order to find and massage the skeleton one must use the fingertips to reach through skin and flesh, rubbing as if to liberate its energy. It is recommended that delicacy be used when entering into the depth of the joints to search for possible spirals and rotations. By use of loving attention such exploration can reveal details of bone shape in areas like the eye socket, pubic bone, the skeletal structure located behind the ears, even the skull. When doing this, the masseuse must be attentive, since all shapes that exist in nature are also found in the human skeleton.

Open the Seven Chakras

Many spiritual and medicinal traditions include an energetic description of the body. Without entering into a debate of whether the energy body actually exists, or what its precise structure is, we can consider these descriptions to be very useful symbolic biology.

For this massage we refer to the chakras located at the level of the seven nerve centers, and consider them to be notable links in the body where fluid or stagnant energies can converge. One can rely on this configuration to successively wake up seven areas of the body.

- **The root chakra (perineum).** The person stands with knees slightly bent. The masseuse's fist rests between his sex and his anus (the fist is positioned like a hand gripping a candle, thus it is essentially the root of the thumb and index finger that makes contact with the perineum). This pressure, which is both a support and a resistance, allows the person to feel his own power and to gather in this place of anchorage where, among others, the muscles and organs of sexuality, urination, and defecation are found.

- **The sexual or sacred chakra.** Found at the level of the pubis, for a man this is right above the penis, and for a woman at the level of the uterus. The person lies down. The masseuse's fingertips press down on the chakra and move as if opening toward the right and left, following the rhythm of respiration. The goal of this movement is to dissolve the sexual prejudices of the genealogy tree, the reduction of desire and the creative force.

- **The center of gravity.** Located one inch under the navel, this point corresponds to the site of *ki* or *chi* in martial arts. It is the center of all harmonious body movement in union with the planet. The person lies on his back and the masseuse makes spiral movements, both clockwise and counterclockwise, beginning at the center of gravity point. These spirals gradually extend throughout the whole body and then return to the center of gravity. The consultant is then massaged in the same way with lines radiating out from the center toward the arms and legs, the torso and head, and back again. This center should also be massaged on the back at the level of the fifth vertebra.

- **From the solar plexus to the heart.** This massage is performed with the consultant standing up, the masseuse behind the person and hugging him with palms flat on his chest roughly between the diaphragm and the heart. The massage is performed as a gentle "pull" from either side of the sternum to dissolve the emotional armor. It frequently happens that the person being massaged may cry or express strong emotions. The end of this massage must include an "integration of the heart" where the person, accompanied by the masseuse's hands, feels his whole body as a beating heart.

- **The throat (chakra of expression).** In this case we avoid applying strong pressure because the throat is a fragile and crucial zone, the channel of both respiration and nutrition. Any use of force can produce anxiety and a feeling of strangulation. In order to open the channel of communication and purification between heart and spirit, this massage must be done with great gentleness. Skin to skin, as if one is creating a jewel by massaging the cavity, use a counterclockwise movement in the space between the clavicles with the intention of dispelling all anxiety and establishing a feeling of goodwill. This positive sensation will then be stretched out, like a necklace or a collar, all the way around to the nape of the neck. Then the hands reverse, thumbs and fingers toward the bottom, edge of the hand against the ears, while the masseuse makes the energy go back up toward the nape, chin, and ears, to the top of the head.

- **The third eye and crown chakra.** The goal of this massage is to open the metaphorical window in the brain in order to let light enter, as much from the sky as from the center of the earth. The masseuse can suggest that the person concentrate on this image. With fingers gathered together like a beak as described earlier, one hand is positioned on the top of the cranium, the other between the two eyebrows, with the masseuse remaining in support of these two points until the massaged person can concentrate his attention there. Then, the masseuse opens his fingers slowly outward, like the petals of an opening flower. The same massage is then repeated with one hand on the top of head, and the other on the back of the head.

Massage the Face

The face is the most important site of the acquired identity. Like a person's name, it represents one of the strongest signs of individuality. The goal of this massage is to change the conception that the person has of his face. The masseuse must use his hands to explore all the details of the bone structure, muscles, and soft flesh in order to present to the massaged person a complete image of his face precisely as it is. Then, according to the desires the consultant expressed beforehand, when he described his "perfect face" as he visualizes it, the masseuse can massage this perfect face and "lengthen" the nose, "widen" the eyes, even "strengthen" the jaw—whatever it takes to make the appropriate adjustments. For the massaged person, the face then becomes a landscape of imagined feeling that corresponds to his essential self. Fulfilled Consciousness does not have a face, but it can wear a sacred, transpersonal mask that defines an archetype rather than an individual.

Massage the Genitals

A person in whom the consultant has absolute trust (not to be confused with the erotic complicity of lovers) must carry out this massage with the goal of restoring the sexual organs to their essential dignity. We have chosen to include this in order not to encourage any taboos that would exclude the genitals from the global sensing and feeling of the body. The following instructions concern the initiatic massage of the female and male organs.

- **Intravaginal massage.** The only fingers used are the index and middle fingers, the two fingers attributed to blessings in Christian imagery. This massage of the interior of the vagina is associated not with penetration, but rather with the goal of releasing all negative memories from the female sexual organ. Thus emphasis is not placed on pushing toward the interior. Instead, with the aid of a lubricant if necessary, the masseuse or partner introduces the fingers as tenderly as possible, first toward the interior, then with spiral movements metaphorically "peeling" the memorial traces that were attached to the mucous membrane. The massage continues with movements that go directly to the exterior from the interior, as if emptying the vagina of a burden that has accumulated there. If, as is frequently the case, the woman sees images of her own sex congested with objects or painful memories, she can visualize these objects coming out as the masseuse's fingers clear the concerned zone. This massage can be very useful for accomplishing a "cleansing" of trauma and guilt.

- **Penis massage.** Most men establish a differentiation between the body and the penis, resulting in the sexual functioning becoming limited to the zone of the penis alone. This goal of this massage is to root the sex in the rest of the body. Beginning in the area of the glans, one descends the length of the penis as if tracing a path that continues without interruption into all areas of the body: palms of the hands, soles of the feet, nape of the neck, the heart, and the top of the head.

Symbolic Massages

These do concern not the physical body directly, but rather the visual or imagined extensions.

- **Comb the aura.** This massage is designed to create calm and untwist tangled energies. With the fingers opened like a comb, stretch the person's aura downward as if combing long hair.
- **Wash the shadow.** This has to do with reconciling the person with his Unconsciousness and its "obscure" contents. The person stands in front of a light source with his shadow projected before him on the ground in a place where it is possible to use a brush, water, soap, essential oils, or other substances that are symbolically pertinent. The consultant then watches the masseuse "wash" the ground within the shape of his shadow.
- **Enrich the skin by rubbing it with symbolic elements.** We have already mentioned that as far as the Unconscious is concerned the skin will absorb experiences that are repeated over time. The healer Pachita rubbed the sick with an image of Christ or the Virgin Mary, but one can apply this principle by

massaging a person with a photo of his parents, with money or a gold ingot if she feels poor, with all symbols that the consultant feels necessary to be absorbed. Similarly, we have found that the psychomagic act of walking in shoes whose soles contain an effigy of the parents or a divine couple (the female element being placed under the sole of the left foot, the male element under the right) often has a surprising effect on the pain of the compromised body parts and on the feelings of not belonging, abandonment, exile, and so forth.

Scratching

The goal of this initiatic massage is to allow a person to undo everything "glued to his skin," especially his fears. The ancient warriors of the Caucasus scrubbed themselves with the dull side of a knife in order to overcome anxiety before going into combat. Essentially, this massage is designed to eliminate negative feelings inherited from the past that one cannot undo in any other way.

The masseuse must be equipped with something that imitates the shape of a knife, like a bone letter opener or other dull blade-shaped object made of natural materials. The massage begins at the top of the head, which one scratches gently using a spiral or with movement that goes in the four cardinal directions. Not an inch of skin must be forgotten because all negative memories can relocate there. The masseuse establishes a path over the body, being absolutely sure that all parts are included: eyelids, genital organs, soles of the feet, and backs of the ears. This massage lasts at least three hours, and may be accompanied by some unobtrusive music.

Venting Anger

Massage can sometimes help a person express and expel a recurring anger, but this will require that the masseuse has carried out the work on his own negative emotions because it takes a certain kind of physical and psychological strength, as the consultant could hurt the masseuse while unleashing the anger.

The masseuse supports his closed fist against the standing person's perineum, as previously described for the root chakra massage, sustaining the fist with the other hand to assure an extremely solid support. The consultant strongly supports himself against the fist and roars, with or without articulated sounds. The masseuse's physical strength is important because the pressure must be significant enough to allow the person to wholeheartedly express himself. The perineum is the only part of the body that one can constrict for someone in a standing position without that person feeling pressure; instead the person receives this pressure as a supply of energy. This massage excludes contact with any other part of the body because the consultant would feel crushed or forced, rather than supported, during the process of liberating expression.

Massage of Reparation with Four Hands

This massage can be done as part of the psychoritual of birth that we will describe next. It asks for the participation of two masseuses, a man and a woman, whose task is to represent the parental archetypes.

Many people have never known good relationships with their parents. When a parent had a difficult relationship with the child, or when one parent was the winner in a battle between the parents, the body lacks the essential information of feeling the significance of the union between father and mother.

The masseuses can each wear a photograph of the parents, one the mother and one the father, around the neck. Before touching the consultant, they make a series of gestures in the mirror in the air above him to place them in agreement and alignment: the greatest danger of this massage is that the consultant finds himself once again confronted with the couple's conflict. The two people then practice an intuitive and balanced massage. First the man massages the right side and the woman the left side; finally, both bring their hands toward the regions to which their intuition calls them, but always with great attention to remaining synchronized.

THE NATIVITY PSYCHORITUAL

The psychoritual is a ceremony composed of both **Psychomagic,** a precise scenario permitting the integration of missing information and the metaphorical fulfillment of repressed desires, and **initiatic massage.** All psychoritual must be performed by a collaboration of people of goodwill who must serve without reservation in an effort to offer assistance in the consultant's healing. The consultant will be the central subject of the ritual and the master of ceremonies at the same time. One could say that the **psychoritual's purpose is to heal and to modify the acquired personality,** but that it performs under the **authority of the essential Being.**

Sufficient planning of a psychoritual is necessary in order to ensure that the persons who collaborate are prepared, and because the consultant, who is also the director, must be able to interrupt the psychoritual at any point during the process to correct the actions of these collaborators.

Psychomagic acts of burial that were discussed in earlier chapters can be considered psychorituals.

We will now describe the psychoritual of nativity, or the second birth, the staging of which allows physical Unconsciousness to receive the vital information that is contained in a successful birth.

For this psychoritual, which lasts three hours, the consultant (who will play the role of the child) must choose two collaborators to be his metaphorical parents, and who are designated herein as the officiates: they can be therapists, or actors, or simply two people of goodwill. They must be capable of the following:

- To act in a convincing way, and without reactivity
- To comprehend the role they are playing, to be attentive to the importance of preventing the neuroses of their own history from interfering, and to have the accompaniment of the consultant in his healing be their absolute priority during this act

- To have a good concept of massage, with a sensitivity and a subtle, varied touch
- To be able to live the moment in a transpersonal way, at the service of universal Consciousness, regardless of personal beliefs or concepts of the divine

Naturally, in the absence of all practical training, these recommendations remain abstract. But ultimately it is the consultant who is the active authority in this therapeutic ceremony. At every moment of the psychoritual he must be able to express his needs and can, where appropriate, agree to a codeword with his symbolic parents that says: "We suspend the psychoritual and will listen to what we hear you saying."

These exercises are not meant to revive traumatic experiences; the goal is to imprint an **alternative memory of a fully accomplished experience.**

The "parents" should prepare by performing the perfect body exercise in part 5 in order to have a foundation they can refer to while playing their role as parental archetypes. In addition, this will help them to avoid the traps of their own genealogy tree, which could interfere in the psychoritual.

They must also present themselves in the most neutral manner possible. They must be dressed simply in white, black, or beige, avoid the wearing of useless ornaments or strong fragrances, have pleasant breath, and use restrained movements. Everything must be done so that from the beginning the consultant can project his real parents onto the couple, followed by his ideal parents. Similarly, the psychoritual must be fulfilled in a neutral, pleasant, temperate room.

This exercise unfolds in nine stages.* It is recommended that you omit nothing, but you can add elements that are necessary for your individual needs (details, particularly important actions, repairs of specific traumas).

---

*Alejandro Jodorowsky's *Manual of Psychomagic* contains a more detailed form of the words "parents" can use during the psychoritual, particularly during the nine months of gestation.

The consultant should arrive dressed in old clothing that represents the weight of the past, but he must also bring brand-new clothes, undergarments, and shoes. He should bring a cord or a ribbon that will symbolize the umbilical cord, and some kind of nondairy milk in a tube or in a carton with a straw with which to be breastfed. If necessary, he can also bring a foundation of golden body paint that may be used to counterbalance a devalued strength.

He also needs to provide a copy of a photo of his father and one of his mother that can hang on each officiate's neck, a black envelope, and seeds of two plants of his choice.

1. Confrontation

The consultant, dressed in old clothes, places himself in front of the two officiates, who can be seated or standing, the "mother" in front of him to his left and the "father" to the right.

He asks them, "For this ritual of birth, do you agree to represent my mother? My father?" (He states their first names.)

The officiates reply, "Yes, for this ritual of birth, I agree to represent your father/mother" (and also states their first names).

The consultant then places the photos of his mother and father around their necks. Following this he expresses his grief, rage, shame, pain, and need to be loved, during which he has the option of striking a cushion. These complaints are rarely ever clearly articulated because filial love is mixed with primitive terror: a child knows that his parents hold the power of life and death over him.

This confrontation will be similar to the one described in part 8. We recall the five stages:

- "This is what you did to me, and/or what you did not do, and therefore I need."
- "This is how I felt."
- "These are the consequences it has had on my life."
- "Here is how I still suffer from it today."
- "You owe me this as compensation."

The "parents" acquiesce to everything and can say reassuring phrases like "Yes, I understand. I was wrong."

2. Symbolic Death and Transmutation of the Parents

Once all the grief has been expressed, the consultant says to the officiates: "Now, to repair all of this, you are going to die and be reborn as the parents I truly need." If the aggression felt is very strong, the consultant can even metaphorically kill the "parents." Otherwise, words suffice as the "father" and "mother" lie down on the ground, close their eyes, and imitate death.

The consultant can express an emotion if he experiences something. He then removes the photos from the officiates' necks and puts them in the black envelope together with the two seeds, which will sprout later, after the envelope is buried in the earth. The consultant pronounces the formula for forgiveness: "What is done is done. I ask your forgiveness for not having been the child who met your expectations, and I forgive you for not having been the perfect parents I wanted." Then the consultant seals the envelope, and the toxic aspects of the parent-child relationship are now deactivated. It is time to make the parental archetypes emerge.

3. Birth of the Parental Archetypes

Piece by piece, the consultant removes his old clothes while pronouncing in a loud voice what he expects of his "parents," who are still lying on the ground: "I want a mother who . . ." "I want a father who . . ." All demands are possible here.

This moment is very important because it anchors the positive parental archetypes in reality: the perfect parents that the consultant awaits according to his level of Consciousness. He can now read aloud a list of qualities and demands he may have prepared beforehand.

Once the new identities of the "parents" are complete, the birth act can begin.

4. Conception

Both officiates stand opposite the consultant, who is now either nude or in undergarments, depending upon his culture and personal modesty. Similarly, the "parents" can be more or less dressed, but it is desired that the skin of the "mother" touch that of the consultant during the gestation portion of this psychoritual.

The officiates are face-to-face, and the consultant dictates the way in which he wants them to be united in the four centers (intellect, heart, material life, sexuality). He also chooses the position in which he wants to be born, which the "parents" must accomplish in a delicate and dignified way by expressing a feeling of ecstasy in their whole beings. Here again, it is the consultant who decides beforehand how the representation of the sexual act of his creation will be carried out, which may be accomplished with varying levels of symbolism and explicit gestures. While the officiates portray their climax, the consultant slides between them, feeling integrated with them and manifesting their joy and Consciousness before his life began.

5. Kneading and Nesting

The consultant lies down and the two "parents" massage him, giving him the feeling that his body is a shapeless mass: the "mother" massages the left side, the "father" the right. Metaphorically this massage represents fertilization of the egg by the sperm, and all cellular proliferation that occurs during this phase.

Little by little, the consultant gently gets into a fetal position with the ribbon or cord tied around his waist. The "mother," as nude as possible, sits on the floor with her back against a wall as comfortably as she can. The "father" deposits the consultant against her abdomen, and she knots the other side of the cord around her own waist. The "father" covers them with a sheet or other soft cloth, which symbolizes the walls of the uterus and the nest in the wider sense.

6. Gestation

The "parents" caress the body of the "baby" under the sheet and "live" the stages of his growth month after month by performing a previously written script about the relationship between the parents, the relationship between the mother and the baby, and the relationship between the father and the baby. If the consultant wishes he can be the one to write this script. The words must be spoken in a soft, slow voice, which reassures the consultant during his "gestation." This phase should last for a minimum of half an hour.

7. Childbirth

Ideally this will be carried out nonverbally, with an agreement between child and mother. An important part of this psychoritual, this is when the consultant is going to feel that the moment has come for him to be born, and the two officiates must be paying attention to what happens. Here again, the consultant can have planned certain details of the "birth" in advance and described them beforehand. The consultant comes into the world with feelings of great pleasure, supported by the hands of his "father," who then puts him in the hands of his "mother," who cuts the umbilical cord with the consent of the "father" after he hands her the scissors.

8. Breastfeeding and Care of the Baby

The "mother" breastfeeds the "baby" directly from her breast by making milk flow from it with a straw from a container to get the milk into the consultant's mouth. The use of cow's milk is not advised because it is generally prescribed as a substitution for maternal milk. Therefore, non-animal almond, soy, coconut, or rice milk is used. If the consultant wishes, his "father" can also give him the bottle.

Once the "baby" is satisfied, the "parents" ask: "What do you want to be called?" The consultant then chooses to keep his name or adopt a new one. Once the new name is given the officiates wash the "baby" in warm water that has been perfumed with rose or other fragrance.

During the cleaning, the consultant can ask for all that he thinks was lacking in his childhood: to spend time playing with his parents, to be dressed in a certain way, that they teach him to speak, that they toilet-train him in a particular way. . . . It is also at this stage that the "parents" paint the "baby" partially or entirely in gold. The parents say, "You are a treasure," and show him his splendor in a mirror. For the consultant, this has to do with finally having all that he felt had been missing.

9. Autonomy

The consultant, now dressed from head to toe in new clothes, can choose to leave alone or in the company of his "parents," who are then placed on either side of him, with "mother" on the left and "father" on the right. With all three holding hands, they can go have a pastry together. If the consultant is painted in gold, the officiates can declare to everyone on the street, "This is our child (saying his name), he is a treasure."

When the consultant feels ready, he takes leave of his "parents" without looking back, carrying his umbilical cord and black envelope with him. He then buries these items under a plant with the photo of the parents placed face down. The two seeds can eventually germinate if that is their destiny, but the consultant must immediately see life growing over the abolished past, which is why he must bury them under an already blooming flower or shrub.

If possible, the old clothes should be recovered from the officiates eight days later, so the consultant can clean them and donate them to charity. If they are charged with too much suffering, they should be burned. The act of cleaning and recycling the clothes suffices in general to purify them.

The success of this psychoritual depends both on the preparation by the consultant of the scenario that suits him and on the quality of the work of the "parents." While the goal of this act is to stage a birth as close as possible to the ideal, one can perform more than one psychoritual of birth, particularly if something went missing from the first one. However, for long-term effects of this act to become apparent, it is advised to wait at least six months before deciding whether or not another staging is needed.

It is quite possible that during the ceremony the intellect will protest, judge, comment, and refuse to believe in what is occurring. The role of the intellectual center is to function as the critic, but it will not necessarily interfere with what the body is in the process of absorbing. In other words, it is not necessary to believe in or to adhere to the act for it to be a success, but **it is absolutely essential that the scene of this experience be completely satisfying to the senses of the body, the comfort of the emotional center, and the tranquillity of the sexual and creative center.**

It also happens that well-intentioned parents can be deceived by the way in which the birth of their child took place: because the medical institution violated them by use of an abusive cesarean, robbing the birth from the child for the convenience of the obstetrician; because the child was breech or extracted with forceps; or because of an "accident" where the tree's trap was stronger than the parents' goodwill. It is therefore possible to offer one's baby, even very young, a psychoritual of birth that resembles the manner in which the parents wanted him to be brought into the world. Naturally, in this case it is mainly gestation and birth that one must stage, since the baby's security and comfort is the main purpose. Even if the child is very small, it is recommended that the parents speak out loud. The intentional communication is a large part of what his senses will receive, and the essence of it will reach him. And if he is older, from the moment he agrees to "stage his birth as he deserved to be born" this psychoritual, more like a game and a pleasant massage for a child, is extremely useful.

PSYCHOSHAMANISM

We have seen that psychomagic assists people who are conscious of their problem(s) and want to heal. But some consultants are not ready to experience an awareness of their illness because their defenses are too solid, and they are not in a state where they can become their own healer. They come to ask for direct intervention on their bodies or, more often, through their body on the deep mechanisms of the Unconsciousness.

Initiatic massage and psychoshamanism are linked, but there is a fundamental difference: the initiatic masseuse works with the body without the use of "surgery," the goal being to modify the body's organic function, while psychoshamanism, initially derived from the work of the Mexican healer Pachita, is inspired by practices of shamans from diverse cultures.

The place where Pachita gave her consultations mimicked an operating room and was illuminated by the dim light of a candle. The scalpels were replaced by hunting knives and a pair of nail scissors, the blood that she "transfused" into her patients was invisible, and she imitated a heart transplant with an invisible heart. Essentially, like many of her colleagues she used the terror produced by the idea of an operation, and the relief that followed a "successful surgical procedure," for therapeutic results. She was capable of threatening the person who was lying on the table, waiting for a few minutes while he felt that his abdomen had been opened or that his body was emptied of blood like an accident victim. The patient, seized with terror, felt his whole body freeze the moment this anxiety of death was most intense. Healing mimics a blood transfusion. The terrified body accepts the placebo because it is convinced the feigned feeling of being incised was real. When the act had to do with a sick organ, Pachita placed on the body of her patients viscera that, according to her, came from the local school of medicine but could just as easily have been purchased from the butcher. Even if the person was vaguely aware that a dead heart was pressing against his chest, the symbolic substitution of a sick organ with another that the "magic" operation sanctified allows for the cure. This illustrates, once again, the fact that the body can accept all objects that one provides to become part of it.

Contrary to initiatic massage, which heals the person by ridding him of the body's illusory limits and allows him to completely feel his expansion, psychoshamanism always imitates an operation with a direct action on the body but without the elements of conjuring (or magic, according to one's point of view). The healers perform the "operation" with their own hands. **The person is specifically warned that this is a false operation,** that the blood is water (colored or not), that the pyschoshaman is going to "open the body" by sliding a letter opener over the skin.

In initiatic massage the role of the masseuse limits the concrete transmission of a certain quality of Consciousness. The masseuse is the channel, but he **remains himself.** Inversely, in psychoshamanism, as in shamanism, the person who operates **is not himself:** he cedes his power to one or more allies who take possession of acts and intentions. That is why it is not the object (the dead heart placed on the living heart) that allows the healing but the intention that accompanies it and the fact that this process is accomplished **via the shaman by an entity** that is located beyond life and death.

As we have already seen with initiatic massage, the Consciousness of the body is independent of the intellect. During a shamanic operation none of the intellectual doubts will be accepted as an experience of the body. This is especially true for the consultant with a dominant personality whose intellect is very strong, which prevents certain awareness and transformation that are sometimes hard to overcome, and hardest to put distance between. This person may choose to remain a prisoner of the family trap instead.

The transpersonal being is healed and free to absolutely be itself. Even though the intellect may obstinately refuse to believe that the most effective path to healing passes through the body, which becomes **a privileged ally of the Unconsciousness,** at the preverbal level the person can experience a lasting change thanks to this act of healing.

Obviously, psychoshamansim is not a substitute for medicine. Rather, it allows a person whose intellectual resistance is very strong to be convinced of the possibility of healing. This may be appropriate where medicine is powerless, like a chronic illness with no known treatment, or to complement a medical procedure.

Psychoshamanistic acts have a strong dramatic character. This has to do with a kind of sacred theater designed not only to demonstrate the capacities and talents of the shaman, but to provoke an **unconscious leap capable of releasing the consultant's self-healing.**

In order to be able to practice this kind of therapeutic theater, there first needs to be a great authority present. The archetypical scene represents a level of authority that the Evangelists spoke of when Christ expelled demons from the body of the possessed. In the Unconscious one feels like one's illness is a separate being, and stronger than one. By definition one says "my cancer" or "my tuberculosis." In the Middle Ages it was said one could assimilate the image of the Devil, who was reputed to possess the body. Only a priest who conducted exorcisms would have sufficient authority to carry out this expulsion successfully, being both an authority of personal courage, strength, and determination as well as an authority emanating from God and allied entities like Jesus, Mary, saints, and angels.

One can hypothesize that all illness inflicted upon us by society and the genealogy tree comes by way of the commands and prohibitions imposed on us by our parents. The psycho-physical link that attaches us to the illness is therefore as powerful as the attachment to our parents. The sick person is attached to the illness, to the deep cause, although often unconscious of this. Even if he wishes for relief of these symptoms he has difficulty determining the causes, which is often very painful. He needs the power of an outside person, working in the name of superhuman entities, to undo the chains attached to evil. We have already seen that love links the child to the mother, then to the father, and is accompanied by its shadow: the terror from the child's obscure knowledge that his life depends on the goodwill of these parents.

Also, people capable of wisely using this terror for good orient themselves toward relief immediately recognized in the Unconsciousness as a power equal to that of the parents. In awakening the terror one can at the same time awaken a filial love. Pachita was conscious of this, so she called all in her patients "my child" no matter what their age.

In providing examples that illustrate the way in which a psychosha-manic operation unfolds, it is not our goal to give advice about whether one should become a psychoshaman. This therapeutic art is complex and demands a long training first; one can no more improvise psy-choshamanism than one can improvise a clinical surgery.

Psychoshamanism Cleanse

Inspired by limpias (cleanses) of the Mexican healers, the purpose here is to unburden the person of toxic or painful attachments and to even-tually prepare for deeper work. This energizing cleanse is accomplished in four phases:

- **Sacralization of space.** No matter what acts of inner transforma-tion are intended, it is appropriate to create a sacred place where the conflicts of exterior life do not enter. As the brain accepts and incorporates symbols, it suffices here to trace a circle counter-clockwise on the ground with the index finger, repeating this four times for the four energies. The consultant immediately visualizes the circle on the ground, and others are then invited to enter by lifting one foot over the circumference, which makes the sacred space something tangible.
- **Cutting the lines.** The officiate's hand is held open with stiff fin-gers. He announces, "This hand serves as a knife to detach from all that imprisons you." This is followed by a series of very precise "cuts" made in the air an inch above the skin accompanied by the sound "Ssssss!" which mimics the sound of a knife cutting or a serpent hissing. This has nothing to do with touching the consultant's skin because the act of freedom would then become an act of aggression. Do not forget to "cut" under the soles of the feet, asking the person to lift them one after the other.
- **Energizing.** The person inside the sacred circle who received the series of "cuts" is now free from exterior attachments. The next step is for the officiate to use the hand egg that we described ear-lier: hand closed in a fist with the thumb on the inside to sym-

bolize the spiritual force materialized in its highest degree of concentration. He proceeds to massage the whole body, rubbing the consultant with his closed fist as described earlier to charge him with concrete energy. This energizing massage is accompanied by a deep "O" sound, which originates in the hara.

- **Sweeping.** While murmuring the sound "Mmmmmmmmm," the officiate uses his hand, which is opened wide like a fan moving through the air, to casually "sweep" the whole body to ventilate, lighten, and put the energies back in motion. In this way the hand represents the maximum gift, maximum lightness, and maximum communication.

Psychoshamanic Operations

These interventions concern two kind of ill health: tumors and cysts.

Tumors

For a person suffering from a tumor in, for example, the liver, the surgical operation practiced in a hospital consists of opening the body to remove the tumor. A shamanic healer will mimic the act of opening the region of the liver, letting a stream of blood flow from the knife while brandishing a piece of chicken liver, claiming, "I have extracted the liver."

The psychoshaman will show the consultant a piece of liver or beef, even a crumpled ball of paper or a metal marble, and say: "This symbolizes the tumor." Then the psychoshaman will put it in a glass of water, saying, "This water symbolizes your blood." A plastic knife: "This will serve as a scalpel." Then he will place the object symbolizing the tumor on the consultant's belly and, with the plastic knife, pretends to incise the flesh at the level of the liver, mimicking a difficult or painful act. The assistant will then pour water on the "operated on" region, and the psychoshaman comments, "There is a lot of blood." Finally, while pretending to use an excessive amount of effort, he pulls the "tumor" out.

In these circumstances, one observes that the consultant screams as if he felt the pain of this operation, which he did indeed feel. Once the tumor is symbolically extracted, it serves to wrap it in black paper and bury it. To finish the operation, the psychoshaman passes his hand around the "operated" zone and says, "The wound is closed." The consultant feels immediate relief. It is then possible (but not certain) that the body Unconsciousness, touched deeply by these mechanisms, can create a process of self-healing.

Psychic Cysts

When a person is literally possessed by fear, grief, or attachment, when the psychic elements or emotions transform into "cysts" that affect daily life, it can be useful to resort to a psychoshamanic operation. We take for example a person who has a "closed heart." Reflecting the word image, the operation will consist of "opening the heart" by placing a stack of several porcelain saucers on the pectoral region and breaking them slowly, one after the other, with a hammer. This act was inspired by a Grimm's fairy tale where a prince carries three iron rings in his heart. One after the other breaks in the twists and turns of the tale, and at the end of the story he becomes capable of loving.

In the same way, one can "wash the heart" of a person afflicted by a hopeless heartache. One solemnly asks the consultant if she is ready to let her heart be freed from this old attachment, her consent actually being essential to this operation. One can then place a sponge or an apple on her chest and say, "This is your heart," then mime opening the chest to remove the heart and wash it. The person cries loudly while the old love is diluted in water. After having metaphorically or actually perfumed the "heart," one places it back on the chest and mimics shoving it back in, finally removing it without attempting to hide it.

Contrary to what happens in Psychomagic, it is not the consultant who will then manage the operation's physical waste. In a psychomagic act it is recommended that the consultant bury, throw into a river, or send into the sky attached to a helium balloon the objects that she has carried or expelled. In psychoshamanism the object is only a support in the intention of healing. In the act that we have just described, the apple will simply go into the garbage since the "cleaned heart" that it represents is nevertheless installed in the consultant's chest. Similarly, the water in which it was washed remains the responsibility of the shaman, who, like a surgeon, has no qualms about throwing it out since it has become useless.

All of these techniques have a goal of **metaphorically purifying the body** and allow us to become aware of the existence of a **material and spiritual double body,** the two aspects being equally important. The body functions as mysteriously as the universe. It makes sense therefore to approach it with experimental practices designed to enable us to begin to shift the limits of our perception. In the same way, the essential Being seeks to manifest itself in the ego, and the spiritual body seeks to manifest itself in our daily physical sensations. Illnesses and tensions can ultimately be interpreted as a battle of the material body against the call of the sublime body.

PART TEN

Healing the Tree

The Rebellious Heir Saves the Lineage

NINETEEN

From Filiation Delirium to Fulfilled Consciousness

By Alejandro Jodorowsky

After studying the genealogy tree, we may respond in two ways. If we have sensed the negative aspects in our familial genealogy, we may become anxious, which therefore interrupts any further understanding. Or, contrarily, we may courageously move forward in healing, which forces us to face the pain we have long sought to bury in oblivion.

One day at age forty I began to cry like a baby as I suddenly remembered a phrase that my mother had thrown at me thirty years earlier as my father slapped her: "Just after delivering you, I had my tubes tied so this monster would never get me pregnant again! Everything that comes from him disgusts me!" I then realized that even if my intellect was adult, I was living on the emotional plane as a little boy who felt unworthy of being loved since my existence itself disgusted my mother. Once all my tears of pain had poured out I told myself, "Now that I am aware of this aberration, what can I do to love myself?"

At the core I understood that all this work on the genealogy tree, beyond a survey of the responsibilities of members of my family, actually proposed a change in my level of Consciousness. As long as this infantile suffering stayed nestled in my heart I would remain locked in my limited and selfish ego, and all my deeds would be distorted by my belief that I was not wanted in this world and unworthy of the appreciation of others. This unconscious feeling pushed me to couple with women who were incapable of loving me and, for the same reason, to do everything possible to deny myself the applause my theater pieces deserved. I told myself, "If I want to heal, I must free myself from this which I call 'my individuality' and, by way of a ritual ceremony, die to rebirth with an adult, objective, loving vision of myself."

I chose a pleasant place in the country, and accompanied by a compassionate partner I read my eulogy and was buried. There, completely covered except for my face, I let myself detach from the victim child. I felt this symbolically anxious moment as a reawakening. In recovering the love of myself that I had lost at ten years of age I became conscious of the suffering that I had inflicted on the women who had shared part of their life with me, together with tense situations that I kept creating with my collaborators. With shame and healthy regret I found that not only for me but for the majority of human beings the search for oneself is a lot like an absurd and dangerously distressing project. I understood that when facing our illnesses we strive to eliminate painful symptoms but avoid healing the deep wound that was the cause and kept us buried in a persistent childhood. But I never thought that we emerge from this limited and selfish level of Consciousness to access a superior, transpersonal Consciousness that unites us to the great energy of the cosmos, the creative constant of all of life.

The infantile ego seeks not to be, but to have: "I am what I possess, I refuse emptiness, I fight to not be expelled, despised, eliminated, or ignored." People who worry struggle because the individual ego is an illusion: it cannot be, therefore it cannot possess anything. Failing to be replenished by this mysterious force that can be felt but never defined, that according to our system of beliefs is called "the Absolute," "God," "the Universe," or "cosmic energy," the individual ego is endlessly tormented by nervous emotions and sees itself incapable of building anything lasting. It occurs to us that when we truly become an adult we discover the divine within us and free ourselves from the emotional, mental, and sexual obstacles that constitute the personal ego. However, this "little me" has more than one trick up its sleeve and can disguise itself as the "saint ego."

One of my friends, who initially carried a pleasant youthful energy, made the mistake of wanting to imitate a spiritual master whom he admired. He shaved his long hair, hid his body's flexibility by adopting a rigid posture, and believing himself to be "chosen" thought that he had received an expected "transmission." He began to recruit disciples who, lacking a father's affection, stuck to him to fill an emotional void. Convinced of his divinity, he declared in a tone too humble to be honest, "I am an ocean of wisdom hidden in a dewdrop." The day his wife left him, taking with her their two children, his saint ego shattered into a million pieces. No longer able to bear the responsibility of conducting so many meditation sessions, he let his mask fall, and in a rage he kicked out his disciples. Then he came to me for a psychomagic act to find a joy for life. I worked with him on his genealogy tree. He studied it with a fury. When he understood which trap he had fallen into, he broke out laughing, saying, "Actually, I was a dewdrop imprisoned in an ocean of wisdom—that is to say, an insecure individual who collected his stereotypes."

Once the mirth passed, he sadly continued, "In his sermon on the mountain, Christ was right when he said, 'A good tree doesn't give bad fruit and a bad tree doesn't give good fruit.' One chops down the whole tree if it doesn't give good fruit and one throws it in the fire. There are so many mistakes, so much abuse, such a lack of Consciousness in my tree that I am condemned to a prison of a useless and meaningless life. The best I can do is to commit suicide."

"You cite the Gospel in an incomplete way," I told him. "After having said those words, Christ added, 'It is therefore by their fruits that you will recognize them.' Do you understand? It is not the tree's beauty or ugliness that defines it. As splendid and as strong as it may be, if it gives bitter or poisonous fruits, it's a bad tree. On the other hand, if the branches are twisted, if its appearance is weak but it gives sweet and nourishing fruits, it is a good tree. The **fruit defines the tree, not the inverse.** Your family can have committed immense errors, but if you develop your Consciousness and your individual ego bows before your transpersonal being, the whole tree, as harmful as it is, becomes a sacred organism and worthy of respect. From the time you change, the life of your ancestors acquires a new direction because in spite of the traps into which they fell, they engendered a descendant capable of seeking his true Being with patience and perseverance as far as raising the I to Nous, becoming by that alone the 'good fruit.' Every fulfilled being is a source of healing for his social circle and ends up incarnating the treasure he has long sought."

When we identify with the artificial me we live in dissatisfaction. Lacking any change in this, nothing can satisfy us intellectually, emotionally, sexually, or materially. We always want more. The only thing that can truly satisfy us, or offer us peace, is fulfillment of our divine Consciousness. The desire to hold onto the person we believe ourselves to be locks us in a constant repetition and plunges us into a frenetic defense of our ideas, feelings, desires, and selfish needs. But the strength that secretly appears from our essential Being by way of intuition and dreams continually directs us to act as we truly are, to live completely, to expand our perception of the world. If we remain identified with our inferior egos without obeying the will that requires us to change, or if we conceal our anxiety at all costs, we risk making our loved ones miserable.

This intense resistance to the call of the inner divinity provokes confusing desires, revolts, destructive appetites, irresistible passions, mania, suicidal depressions, and illnesses. Sometimes certain people delude themselves by thinking their limited ego is their essential Being, attempting to evade their painful realities by developing a **filiation delirium.**

Doctor Alfonso Millán invited me to his private office in Tlalpan, Mexico, in 1970. Because of my knowledge of the art of pantomime he wanted my help in deciphering the gestures of his paranoid and schizophrenic patients. I have never forgotten Don Pedrito, a man who maintained a certain kind of elegance and whose behavior was apparently normal. He could simultaneously play a tango on one hand and a mazurka by Chopin on the other hand. Pleased by my applause, he gave me a hug and explained to me that the people who said his parents were actually members of the Communist party had decided to keep him incarcerated in the Floresta asylum because he was the son of the ex-emperor of Russia. He believed the royal blood flowing through his veins gave him the exceptional musical gifts that were proof of the truth of his words.

Speaking to the other patients, I observed that one of the essential manifestations of their illnesses consisted of the filiation delirium. They believed themselves to have illustrious origins, proclaiming their links to the great of the world, insisting they had an important role in politics, religion, or science. They invented heroic acts of the past or revealed heroic missions they intended for the future. They attributed all sorts of qualities and powers to themselves, boasting of being authors of revolutionary inventions or immortal works of art, inventors of things that would save the world. They attributed these to gifts of clairvoyance, the capacity to see into the future, as if the belief of having discovered the secret of their origin allowed them to also access the mysteries of their destiny. While they arrived at the certitude of having recovered their place in the genealogy tree, they manifested a supernatural psychic fertility. These euphoric states were darkened by thoughts of persecution, and they believed they were victims of sordid schemes because of their high social rank or because they were heirs to fabulous family riches.

In giving them pantomime classes for a year, I understood that those who are called "crazy" reveal anxieties that are also present in individuals considered to be "of sound mind." Locked in the selfish Me, we only nourish the past. Without transcending the personal dimension, without the goal of cosmic fulfillment, without seeking total union, we strive to look like others and we create family relationships that differentiate but little from the madness of filiation.

When megalomaniacs who are isolated in depression, anxiety, confusion, and dissatisfaction transform their parents and ascribe a prestigious lineage to them, through their madness they express the desire to descend from parents who incorporate the essential Being into their cultural being. In saying they are born of a famous man and woman, they actually affirm that they are the product of divine Consciousness. When they claim to have been abducted from their real families and placed in surrogate families, they show what the majority of human beings feel: "We were born into a clan that knows nothing but imitation and has only ignored creativity. We have been deprived of our essence and submitted to cultural tyranny. If those who educate us instill in us that this fragmented reality is true reality, we feel that they are wrong, that they lie to themselves, and consequently, we lie to ourselves. If our parents did not teach us how to get to our inner god, they are not entirely our parents."

While the mad proclaim their lineages with the greats of the world, insisting on their role in determining politics, religion, or science, they are doing nothing but manifesting their desire to join with the whole universe. We are the creators of Consciousness; we have a preordained role in the possible evolution of the human species. If our spirit stagnates, if we become a spoke in the wheel of evolution, we collaborate in the extermination of humanity. The Messiah, so awaited by the Jews, is not an individual but a day when all human beings reach divine Consciousness.

When psychotics reveal the missions of spectacular characters who will become reality in their futures, they have an intuition of the mission engraved in the Supraconsciousness of each one of us: to engender mutant children who will transform the decadent society in which we live. The megalomaniac interprets the divine plan of a human being's fulfillment as a task falling to him to save his fellows.

When the mad claim that only royal blood flows through their veins, which awards them exceptional gifts, they reveal that all blood is of royalty. Just as our planet is shared for the common good, and so we should live without polluting or destroying it, human blood is not individual but collective. Those who pollute their own blood with drugs, toxic foods, or an excess of alcohol do harm not only to themselves but to the whole species. Our civilization, in destroying the forests, in covering our cultivable areas with cement, has usurped land from the vegetable kingdom. And what if vegetation, unable to grow on the whole surface of the earth, turns to human blood in its intention for expansion? We carry fatal parasites in our bodies: the égrégore (collective spirit) of tobacco, coffee, tea, marijuana, poppy, grapevine, hops, cocoa, sugarcane, the vine from which ayahuasca is made. In order for the necessary spiritual evolution to occur, we must cleanse our bodies of these invasions.

If the mad attribute all kinds of powers to themselves, if they boast of being the creators of revolutionary inventions and immortal works of arts, of having discovered universal remedies, it is because they have the intuition of that which a fulfilled humanity would be capable of achieving if it used the full potential of its millions of neurons.

The rest of us, who are considered to be "normal" individuals, are trapped in the ego and live unsatisfied lives. Anonymity weighs on us; we would love for our friends and family to acknowledge us before we die, and therefore have the burning desire to achieve something important—but we find it impossible to define that "something." Deep down we know that no one, without achieving divine Consciousness, can achieve immortality. The occultist Gurdjieff thought that we are born with only one grain of soul, and that it is our responsibility to make it grow or we will pay the consequences. "Those who live like pigs," he said, "die like dogs."

When megalomaniacs claim gifts of clairvoyance and prediction, they only transform into madness that which our essential Being attempts to make all us "normals" hear. If we rely on divine energy, which constitutes the luminous center of our innermost selves and which we call our **inner God,** we can expand the limitations of the brain and achieve our cosmic purpose, living in continuous expansion. By remaining prisoners of the familial trap we repeat the past, repress our authentic drives, and carry feelings, desires, ideas, and needs that are not ours. Seeking solutions outside of ourselves, we will feel mutilated; we will feel the need to be someone or something else, focusing excessively on appearances. Or we will vegetate, locked in absurd systems, inhabited by the feeling that the world in which we live is not a true world and that the worst thing that ever happened to us was being born.

When the euphoric states of the mad are overshadowed by ideas of persecution and the certitude of being the victim of sordid plots, they show us an exaggerated version of how we feel, immersed in the cultural trap. At every moment the inner God pursues us with miracles designed to reveal higher levels of Consciousness, but we transform them into "chance," "strange coincidence," or "accidents," projecting onto the exterior that which actually emerged from the depths of our spirit. The essential Being pursues us, but we fight against the miracle with the same projections that paranoiacs experience in their opposition of imaginary conspiracies.

During the year in which I shared daily life with psychotics I had pleasant conversations with Don Juan Muñoz, alias San Calixto, during his rare calm moments. For the majority of the time he felt possessed by a demon who put curse words into his mouth, and he would become very strongly agitated, demanding that someone sew his lips together with string blessed by the Pope.

After a pantomime lesson in which I taught him to mime walking against the wind he told me, "Some years ago, before my enemies, Satan's henchmen, locked me in this castle, I traveled a large part of Mexico to spread the Gospel to my brothers. I did this on foot because I had no means to buy an ass. Very often the Devil sent me storms to prevent my advancing. Maybe because I was so skinny and all I had was one bag with bread in it, I could always cross these storms with ease. One night, I stopped to sleep on the side of a little church. When morning came, I continued my journey. After about four hours of walking, I sat down to eat. Upon opening my bag, I realized that my bread was full of ants. I thought, 'These creatures are now far from their home. Maybe they have parents, children, friends. What I must do is bring them back to the place from where I took them.' I thus retraced my steps for four hours, opened my bag, and deposited the ants in their anthill. At that very moment this invisible halo that surrounds my head descended from heaven."

I interpreted Juan's story like this: The pilgrim symbolizes a man with a high level of Consciousness. When he realized that he lives in the destructive trap of the genealogy tree—that is to say, his bread, his authentic being, is invaded by a swarm of strangers—he does not see the ants as enemies, he does not despise the clan for its egoism, but he decides to bring them to his first essence, the divine filiation, by bringing the ants to the temple. By restoring his genealogy tree in its celestial roots, he obeys harmony and spiritual health.

In these calm moments, when he was San Calixto, Juan expressed himself in a prophetic way: "In my abysmal energy, the thought loses its limits. I look at everyone and everything with the love of a father. Intense is my tenderness for the ephemeral existence. Nothing begins, nothing ends, nothing is born, nothing dies. I accept with love the sacrifice of my illusory figure."

Through the words of San Calixto, I understood the deep significance of the numberless Arcanum of the Tarot, Le Mat (the Fool, in popular language). By penetrating the territory of the Unconscious—if we do not go astray, if we remain linked to the rational world—we encounter not insanity but an intermediary state called **trance,** a deep connection with the transpersonal Unconscious—that is to say, the Supraconscious. It is in this state of trance in which great artists and great scientists travel, and perhaps that is what Einstein was referring to when he said, "The imagination is more important than knowledge." Great healers like Maria Sabina, the shaman of hallucinogenic mushrooms who is said to have visited patients in their dreams in order to cure them, also use trance. These talented beings enter into a dimension of the spirit that is located beyond the **individual ego,** and what differentiates them from those who are mad is that while the latter open the same mental doors that allow them to communicate with the indefinable, they nevertheless remain prisoners of their anxiety instead of joining humanity.

When asked, "Master, what is enlightenment?" a Zen monk responded, "Opened door to the north, opened door to the south, opened door to the east, opened door to the west!"

The Conscious being defeats identification with words, and in his mind reigns silence: **he knows how to be.** In his emotional center, objective judgment replaces criticism: **he knows how to love.** In his sexual center, passions are well channeled and dissatisfaction is defeated: **he knows how to create.** In controlling his useless needs he reduces them to the essential, and he does not self-destruct: **he knows how to live.** He has ceased to think that to take action is to triumph over another. He pushes his limits endlessly and without rest. He adds trance to his rational capacities: he does not lose consciousness in the awake state, but he allows it to be possessed by his essential Being, impersonal because it speaks the sacred madness that inhabits its spirit. The Conscious being ceases to be his own witness, no longer observes, is an actor in the pure state, an entity in action. His daily memory stops recording facts, words, and fulfilled acts. The island of reason expands and unites with the ocean of Unconscious. In this Supraconscious state he does not fail and is not provoked by accident. He does not conceive of space, he becomes space. He does not feel time passing. In this extreme state of lucidity each gesture, each action, is perfect. He cannot deceive because he has no project and no intention; he experiences pure action in the eternal present. He is not afraid to free his instinct, no matter how primitive it may be. For him, going beyond the rational does not mean denying mental strength; he remains open to the poetry of intuition, to flashes of telepathy, to voices that do not belong to him, to the words that come from spirit's other dimensions. These words join together in the infinite extension of feelings, of inexhaustible creative forces bestowed on him by his sexual energy. He experiences his body not as a concept of the past but as a subjective and vibrant reality of the present. Rather than being dominated by rational concepts, he allows himself to be moved by forces that belong to sublime levels: by the totality of reality. An animal in a cage has movements similar to rational perception; the free movement of an animal in nature is comparable to the trance. The prisoner animal must be fed at fixed hours; the rational, to act, must receive words. The wild animal feeds himself and never feeds incorrectly. The being in a trance is moved not by what he has been taught, but by that which he is, and **he searches not for the truth but for authenticity.**

In order to heal and to know how to guide others toward their own healing, it is absolutely imperative to familiarize oneself with the state of trance, and to abandon oneself there without fear, knowing that one can enter and leave by one's own will. The trance begins with an extreme perception of oneself, an exacerbation of the internal intention, which directs one toward the abolition of the duality of spectator-actor. In trance, one ceases to observe oneself, and dissolves into oneself. And melting into oneself, one also melts into exterior reality: all of space is one's body, without possibility of error. Fans of the *corrida* (bullfight) are aware of the moment in which the *torero* "enters the place" (*entra en el sitio*) where he unites with the bull, the point when there are no longer two adversaries but two complementary bodies that dance, uniting life and death. Man and animal, with movements that seem to be dictated by the public, live in a distinct dimension that one calls "real" in which there is no longer room for fatal error, where everything is fair, perfect, and beautiful. This is how the shamans and healers proceed. For them therapy is not a science but an art. The healer dissolves into the patient, and together they "enter the place."

Watching my cats pretend to bite each other's jugular, I observe that they know perfectly well where the vital points are. They also know which herbs to use to purge. Similarly, we know instinctively where health and disease reside in the human spirit. It is only through trance that we can guide a consultant, or our genealogy trees, to healing.

So that is how one day in a moment of extreme crisis I was pushed to sit in front of a typewriter, and I began to draft a book with the feeling that it was being dictated to me. The book was *L'Arbre du Dieu pendu,* in which all the characters belonged to my genealogy tree, and although they were real I transformed and exalted them in order to convey their story as myth. To each I gave what they had unconsciously aspired to without having been able to achieve. For example, I transformed a prostitute aunt into the mistress of the president of the republic. To those who died prematurely, I invented a sequel to their existence. I allowed my mother to fulfill herself artistically, something she had never been able to do in her life. Better still, I let her spend time with her father, whom she had never known, and to have an affectionate relationship with him. This work, other than its quality as artistic fiction, allowed me to use creativity to transform my familial memory into a heroic legend. And I understood in this moment that everything I gave to my genealogy tree, I gave to myself. In finishing this book, my existential crisis ended and my life was enriched: I was able to love.

TWENTY

The Healed Tree

The Role of the Creative Imagination

At the beginning of this book we presented a path of studying the genealogy tree as a "hero's journey."* Actually, if we refer to the ultimate fulfillment of the human being's four energies, the hero is also a genius, a saint, and a champion. This has to do with the highest degree of intellectual, emotional, creative, and physical capacity. This journey thus goes from **oneself to oneself**: from the being caught in the familial trap to the being liberated from the trap. The acquired individual personality does not disappear but rather accepts, on the one hand, **seeing his limits broaden and, on the other hand, putting himself at the service of the transpersonal being,** the part of us that thinks "Us" and not only "Me." But this "Us" is not the clan's limited beliefs, the family legend, which in essence opposes union with the world because individual or familial egoism is that which essentially separates us: me from other individuals, and my clan from other clans. When we arrive at the transpersonal "Us," the identity becomes a collective affirmation commensurate with humanity.

This journey is also the passage from an infantile attitude to a

---

*The model of a "hero's journey" was first expressed by Joseph Campbell in his book *The Hero with a Thousand Faces* in 1949. It has since been widely used by various authors, especially for screenwriting methods.

mature attitude. At the opposite of the infantile being, the mature being accepts the fact that others may not change and seeks **to modify his own inner reality,** which has an impact on all his relationships.

This voyage of the individual being to the transpersonal being requires many trials that we have detailed. We must first detach from the familial legend in order to clarify the situation and the relationships, experiencing them such as they truly are. Then, with an adult Consciousness, we go into old childhood wounds to face the shortcomings and abuse, confronting anew the fears that paralyzed us before, and also—dare we suggest, at least in the imagination—confronting all solutions that might raise the genealogy tree's level of Consciousness. We challenge our conception, our birth, all our bonds, and even our own parents' and grandparents' upbringings in our fight against the rigidity of the past, which leads us to the ultimate face-to-face with death. In terms of this voyage, each person must in fact pass through the symbolic death of his or her acquired personality, forged by the past, with which it has become impossible to identify.

At the end of the path, the reward is then to have at our fingertips something similar to the Golden Fleece from Greek mythology, or the treasure from traditional tales. This elixir of long life, this priceless gem, is simply Consciousness, the **reunification of the self with the Whole.** Once we recognize what we truly are, we also understand that through the genealogy tree Consciousness entrusts us with a body that little by little learns to respect this recognition. Such is the nature of the work on the body that we have presented in the preceding chapter. But so that the voyage is complete, the hero has the task of bringing his precious booty back to the world from which it originated. The final healing consists of this: once the individual path is accomplished, each of us must **return to the origin and heal the tree from the inside.**

We frequently feel cut off from our clan of origin at some given moment during our work on the self. In discovering our true nature, we will also discover at what point the family ignored and neglected us. When undergoing the abuse, we feel like an orphan, yet the fruit and the tree are still joined by bonds of obvious or underlying love. Even if we leave behind the definitions of the past, the relationships, the character, and the inheritance of the tree can be **integrated just as much as any contribution of energy** once they have been transformed by our work on Consciousness.

Just as we have discovered the impersonal and essential Being residing in the center of our person, so it lies, latent or obvious, in each member of our family. It is therefore possible to establish a relationship (concrete or intended) from essential Being to essential Being with each member of the tree.

We build a shared experience with the members of our tree who are individuals in their own right, in the same way as others who share collective bodies, like beehives. But instead of being dependent on the risky fates of this collective and its limited level of Consciousness, it behooves us to actively participate in its advance toward higher Consciousness. "It is the fruit that defines the tree, not the inverse"— our personal realization becomes the level of healing to which the tree can also reach.

In the same way that on the return path the hero encounters his ultimate opponent over whom he must triumph in order to achieve his destiny and save his world of origin, a series of traps are presented for the person who wishes to obtain his own healing and that of his genealogy tree. One of these traps consists of thinking that the hero should sacrifice himself to "save" his parents and other members of the family. Actually, the redemption of the tree can only occur through our personal realizations, that is to say, through the full unfolding of our capabilities and talents. That is why we begin this chapter with a study of the failure neurosis and its main causes.

The second trap, subtler, is that of the blind points where our old personality comes to take refuge. We can call this part of the ego that obstinately refuses to serve Consciousness the **mental island,** and its elimination will be the work of a lifetime. The question of when a person is "cured" is an integral part of all therapeutic approaches. If, in artistic practices, the question is in knowing when the work is complete, on the spiritual path it has to do with determining when enlightenment has been attained. In the metagenealogical approach, we define a state of healing as a state sufficient to allow the person to devote himself to healing his tree.

Once this state is achieved, work will take place on the inner characters that we carry like many inherited formations of our personal and familial histories. Following this, we will focus on transmutation of their sublime expression in order to allow us to work with our allies—how can we use our creative imagination to awaken our essential psychic energies? The development of the sublime tree will be the final artistic act that seals completion of the work. This healing of the tree consists of endowing each character with the fulfillment that he or she was not able to achieve in his lifetime. Once elevated to their highest potential, our ancestors all become transpersonal and transform into an energy that we can somehow absorb into our own hearts. Then the tree disappears and melts into us, and to some extent we also accept our own disappearance as an individual, ultimately recognizing ourselves as pure Consciousness.

We then no longer act as "having" a family but as "being" a family, which can transform into a completely healthy society, even humanity.

OVERCOMING THE FAILURE NEUROSIS

Ultimately, it is not what we think or say that determines our reality but **what we are or are not capable of doing.** Even when we use different strategies, each time we experience failure on the path to a goal that is close to our hearts we face the ultimate trap of the acquired personality: the failure neurosis.

This can take different forms, from the most flagrant to the most subtle. At the moment that we think we have succeeded, we encounter an interior or exterior obstacle that calls this apparent success into question. Accident, depression, helplessness, procrastination, paralysis—the conclusion is always the same: "I can't do it." The failure neurosis can also express itself in a collective enterprise, such as when someone suddenly throws himself headlong into conflict with another, immobilizing the joint effort, or when a person decides to leave a cooperative, knowing very well that her departure will produce a crisis that will damage the success of the work. The failure neurosis also manifests when, once the work is produced, one retrospectively demolishes it, perhaps by falling into a deep depression, or by sabotaging whatever is left to sabotage, like the publicity that will carry the project to the world. The failure neurosis expresses itself as an indefinable malaise, feelings of guilt, the notion that one is ugly or incompetent in spite of all objective proof to the contrary. In extreme cases, the person kills himself or sinks into madness after having attained his goal.

Under all these faces, the failure neurosis boils down to a fundamental prohibition: **that of being and experiencing outside of the genealogy tree.** One is driven to failure by six main causes, six beliefs that are encrusted in the Unconscious. We present each of them below, accompanied by a suggestion for a positive visualization to use to move beyond them.

"I Am Fundamentally Bad."

Under one pretext or another, the genealogy tree did not accept me for what I was. The clan wanted a child of the opposite sex, of another appearance, with other qualities, quicker, slower, more tranquil, more energetic. This rejection, reiterated many times, deeply affected me and drove me to attempt, without success, to be what the tree wanted me to be. This was obviously impossible because I can only be myself. However, at any given moment of triumph when I gave myself the right to exist just as I am, I tried to drive myself to failure—making the clan right about me.

Positive visualization. I imagine the whole tree is just like me. What marvelous relationships I would have with each member of the clan if the characteristics held against me where common to everyone. For example, I am delicate and spiritual in a virile and materialistic tree; I imagine the whole clan endowed with my delicacy. I am a girl and they wanted a boy; I imagine the whole tree sensitive to feminine qualities: my father, my grandparents, my uncles, all family members, are endowed with great inner femininity.

"I Was a Burden or an Obstacle."

The genealogy tree makes me responsible for its own inconsistencies and incapacities. I was born "by accident," or in a family already mired in material problems. My parents abandoned me into the hands of others or, to the contrary, they claimed to have "sacrificed" for me: they accused me, overtly or not, of preventing them from fulfilling their goals. So I feel incapable of bringing anything good to anyone. In order not to betray this belief, at any given moment of triumph I sabotage my own success that would be a solution, a joy for the world, contrary to that which identifies me today.

Positive visualization. I am a contribution; with me comes miracles. For example, the moment I was born I imagine my parents received a prize, a government grant, a gift for my birth. If my mother missed a career as a singer because of my birth, I imagine that my mother's voice mutated in a miraculous way during her pregnancy and that she became a celebrity thanks to me for her golden voice—she even did a duo with me.

"I Do Not Have the Right to Betray."

The clan apparently accepts me. It is possible that I had a happy childhood. But my existence is based on the condition of loyalty without fail. I must adopt their ideas, their social behavior, their religion, their ideologies, aesthetics, and emotions as mine. In reality, I do not exist and my family does not love me unless I remain a completely supportive, indistinguishable element. If my mother inculcated me with hate toward men (for a girl), or convinced me that no woman was good enough for me (for a boy), I will make my amorous relationships fail in order to not betray my mother. If my father thinks that all activity outside commerce is unacceptable, I will fail in everything that is not commercial. National cohesion also functions according to this model.

Consequently, I do not give myself the right to live except as an element of the clan, which deep down, absolutely denies my unique existence.

Positive visualization. The whole genealogy tree takes on my new ideas, my new initiatives, my discoveries. For example, if I change my political opinion, they register with my party and vote with me; if I fall in love with a person of another race or religion they fall in love with my partner's culture or convert to the religion.

"I Do Not Have the Right to Leave."

Here again, the family ambience was apparently happy. But my parents raised me not to guide me toward independence but to keep me (actually or symbolically) near them. The deep dissatisfaction of other members of the clan reflects on me. If I leave my parents, they will die, or (in the case of a parental couple with a sadomasochistic knot) they will kill one another; or else one will sink into a depression. I am guilty. I must put in a lot of effort for everything I have received because I carry an artificial responsibility. All success is a step toward the world and in effect consists of leaving my family to enter into the human community. Consequently, I am not allowed to triumph.

Positive visualization. All the members of my family go toward an ideal place on the planet, outside of familial roots. I visualize my whole genealogical tree peopling the planet, full of joy, emigrating successfully here and there.

"I Do Not Have the Right to Surpass My Parents."

I carry my clan's defeat. Either the clan is composed entirely of failures or there is, among my ancestors, a (generally very narcissistic) "big man" or "exceptional woman" whose success is considered unsurpassable. They inculcated me with limitations for any possible success: it is not possible to be rich, happy in love, talented, adventurous, beyond whatever limits. If, for example, my father and grandfather were failed doctors who became nurses, dentists, or physiotherapists, I will consciously fail my exams at medical school in order to refrain from showing them that it is possible to succeed, because in exceeding them I would destroy their authority, their superiority established on my voluntary inferiority, and would find myself symbolically to be an orphan. The pain of failure stings less than this abandonment.

Positive visualization. I raise everyone to the level of my own fulfillment. Each, in his own domain, encounters success equal to mine and enjoys his triumphs in the great collective party where everyone accepts success and talent essentially as an individual, and where no one can be compared with anyone else.

"Pleasure Is Dangerous, Dirty, and Prohibited."

Triumphing in my true vocation is the greatest pleasure there is. If the genealogy tree suffers from a strong sexual repression, all pleasure will be considered suspect, even diabolical. Generation after generation, my clan prohibits its descendants from enjoying life and their own capacities. At the moment of triumph this fundamental prohibition descends, preventing access to fulfillment, and can also affect sexuality, causing one to be frigid, impotent, or a premature ejaculator.

Positive visualization. I imagine a huge carnival. My whole family participates, each of us with a costume and a mask that allows us to act out something previously kept secret and prohibited from our personality. Each enjoys the pleasure of this warm, delightful ambience.

Thus, once again something forces us to define ourselves as limited beings in need of the narrow framework of the familial clan. No matter what the configuration of the trap straining the genealogy tree, it amounts to a prohibition of any connection with our Consciousness, our inner God, our joy of living, our creative capacity.

Each time the failure neurosis manifests it causes the individual to lose sight of his goal, his personal sense of his existence, and the mission of his particular life that only he has the power to realize. The basis of the failure neurosis is a devaluation of self, based on family membership, which resides in us as orders and prohibitions. At the end of the day, we feel empty. The only way to radically oppose this harmful illusion is to accept the inner diamond, our own essential value, and to draw from the source of ourself this unalterable happiness that resists all obstacles.

From time to time it is possible to achieve results using different acts, Psychomagic* among others. One can, for example, devote the work to a specific family member. But the real work on the failure neurosis consists of identifying it whenever it is found at the crossroads, each time it appears. One can then consciously choose to be driven by or to turn away this failure, this call from the past. By way of colossal inner effort one can then proceed in Consciousness until fulfillment. This implies having a concept of God or a superior force, which is the compass for our action because a lack of faith in one's self is aligned with a lack of any faith. Our clan has asked us to be something other than be ourselves, and in yielding to this order we have lost sense of what we truly are.

The acceptance of one's self is heroic because it means the collapse of inner restrictions created by the family, society, and culture. Our acquired identity is always insufficient and defective: it is the container and not the contents. But the collapse of these worthless remains, or the crack in this mask, terrifies us and we tend to reject it. Our greatness, our capacity to shine, to love without limits, to triumph, is more frightening than our smallness. To overcome this fear implies having a more elevated purpose. We can call it love of oneself, love of the work that we are in the process of accomplishing, love of all those whom this work will benefit. It is therefore when gratitude enters the game, when we accept the collapse of the limited me, when we enter into contact with gratitude and grace. This essential appreciation opens the path to our own qualities.

Actually, it is never the limited self that triumphs, but the transpersonal self. An artist is inspired by his Unconscious, which exceeds him; his deep creativity does not come from himself. Triumphing in business assumes an appreciation for all the clientele who make the success possible. Triumphing in a collective implies an appreciation for all the collaborators.

The failure neurosis is basically inseparable from the familial ego.

---

*See Alejandro Jodorowsky's *The Manual of Psychomagic,* particularly the chapter dedicated to this subject.

It will manifest throughout life in more and more subtle shapes. To solidify the state of being that will overcome the inevitable onslaught of this neurosis, we propose some exercises designed to reinforce faith in one's self, gratitude, and intentions for the future.

Work on the Future

We have presented the hypothesis that we carry the future within us, that our brains are potentially limitless, just as the universe is, and have more capability than we use. The future is therefore inside us, like an immense reservoir of potentiality, and we can postulate that there exists in us an energetic destiny inviting us to become that which we are able to be, guiding us toward positive fulfillment. We can work on the future like we work on the past. An unhappy, neurotic person locked in restrictions from the past cannot open his attention toward future possibilities.

Project Oneself into a Fulfilled Future

Concentrate on what you want to accomplish in the upcoming year. What will your living environment be like? Your physical shape? How will your finances be? What will you have created? How will your creativity be? What will your desires be? Who will be part of your support group? How will those relationships have evolved? How will you think? What will your ideas be like? What is the most positive vision you are capable of imagining, corresponding to your true Being, to your deepest wishes? Now transport yourself to ten years from now. What can you best imagine for yourself? For your surroundings? For your world? And in twenty years? In thirty years? Push the boundaries to your peaceful death. What kind of death do you wish for yourself? In what context? What kind of world do you want to leave behind?

Enrich the Past with Contributions from the Future

Return to an episode from childhood with the adult Consciousness that you have today; pay a visit to the child you were and give that child the keys to handle the situation along with information on what good awaits in the future. For example, "It is marvelous to be forty years old! It is wonderful to become fully oneself." Or "You are going to have children and you are going to love them more than you can imagine." Then, project yourself further back in childhood, visualizing a life of happiness and returning as a very wise person, filled with great life experiences; now visit several episodes of your past and sow seeds of hope and wisdom there, which will allow you to fulfill this future you desire.

Get Out of One's Self

One of the problems of the failure neurosis is that one lacks an inspiring goal. We have seen that when a person does not know his goal in life, in all likelihood it means his parents did not desire his birth. It is therefore useful to make a psychoritual of rebirth to find his capacity to project himself into the future. But it is also important to be able to represent **a goal that goes beyond the framework of one's destiny.** The goal of the human species could be to "live as long as the universe, to know the totality of the universe, to become the Consciousness of the universe." Between the individual goal and the universal goal one can imagine a whole range of propositions designed to provide for the collective good.

Solve a World Problem

Choose a problem that is beyond you, like world hunger, religious or cultural wars, the condition of women around the globe, child slavery, deforestation, global warming. Examine whether this problem concerns you in your daily life or in your transpersonal being. To some extent, a problem on this scale will not concern you directly but affects you on another plane.

Each of us is capable of designing a solution to a global problem, and this kind of drafting takes us out of ourselves. All solutions have value, even if they are different. The solution of a man is not necessarily the same as that of a woman, that of a homosexual is not necessarily the same as a heterosexual, the solution of an artist is not the same as the solution of a scientist, but each solution carries a power of personal solutions for the world.

Push the Limits

We will now develop to its completion the exercise proposed at the beginning of this book. As with all the visualizations we have suggested, you can record yourself reading the text aloud and then carry out the exercise while listening to it with your eyes closed, or you can read it for someone else. The body is going to serve as a point of departure for the expansion of three other energies: intellectual, emotional, and sexual-creative.

- Sit comfortably on a chair, in a balanced and neutral position, feet on the earth, eyes closed. What do you see? Wait to see complete darkness. Does this darkness seem vast, or, contrarily, do you have a black wall in front of you? If you see a wall or a boundary, imagine that it is infinite space that you face and that surrounds you. At the center of the obscurity, at the height of your skull, visualize or imagine a point of light that represents a concentration of your mental energy.

- Begin by projecting this point forward. It can leave a trace, like a ray of light, or simply move forward toward the horizon before you. If you have difficulty making it progress, note how far you can go, and thank this border that allows you to make a topographical survey of the actual border of your intellect, and from which you can move further from now on.

- Then come back to the center of your skull and project the point of light backward, as far back as possible. See if raising your eyebrows, with your eyes remaining closed, helps you to project in a direction that is not straight ahead.

- Now project the point in front of and behind you, simultaneously toward right and left. Go as far as you can. In addition to these four directions point toward top and bottom, always as far into the distance as you can.

  Once you shine in the six directions, begin to make these six rays of light turn around you in a spiral that moves in a counter-clockwise direction. As the coil's movement is amplified, little by little, find yourself in the middle of a sphere of light and emit the sound "iiii." Allow this sound to resonate in your head in one or more notes, increasing the volume with each breath but without forcing the voice.

Then bring the six directions of light back to you with the notes that you sang, and take a bit of time to gather the energy that you yourself put into motion. Imagine the whole inside of your skull is lit by this light, and at this moment of integration set the intention to allow yourself to enjoy the feeling of this state of excellence, of **compassionate silence,** as often as possible.

- Now place your attention on the center of your chest, visualizing or imagining an increasingly powerful source capable of giving birth to a river. First the river flows forward. It is the limitless force of your emotional energy. Let the river sink out of sight in the horizon, and follow your heart as far as you can. Then add to this first river a second one, derived from the same source, which rises in back of you. Once these two rivers are on course, add two others, toward the left and right, and then two more that go up and down. Once six rivers flow from this source of absolute love, put them in motion in a counterclockwise circle. As the rivers turn around you, they surround you in a sphere of dancing water. You can give it a temperature that feels appropriate to you. Emit the long "ā" sound, "āāāā" . . . then the short "e" sound, "eeee" . . . then the short "a" sound, "aaaa" . . . increasingly strong, increasingly more open, but without forcing the voice, letting it resonate in your chest.

  Then recall the rivers of love into the center of your chest, letting the sound you emit resonate in the echo of silence. Keep your heart full of this inexhaustible source that gives everything and asks for nothing in return. It allows you to return to a state of excellence in the emotional center: of **compassion without judgment.**

- Concentrate on a point about four fingers' width below your navel, at the level of what those in the Oriental cultures call *hara, dan tien, dantian,* or *tanden,* which corresponds to what Western physics defines as our "center of gravity." You imagine or visualize a transparent tentacle, capable of stretching into infinity, that emerges from the center and is directed forward, charged of a formidable energy. Let it go as far as possible, communicating its energy that runs through everything. It is an invigorating force. Think how this power that emerges from your sexual and creative center originated from the same energy that created the universe. Now a second tentacle comes out of this same center toward the back, then two more toward the left and right, then two more going up and down. Draw out in these six directions this generous power of life and of creation, which starts to spin, forming around you in a sphere of infinite energy. Then your with mouth closed begin to chant the sound "mmmm," feeling the resonance descend into your pelvis. Little by little, this is replaced by a low-pitched "oooo" that you can also make with the nasal sound "awn." You can feel your voice resonate in your skeleton.

When you bring these energy tentacles toward you, their strength nests in the center of your pelvis and releases an energetic body into the totality of yourself, which contains all of the stars in the universe. This excellence, which is nevertheless yours, is that of **genuine desire,** and it is capable of continuous creativity.

Spend some time in silence, listening to the echo resonate from the sounds that you have produced, tasting this force that is henceforth yours. Upon opening your eyes, raise yourself up and walk around the room, noting how your perception of the environment and of yourself has changed after doing the exercise. You can, at will, charge everything you see with light, love, and energy.

SUFFICIENT HEALING
AND THE TAMED EGO

Undertaking the healing of the tree does not makes sense if one has become one's self simply by stitching up the wound without disinfecting it. It is very difficult to judge from the exterior whether a person has attained the minimal level of psychic health necessary to help himself and to eventually help others, but to some extent each person can examine his tamed ego and is capable of differentiating between the objective and the subjective. One can have a reduced but completely egocentric personality or, inversely, a strong personality that achieved a level of transpersonal Consciousness. The point is not to eliminate the ego or past history but to be able to radically apply it in daily life with the maxim, "Nothing for me which is not for others," and to practice a radical recognition that accepts present reality without mental judgment and intrusion from the emotional center.

As such, at any moment the experience of past trauma in our memory is susceptible to plunging us back into the inherited emotional state of childhood, which causes us to lose sight of the common interest or the objective situation and refocuses us exclusively on ourselves. It is not desirable or possible to eradicate our histories. The question is to know with what flexibility a person is capable of returning to himself: to his genuine emotional age and to a mature interaction with the situation.

Example: In a group working on the genealogy tree one participant, suddenly seized by a kind of nervous breakdown, threw herself to the ground crying and shouting. Nothing could draw her out of the breakdown; a persistent little girl inside her possessed her entirely and any sign of attention did nothing but reinforce her state. So that the collective work could continue, the solution was to ask all of the more than fifty people who were participating to lie down and take turns mimicking her actions. In a matter of a few seconds the young woman got up and calmly continued the work, understanding that the world would become uninhabitable if everyone behaved like her.

We will now present some key elements that are necessary for examination of the individual me: autonomy, acceptance of one's self as an adult, relationship to the interior and exterior liar, and coming face-to-face with the fact of our own death. This ultimate revision of the ego can in no way serve to gauge the degree of realization of another person.

This has to do with intimate and personal work that allows us to see if we are capable of initiating the healing of the tree on our own. If this is not the case, it suffices to focus on the area where we have discovered the insufficiency.

Several signs indicate that **sufficient healing** has taken place. The mature human being is capable of putting himself in another person's shoes and of taking either the lead or a secondary role according to the demands of a specific situation. Simultaneously, the mature person is indifferent to criticism or praise and is independent of the old judgments that his genealogy tree imposed on him in childhood. He is as capable of expressing himself clearly as he is able to expertly and attentively listen without criticism. The general tone of his existence, in spite of failures and obstacles, is a deep joy of living, independent of circumstances. This person knows gratitude and practices generosity but is capable of defending himself and preserving his dignity if someone unjustly attacks him. This person feels a sense of responsibility toward everything in his environment, including social and planetary concerns. The person is capable of not encroaching on the space of others and accepts the need to bend to circumstances rather than to his all-powerful desires. This person does not need to exploit or possess another and does not base his superiority on others being dragged down. This person does not compare himself to others, has replaced competition with emulation, and strives to embrace an appreciation of the diversity in human experiences as much as possible.

Here, we propose paths that can be used to help us move beyond our own blind spots. If we are not at peace within, nothing can be accomplished, even if we have the desire to heal the tree or to help others. Without autonomy true union is not possible; all woven bonds will be links of dependence, strained by genealogy tree neuroses.

Autonomy: Prosperity and Health

The body is the foundation upon which we establish our three other energies (desires, emotions, ideas), so it is essential to clarify our relationship with the material world in order to assure autonomy.

- Am I financially autonomous? What is my relationship with money? Am I independent from the concepts of money prevalent in my genealogy tree? In regard to work, am I in a domain that pleases me? What is my concept of prosperity?
- How do I treat myself physically? Is my nutrition as good as I want it to be? Do I still consume certain toxic products to which my lineage is addicted? What is my degree of personal hygiene? Do I choose only the same type of diet that was followed my family?
- Does the place where I live please me? How is my space organized? Is it in order or disorder? How much territory do I have? Am I at ease everywhere?

Here are some basic psychomagic acts concerning the relationships to territory and money.

Terrified of Poverty

For this act, turn to "Psychomagic Resolution" in part 7.

Regain Money

In each genealogy tree money has its own "color" or "taste." There may be "dirty" money, "easy" money, money won through pain and effort, parental money, the salary of an honorable profession, inherited money that may be connected with generosity or stinginess, money snatched by humiliation or theft, and financial ruin. One must clean the money of any subjective meaning and reestablish its initial qualities: the actualization of an energy exchange.

- One can iron and perfume bills in order to "clean" them and symbolically "bless" them. Rub the body with these exalted notes, or take a walk with a bill glued to one's forehead; or hanging from one's neck like an amulet.
- In a case where the notion of dirty money or unmerited money is particularly strong, one can adapt this act of Mexican magic.

In a specific place in the house, perhaps under one's bed, put a chamber pot into which one urinates, each time throwing in a coin. Allow the urine to accumulate for six days, and on the seventh day empty the chamber pot and thoroughly wash the coins before putting them in your mouth. Then use this money to buy the most desired sweet pastry, candies, or another delectable food.

• When one does not feel powerful in regard to producing money, place three gold coins in one's anus and retain them there for as long as possible. Then, excrete the gold coins with excrement into a chamber pot, burying the excrement and gold coins in the ground with a shrub over it. The shrub will grow on this natural fertilizer as well as on these gold coins, which are both sacrifice and symbolic investment in future wealth.

Take Possession of Territory

Urinate into a dropper bottle, then deposit a drop of urine in each corner of the place that one wishes to appropriate. Within its apparent simplicity, this act gives stunning results.

Exile or Lost Territory

Have someone send you soil from the country or place that you had to leave, or from which your ancestors were ousted. Sink your feet into this earth every day for about thirty minutes. Once you no longer feel the need to unite with this land, pour it into a river that joins the sea, thus returning it to its origin.

Maturity: From Baby to Adult

Emotionally, the infantile attitude consists of depending on another to be the agent of one's emotional well-being, "If only this person would change, my life would be simpler," "I cannot live without love from this person." As such, when one places "me" in the other, like a baby clinging to the mother's neck, one remains empty of oneself: the other becomes an idealized me, and one becomes completely dependent on the other's actions. One can then feel betrayed, unsettled, or abandoned at any given moment.

When one becomes capable of entering into contact with one's self as an adult, capable of taking full responsibility for one's life, one is no longer in a relationship of emotional dependence on another and learns to love unconditionally.

Here are some questions to ask in order to evaluate one's degree of emotional maturity:

- What is my attitude when I am faced with emotional shock? Am I capable of applying my adult Consciousness in these moments where a wound from the past reemerges? Am I capable of using this old trauma as a fertile obstacle that allows me to better know myself?
- Am I capable of listening to others, of assisting them without judgment? Do I still have enemies? (The enemy is no one other than myself. If I no longer have enemies, I am no longer my own enemy.)
- "Love thy neighbor as thyself." Am I capable of loving myself? Am I capable of loving another without wanting to possess him or her?

Here one can develop the exercise regarding abuse proposed in part 8 and question oneself, center by center, to know one's age intellectually, emotionally, creatively and sexually, and materially. In each of these four energies there are traces of the persistent child. The questions are meant not to shame or repress, but to help one better know one's energetic centers.

Over the course of three weeks ask yourself, center by center, what event most revealed your immaturity:

- Intellectual: perhaps due to hasty judgment, unbridled enthusiasm, confusion, or uncertainty

- Emotional: possibilities include an invasive "ego crisis," emotional confusion, anger, panic, jealousy, or sadness
- Creative-sexual: could be from blocks, or perhaps an abundance of uncontrollable energy
- Material: a regression in eating habits, conflicts over territory, or irrational fears

On what occasion did the persistent child manifest, and in what center? What age are you now, intellectually, emotionally, in your sexual and creative energy, in your body, in your territory, even in your daily life?

Visualize your "ideal age" in each center. What would a millennium be, creatively? What would the age of feelings be, charged with several centuries of experience? Or an intellect that is as old as the universe itself? According to you, what physical age would be ideal in a body that does not decay over time?

Truth or Lie

G. I. Gurdjieff created a movement called "Seekers after Truth," an ambitious enterprise mostly, doomed to fail because, to the limited understanding of our ego, Ultimate Truth is unknowable. However, we can strive to flush out the opposite, the lie, which entails a focus on nurturing one's attention.

This quest can stretch out into all domains, beginning with the society in which we live, the education we have received, and the dominant political or religious ideologies. When we fix our attention on a subject it is easy to flush out the false elements, but moreover this implies living our deepest vocation: differentiating our self from the masses is possible only if we are solidly anchored in personally satisfying activities. Subscription to uniformity is a by-product of dissatisfaction.

The most important work actually concerns our **interior lies.** We might say that the main lie comes from the ego when it does not serve the essential Being. All serious therapeutic, artistic, or spiritual work is a path toward authenticity. From the metagenealogical perspective this authenticity consists of relentlessly seeking to reveal our wild ideas, pathological feelings, implanted desires, and absurd needs.

In order to be our self, in order to flush out the lies, it helps to stop being self-critical. Disintegrating the inner judge is advisable, as is replacing this judge with a vigilant, objective observer that serves our growth.

This implies entering into an understanding of our self, totally accepting what we are without fail, in the same way that in order to succeed in Alcoholics Anonymous one must begin by publically declaring oneself an alcoholic. After verbally clarifying our defects, "Yes, I am a jealous, envious, social climbing egoist," we must then face our shame, disgust, guilt, and the many other negative feelings we inherited from childhood. A major obstacle to the future path consists of defending ourself constantly, which prevents us from seeing ourself.

- How can I radically differentiate myself from the masses without becoming imprisoned in a revolutionary attitude? If I am free from all ideology, how can I find something that interests me in everything?
- Am I capable of thinking objectively? What is the critical part in my daily thoughts?
- What ideas and ideologies do I still have attachments to? What social and religious morality does my tree hold over me?

Learning to Die

All work is based on being conscious of the fact that we are mortal. The ego must know it is going to disappear without any metaphysical comfort that sounds like a paradise: another world over there, reincarnation, resurrection. These possibilities are uncertain, so we must therefore leave them where they are: on the outside of our present being. If we manage to dominate, to destroy all hope in the future, if we accept our ephemeral nature, then we are truly our self. The only hope to which it is useful to adhere is of the immortality of Consciousness, which may then help us achieve our supreme goal of entering into contact with our source: the creative energy of the universe.

On the other hand, a personal goal of making the body immortal falls under selfish narcissism and is, in some way, a crime. To achieve our own immortality we must apply death to everyone but our self, seeing everyone and everything die since everything except us is ephemeral. Genuine maturity lies in the acceptance of this impermanence without clinging to the hope of an "over there," but without denying it either. Once the deep feeling of our own mortality is acquired, along with that of others, the mature person lives compassionately with the understanding that to be alive is a privilege, that time is precious, that gratuitous criticism does not make sense. We live among beings that disappear, but in a world where new life constantly shows up.

People who are apparently strong and mature can get to advanced age without having completed this work and have a kind of wisdom, but they will crumble when their parents disappear. Actually, it is normal to see our parents die, as evidenced in this Zen tale: The master says to the disciple, "Your grandfather dies, your father dies, you die, your son dies." The disciple protests, "How can you tell me such a thing?" The master: "Look at the order in which I told this to you."

The true desire in the genealogy tree is that death arrives in its appropriate time and order. One of the most important of the 613 mitzvot of the Jewish tradition consists of visiting the sick: accepting illness and death comes back to accepting eternity, which is in us. It then becomes clear that **infinity and eternity are part of us.** But before defeating death, we must encounter the fear and horror it inspires in us and understand that each of our four centers reacts differently toward death:

- The intellect agrees to dissolve it and is capable of total acceptance because death is synonymous with emptiness.
- For the emotional center dying means loving everything without limits, submerging in the Whole. It is the death of the other, or the definitive absence in our lives, that can create pain.
- For the sexual and creative center death consists of ceasing to create, ceasing to desire. The way of Buddhism proposes to break this link and advocates for the abolition of desire.

- The body itself manifests a total refusal of death: it does not want to die or age, and it cannot learn to be resigned to it.

The following exercises allow us, to a certain extent, to get closer to achieving detachment.

Undoing the Spell

If you find yourself still in compliance with the genealogy tree in one center or another, you can deliberately choose a theme and talk to each family member about it. This will serve to remove any remaining hidden content and return opinions, needs, emotions, or desires to their true ownership.

Example: Today, I want to treat the problem of money. I speak in the name of my own grandfather: "Money is hard to earn. One must not be ambitious but work modestly each day." My grandmother, who remained a widow, said, "My husband was a saint and shared everything he had. He left us financially ruined at the time of his death. I quickly understood that what was so lavish was actually very difficult to obtain: the world is populated with egoists and misers." My grandfather also said, "Earning a living is a combat! To make money, one must battle, compete, swindle, or crush others." My mother said, "Disgusting! All these filthy bills dirty my hands." My sister believed, "Thanks to my beauty, I deserve all the generosity of the world. I do not need to put any effort toward earning my living. A man will look after me because I deserve it."

One can make this exercise with any theme. Write the statements belonging to each member of the family on a sheet of paper, burn it, and then spread the ashes at the base of a plant for which the ashes will serve as fertilizer.

Detachment

Learning to detach from things enables us to allow them to be free to be what they are. So we live and act lightly, without anxiety. We let beings and events come freely.

In a comfortable position, with eyes closed, concentrate on this affirmation: "I do not need this or that, or to be this or that, to be me. To be this thing, this person, or this state, this thing, this person, or this state does not need me." Continue until you get to your final resistances.

Three Days of Nondiscrimination

- **A day of silence:** This is a fast from all distractions, including reading, television, music, and verbal interactions with others—are you capable of living in silence for a whole day?

- **An objective day:** Do not make any affirmation or negation that is not valuable to everyone. For example, one can say, "Today the temperature is twelve degrees." One cannot say, "It is cold." Also, one cannot say, "This person is good looking," or "This is delicious," or "You are naughty," or "You bore me." Ideally, the day should unfold without one saying the words "me" or "I." Note how many times you fell into subjective wording, if this is the case.

- **A day without criticism:** This is a day during which one does not say or think anything that constitutes a criticism, whether aesthetic, emotional, or ideological. Criticism cannot surface toward others, the world, or oneself. The day's mantra is "Yes."

Facing Death

Begin by asking yourself what age you want to live to. Compare this age with the eldest of the deceased from your genealogy tree. In what state do you imagine ending your days? Compare that with the end of life of others in your tree. Now, what is the longest duration of life achievable in the best possible conditions—what are you capable of imagining? To what point are you able to allow yourself the right to live and have joy in living? Write your own eulogy, imagining dying at the most advanced age possible, describing in detail how you got ready to peacefully die and the things that you fulfilled in this lifetime.

Concentrate in silence and stillness on the following affirmation for fifteen minutes: "I am going to die now. Everything I am, everything I have done, everything I gave, everything I accomplished—that's it and nothing more."

Laugh at Everything

You must first practice doing something for no reason. Study laughter as a purely physical action. Observe the movements of the diaphragm, respiration, the length of the bursts of laughter, the sound you produce. Continue to laugh, overcoming the inhibition that comes from "pretending." Once you are able to laugh voluntarily, begin to precede each burst of laughter with a phrase that expresses a problem, a personal or collective sadness.

"I am mortal, I am going to die! Ha ha ha." "I feel useless! Ha ha ha." "I am too old to (complete this phrase as you wish)! Ha ha ha." "I have problems with money! Ha ha ha." "Someone stole my car! Ha ha ha." "My parents don't love me! Ha ha ha!"

Gradually you are going to increase the gravity of the affirmations, laughing more and more, longer and longer.

"The planet is heating up and we are all going to die. Ha ha ha." "This person I love is dead. Ha ha ha." "This catastrophe killed so many people. Ha ha ha." "I am sick, I have cancer. Ha ha ha!"

Go as far as you can until you make the most awful statement possible that can cause a laugh, one which is more and more honest, more and more sincere, more and more overwhelming.

OUR INNER CHARACTERS

Obstacles and Allies

Earlier in this book we described the ways in which each of our centers can be colonized by another center. If we move from the theoretical plane to the symbolic plane these deviations of the ego can be assimilated by the inner characters who take turns commanding our lives. When we are not unified, and our actions are not in service of the transpersonal or essential Being, there is a strong chance that these fragmentations are still at work. Identifying and sublimating our own characters is a necessary stage before we can work on the exaltation of members of our genealogy tree. This will be our first step in the integration of deep forces of the Unconscious.

Actually, our genealogy tree deposits hierarchical structures and models of future archetypes in us, therefore modeling our conceptions of ourselves and of the visible or invisible worlds that will then influence all our spiritual imagination. According to the manner in which the relationships between the children and adults in the tree unfolded, a pantheon of incomplete archetypes formed within us in an obscure, even toxic way. Father, mother, and others are the framework on which we later weave our concept of the divinity, whether as a multitude of gods or as one unique God transmitted by angel, saints, sages, and prophets.

The work on the characters constitutes a first step in identifying this pantheon. We might say our characters are minor deities who possess us. In the same way that the multitudes of gods in polytheistic religions lead to intuition of the divine energy central in monotheism, **we have more "me" than it behooves us to identify and gather together to get to the transpersonal self.**

P. D. Ouspensky, paraphrasing Gurdjieff, said, "Man is never an *a*, he continually changes. He rarely remains identical, even in a half hour. . . . Now he is Ivan, one minute later he is Piotr and later still, Sergeï, Nicolas, Mathew, Simon. But you think all are Ivan. . . . You discover that Ivan lied and you are very surprised that he, Ivan, could do such a thing. It's true, Ivan cannot lie: it is Nicolas who lied. And, on each occasion, Nicolas will lie again because Nicolas *cannot stop himself from lying*. You will be amazed when you realize the multitude of these Ivan's and these Nicolas' who live in just one man."*

This continuously happens to us in daily life. How many times have you heard partners who break up say, "How could he or she have done that to me? I do not recognize him or her!" Similarly, when a

---

*Ouspensky, *In Search of the Miraculous*.

crisis situation occurs, one frequently discovers a completely unexpected aspect of the otherwise well-known person.

All of us carry a series of characters with somewhat defined contours who are active to varying degrees in our daily lives. Eventually and with constant effort all these aspects of me can be absorbed into a single person who harmoniously presents several faces emerging from a unified center. Frequently a person who has reached a high level of Consciousness is described by others as being extraordinarily present, but also gifted with many faces that coexist in a non-chaotic but harmonious way. For example, many disciples of the Indian saint Anandamayi Ma, who died in 1982, describe the way their guru constantly changed her expression and energy—in just a few seconds passing from childlike to the concentrated wisdom of a teacher or to the deepest mystical ecstasy. In the same way Characterology, astrology, and the Enneagram describe different "types" of characters, but fulfilled people will relate their experience of being human with the whole zodiac, with all of the types.

In the first place, the characters embedded within us are **obstacles** because they freeze aspects of the active identity, which then breaks up into several egos. We chaotically jump from one to the other according to circumstances, adopting elements of an old repertoire of preestablished solutions, facing endlessly changing conditions of life in a helter-skelter way. All the characters represent solutions from the past that we apply once again, but in a more or less useful way. As long as we are the toy of this succession of scattered characters, we can compare ourselves to an empty throne before which several contenders squabble to each take a turn.

But each of our characters has the **potential to return to the source;** each one is a piece of the puzzle that ultimately will form a complete image of our personality. In other words, an archetype nests behind each character, an ally who can help us move toward a closer union with the essential Being. We must embrace the obstacle, clearly identifying each character to lead it to its ultimate fulfillment, discovering in each of these fragments of ourselves the inner resources that drive us toward excellence.

Moreover, each character that makes us up is an inner survivor of the genealogy tree. Each character is shaped by imitation, compensation, opposition, or interpretation of perceived heritage. Work on these characters allows us to dissolve the last elements of "identity" that are in reality many contracts with the past.

For example, if I had a hard and crushing father who terrified me, several inner characters can be derived from my relationship with him. It is possible that I have developed a slave character, servile and full of rancor but incapable of rebelling. It is also possible that I carry a character similar to my father inside of myself, capable of manifesting a terrifying rage but unable to control it. In my relationships, one or the other of these two characters emerges according to the way in which the other treats me, but the characters will be useless and neurotic as long as they remain a mere imitation of my father or a reproduction of my own scared-child attitude.

My work then will consist of identifying the slave character and the tyrant character, giving them each a name of my choice, and recognizing them whenever they manifest. To do this, I must create or consolidate a **central character,** guide and moderator of the multitude with which I live. In distinctly naming the "slave me" (Moochy Rat, for example) and the "tyrant me" (Captain Cannon, for example), I begin to de-identify from my own acquired identity. I am no longer only J. Doe, but rather I am this multitude of individuals whose behavior I can leisurely observe. Bit by bit the characters begin to reveal their unsuspected potential. It is possible that Moochy Rat, who is usually a quiet, non-active observer, is capable of extraordinary thoroughness and reveals his artistic talents, gifted mathematician's mind, or diplomatic skills. At the point where I no longer merely react when in situations similar to those of my childhood, but I reinforce peaceful or productive situations, it will be possible to activate his talents.

Until now, Captain Cannon did not explode unless he was sure to win. If I intentionally decide to call him when faced with a person who scares me (as my father scared me), I recruit him to stand my ground in front of the enemy, and he becomes the best ally to my authority as I learn to win battles under his guidance. It may also be useful for courage and perseverance, inner work, or a healthy confirmation to put the qualities of healing into service for personal growth.

All knots and cores, by making us act under compulsion, keep us from identifying our inner characters. Inversely, our awareness of these characters allows us to face the knots and dissolve them. Frequently, we are possessed by characters created by the genealogy tree that we have adhered to in order to not be excluded.

Example: A consultant still suffered at forty years of age from a strong devaluation. At his birth his mother had exclaimed, "It's a devil!" She then named him Giuseppe (Joseph, like the biblical character) in order to deactivate his predicted diabolical nature. But actually his first name, which is a reference to the supposedly asexual spouse of the Virgin Mary, negates the little boy's masculine identity. The study of Giuseppe's genealogy tree revealed the fact that he was the second son among his siblings, the first having been named Salvatore after their maternal grandfather, whose name was Savior. One may then deduce that the first son was considered as the Christ child, and with that role having already been distributed, Giuseppe was entrusted with the role of the devil: the dark side of the male.

A lot of sexual abuse had been perpetrated in Giuseppe's genealogy tree, and it can be argued that his mother carried an unconscious hatred toward men as a result of this abuse, which she had projected onto the little boy since his birth. Nonetheless, Giuseppe's psyche contained the remains of an encrusted maternal rejection, and the devil "character" haunted him, accompanied by a feeling of intense ugliness. His psychomagic act consisted of making this devil character exist in reality, and not just any devil but his own, to which he gave the name Judas. He dressed in the skin of this character for one week, walking in the streets wearing a red costume complete with horns and a tail while carrying a trident. He took many photos of himself in daily life situations, which he then sent to his family. At the end of this work, he buried the devil costume and raised this infantile character to an angelic dimension: if a devil is just a fallen angel, one can imagine that the devil rises up to become an angel. In the case of Giuseppe, this experience allowed him to recognize his vocation as a poet and to publish his first collection of poems.

Work on Inner Characters: Seven Steps
Identify Them

Identify as many characters as you can that are inside you, and name each of them individually. It is essential to name them because otherwise the characters remain fragments of your acquired personality. If you are Alice, your characters cannot be "shy Alice," "intellectual Alice," or "traveling Alice."

Distinctly naming these "me" instances allows for the dismemberment of the acquired "I" or false self and facilitates the diminishment of its power.

The characters must have at least one first and last name, a title and a last name, or a title and a first name. They are not necessarily all the same sex (a man can have one or more female characters and vice versa), and they can be different nationalities, or even half human, half animal. One person could have, for example, characters by the name of Luisa Sainthypocrite, Tiger Lionhunter, Doctor Bling, Jealous Dog, and Rosita Tamales.

Define Them

Define each character as precisely as possible according to the following questions:

- What is its motto, its favorite maxim for life?
- In what circumstances did it emerge? What are the situations in which it feels competent? When does it disappear? What scares it the most?
- In the situations where it shows up, what is its usefulness (real or imagined)?

- What are its qualities or defects?
- What does it physically look like? What kind of voice does it have, what does it eat, how is its body, how fast does it die?
- What are its opinions? How does it vote? What does it read? Where is it from?
- What gives it satisfaction? What are its pleasures and its tastes?
- Who are its friends? Enemies? With whom would it like to align? Whom does it admire? What occupation gives it most joy? What are its preferred travel or vacation destinations? What is its favored mode of transportation?

Bring Them to Life Artistically

Write a short story or monologue, paint, draw, or represent each character you have successfully identified in some way. You can also imagine that each day of the week a different character will do the cooking.

Live in Consciousness with Them

Once each character is clear to you, you will have the opportunity to observe their appearance in your reality for a given time period. When they show up, recognize their existence and give them free reign to act (within reason; if a violent character appears, it is not necessary to demolish a car or slap someone). Then examine their actions. If a character is positive, give that character credit. If negative, identify to what deviation of the ego it belongs, as you did earlier when defining each character.

Relate Them to the Genealogy Tree

Can you identify what your age was when each character began to develop? What relationships or familial circumstances led you to create it? Does it have any resemblance to a member of the genealogy tree? Is it diametrically opposed to anyone in particular?

Summon Them in Difficult Situations

Once you can identify the characters, imagine situations where the competencies of each one can be useful. Even if you do not feel capable of acting as the character in such situations in reality, visualize yourself trying to solve them. For example, give a sweet and diplomatic character the opportunity to resolve a conflict that is overwhelming you now, or give an intellectual character the opportunity to solve a problem in an area that is foreign to you.

Exalt Them

Ask each one, "What is the characteristic, the energy you need, to truly become a hero, a genius, a saint, a champion? And through what experience or what alliance could you achieve this quality?"

Even if the character is, on the surface, ridiculed or limited it still possesses the potential for fulfillment. What you agree to give to your characters will actually be a contribution to your united me.

Allies and the Creative Imagination

In the same way that we can differentiate between the characters inhabiting us so we can transform them into tools for the service of our fulfillment, we can summon seemingly exterior archetypes to allow them to breathe the life of transpersonal qualities into us. The practice of forming an alliance with suprahuman forces is the basis of shamanism, but it is also present in universal imagination through fairy tales and legends where the hero receives help from supernatural allies. Once we recognize the acquired personality in its caricatural multiplicity, we are ready to integrate an ally.

At this point we must define the term "ally" from the metagenealogical perspective. Our basic assumption is that we possess knowledge that we are not aware of. Whether it is latent content in the human brain, in the form of "cellular memories" inscribed in the body or in the collective Unconsciousness, or the memory present in humanity from our experience in the larval state, we can postulate that there exists an immense reservoir of knowledge within our reach that is available but hidden. Similarly, energies that the intellect cannot grasp are obviously circulating in the universe. Also present in minerals, vegetation, and animals, these energies are represented in a more advanced form by the mythical beings of human or divine nature, some specific to a particular culture and others belonging to all of humanity. In attempting to identify these energies, symbolic disciplines often join forces with seemingly distinct elements (for example, in certain astrology manuals Aries is associated with Mars, sage, the color red, and the head), as if some energy exists between them. Traditional magic is fond of these lists of analog correspondences.

When a task seems to be beyond our known abilities and we feel powerless to accomplish what we need to, it becomes necessary and possible to **awaken a latent energy** as an alliance with a specific element that represents it. Only a superhuman entity, an accumulation of transpersonal energy can impart forces that transcend our individual identity. In reality, the ally is an energy without a fixed contour: not something like a tiger or an object made of gold, but the energy symbolized by a Tiger, the energy connected to Gold. Thus the shaman is associated with the eagle (and, through him, with the collective spirit of the Eagle) to enable us to rise above daily concepts to develop a broader vision. Before appearing on stage, an artist may call upon a saint or a divinity to give him the strength to carry out an extraordinary performance. In a similar way, when Jacques Lacan said, "You all can be Lacanian, I will remain Freudian," he shows in a Western fashion a rationally acceptable truth that the shamans know: one cannot be one's own ally. **The archetype is a point of symbolic accumulation of energy that we summon to take action.**

The human psyche has the capacity to put itself in the place of another. Whenever we live as finite, defined beings and see ourselves confined by physical existence we set a limit (desirable in certain activities of daily life) on our energies, our time, and our space, on our life and our capacities. When we put ourselves in another's place we begin to understand and imagine attitudes and feelings that are not "ours," but that reside "in us," all of which have the capacity to enrich us. If actors or singers gets so deeply into a character that they become Hamlet or Norma for two hours, completely living this momentary incarnation, it allows them to access guides, a

Consciousness, emotions, and a capacity of communication whose agent they do not know.

Similarly, we can all put ourselves in the place of a sublime character. The most powerful archetype will be the creative Consciousness of the universe that monotheism defines as one God. This king archetype can subdivide into a multitude of secondary divinities, angels, saints, and symbols that represent more individualized fragments of the same energy.

We have seen that all illness, all suffering, results from a lack of Consciousness and its "secondary divinities": love, beauty, creativity. As such, we can postulate that in our Supraconsciousness these levels of Consciousness, and very elevated energies of divine nature, exist in the latent stage. The question is how we can get to them.

The proposition that we make here is that we can imitate them, put them "in the place of," but also that we can give them a place inside of us. All work on the allies is made of this double movement: defining a space inside ourself so the ally can reside there, while simultaneously obtaining permission to put ourself in its place through an alliance with it in order to speak on its behalf. The ally can just as well be a teacher who guides us as an assistant who helps us. It is not necessarily a superior archetype according to the dominant ideology of the world in which we live but is quite capable of being useful. A cow or an ass is as valuable an ally as an angel or a wizard.

Up until now we have worked with analysis, guided by the intellect, and with the intuitive aspects that allow us to identify our characters. Another instance now comes into consideration: the **creative imagination,** which is our capacity to create scenarios in which the coherence and authenticity fall within us with the same strength as a living memory.

The term **imagination** integrates two main activities of the spirit. One is nomadic and functions according to "principles of production" from already existing elements. This imagination, in which we are spectators, proceeds by multiplication (agitation), reduction (dwarf characters), or association (monsters that are half man, half beast). The other, which Henry Corbin called "Imaginal," designates an imaginative capacity that consists of creating situations that exceed reality, and can go as far as experiences produced by hallucinogenic drug use. It is a kind of voluntary awake dream where the imagined experiences incarnate in us. Instead of dreaming an adventure about a hero outside of us, we become the hero; instead of seeing a sleeping virgin whom a prince awakens with a kiss, we become this young woman who is awakened by the feeling of her lover's lips on hers.

For Islamic psychology (or better, psychosophie), the creative imagination constitutes the central faculty of the soul. For this philosophical tradition Corbin tells us that the imagination possesses "its own Noetic and cognitive function, that is to say it gives us access to a region and a reality of Being which without that function remains closed and forbidden to us."* This power of the soul opens the being and its experience to a supersensible world: not the world known by the senses, or that known by the intellect, but a third space that is an inter-world between the perceptible and the comprehensible. Some authors call this the "world of the soul."

In order to exist with the sublime integration of entities in ourselves as a decisive experience, and later in the totality of the tree, we must use this form of imagination. It requires a complete indifference to the doubts formulated by the intellect, an extreme concentration of attention like we use in meditation, and therefore a constant contact with our capacity to **imagine physical sensations:** to see with the eyes closed, to sense an odor that is absent, to taste imaginary flavors, to feel imagined movements.

The work of integrating an ally is both **active and receptive.** This has to do less with leaving oneself open to being possessed by any entity, and more with the question, "If I could provide myself with an available energy in the universe that I need in this moment, what would I

---

*Corbin, *Spiritual Body & Celestial Earth.*

choose? And what is the element, vegetable, animal, character, or archetype that spontaneously incarnates this energy for me?" The choice of ally is therefore a rational and reasoned method that must represent a quality that we lack, possessing a strength symbolically sufficient to exist on a plane that goes beyond the genealogy tree, society, or culture. The spirit groups of animals, plants, sacred places, divinities, or memorable historical characters are all possible allies that they have a universal dimension. As a beginner in working with energetic allies, it is more hazardous to call on a movie star, cartoon character, or person you once knew since these symbolic representations are susceptible to being marred by remnants of abuse and knots present in or around the tree. As a general rule, it is better to secure the strength of strong archetypes before forming an alliance with a secondary archetype.

Then, in the next step you will be able to realize that all the characters or people who sparked your admiration are actually reflections of qualities that want to grow in you. You will therefore be able to make an alliance with these kinds of characters: a writer or a celebrated artist, a politician, a person who helped your family, a television star, an athlete, or a character in a video game.

An important phase of mourning consists in integrating a departed person as an ally. If the deceased person was a parent or primary caregiver in your childhood and was an adult when you were a child, it is best to first complete all necessary work on the genealogy tree in order to receive only positive energy from him or her.

Here are some paths to use to work on these allies.

Steal the Light

It is permitted to "steal the light" (Consciousness, beauty, charisma), since this theft does not deprive anyone. For this exercise, choose an archetype or a real person who possesses a talent, grace, or quality of being—these transpersonal qualities are endless—to which you respond.

Lie down on the ground and concentrate on this person. Visualize his movements and his actions, listen to his words, feel the quality of energy that this person brings. Then begin to integrate these elements that you first saw as being outside of yourself into sensations in your own body, bearing in mind that you can only be sensitive to qualities that lie latent within you. If the character of your choice dances or sings, imagine you dance or sing like him. If he is capable of remaining in deep meditation for hours, feel this state. Regardless of the activity that he is capable of, imagine that it is you who functions with this same mastery. Then visualize your model again, bow before him, and thank him for having revealed your own qualities. Conclude this exercise with the statement, "The light that I see is the light that I carry in me."

Creative Imagination for Feeling the Body of an Ally

This meditation provides a practical way to integrate the energy of a meta-terrestrial force that moves beyond family, society, and culture and can serve as a mediator with the sublime part of oneself. An ally can fill gaps left by the genealogy tree; for example, in the absence of a father, one could integrate an ally who constitutes a strong paternal presence. An ally can also wake up energies that are blocked or dormant within us, like the capacity to love, courage, creativity, authority, responsibility, clairvoyance, and strength.

We note that like any living being, the ally that one chooses has a heart and a **breath**. If the ally is a metal or a plant this breath and this heart are part of a collective and are united to the whole planet. The base of the heart is love; the base of the breath is **union, introversion, and sharing.**

For example, three possible allies are an oak tree, a lion, and Christ:

- Concentrate on the heart of the ally that you wish to call. In the case of an oak tree, its heart is the union of all the roots of the oak trees in the forest, and it is an essentially collective being. The heart of the lion is strong and powerful, and it corresponds to the needs of a carnivorous, solitary predator. The heart of Christ himself is much stronger than that of a wild animal, but its heartbeats are not those of a hunter; they are full of compassion for the world, impregnated with a charitable energy. Feel the heartbeat of the ally in unison with yours.

- Now concentrate on the breath of the ally. The oak breathes from all its leaves. During the day, thanks to the light of the sun, it produces oxygen, which allows other beings to breathe; at night, it breathes like us, absorbing oxygen and giving off carbon dioxide. The air inhaled by the lion strengthens him, while the exhalation comes from his lungs like a weapon and allows him to roar. The breath of Christ draws in polluted air, purifies it in his heart, and exhales it as a gift of purity to the world. Unite your breath with that of the ally you have chosen.

Imaginative Meditation of the Integration of an Ally

Stretch yourself out on the ground. Imagine that your body relaxes little by little while you identify the colors of the rainbow, which will allow the spirit to relax by freeing the mind of words and helping it become more receptive to images. Physical relaxation consists of letting the body live its own life, leaving aside the tree's cellular memory and your individual memory of abuse, pain, and deprivations, allowing space only for the present and its possibilities.

The color red is imagined for the feet, which gradually relax. The color orange relaxes the legs; they live their own lives. The color yellow allows the whole region of the hips, pubis, genitals, and lower back to relax. Green relaxes the entire abdomen, including the stomach and viscera; the muscles of the back also rest little by little on the ground. Light blue allows the lungs, chest, shoulders, arms, and hands to relax. Indigo relaxes the throat, neck, and the whole spinal column. With the color violet the head and face relax, the tongue loosens, and in the image of a muscle, the brain rests too.

Once this relaxation is accomplished, count backward from nine to enter more deeply into yourself. Arriving at zero, imagine that an axis of light emerges from your navel that lifts you as high as the sky, feeling, not seeing, the ascension of your phantom body (your perfect body) as it rises the length of this axis of light into the sky. The area of the sky where you arrive is calm, clear, lighted, and tranquil. You are naked and light, and you feel a pleasant breeze take you toward your inner territory. This landscape can be a country, the woods, a body of water, a mountain . . . it is you who discovered it, so trust yourself. In this space there is no danger. You see your personal place emerge from the ground: temple, laboratory, palace, or house. You enter into this place as it pleases you, walking or flying. There, at the center of this private place, summon your ally and see him arrive.

You then make contact with him. He gives you a gift that you integrate into your body, which can be any of a variety of things: a key, an object, lines he writes in your book, or simply a state of being like joy or love that he communicates to you. But do not ever forget that this ally makes up part of the superior dimension of yourself, your Unconsciousness, from where he descended to grant you this grace in the space that you have prepared for him. You can embrace your ally, make love with him, dance with him—the encounter unfolds as you wish.

Afterward, the ally enters into you and melts there. You then return in the same way as you arrived: you leave your private place, letting the breeze carry you, finding the axis of light and descending toward your physical body, which you reconnect with on the ground. Then, starting with your feet, you begin to feel your present life again by imagining the colors of the rainbow. You can now return to your usual state.

Make an Altar

Once the alliance is complete, it may be useful to sanctify a place (which symbolizes your ally and beyond, the whole world) to gather representations of the forces with which you work. These figurines, photos, pebbles, and other objects of your choosing are actually a point of completion and an anchoring of energies allied with those with which you work. They may also be considered to be places of "energy storage." Little by little you can add representations that call to you: little sculptures, images, mineral or vegetable elements, incense, perfumes, candles. All of these items are actually metaphorical representations of energies that you wish to keep present in yourself as a kind of reminder of self.

An established altar, clean and maintained, is a place where you can deposit questions or problems that you cannot solve alone in the form of a letter, a photo of a person who is dear to you, or anything that relates to your situation. The altar will "work" for you if you maintain it. From the moment you dedicate a consecrated place, be it a small shelf, mantle piece, or table top, if you dedicate yourself to the representation of the forces with which you made an alliance, it becomes possible from that point on to little by little sanctify the whole world.

Let Your Allies Talk, Act, Decide

From the point at which the relationship with your allies is established, you can spend quality time letting them talk or act in you. For example, you can allow them to write in your place, to speak to you during meditation, or to dance to your choice of music. Later, in difficult situations, you can rely on them to help in a variety of ways. When consoling a person who has suffered a loss that overwhelms you, it will be possible to invoke a wiser ally who is more experienced than you, allowing this ally to speak and act.

Each person discovers the forms and pertinent rituals for the allies he or she has integrated in his or her own time. A number of processes for this are described in the religious or magical practices of the world.

FROM GENEALOGICAL TRAP TO TREASURE

The Tree Altar

In order to heal the tree we must begin by posing the question, "Who are the members of the family that I wish to include in this work?" There must be at least fourteen: the two parents, the four grandparents, and the eight great-grandparents. But we can add brothers, sisters, uncles, aunts, godfathers, godmothers, or other important people.

As with all the characters we carry within us, there are inherited aspects of the genealogy tree that contain certain qualities and neuroses. And as with all the allies that we are capable of choosing, these reflect the latent, sublime aspects in the tree. It is in this capacity that **the tree becomes a treasure and not a trap:** when we are capable of facing the facts of these shortcomings and of invoking their positive, creative, and healing forces they can provide for us. None of these energies are actually foreign to the tree. As we have previously stated, the deepest bonds that circulate in the lineage—in spite of the abandonment, the betrayal, the humiliations, and the abuse—are bonds of love. Very often, however, the people who have preceded us did not live in service to the essential Being, and these qualities have remained in a potential state.

Thus, the tree's ultimate healing always consists of the work of the creative imagination to disperse these latent qualities and to give each ancestor the **ultimate fulfillment of his destiny imaginable.**

Indeed, as we have seen, my brother or sister's tree—even if all the members are the same—is not the same as mine. As such, my healed tree will always be unique because I am the only one with my specific ability to decipher and fulfill the destiny of my ancestors, and to bestow upon them the forces they lacked. This work will consist of injecting these qualities and/or these allies into the genealogy tree and imagining the fulfilled destiny of each of its members.

For example, a great-grandmother who was a frustrated singer, an unloving mother, a woman confined to a house and cheated on by her husband, who grew bitter with age, might be exalted in various ways by a great-grandchild according to how she was fulfilled in her own life through artistic, emotional, or relational qualities. For one, the ally who can heal her great-grandmother will be Maria Callas; for another, it will be the archetype of the female divinity; for yet another, it will be a great explorer, and so on. Just as the altar is a specific, finite area from which it is possible to sanctify the whole world, the healed tree is a specific group of humans from which it is possible to sanctify all of humanity.

A number of shamanic practices advocate healing the ancestors with dances, chants, rituals, or other endeavors accomplished by the descendants and dedicated to the ancestors. From the moment where the ancestors are healed, cleansed of their faults or their errors, they can become divinities or allies. Native Americans assimilate natural elements into their genealogy trees; for example, the river is the grandfather, the prairie is the grandmother. This means both a reverence toward nature, which begets and nourishes us, and a sacralization of real ancestors who, once disappeared, return to get involved with natural elements and therefore in their turn become a source of life and energy for those who follow.

When the forces of the past are very active and draw us toward our origins and already-known models, the ancestors are harmful and can be related to demons. When our genealogy tree pushes us toward the future, toward the creativity inherent to Consciousness, our ancestors become allies, collaborating in the development of humanity. In the same way, this allows us to consider all the beings that have worked for Consciousness, progress, beauty, and love to also be our ancestors. We can symbolically integrate Michelangelo and Buddha into our tree if we consider that they too have made contributions that help us create. Works of sacred art and the creation books of the great religions can all become allies.

Healing our tree includes conferring on our own ancestors, by way of creative imagination, a dimension similar to what we attribute to these saviors of humanity. To accomplish this we must offer one or more archetypes to each member of the tree in order to complete them and to allow us to exalt their destinies.

We must not confuse this individual work with a situation that we have already briefly mentioned: the presence of an exceptional character in the genealogy tree. When the familial story presents us with a genius of the past with an unsurpassable human achievement, we may be left with nothing to live for. As such, this ancestor who is "richer," "smarter," "more beautiful," "more creative," or "stronger" is not useful to his descendants, but he becomes, to the contrary, a heavy model to carry because his energy remains stagnant in him and is not transmitted to the lineage. Our goal is to integrate all the values of the tree by offering these unsurpassable ancestors further development in the future. If a genius, saint, champion, or hero existed in the family, the trap would be to think that his biography, values, and individual me that is consequently inimitable are the tree's riches. In this way, we would mistakenly believe this ancestor must be considered to be a carrier of energy for our personal fulfillment. However, there are many ways to avoid this trap: the son of a great artist can become a grand financier who manages the inheritance of his father, exercising his personal talent as a man of business; the son of a philosopher can become a monk, and the daughter a great therapist; or the child of a saint can become a fashion designer.

By definition, **everything we give to the genealogy tree we give to ourselves.** There is no lack or rivalry. If I "offer" a strong ally to an abusive or absent ascendant, I do not deprive myself. On the contrary, I strengthen myself. Once each character of the tree is fulfilled, the tree dissolves in me and disappears. We might say that the goal of all the work is to forgive God, the Universe, or nature, for killing us. No one readily accepts death; for our individual egos it is a huge injustice, and the tree's healing is not possible without this forgiveness. Acceptance of death, being able to feel gratitude for the perspective of our disappearance, requires that we realize it is a gift that allows humanity to attain immortality. And, at the same time, it allows us to let the genealogy tree "die" in order for it to live through us and through our fulfillment during our existence. That is why we can heal the tree only after having integrated all the allies that are needed for ourselves.

Similarly, it not possible to live with a tree in which some people who remain do not love us, cause problems for us, or cause us shame or horror. The genealogy tree gave us life and we carry it within us. All criticism or residual rejection from it corresponds to a non-acceptance of our selves. The work then consists not of accepting the tree as it is, which would actually provide for a lower level of Consciousness, but of understanding the tree, which is the whole point of this book. Exalting each member by way of reinvention, especially those who carry the darkest parts, gives their destinies and vital energies an outlet that we can accept.

To accomplish this, here are some suggestions for actions that can assist you in reconsidering and re-creating your lineage:

- Examine your own actual level of Consciousness, then that of each member of the tree. Each member who has experienced an inferior level of Consciousness to yours can be symbolically elevated by, for example, adding an anecdote to his life. If a member of the lineage attained a superior level of Consciousness to yours, what efforts can you make to raise yourself to that level?

- Once a successful effort has been made, return to work on the purpose for you. What is the goal of supreme fulfillment available to all human beings? Do not judge, but honestly express this aim. For example, if your universal and personal goals are to become a millionaire, find a path for each character of the tree that will allow them to attain this goal (perhaps by finding oil, playing the stock exchange, building a company). If your supreme goal is sainthood, genius, enlightenment, or immortality, use the same approach to create a kind of familial novel where each attains this goal in their own way, all the way back to your great-grandparents.

- Apply the exercise of the perfect body to everyone in the genealogy tree. Begin with your parents. Meditate on the perfect body for each member of the family, noticing which mineral, vegetable, animal, or archetypal allies spontaneously come into your thoughts for each one.

- Offer your own talents to all the members of your family. If you are a painter, ask if you can paint each of the members of the tree; if you are an athlete, imagine what excellence they could achieve in this area; if you practice a religion or if you meditate, imagine reaching perfect union with the divinity or one's Self; if you are an actor, give each member a role in a real or imaginary production. Example: A cartoonist felt blocked in his work and suffered inexplicable physical pain. His genealogy tree consisted of twenty-four people; he therefore asked twenty-four people to massage him, each representing a member of the tree. During the collective massage, he felt his body was a spaceship (like those he loved to draw) and all twenty-four people were part of his oeuvre. This act gave him energy to create and to live.

In order to complete this work, we can learn or deepen our understanding of some of the exercises already discussed.

The Race of the Tree's Characters

While you are meditating, imagine a long road in the landscape of your desire. Put all of your family on a starting line there, including yourself, and start a race. You are going to discover what happens, what doesn't happen, who cheats, who fights with whom. First, envision that members of the trapped tree become involved in a conflict that includes injuries, deceptions, and a winner. Then, begin the race again with a new vision whose goal is not that only one person wins, but that everyone arrives at the finish line. The family begins then to help one another, and you imagine how through this familial solidarity everyone reaches the goal.

The Ball

All members of the paternal and maternal trees are seated in an enormous ballroom. First have one branch dance, then the other, as if two balls were juxtaposed. Little by little members of the two branches of the tree mix and the ball becomes a combined circle of dancing, in the center of which you find yourself, surrounded by your whole family.

Make a Collage of the Healed Tree

Once you have explored all the members of your genealogy tree and discovered how to exalt them, you can make a collage that represents the healed tree in a useful way. The outline of the tree will be the same as that which we presented in part 2, but reversed.

Place your fulfilled goal, and the consequences of the realization of this individual purpose on society, culture, and the whole of humanity, at the base of the tree. For example, "I am perfectly happy and fulfilled in my emotional life. My company prospers and I participate in sustain-

Me and my allies							
Mother and allies				Father and allies			
Maternal grandparents and allies				Paternal grandparents and allies			
			Great grandparents and parent allies				
My fulfillment: Society, culture, and humanity are fulfilled as the result of my fulfillment. Immortality of humanity.							

able development. Thanks to my actions and those of my associates, the planet has become a marvelous garden, the economy has been purified, science has evolved, and human beings can live in abundance, creativity, and brotherhood."

You can place your fulfilled great-grandparents on this new terrain that you have built: their past existence, all the historical circumstances, social taboos, and traditions to which they are attached are now in contact with the world you have created. Your great-grandparents are therefore retrospectively free to completely fulfill themselves and move beyond the abuse, trauma, and injustice they had been victims of during their lifetime.

"My great-grandparents recovered their land, and instead of being agricultural workers they were independently wealthy. They were able to travel and discover the world. My great-grandmother, inflicted by a degenerative illness of the joints, was cared for, lived to be one hundred, and became a famous painter."

You can establish the fulfilled destiny of your grandparents, then your parents, and finally your own, by using the fulfilled destinies of your great-grandparents. Each member of the tree attains his or her personal accomplishments.

At each stage of the tree, choose one or more images that symbolize the allies you wish to "offer" to each member of the tree. Make the collage with each one receiving the image to which they correspond.

This imaginative work for healing the tree does not guarantee that all the relationships among living members of the clan will become harmonious, but it can contribute to it. When individual Consciousness awakens in each one of us, we become capable of elevating the clan's Consciousness. Even if conflicts or misunderstandings appear to persist between members, the work of healing the tree produces a real transformation, preparing the terrain for a progressive mutation of the relationships. It comes back then to each person making their own life path. Obviously, we cannot influence the awakening of Consciousness in another, but the ultimate goal of this work is that truth and love circulate between members of the same family.

Moreover, even if this seems like a utopia for the disgruntled spirits, this work also advances a positive transformation of society. From the point of view of the past, all society is a union of individuals driven by a common will on the material, cultural, religious, political, and ideological planes. But even if each of us vaguely seeks to fulfill our essential Being, to live according to the most elevated level of Consciousness, the deep desire (Supraconsciousness) of the clan, and therefore of society, is to attain collective Consciousness—which is union with the totality of humanity. As such, it is only possible if a significant number of people reach transpersonal Consciousness. Below this level, the clan and society exist only in the defensive mode, united against a common enemy.

The motto inscribed in the roof of the Greek temple of Apollo at Delphi is extremely famous: "Know thyself." But Greek wisdom added a corollary: "Nothing too much."

The work that we have accomplished can be summarized by this dual maxim. Thus, first know yourself as an individual with four centers, and as a product of a genealogy tree. Then eliminate all of your baggage by overcoming harmful habits from all four centers, and endeavor to not live a life of repetition. The parents become "too much" one day and the child must leave the familial space. Even a spiritual or religious theory can become "too much" at a given moment of growth of Consciousness. Social ostentation in all its forms is "too much" as one moves beyond.

After letting go of ideas, feelings, desires, and excessive needs, one gets to greater obstacles: the me is also "too much." This is what awakens the until-then buried transpersonal Consciousness. Once one has discovered all that was unnecessary in one's self and overcomes it, one can begin to help others do the same. That is how the Nous makes sense: union between two beings; union between man and the divine; union between two instances of oneself, the individual personality and Consciousness.

> *In truth, we are only one soul, you and me*
> *We appear and we hide in one another, you in me,*
>   *me in you.*
> *Here, the deep sense of my relationship with you*
> *Between you and me, you and me do not exist*
> *we are the mirror and the face at the same time*
> *we are the drunk and the eternal cup*
> *we are the salve and the healing*
> *we are the water of youth and the one who pours it.**

---

*Jalāl ad-Dīn Muhammad Rūmī, *Roubâ'yât*. (Translated from French here by Rachael LeValley.)

EPILOGUE

From the Soul to the World

By Alejandro Jodorowsky

A person who heals his tree by dissolving the names, physical appearances, and personal histories of each parent, transforming it all into vital energy, becomes filled with a healthy joy for living, free of the ties that bound him to the past. This person can feel the sacred character of everything surrounding him, knowing that everything is linked to everything else, everything is possible, everything is living and can respond, there is always a way to loosen what is stagnant, and the world finds its way. Abandoning hope and goals, this person lets the way guide her, and she trusts life. The person with a healed tree knows that every thought in the world attracts its equivalent, that in a certain way reality is his mirror and, at the same time, the result of that which we are and that which we believe we can be. If we desire defeat, the world becomes our enemy and helps us to fail. If we hope to triumph, the world becomes our ally.

The person who healed his tree also knows that real experiences and dreams imprint in the memory in a similar way, and therefore, treating reality as if it were a lucid dream, he introduces acts to transform events in a positive way. This person is sure that by eliminating mental limitations he will pacify these emotions, cleanse his desires, and become useful to others.

An abundance of psychological problems, emotional and sexual dissatisfaction, and becoming a slave to useless desires promoted by the media can all distract individuals who are attached to the past and an illusory future created by illusions and infantile terrors. Once the tree is healed, those who reach spiritual health know that the moment in which something can be accomplished is here right now—not yesterday, not tomorrow. The totality of the past exists in the present, as does the powerful seed of what will be in the future. By abandoning all distraction the person can focus her thoughts, feelings, and desires on what she really needs to know or fulfill. There, where she concentrates her attention to the maximum, she can capture the miracle.

I do not speak of extraordinary phenomena like levitation, statues that cry blood, the odor of sanctity, the multiplication of loaves, changing water to wine, the capacity to walk on water and bring the dead back to life, or walking on hot coals. Spectacular events that are impossible not to notice can be considered by anyone with sufficient faith to be indicators of the existence of God.

When I speak of **miracles,** I am referring to the whole universe seen from a new level of Consciousness. The person who has tamed his personal ego and put it into service of the essential Being, who has ceased to live on his mental island, harnesses the outer world and himself as a unit. The person does not have to live in a reduced space but feels at every instance that he lives in a combination of infinite universes, that the time of clocks is a miniscule tick-tock between an eternal past and future, that his body is a mysterious machine operated by an all-powerful energy that one calls **life.**

This life exists everywhere, from the smallest particle of matter to the exorbitant stars that populate the cosmos and dance there. Every beat of the heart, every breath, every cell, every thought, every emotion, every desire is a miracle, in the same way that all leaves, every blade of grass, every flower is a miracle. To see, to hear, to touch, to smell, to eat, to digest, to excrete, to birth, to die—all are sublime miracles stirred by an unimaginable creative force. A conscious being of immense and extraordinary character lives in the world with gratitude, blessing every second of his existence in this endless wonder. If he stagnated previously in rational confinement, a prisoner of his body and separated from the exterior, nevertheless he and the world are on the same wavelength as a strip of light, an infinite ensemble whereby all parts resonate in unison. What is important is not applauding or producing extraordinary phenomena, but **learning to consider the world and oneself as sacred work.** Generally, people consider life to be a natural phenomenon in which one profits without giving anything in exchange. But the miracle requires an exchange: what we were given, we must share with others. If we are not united, we cannot grasp the miracle.

Once she has attained a high level of Consciousness, a person can help those who have not yet reached this level by teaching or sharing without asking for, or expecting, anything in return. This creates psychomiracles and sets off a positive reaction in others.

At twenty-three years of age I dedicated my whole life to the art of pantomime. One month before getting on the boat for France, I had my first encounter with free generosity when I met an extraordinary woman by the name of Chabela Eastman. Tall, dignified, and elegant, fitted with an abundance of curly white hair, with beautiful lines outlining her face, she was the spouse of a multimillionaire who owned a chain of newspapers. A lover of classical music, it was she who brought the famous conductor Sergiu Celibidache to our distant Chile.

Chabela attended a mime show that I gave in a little theater, to a paltry audience. She paid me a visit in my dressing room and enthusiastically invited me to dinner in the garden of her immense abode. The splendor of the dishes, the excellent roast duck with orange sauce, the liveried servants in white gloves—all increased my shyness. I went mute and began to shake. She thought I was cold and ran inside and returned carrying an enormous vest of black wool.

With best wishes she forced me to wear it, saying, "It belongs to Celibidache. He left for Italy and forgot it here. Let your body absorb the energy of this cloth. It belongs to a great artist, and you too will be known throughout the world one day." Then she took me for a ride in her powerful sports car. She drove it so fast that I almost urinated in fright. Her mane tousled in the wind, she recited the poems of Rilke in a solid voice. Noticing my face's intense paleness, she lowered her speed and took the road back to her abode, affirming joyously that in order for poetry to touch the sublime it must be recited at 120 miles per hour.

I did not see her again until the eve of my departure for Europe. She sent her chauffeur in uniform for me, driving a white Rolls Royce, and received me in a small golden room. There, she made me sit down and without a word set two women to sand and polish my fingernails and toenails, to which they added a coat of clear polish. Once their task was complete, the young women left us alone. Chabela then opened a safe and put a big stack of dollars into my hands.

"This will allow you to live for a year. I don't want you to waste your talents working. You must dedicate yourself exclusively to your art."
"But I will never be able to repay you."
"You're wrong. You're going to reimburse me immediately."
Then she gave me a ten-dollar bill and a fountain pen.
"Write a poem here, and sign it."
I complied. "Birds fly without fear of crashing into the ground."

Chabela exclaimed, "I am going to frame this bill. In a few years, it will be a thousand times more valuable than the money I gave you today."

Her attitude was devoid of all desire and seduction. She behaved as if driven by a great goodness and an extraordinary admiration for art. Her freely given generosity changed my life. She gave me faith in the human being, and consequently faith in myself and in the world.

Some years later, passionate about the study of the Tarot and reading books on psychoanalysis, it occurred to me that the doctors and therapists of university psychology, trained as scientists and not as artists, make the mistake of turning spiritual healing into commerce. Making psychoanalysis or psychotherapy a profession drives them to stretch the time for which a patient must receive therapy for the longest duration possible, sometimes years. They have to have a certain number of patients, enough to live comfortably. The group of consultants becomes a herd. Or, since they live off their patients, the "sick" are symbolically turned into foster parents. It follows that treating a person so that he will remain a patient for the rest of his life is excellent business, while leading a person to healing represents a financial loss.

To be a healer requires deep humility. A true therapist knows that he cannot heal the world but can only begin, step by step, to heal one individual after the other, striving to show that life is a magnificent gift and that the universe was created with a love without limits.

Mother Teresa understood this very well, and it is an image of her that showed me the way. One sees her in the middle of a road full of garbage, squatting before a nearly dead child, all her concentration focused on him, giving him energy with the warmth of her hands. Obviously, she did not make this moral act a profession, she did not claim to be paid by the dying whom she collected, she was not a tradeswoman gathering a herd to milk for as long as possible. From what did she live? From work fulfilled in her community or by donations. The only possible solution for therapists to avoid exploiting the suffering of those who ask them for help is for governments to finance them, but that is utopia; these supreme powers are at the service of economic greed and not universal Consciousness.

Thanks to the example of this woman saint, it seemed a shame to live off Tarology, Psychomagic, Psychoshamanism, or Metagenealogy. The role of a conductor exploiting a herd, or the role of a child who lives off his symbolic parents, seems immoral and disgraceful to me. I am assured other sources of revenue in cinema, literature, theater, and comics, and I opted for the solution of practicing therapy as a free art.* I decided to give my Tarot readings and psychomagic advice publicly once every week. It seemed important to me that people who suffered could find, as if by miracle, in the most common a place possible (a bar, for example), a well-intentioned person who could give them useful advice to better their lives. In our materialistic society, if one offers something freely it is generally taken either to promote a commercial enterprise or to pull people into a sect. When we truly give without asking anything in return, we uncover the sublime and miraculous part of the human relationship. This enables us to rediscover faith in one another, a necessary principle of all healing.

During a conference that I gave in Bologna, Italy, I declared that the artist of Metagenealogy must first be an independent person dedicated to guiding others not for personal benefit but from a transpersonal perspective, with the goal of participating in the evolution of humanity. I proposed then to analyze someone's genealogy tree in public. A man in his fifties raised his hand immediately, asking to be the subject of this study, which I accepted. He ascended the platform with a condescending smile, incredulous. He was a homeopathic doctor, very respected by hundreds of his patients. When I asked him what his purpose in life was, he responded, "I want to find faith in humanity and stop hating money." I began to analyze his emotional relationships with his family. This consultant, in spite of his delicacy, intelligence, culture, and goodness, lived in an emotional bunker, confined to an intellectual terrain without being able to express any emotion. After extensive questioning, he revealed

---

*At the age of fifty, when in financial ruin, I had no choice but to temporarily accept consultants paying me what they could, without imposing a fee, as do honest healers and shamans the world over.

that his father was a very cold man who was afflicted by a sordid miserliness. He required his son to excel in studies but never took his son into his arms or touched him.

I offered him a seat and asked him to sit down. Then I plunged my hand into my pocket with the intention of extracting a fifty-euro bill that I always had on me: a psychomagic habit to absorb the energy of money. I announced that I was going to rub the bill on him until the infantile hate of money disappeared. But in taking my hand from my pocket, I realized that instead of a fifty-euro note, I had pulled out a five-hundred-euro note. As a healer, I could not back down and return this bill to my pocket to look for one of lesser value. That would have been interpreted as a repetition of the paternal stinginess. Good heart working against bad fortune, I rubbed him tenderly all over with the bill. The man, imprisoned in his defenses, let me do it with the same incredulous smile. When I finished (and not without a certain pain, because the act obligated me to depart from a paper of great value!), I put the bill between his hands and told him, "This is a gift for you . . ." He began to cry convulsively. I took out a handkerchief and dried his eyes like a child. He hugged me. In obtaining the generosity of a paternal archetype, he was liberated from the miserliness of his father and he ceased to project it onto the whole human race. He left the emotional bunker. In leaving the stage, he mingled with the public, having recovered his faith in his fellows.

When I realized that suffering prevented the ability to see beauty in the world, I decided to invent the psychomiracle: a surprise act, but one that had been awaited for one's whole life and could have an illuminating effect. This consists essentially of helping a person in an anonymous way, without getting anything out of it. The simplest psychomiracle consisted of my sending ten dozen roses to a woman who was sure she would never again encounter a suitor because some years earlier her husband had abandoned her. In receiving this volume of flowers with no sign of a sender, she thought someone loved her without daring to say so, which provided her with self-esteem. Not long after, she introduced us to her new companion.

These acts, which I very often achieved while fighting against inherited resistances of my upbringing in the home of merchants, where generosity was regarded as nonsense, led me to a joyous satisfaction as I reflected on the possibilities of generating social psychomiracles. One day when I was received by Michelle Bachelet, then president of Chile, I proposed, without asking for anything in return, that Chile offer Bolivia access to the sea, thus creating a historical example of one country helping another purely for love of humanity. She told me Chile was not ready for that yet, and that it would create problems with Peru.

While Marianne Costa and I were writing this book, I proposed to the Argentine association of the mothers of the disappeared (whose children were executed in secret by the military government) that they ask the government, apart from trying the assassins, to give these mothers a space in the middle of Buenos Aires where they could build a metaphorical cemetery. Here each mother, with the generous help of sculptors and architects, could build a grave in which to symbolically lay her child to rest. This would allow them a place to express their pain and to mourn.

Just like the Tarot and Psychomagic, Metagenealogy is an art and not an occupation. With willpower, work, time, and good teachers, anyone can learn a profession. But to be an artist suggests a gift. It is not enough to have good intentions in order to become an artist-therapist; lack of talent actually hides the desire to be admired or to achieve financial gain.

The artist, instead of imitating others, works above all to develop Consciousness at its highest level in himself, knowing that he cannot ever take his consultant higher than the level that he himself has attained.

From the point of view of a professional doctor, illness is an invasion or a dysfunction of the body that transforms someone into a sick person. This doctor considers the person's ego but not his essential Being. The illuminated Consciousness is in a state of permanent health. At this level the person is no longer ill, **he is a being who has an illness,** but the illness does not have the person.

All physical and mental illness falls under a certain level of Consciousness. When we attain supreme happiness, even if we have cancer, we are not ill. The illness, which resides in us, becomes a teacher that makes us evolve. If we live identified closely to the ego, the illness invades us and plunges us into depression.

The doctor tries to heal an illness. The artist-therapist, whatever the gravity of the diagnosis, works with a healthy being in which an illness nests. The consultant is a whole being who has lost contact with his highest level of Consciousness. This sublime dimension, stifled or hidden, must be developed or revealed.

Through naïveté, narcissism, eagerness, desire for power, or some other impure motive, a person without artistic talent can self-proclaim himself a therapist and begin to treat naive patients, causing serious harm. This is because the self-proclaimed therapist is incapable of self-criticism and has not moved beyond the illusory ego to get to his authentic, transpersonal identity.

The ego faces constant resistance; it defends traces of the past. If we want to fulfill ourselves spiritually, we will have to fight against the ego all of our lives, until our deaths. Doing so, the ego eventually becomes an ally. To the extent that we arrive at this invisible teacher who joins us in totality, we see with increasing clarity this persistent child in ourselves: impossible to eliminate, but able to be tamed.

Those who feel satisfied with their "acquired impersonality," their "divine ego," or their "deep wisdom" are prey to an illusion. There is no perfect individual fulfillment. There is only an incessant battle against the limited individual who hinders the functioning of the community of conscious beings who are undergoing constant transformation.

In guiding others toward health, an artist-therapist heals himself. This state of self-healing allows the transformation into psychothaumaturgy. Even if he knows that it is impossible to propel all of humanity to health, or to transform the world, he works toward this ideal while accepting with a deep humility that he can begin the task but will never be able to achieve it.

How can an individual heal if humanity does not? As the Japanese poet Yokomitsu Ruchi wrote, "An ant dies of hunger at the top of a tower: the moon is so high."

Glossary

Consciousness/consciousness. These terms are often confused. "Consciousness" is interpreted as "that which I am conscious of" (that which I notice while awake). In reality, that which we are conscious of is what we wrongly call "unconscious," and we are more unconscious than we are conscious. If we free ourselves from the concept of "to be conscious of," Consciousness is what we truly are: an indefinable nature (often called soul or spirit). On the other hand, what we call "consciousness" is the personality in wakefulness, a prison of rationality that tells us we are only that which we notice.

Core. An infantile impulse that will develop into an adult psyche. Potentiality, full of life energy, libidinal energy, emotional energy, and intellectual energy; also very fragile and expressed candidly and uncontrollably at the same time, with an urgent force and without any self-censorship. If, instead of supporting the development of this core, the caretaking adults stifle it—establishing relational knots—the core will persist beyond childhood, turning into a limitation in the four energies (intellectual, emotional, physical, creative-sexual). A stagnant or calcified vitality will prevent the person from living out his destiny as an adult. Most of these polluted cores come directly from a knot transmitted from a close relative in the family who is suffering in turn from another polluted and doubtful core. See also "knot."

Creative power or creator. The power of the cosmic or universal Consciousness that allows us to enter into pure Consciousness without any opposition to our future design.

608

Essential Being. Sublime and creative individuality, independent of heredity: our essential Being, the God within.

Genealogy tree work. More than a simple search for our family members' responsibility in our lives, the work proposes to change levels of Consciousness.

Introjection. The means by which parents and other members of the family enter into our Unconscious as archetypes. Psychoanalysts define introjection as some part of the ego absorbing a characteristic or feature from the exterior world. This is therefore about appropriation.

Knot. A pathological persistence of an infantile core into adulthood that creates a fixation on the past, forming when the parents and other members of the family are incapable of accompanying the child's growth in a balanced way due to two principal mechanisms: shortage and excess. See also "Core."

Metagenealogy. 1. It is not strictly a "therapy" but a work of awareness, which means the comprehension of the elements of the past that have formed us, as well as the beginning of an impulse in the future to which we give shape. 2. Individuals can have at the same time, from their great-grandparents, grandparents, and parents, a negative and a positive vision. As such, this can turn each family member into a double entity where one entity is luminous and one obscure: two complementary energy fields, in spite of their opposition to one another. In the present, the soul that materializes collides with material that is spiritualized; the Supraconsciousness collides with the Unconscious; the attempt to carry out plans for the future collides with the attempt to repair the past; the essential Being collides with the sociocultural being; the desire to create collides with the desire to imitate. The study of the genealogy tree under simultaneous and complementary aspects (treasure traps) is what we call Metagenealogy.

Nous. The transpersonal identity.

Persona. The artificial image of one's self created by family, society, and culture.

Personal self. The individual ego, although somewhat sick due to the influence of society, culture, and family, that can rediscover the essential Being thanks to work with the tree.

Power of repetition or impersonator. The power derived from a familial group that has influenced our beliefs, habits, traditions, restrictions, and so forth.

Projection (psychoanalytical term). Attributing to another person feelings that emerge inside of us in order to protect ourselves from an emotional situation that we cannot manage to control. This bestows on that person defects or qualities that do not exist but serve to shape the person in accordance with the preexisting familial model.

Psychomagic. Therapeutic technique developed by Alejandro Jodorowsky that consists of staging a healing act to free an unconscious block. The act, which takes place in everyday life, is experienced as if in a dream.

Social self. The acquired personality formed by family, society, and culture through which we regularly communicate with others, albeit with feelings of inadequacy.

Supraconsciousness. More than anything, the human spirit aspires to two things: wisdom and immortality. The Unconscious must then be designed with two zones: that which is the product of past experiences, including our animal traces, which one might also call Unconscious; and that which contains potential possibilities of mutation designed to develop beings with cosmic Consciousness, composed not of past experiences but of future possibilities to which poetic and prophetic statements are attracted.

Transpersonal self. The adult self: conscious of the existence of others, able to identify with the essential Being.

Unconsciousness. Opposite the psychoanalytical approach of transforming the language of the Unconscious (dreams, slips of the tongue, synchronicities) into an articulate language with rational explanations, Psychomagic teaches the intellect the language of the Unconscious, composed mostly of images and actions that defy logic. The Unconscious contains information (images, experiences, etc.), that essentially opposes all logic. But in the way in which Alejandro Jodorowsky conceives of the Unconscious, this is not an enemy: when obeyed, it is an ally.

Bibliography

Bartley, William Warren III. *Wittgenstein*. Philadelphia: Lippincott, 1973.

Campbell, Joseph. *The Hero with a Thousand Faces*. London: Fontana, 1949.

Ch'ing, Chen Man. *Lao Tseu: Mes Mots Sont Faciles A Comprendre*. Translated by Tam C. Gibbs. Paris: Le Courrier du Livre, 1998.

Corbin, Henry. *Spiritual Body & Celestial Earth: From Mazdean Iran to Shi'ite Iran*. Princeton, N.J.: Princeton University Press, 1977.

Derlon, Pierre. *Secrets of the Gypsies*. Paris: Robert Laffont, 1975.

Descartes, René. *The Passions of the Soul*. Translated by Jonathan Bennett. New York: Charles Scribner's Sons, 1927.

Feldenkrais, Moshé. *Higher Judo*. London: Frederick Warne, 1952.

Freud, Sigmund. *An Outline of Psycho-Analysis*. London: W. W. Norton & Co., 1949.

Grad, Adolphe D. *Le livre des principes Kabbalisticques*. Paris: Robert Laffont, 1974.

Janov, Arthur. *Le corps se souvient*. Paris: Éditions du Rocher, 1997.

———. *Sexuality and the Subconscious*. Paris: Éditions du Rocher, 2006.

Jodorowsky, Alejandro. *Manuel de psychomagie*. Paris: Éditions Albin Michel, 2009.

———. *Mu: Le maître et les magiciennes*. Paris: Éditions Albin Michel, 2008.

———. *Psychomagic: The Transformative Power of Shamanic Psychotherapy*. Rochester, Vt.: Inner Traditions, 2010.

Jodorowsky, Alejandro, and Marianne Costa. *The Way of Tarot: The Spiritual Teacher in the Cards*. Rochester, Vt.: Destiny Books, 2009.

Jung, Carl Gustav. *Commentaire sur le mystère de la Fleur d'Or.* Paris: Éditions Albin Michel, 1979.

Lacan, Jacques. *Encyclopédie française,* vol. 8. Edited by A. de Monzie. Paris: Larousse, 1938.

Lalouette, Claire, trans. "La naissance divine d'Hatchepsout." In *Textes Sacrés et textes profanes de l'ancienne Égypte.* Paris: Gallimard, 1984.

Leboyer, Frederick. *Birth without Violence.* Rochester, Vt.: Healing Arts Press, 2009.

Nilsson, Lennart, and Lars Hamberger. *Naître.* Paris: Hachette Pratique, 2003.

Orage, Alfred Richard. *On Love with Some Aphorisms and Other Essays.* New York: S. Weiser, 1969.

Ouspensky, P. D. *In Search of the Miraculous: Fragments of an Unknown Teaching.* San Diego: Harvest Book, 2001.

Rūmī, Jalāl ad-Dīn Muhammad. *Roubâ'yât.* Translated by Assaf Hâlet Tchélébi. Paris: Éditions Adrien Maisonneuve, 1950.

Wieger, Léon. *Récit de l'apparition sur terre, du Buddha des Sakya.* Compiled by Pao-tch'eng in *Les vies Chinoises du Buddha.* Paris: Cathasia, 1951.

Index